# Anarchist Pedagogies: Collective Actions, Theories, and Critical Reflections on Education

Edited by Robert H. Haworth

Anarchist Pedagogies: Collective Actions, Theories, and Critical Reflections on Education
Edited by Robert H. Haworth


ISBN: 978-1-60486-484-7
Library of Congress Control Number: 2011927981

Cover: John Yates / www.stealworks.com
Interior design by briandesign

10 9 8 7 6 5 4 3 2

PM Press
PO Box 23912
Oakland, CA 94623
www.pmpress.org

Printed in the USA on recycled paper, by the Employee Owners of Thomson-Shore
in Dexter, Michigan.
www.thomsonshore.com

# CONTENTS


Introduction 1
Robert H. Haworth

**Section I** **Anarchism & Education: Learning from Historical Experimentations**

DIALOGUE 1 *(On a desert island, between friends)* 12
Alejandro de Acosta

CHAPTER 1 Anarchism, the State, and the Role of Education 14
Justin Mueller

CHAPTER 2 Updating the Anarchist Forecast for Social Justice in Our Compulsory Schools 32
David Gabbard

CHAPTER 3 Educate, Organize, Emancipate: The Work People's College and The Industrial Workers of the World 47
Saku Pinta

CHAPTER 4 From Deschooling to Unschooling: Rethinking Anarchopedagogy after Ivan Illich 69
Joseph Todd

**Section II** **Anarchist Pedagogies in the "Here and Now"**

DIALOGUE 2 *(In a crowded place, between strangers)* 88
Alejandro de Acosta

CHAPTER 5 Street Medicine, Anarchism, and *Ciencia Popular* 90
Matthew Weinstein

CHAPTER 6 Anarchist Pedagogy in Action: Paideia, *Escuela Libre* 107
Isabelle Fremeaux and John Jordan

CHAPTER 7 Spaces of Learning: The Anarchist Free Skool 124
Jeffery Shantz

CHAPTER 8 The Nottingham Free School: Notes Toward a Systemization of Praxis 145
Sara C. Motta

CHAPTER 9 Learning to Win: Anarchist Infrastructures of Resistance 162
Jeffery Shantz

CHAPTER 10 Inside, Outside, and on the Edge of the Academy: Experiments in Radical Pedagogies 175
Elsa Noterman and Andre Pusey

CHAPTER 11 Anarchy in the Academy: Staying True to Anarchism as an Academic-Activist 200
Caroline K. Kaltefleiter and Anthony J. Nocella II

**Section III Philosophical Perspectives and Theoretical Frameworks**

DIALOGUE 3 *(On a mountaintop, between two who are in fact one)* 218
Alejandro de Acosta

CHAPTER 12 To Walk Questioning: Zapatismo, the Radical Imagination, and a Transnational Pedagogy of Liberation 220
Alex Khasnabish

CHAPTER 13 Anarchism, Pedagogy, Queer Theory and Poststructuralism: Toward a Positive Ethical Theory, of Knowledge and the Self 242
Lucy Nicholas

CHAPTER 14 Anarcho-Feminist Psychology: Contributing to Postformal Criticality 260
Curry Stephenson Malott

CHAPTER 15 Paideia for Praxis: Philosophy and Pedagogy as Practices of Liberation 283
Nathan Jun

CHAPTER 16 That Teaching Is Impossible 303
Alejandro de Acosta

CHAPTER 17 Against the Grain of the Status Quo: Anarchism behind Enemy Lines 312
Abraham P. DeLeon

AFTERWORD Let the Riots Begin 326
Allan Antliff

CONTRIBUTORS 329
ACKNOWLEDGMENTS 334
INDEX 335

# Introduction

**Robert H. Haworth**

As I sit to write this introduction I am reminded of a particular teaching experience I had almost a decade ago. During class, I was passing out the dreaded federal standardized test when one of my students who considered himself an anarcho-punk yelled out, "Hey . . . Mr. Haworth, you are a fucking sell-out!" I couldn't help but think about the two decades I had been involved in punk and hardcore, as well as the intense collective work many (including myself) had participated in throughout those years. How could I be a sell-out? I stopped everything and asked him what it meant to be a "punk," and how he identified and acted as an anarchist within the overwhelming functions of the state and capitalism? I went on to ask the rest of the class specifically, "If I don't have a certain punk aesthetic and work as a teacher in the public schools, is that considered selling out?"

After that experience, I went home frustrated. As a student, I didn't like high school or the ridiculous standardized tests either, but I asked myself an important question: "Was I doing something different in my classroom or just reinforcing and reproducing state and corporate interests?" As an educator, I worked diligently to teach through a more creative, dialogical, and critical framework. I worked as a social studies teacher because I felt it was a space where I could engage students in important discussions surrounding the problems of capitalism and the injustices in the world. I believed public schools were potential spaces to experiment in different pedagogical practices and at the same time cultivate dissent against a system that has been so oppressive to young people and anyone living outside of dominant cultural practices.

I have to be honest that I don't agree with my student's judgment that I am a "sell-out," although there are times I feel differently. Throughout my transition into academia, I have realized how much those comments and that conversation with the class had an impact on my thinking. Experiences such as these have led me to think more critically about the complex relationship anarchism has with education. In fact, the more we engage in conversations about these intricate relationships the more we see that they are filled with tensions and ambiguity. Should we place our bets on a state-run educational system that anarchists have always been skeptical of (including my student)—one that is hierarchical and extremely authoritative? For me, and probably my old student, the answer is no, but I don't make that decision lightly or without bringing up more inquiries.

For example, scholars within critical pedagogy (see Paulo Freire) have not only written extensively on pedagogical processes that question and resist authoritative structures, but they have also taken into consideration the transformative possibilities and spaces of resistance that teachers form within different public school settings. Tensions definitely emerge with the deskilling of teachers (Giroux, 1988) as our schools are inundated with prescribed curriculum and there is very little room to discuss ideas and critical perspectives outside of the scripted materials. On the other hand, anarchists have taken a different direction. Historically, anarchists have steadily criticized the state and public schools and have considered them mundane institutions that uniformly reinforce capitalism and hierarchical models of control. However, over the last century, anarchists have made numerous attempts to create educational processes that transgress authoritative factory models and deterministic curriculum of the state and corporate entities (see Paul Avrich).

The early twentieth century was full of criticisms and philosophical discussions surrounding education. John Dewey and others brought into question the very nature of schooling and what it means to be an educated person (see *My Pedagogic Creed*). Unfortunately, many progressive criticisms and pedagogical practices had limitations. Their notions of education were more in line and embedded in school reform under the state and limited to what can be imagined and created within a managed or representative democratic society. One of the many significant anarchist voices that challenged state-run schools and their oppressive pedagogical practices was that of Emma Goldman. Inspired by Francisco Ferrer's (1913) work in Spain, Goldman wrote scathing critiques of classroom teachers, specifically their troublesome teaching practices under capitalism and the suffocating implications they had on the larger society: "The ideal of the average pedagogist is not a complete, well-rounded, original being; rather does he seek that the result of his art of pedagogy shall be automatons of flesh and blood, to best fit into the treadmill of society and the emptiness and dullness of our lives" (p. 8).

Clearly Goldman's statement is not limited to that particular time period. Her foretelling words resonate deeply into schools in the twenty-first century. In many cases, schools are still dull and lack inspiration, creativity, and spontaneity. From an anarchist perspective, public schools are connected to and guided by the state, whereby they are infused with authoritarian relationships between the student and teacher, they uphold corporate structures and are inundated with standardized curriculum. Under these particular state structures, teachers' work lacks autonomy and many (particularly failing schools under federal mandates) are forced to conform to curriculum standards, meritocracy, and quantitative outcomes.

Therefore, important questions need to be addressed. For example, "Are there spaces where discussions surrounding education and connections to anarchism are occurring?" and "Are there movements to create alternatives to schooling under capitalism and state structures?" It is quite evident that the body of writings by Goldman and others who challenged the dominant practices of state-run education are considered less frequently within academic settings and in the larger public school discourse. However, there are locations where alternative learning spaces are being created and where discussions are happening surrounding anarchist pedagogies. This is particularily evident in the struggles against neoliberalism and in the current Occupy movements. Yet it is still not seen as a relevant philosophy or theoretical framework. This should probably not be a surprise to anyone. For over a century, anarchism has been predominantly misunderstood and definitely misrepresented in political, economic, social, and cultural spaces. Graeber (2004) points out that "most academics seem to have only the vaguest idea what anarchism is even about; or dismiss it with the crudest stereotypes" (p. 2). Unfortunately, the dismissal of anarchist thought tends to move even further away when discussing philosophical and theoretical frameworks in education. Although there are many educational researchers who frame their work within critical perspectives (Marxism, neo-Marxism, Autonomist Marxism, and Marxist Humanism), the majority of research and teaching practices are confined to "liberal" and "conservative" ideological debates.

The issues emphasized above are some of the major factors that motivated me create this book. I wanted to emphasize the important contributions anarchism has made to educational praxis. Additionally, I wanted the book to disrupt dominant discussions regarding formal state-run education and explore the more creative spaces of resistance that emerge out of anarchist pedagogies and nonstatist structures. Moreover, from the body of work illustrated by the contributors, it is evident that there is not one defining position on anarchist pedagogy. In some cases, the fluid characteristics of anarchism and the pedagogical processes that individuals and collectives engage in are situated and nestled into the different educative spaces we inhabit. With this in mind, within these pages there are opportunities for anarchists to explore and critically reflect.

## Knowledge and the Marketplace

This leads me to consider another important factor as to why I wanted to create this volume. There is a critical need to realize anarchism within an educational context in order to provide alternatives to the intensive shifts to universalize global capitalism at all levels of society. Part of this shift is due to the fact that, "conservative, neo-conservative, and neoliberal educational reforms are gaining momentum and have been quite successful in making their arguments clear and concise" (DeLeon, 2008, p. 137). As globalization "from above" has dominated the discourse surrounding educational reform so has the relationship solidified between knowledge production and marketplace values. Michael Peters (2009) describes the shift into the "creative economy" as a way of moving the global economic order into one that focuses on "the growing power of ideas and virtual value chain—the turn from steel and hamburgers to software and intellectual property" (p. 45). Education is thus adrift within the shifting tides of capitalism. In fact, Dokuzović and Freudmann (2009) point out that even investors in the music industry are altering their capitalist energies to focus on education, highlighting that "knowledge is a tradable commodity and considered profitable." With the massive international movements to standardize curriculum, commodify knowledge, and privatize public institutions, it is evident that state education has deepened its relationships with capitalism and embracing the move to the new knowledge economy (Giroux, 2004; Saltman, 2007).

But why should anarchists care about how capitalism and the state operate within educational structures? Public schools and universities under state control continue to have oppressive tendencies. They rely on relationships and financial backing by corporations, while operating extensively under hierarchal structures. These modes become intensified under neoliberalism and the attempts to universalize globalize capitalism.

However, it is vital that we not view or discuss these dominating forces as impenetrable (Day, 2007). According to Day (2004) a "multiplicity of new forms of struggle is emerging" (p. 741). Struggles within multiple fronts contest the overbearing reaches of global capitalism. Students, workers, activists and other community members have organized in different capacities. They form creative and innovative interventions that challenge the dismantling of public spaces, while at the same time, "create alternatives to state and corporate forms of social organization" (Day, 2004, p. 740).

At the university level, it is vital to recognize that contemporary uprisings to contest neoliberal policies and austerity are not movements to reclaim these institutions in order to "rewind" them back to some romanticized liberal democratic spaces. In contrast, the movements are much more privy to the complex historical problems of how universities operate, they are working diligently to distance themselves from the reestablishment of these structures of the past. However, if universities operate under rigid and hierarchical settings, why are they important within an anarchist context? Stephven Shukaitis (2009) makes an important argument that "one can find ways to use the institutional space without being *of* the institution, without taking the institution's goals as ones own" (p. 167). Shukaitis's suggestions are important to underline as the movements to contest neoliberalism unfold. As we participate in liberating spaces out of the clutches of neoliberal policies and global capitalism, it is critical that anarchists continue to develop their reflective capacities.

Within an educational context, such discussions bring forth significant implications. Currently, there is an incredible need for anarchists to interrupt the authoritative and deterministic nature of state-run compulsory schooling and at the same time, continuing to immerse themselves in creative reflective actions which are not always present in contemporary movements. Unfortunately, anarchists have been inconsistent in constructing critical reflections surrounding their pedagogical practices. This has led some to criticize, and in most cases dismiss, anarchist experiments in education. Suissa (2010) recognizes some of the pedagogical vulnerabilities within anarchism: "As far as educational practice is concerned, there are several weaknesses in the anarchist account. Primarily the sparse attention paid by anarchist writers to the issue of pedagogy both exposes this account to theoretical questions about the most appropriate pedagogical approach and opens the door to questionable pedagogical practices" (p. 149).

As anarchists negotiate the difficult terrain of shaping different pedagogical practices, they cannot be dismissive of Suissa's concerns. Questions surrounding how power operates within these educational spaces demands ongoing external and internal struggles. Although Graeber (2002) highlights the diverse functionality of consensus and how collective actions enable individuals to create proposals and "allow initiatives to rise from below" and "without stifling dissenting voices" (p. 71), these processes do not occur by happenstance. Within these unique spaces, particular anarchist pedagogies do emerge. But as creative organizers and activists, how do we continue be diligent in confronting the overbearing racist, classist, sexist, and homophobic structures we are so immersed in? One example anarchists may consider is the work of French philosophers Gilles Deleuze and Félix Guattari (1987), who in the past have advocated for a continuous critique of how we take up transformations in our attempts to escape capitalist lines of flight. Thus, stressing the major point that movements wage permanent struggle within their own collective organizations; thus working to guard against the potential of emerging microfascisms.

Similarly, while there is a need for anarchists to emphasize their struggle within their own collective organizations and movements, there is also potential for these processes to offer insights into our pedagogical practices and educational spaces. Similar to how the critical educator (within a Freirian context) uses reflective practices to challenge the authoritarian and antidialogical learning environments in the classroom (and in the larger society), anarchists must value those reflective insights that transform the infoshops, the free skools, the independent media sites and other autonomous locales.

Broadly, this volume seeks to highlight the multiple sites where anarchist pedagogies operate and where they extend throughout the different locales and communities where knowledge is produced. Moreover, because these spaces and theoretical frameworks are consistently being renegotiated and reimagined, I understand that the following contributions are in no way conclusive. These examples are the subjectivities that surface within the cracks and in-between spaces that disrupt the oppressive practices of capitalism (Holloway, 2010).

In the final portion of the introduction I will briefly discuss how the three main sections of the book can help expand our understandings of anarchism's historical contributions, contemporary anarchist pedagogies and experiments, and finally, the important influences other philosophical and theoretical frameworks have on anarchist thinking.

## Learning from Past Experimentations

In the first section contributors provide vital discussions into past experiments in anarchists pedagogies, their implications for contemporary public schools, and new educational experiences and subjectivities. There is a serious need for anarchists and other radical pedagogues to revisit some of these historical critiques and philosophical conversations. Conceptually, the section was inspired by Judith Suissa's (2010) argument that the relationship between anarchism and education has been "undertheorized." I concur with Suissa's assessment. For anarchists, it is important to question, reflect, and further theorize on the wide-ranging historical experiences that anarchists have created. Furthermore, taking into consideration what these practices might mean for those exploring education in contemporary times and future spaces. It is my desire that these critical reflections help rekindle the anarchist "spirit" in not only critiquing compulsory schooling under the state and capitalist structures, but by revisiting arguments regarding education that are outside of hierarchical, authoritarian, and formal state institutions.

## Anarchist Pedagogies: Situated Knowledge and Actions

Anarchists take into account that knowledge is produced through situated processes. On a larger scale, Janet Conway (2006) describes knowledge created in twenty-first-century social movements as "largely tacit" (p. 1). Through Graeber's (2009) ethnographic research, situated knowledge is evident within the movement's diverse organizational strategies and learning processes. In his book entitled *Direct Action: An Ethnography*, Graeber illustrates how individuals and collectives recognize the oppressive nature of hierarchical and authoritative structures, thereby helping to build alternative venues to engage in particular pedagogical practices that represent those horizontal and mutual spaces. Additionally, these situated spaces highlight the intricate and sometimes delicate affinity between the different activists and organizations.

Adding to the literature of direct action and critical ethnographies, Conway, Graeber, and others have engaged in documenting the movement's diverse narratives and organizational experiences. Contributors in the second section of the book add voice to some of the contemporary challenges in these educational spaces. Authors explore ways in which active learning takes place in the streets, free skools, unions, and even the potentialities within the structures of the university. The narratives offer new perspectives into the ongoing challenges of collectively building spaces of learning. At the same time, the discussions also offer some interesting discernments regarding the tensions that occur when entering into these mutual, horizontal, and voluntary spaces. These educational projects help us better understand the complexities of teaching and learning within anarchist spaces, not so as to construct deterministic or objective goals, but rather to envision such projects as ongoing and continuous processes.

## Philosophical Perspectives and Theoretical Frameworks

To help us navigate this section, Jesse Cohn's (2006) description of anarchism as a "theoretical magpie" cannot be overstated (p. 97). In fact, Cohn's remarks not only demonstrate the complexities of anarchist thinking but underline the important need for anarchists to be critical in how anarchism attaches itself to certain frameworks. Because of anarchism's fluidity many anarchists have taken up multiple directions regarding educational practices. Historically, Rudolf Rocker (2004) viewed anarchism as existing beyond a fixed and self enclosed social system. In his discussions regarding anarchism and pedagogy Armaline (2009) suggests not only that anarchism is "fluid" but that "it changes with the needs and will of those who (re)produce it." (p. 136). Similar to Ferrer's (1913) work, Freire was concerned with dogmatic processes that were prevalent within education and in many of the liberation movements of the 1960s. Much of his work embraces teaching and learning as a dialogical process, where education is a processes of exposing and contesting authoritarian power dynamics between teacher-student and student-teacher relationships. Additionally, he describes the importance of having a "respect for the autonomy of the student" (Freire, 1998, p. 59). The naming or exposing of power, as well as acting against oppressive perspectives, becomes an important transformative educational experience toward critical conciousness (Freire, 1972; Kahn, 2009). Although Freire's work is invaluable in discussing liberatory and transformative ways of teaching and learning, it is important to mention the theoretical tensions his work has within some of the current literature surrounding anarchism and poststructuralist thought.

In the mid-1990s, Todd May's (1994) work broadened theoretical and philosophical thinking between anarchism and poststructuralism. Constructing relationships between Deleuze and Guattari (1983; 1987), Michel Foucault (1980), and others, May reopened the conversation surrounding the fluid traits of anarchism and its connections to poststructuralist thought. Other poststructuralist thinkers in education, including Diana Masny, whose work incorporates Deleuzian perspectives on literacy, have critiqued and extended the discourse regarding transformation. Masny does not disagree with Freire that transformations take place within individual subjects, but her work is concerned with how transformations are taken up. For Masny (2006), transformative education discussed within the Freirian context is too linear and deterministic. While Freire was correct that we are "always becoming" in the world, Deleuze and Guattari (1987) contested our understanding of transformation as moving in a unidirectional path of liberation and critical consciousness. Therefore, subjects do not transform into something that is "good" or "bad," but recognizing that, we are "becoming other than."

Additionally, the authors in the third section facilitate important philosophical inquires into anarchist theories that emerge out of constructing complex pedagogical practices. As anarchist pedagogies unfold, important questions regarding national borders and the nation-state, gender and queer theory, the difficulties of working in and around state structures, and questioning our personal assumptions about teaching come into fruition. Within these knotty discussions, the authors are able to discuss some of the challenges and navigate the fluid intersections between the social, political (micro and macro), and cultural spaces. Therefore, this section cultivates philosophical and theoretical conversations about the experiments we are constructing to escape education as an oppressive machine of capitalism.

In closing, it is difficult to say if I could give my old student a definitive explanation of how we can challenge dominant educational practices (or even grapple with the definition of punk). Public schools are still moving in extremely unhealthy directions that are, in many cases, irreconcilable even under state and capitalist structures. The intention of this book is to think differently about some of these complex educational issues and their relationships to anarchism. As Armaline points out, "anarchist theory contains a component of self-reflection and self-critique" (p. 136). With this process in mind, it is important to recognize that our creative responses to construct anarchist pedagogies are not linear or deterministic. Rather, the intricate networks of situated knowledge provide important insights into how we might envision different educational experiences and processes thus offering the potential to transform our collective work.

## References

Armaline, W.T. (2009). Thoughts on anarchist pedagogy and epistemology. In R. Amster, A. DeLeon, L. Fernandez, A. Nocella II & D. Shannon (Eds.), *Contemporary anarchist studies: An introductory anthology of anarchy in the academy*, 136–46. New York: Routledge.

Avrich, P. (2006). *The modern school movement: Anarchism and education in the United States.* Oakland: AK Press.

Cohn, J. (2006). *Anarchism and the crisis of representation: Hermeneutics, aesthetics politics.* Cranbury, NJ: Associated University Presses.

Conway, J. (2006). *Praxis and politics: Knowledge production in social movements.* New York: Routledge.

DeLeon, A. (2008). Oh no, not the "a" word! Proposing an "anarchism" for education. *Educational Studies, 44*(2), 122–41

Day, R.J.F. (2004) From hegemony to affinity. *Cultural Studies, 18*(5), 716–48.

Day, R.J.F. (2007). *Gramsci is dead: Anarchist currents in the newest social movements.* Toronto: Between the Lines.

Delueze, G. & Guattari, F. (1983). *Anti-Oedipus: Capitalism and schizophrenia.* Minneapolis: University of Minnesota Press.

Delueze, G. & Guattari, F. (1987). *A thousand plateaus: Capitalism and schizophrenia.* Minneapolis: University of Minnesota Press.

Dewey, J. (1932). My pedagogic creed. In D. Finders & S. Thornton (Eds.), *The curriculum studies reader.* New York: Routledge.

Dokuzović, L. & Freudmann, E. (2009, November). Creating worlds. Squatting the Crisis: On the current protests in education and perspectives on radical change. Retrieved from http://eipcp.net/projects/creatingworlds/dokuzovic-freudmann/en.

Freire, P. (1972). *Pedagogy of the oppressed.* New York: Continuum.

Freire, P. (1998). *Pedagogy of freedom: Ethics, democracy, and civic courage.* New York: Rowman and Littlefield.

Ferrer, F. (1913). *The origin and ideals of the modern school.* London: Watts.

Foucault, M. (1980). *The history of sexuality.* New York: Vintage Books.

Giroux, H.A. (1988). *Teachers as intellectuals: Towards a critical pedagogy of learning.* Westport, CT: Greenwood Publishing Group.

Giroux, H.A. (2004). *The terror of neoliberalism: Authoritarianism and the eclipse of democracy*. Boulder, CO: Paradigm Publishers.

Goldman, E. (1906). The child and its enemies. *Mother Earth, 1*(2), 7–14.

Graeber, D. (2002). The new anarchists. *New Left Review, 13*, 61–73.

Graeber, D. (2004). *Fragments of an anarchist anthropology.* Chicago: Prickly Paradigm.

Graeber, D. (2009). *Direct action: An ethnography.* Oakland: AK Press.

Holloway, J. (2010). *Crack capitalism.* New York: Pluto Press.

Masny, D. (2005). Multiple literacies: An alternative *OR* beyond Freire. In J. Anderson, M. Kendrick, T. Rogers & S. Smythe (Eds.), *Portraits of literacy across families, communities, and schools: Intersections and tensions*, 171–84. Mahwah, NJ.: Erlbaum.

May, T. (1994). *The political philosophy of poststructuralist anarchism*. University Park, PA: Penn State University Press.

Peters, M.A. (2009). Education, creativity and the economy of passions: New forms of educational capitalism. *Thesis Eleven*, 96, 40–63.

Rocker, R. (2004). *Anarcho-Syndicalism: Theory and Practice*. Oakland: AK Press.

Saltman, K. (2007). Schooling in disaster capitalism: How the political right is using disaster to privatize public schooling. *Teacher Education Quarterly*, 34(2), 131–56.

Shukaitis, S. (2009). Infrapolitics and the nomadic educational machine. In R. Amster, A. DeLeon, L. Fernandez, A. Nocella II & D. Shannon (Eds.), *Contemporary anarchist studies: An introductory anthology of anarchy in the academy*, 166–74. New York: Routledge.

Suissa, J. (2010). *Anarchism and education: A philosophical perspective*. Oakland: PM Press.

SECTION I

# Anarchism & Education: Learning from Historical Experimentations

# DIALOGUE 1

## *(On a desert island, between friends)*

**Alejandro de Acosta**

**A:** Even in the strangeness of our isolation, you want to discuss something you call anarchist pedagogy? Haven't we been circling around this topic for some time now? Well, if I understand your expression, it is already underway.

**B:** Yes, it has been underway for centuries.

**A:** And yet, here in our isolation, we feel the need to talk it over again. What's more, if I know you, you will want to narrate a myth of origin...

**B:** Remember, always, that it is just that, a myth, a story.

**A:** So maybe I am the one who is inclined to fabulate here. We agree that it is underway, but it begins again, is renewed, in the posing of a new problem. Not merely ridding ourselves of the problems whose names are so familiar...

**B:** ...and just why is it that the names "school, schooling" fit these familiar problems so well? ...

**A:** ... rather shifting attention and interest to a new set of, let's say, "unschoolish" problems.

**B:** Is this the concern that made me want to talk? From one problem, one frustration to another?

**A:** Not every problem, not every frustration is identical. There is great virtue, one could even say will power, in selecting one's greatest problems. You have spoken macroscopically, as if from a great distance. But I will remind you that, here on our island, it is wisest to speak microscopically. Have we not been teasing out the fine grain of a redefinition of freedom, endlessly rediscovered, a shift from opposition to invention (and affirmation)? Though neither of us willed this our isolation, is that research not one of the ways that we have come to accept, even desire, our prolonged stay here?

**B:** Well, there is your story, finally: from freedom as the remainder of an agon, a struggle, a combat (the operation impure, the fight always on the verge of returning, a mark, a brand on the body of the free) to freedom as self-invention, creativity, undiscovered potential.

**A:** Now that these first words have passed our mouths, I see the strangeness of this story. We have been speaking with each other for a very long time. Now I want to ask you: invention, creativity, potential—of what? Of the human?

**B:** Perhaps. I have invoked "schools, schooling" and to many this suggests the idea of the child. Of course, though here on the island we have not seen children for some time, surely we have not been here so long as to forget all that. I think the suggestion is deceptive. I doubt that we will discover some pure freedom here. We have long agreed that is nonsensical. The "unschoolish" freedom in question is something else than what we imagine the human animal is doing in its untrammeled youth.

**A:** Yes, what we are after is something other than the infantilization of everyone...

**B:** ...including youth. It is a question of knowing just what a myth, a story, a fable is.

**A:** An adventure of ideas? Not just of images and symbols?

**B:** We are exploring the island, again...

**A:** In this adventure of ideas, we might take up your strange couple: a word that says not-something (an-archy) and one that says... yes, someone, a companion (pedagogy).

**B:** Let us become interested in this unlikely coupling, if only because it is another name for the ever-repeated birth of another people... our silent, invisible companions here?

**A:** It is pleasant to think of them. It is also pleasant to suppose that every generation will amuse itself by cultivating the prefixes no-, un-, de-, an- as so many prefaces to what I call its compelling new problem, rediscovered, reinvented...

**B:** Or to what I will still call a frustration, one which is not humiliating and becomes, in time, a fascination. Remember our arrival here, the first few years...

**A:** What else is there to do, if we agree that it is already underway?

**B:** More or less everything. But, in this myth, which is a little bit more yours than mine, in these birth stories, these genealogies, we might learn how to be fascinated by a series of recalcitrant minorities...

**A:** Our companions, now less silent, less invisible: a fringe that invites us to reconsider where we had placed the center of our island, and so to conceive its problem as our own.

**B:** Yes: for them it is already underway, and, from them, we might learn that the same is true for the rest of us.

CHAPTER 1

# Anarchism, the State, and the Role of Education

Justin Mueller

Education has played a particularly important role in the history of anarchist thought and practice, perhaps more so than any other political philosophy aimed at social transformation. This is in part because, for anarchists of all stripes, education has never been simply a means to achieve a new social order. It has been, rather, part of the very practice and prefiguration of the anarchist ideal of creating freer and more critical minds, and more open, cooperative and nonoppressive relationships within society. As a result, understanding the peculiar nature of the role of education for anarchism can help us better understand the relationship between anarchist educational theory and its relatives in the broader circles of "libertarian" or "radical" education. It can also help us underscore the tremendous differences between the anarchist conception of education and that of historical and contemporary statist and capitalist pedagogies. Finally, a greater understanding of the role of education within anarchist theory can help us clarify the means, aims, and ideas of the wider anarchist movement and tradition. First, however, we will briefly look at what is meant by "anarchism" and provide a basic foundation for further discussion of its values and criticisms of the existing state of education.

## A Brief Sketch of Anarchism

Anarchism has had a rather bedeviled career, maligned by many, misunderstood by most, and marginalized even by erstwhile theoretical allies. In the popular imagination, it is often seen as simply synonymous with chaos, disorder, or violence; more likely to evoke the image of a smashed Starbucks window than a nuanced philosophy based upon principles of economic and political equality (Starr, 2000). However, the anarchist Emma Goldman defined anarchism in this way:

> Anarchism, then, really stands for the liberation of the human mind from the dominion of religion; the liberation of the human body from the dominion of property; liberation from the shackles and restraint of government. Anarchism stands for a social order based on the free grouping of individuals for the purpose of producing real social wealth; an order that will guarantee to every human being free access to the earth and full enjoyment of the necessities of life, according to individual desires, tastes, and inclinations. (1911a)

Such an idea hardly seems to warrant immediate dismissal. Rather than social disintegration, the normative principles and organizational ideas in anarchist theory advocate social, economic, and political arrangements that affirm a strong valuation of individuals as ends in themselves, a commitment to egalitarian and democratic methods, and a staunch opposition to hierarchical institutional power arrangements that subordinate some individuals to others. Fundamentally, anarchist theory operates under the notion that people can and should determine the direction of their own lives, and that social arrangements should be constructed with this aim in mind.

In answering the simple question, "What is anarchism?" it may help to begin by thinking rather of "anarchisms." The term "anarchism" really refers to a cluster of ideologies, movements and theories that share a family resemblance to each other, rather than to a largely enclosed and holistic system of thought (Guérin, 1970, p. 4) like Marxism. In this way, the wide variety of often conflicting opinions that fall under the label of "anarchism," especially regarding along what lines a future society ought to be ordered, should not be viewed as simple internal "contradictions." Rather they represent an experimental "plurality of possibilities" that may be more or less relevant or useful in a variety of different situations (de Cleyre, 2005, p. 48).

There are common principles, however, that unify anarchists. The word "anarchy" comes from the Greek, "*an*," meaning "no" or "without," and "*archos*," meaning "ruler" or "authority." In this sense, the concept does not mean "chaos" but rather an opposition to *hierarchical power relationships*, which are the corporeal embodiment of the notion of "opaque" authority (Sylvan, 1993, p. 221). Thus, opposition to the State and capitalism are appropriately features of anarchist theory, but they are *incidental* byproducts of this primary rejection of hierarchy, of divisions between those who command and those who are compelled to obey (Bookchin, 2005, p. 27). This simple principle of opposition to hierarchy and imposed authority, taken seriously, logically extends to an opposition to all dominating and exploitative social, political, and economic power relationships, including not just capitalism and the State, but patriarchy, racism, sexism, heterosexism, war (and by extension, imperialism), and any number of other manifestations of power disparity as harmful to human development.

Anarchism is not simply a negative critique. Moving beyond the extensive list of things anarchists are opposed to, the anarchist opposition to hierarchy implies a wide variety of positive means of association. Behind any specifically proposed social arrangements, however, are a few general principles, which will be elaborated in the next sections.

## Values, Human Nature, and Other Pedagogies

> Let the universal culture of schooling aim at an apprenticeship in freedom, and not in submissiveness . . . The motif, the thrust of the new age is the freedom of the will. Consequently, pedagogy ought to espouse the molding of the free personality as its starting point and objective . . . That culture, which is genuinely universal in that the humblest rub shoulders with the haughtiest, represents the true equality of all: the equality of free persons. For only freedom is equality. (Stirner, 2005, pp. 19–20)

The above quote by Max Stirner provides an excellent introduction to the anarchist attitude toward education. As Stirner suggests, the role of education in anarchist theory is one of emancipation and cultivation. Its aim is to develop free and critical minds, and in pursuit of this, cultivate the values of liberty, equality, and solidarity (Kropotkin, 1985, p. 128). We must explore what these concepts mean and how they are used for anarchists specifically. Certainly, no pedagogues from other progressive or libertarian schools of thought would deny that they too seek to develop many or all of these traits in some fashion. In order to understand what makes an anarchist approach to education distinct, then, we also need to understand the nuances in anarchist thought regarding the interplay of values, human nature, and development, as well as the relationship between individuals and society.

### Values

As mentioned previously, the major values espoused by anarchists are liberty, equality, and solidarity. While different schools of anarchist thought may appear to emphasize one over the others (as with arguments between "individualist" and "social" anarchists), these differences are largely superficial, with little changed in substantive values (Guérin, 1970, p. 4). In actuality they are inseparable from and mutually inform each other. Rather than a fixed value-slope or hierarchy, these values form a continuum wherein each idea is meaningfully constituted only in association with the others.

### *Liberty*

While distinctions can be drawn between the concepts of "freedom" and "liberty," they are essentially interchangeable in anarchist literature, and for the purposes of this essay. The anarchist conception of freedom is fundamental to understanding the entire thrust of anarchist theory. Unfortunately, it is also one of its most frequently misunderstood, caricatured or oversimplified ideas. Freedom must be understood within the context of the anarchist conception of human nature, which we will explore later. For now, it is sufficient to note that anarchists view human nature as malleable, that we have the potential to do *better*, and that freedom is a necessary condition for the development of one's potentials. Freedom for anarchists, then, goes beyond the classical liberal notions of autonomous, atomized, presocial free persons, as in the thought of Rousseau or Locke. Such liberal notions prescribe formal liberty and equality before the law, but do not provide substantively for the material security and development of individual faculties and expression (Goldman, 1940). As Daniel Guérin (1970) states, "For the anarchist, freedom is not an abstract philosophical concept, but the vital concrete possibility for every human being to bring to full development all the powers, capacities and talents with which nature has endowed him [*sic*], and turn them to social account" (p. vii).

For anarchists, freedom is not simply a lack of external fetters or domination. Nor is it, as occasionally and misleadingly imagined by critics, an "absolute" claim for simple license to do whatever one wants, regardless of wider consequences. As Errico Malatesta (1993) explains, "[Anarchism means] freedom for everybody . . . with the only limit of the equal freedom for others; which does not mean . . . that we recognise, and wish to respect, the 'freedom' to exploit, to oppress, to command, which is oppression and certainly not freedom" (p. 53).

Rather, then, freedom is conceived as part of the development of one's potential, a prerequisite for a person to "grow to his [*sic*] full stature" (Goldman, 1979, pp. 72–73). It is something that is cultivated within, rather than separate from, a given social context, and cannot be understood without reference to society. It is not a goal for a hypothetical and archetypal individual Person, but for actual people to pursue alongside and—ideally—in cooperation with others.

### *Equality*

The importance of the notion of "equality" in anarchist thought is intimately related to anarchism's rejection of social or institutional hierarchy and domination. It is also rooted in a particular understanding of human nature. As with freedom, anarchists support social equality as a necessary condition for individuals to be able to develop their "various faculties" and their potential (Maximoff, 1953, p. 156). Mikhail Bakunin best summarizes this intertwined appreciation for individual freedom and social equality in one of his better-remembered quotes: "Liberty without socialism is privilege, injustice; and that socialism without liberty is slavery and brutality" (ibid., p. 269). However, the anarchist critique of social inequality goes beyond simply decrying the resource deprivation endured by some and the opulence accrued to others under capitalism (or any other hierarchical social or economic order). In anarchist thought, hierarchy brutalizes and warps both those who rule and those who are ruled in a stratified system; the former in being corrupted by their relative power, and the latter by developing servile attitudes and deference to authority (Kropotkin, 1988, p. 83). Although those who are privileged in a stratified society clearly gain many benefits and seek to preserve those benefits, in anarchist theory they too are unable to develop their potential due to the degenerative effects of hierarchical power and privilege. In this way, the anarchist call for social equality is not only a rally-cry for the disenfranchised, but is also rooted in a belief that social equality is an emancipating precondition for *all* to actualize themselves fully.

Substantively, then, anarchists believe with Alexander Berkman (2003) that

> Equality does not mean an equal amount but equal opportunity. . . Do not make the mistake of identifying equality in liberty with the forced equality of the convict camp. True anarchist equality implies freedom, not quantity. It does not mean that every one must eat, drink, or wear the same things, do the same work, or live in the same manner. Far from it: the very reverse in fact . . . Individual needs and tastes differ, as appetites differ. It is equal opportunity to satisfy them that constitutes true equality. (p. 164)

As Berkman suggests, while most anarchists advocate some form of cooperative and egalitarian socioeconomic system, this is not rooted in an aesthetic valuation of "equality for equality's sake," or a conflation of equality with identical goods received. Rather, *equality of conditions and opportunity* are seen as instrumental and necessary conditions for everyone to be able to fully develop and express their individuality.

### *Solidarity*

In opposition to the Social Darwinist advocates of his time, such as Herbert Spencer, who expounded the virtues of competition and elimination of the "unfit" elements of society (Spencer, 1993), the anarchist and scientist Peter Kropotkin argued in defense of "mutual aid" as a natural and important phenomenon in evolutionary biology and social development. In *Mutual Aid*, Kropotkin emphasizes that cooperation and fellow-feeling, not just competition and domination, have been a factor in the evolution of many species, including humans (Kropotkin, 1972, p. 28). In this simple observation, Kropotkin sought to dispel the belief that mutual domination, competition, and destruction were somehow inevitable or even virtuous features of our social and political landscape. This challenge is representative of the core appreciation for solidarity in anarchist theory.

Solidarity, fraternity, or mutual aid are, at their simplest, cooperation and free association between individuals in a social context. In the continuum of anarchist values, it plays a vitalizing role by encouraging active empathy and identification with others. It is, at an individual level, a "moral disposition" or "attitude" toward others, wherein others are seen not as competitors to be defeated or as means to an end, but as moral equals to be respected and valued (Suissa, 2010, p. 67). In this way, solidarity functions in anarchist theory as the means of overcoming the traditional liberal dichotomy of individual liberty and social equality. While not an anarchist, Alfie Kohn (1992) expresses this understanding of solidarity well:

> When we think about co-operation . . . we tend to associate the concept with fuzzy-minded idealism. . . . This may result from confusing co-operation with altruism. . . . Structural co-operation defies the usual egoism/altruism dichotomy. It sets things up so that by helping you I am helping myself at the same time. Even if my motive initially may have been selfish, our fates now are linked. We sink or swim together. Co-operation is a shrewd and highly successful strategy—a pragmatic choice that gets things done at work and at school even more effectively than competition does. . . . There is also good evidence that co-operation is more conductive to psychological health and to liking one another. (p. 7)

In advocating solidarity, then, anarchists are not just appealing in a "utopian" fashion to the "natural goodness" of people (Wolff, 1996, p. 34), or saying that we ought to all get along and work together, in denial of potential conflict or disagreement. Rather, the anarchist belief in the value of the principle of solidarity is grounded in the understanding that even with these possibilities of divergence, organizing our relationships and society along lines of cooperation rather than competition is both possible with humans as they currently are and vital to the maintenance of the principle of "equal liberty for all." If competition overshadows cooperation, then this results in a situation of unnecessary and contrived categorization of "winners" and "losers," of "internecine strife and struggle," and consequently an unnecessary infringement upon the ability of each person to freely develop their potential (Goldman, 1979, p. 118).

Anarchists see the implementation of these freely associating cooperative organizational forms as not just immanently possible, but as an extant and ubiquitous means of association in our day-to-day lives, in spite of contradictory norms in governing structures and the economy. Colin Ward (1973) provides a picturesque description of this perspective:

> An anarchist society, a society which organizes itself without authority, is always in existence, like a seed beneath the snow, buried under the weight of the state and its bureaucracy, capitalism and its waste, privilege and its injustices, nationalism and its suicidal loyalties, religious differences and their superstitious separatism. . . . Far from being a speculative vision of a future society, it is a description of a mode of human organization, rooted in the experience of everyday life, which operates side by side with, and in spite of, the dominant authoritarian trends of our society. (p. 18)

## Human Nature

As suggested in the previous section, there is a recurring motif in critics of anarchism that suggests anarchists have an unreasonably high or even naïve opinion of human nature, and thus bases its political ideals on the "natural goodness" of people (Wolff, 1996, p. 34). While some anarchists might, it would be a mistake to consider such an understanding of human nature to be representative of the whole, or even most of anarchist thought. On the contrary, anarchist theorists have devoted considerable attention to the question of human nature, and consequently have developed a nuanced understanding of how it should be understood. It is important to understand the complexity of the anarchist conception of human nature, both in order to understand the anarchist objections to capitalism, the state, and hierarchical social authority generally, and because this complexity plays a vital role in distinguishing how anarchists approach education compared to the approaches of other "radical" or "libertarian" educators like A.S. Neill and Paulo Freire.

### *Anarchism and Human Nature*

Rather than holding an overly positive or benign view of an "essentialist" human nature (May, 1994, p. 63), both classical and contemporary anarchist theorists have widely understood humans to be capable of violence and selfishness, as well as kindness and altruism. Human nature, for most anarchists, is neither tainted by an original sin nor a *tabula rasa* (blank slate) à la Locke. Rather, it is malleable, and certain aspects of human behavior can become more prominent depending on context. For most anarchists, it is the situations and social structures in which we find ourselves that play a significant role in determining which of these features of our "nature" will be more likely to exhibit. Contrary to the reasoning of Thomas Hobbes and, consequently, most of the modern tradition of Western political philosophy, anarchist theorists have argued that it is precisely *because* we are capable of both good and ill that we should abolish hierarchical political institutions and social relations. As Peter Kropotkin (1988) complained:

> When we hear men saying that Anarchists imagine men much better than they really are, we merely wonder how intelligent people can repeat that nonsense. Do we not say continually that the only means of rendering men less rapacious and egotistic, less ambitious and less slavish at the same time, is to eliminate those conditions which favour the growth of egotism and rapacity, of slavishness and ambition? (p. 83)

Bakunin (1970) too believed that "It is a characteristic of privilege and of every kind of privilege to kill the mind and heart of man . . . That is a social law which admits no exceptions" (p. 31).

It is how our social relations are ordered, then, that delimits which types of behaviors are likely to thrive. One could imagine that neither Bakunin nor Kropotkin would be very surprised at the results of the Stanford Prison Experiment, wherein subjects adapted their behaviors and attitudes toward each other depending on whether they were cast as "prison guards" or "prisoners" (Zimbardo, 2007). Rather than simply hope for a deep-seated human goodness to overcome dominating and violent behavior, anarchists argue that traits like compassion, independence, and a sense of solidarity must be cultivated through properly facilitating environments. This must take place in wider society (workplace, neighborhoods, etc.) for broader changes to occur, but as Bakunin notes, the "environment that [nourishes] and [raises]" a person, like formal education in youth, is of particular importance in determining subsequent social attitudes and behavior (Maximoff, 1953, p. 153). If a child is to grow to value cooperation and solidarity with others, then she must practice cooperation rather than institutionalized competition with her peers. If a child is to grow to challenge received truths and think for herself as an adult, then she must, while young, learn in a way that encourages her to practice individual inquiry and challenge authority.

## A.S. Neill and Summerhill

The original Summerhill school and its founder A.S. Neill are regularly included in accounts of broadly "libertarian" educational experiments and ideas. As one of the longest-running schools (founded in 1921 in the town of Leiston, England, and still running) this should come as no surprise (Neill, 1992, p. 8). The similarities between Summerhill and the anarchist approach to education are quite remarkable. The original intention, according to Neill was that of "[making] the school fit the child—instead of making the child fit the school" (ibid., 9). The fundamental ideals of the school are those of freedom for the child and equality among all members of Summerhill, students and teachers alike. The freedom is that of individual autonomy. Lessons are not compulsory, play is celebrated and self-directed, and creative originality is encouraged. Equality is understood and practiced in a way that every anarchist can understand. At school-wide assembly meetings, everyone gets one vote, students and teachers alike. Teachers are called by their first names or nicknames as the social equals of students and have no real institutional authority over them (Neill, 1977, pp. 4–8). Summerhill is very much, in the words of Neill, a "self-governing community" (Neill, 1992, p. 3).

Structurally, then, Summerhill is very similar to examples and ideals of anarchist educational experiments. Pedagogically and philosophically, however, there are important distinctions. One distinction is that of Neill's understanding of human nature, which rests on the belief that a child is an innately "good, not an evil being" and that "without adult suggestion of any kind" a child can reach her potential (ibid., 9). While anarchist educators certainly don't view children as evil, and share the same abhorrence of traditional notions of "discipline" and institutional authority, they have been less enthusiastic about an individualized and abstract notion of "freedom" that does not take into account the situational and dual nature of humanity. While a child may certainly be freer and avoiding harm when protected from the regimentation and violence of traditional state schooling, such "protection from" is insufficient to provide for a positive ideal and an emancipatory social alternative. As Judith Suissa (2010) notes from her contemporary visits to Summerhill, "One has the impression of a lively group of self-confident, happy children, who may, as one imagines, very well grow up to be happy, but completely self-centred individuals . . . there is little attempt to engage with broader social issues or confront present socio-political reality" (p. 96).

A *laissez-faire* pedagogy is insufficient, then, for the anarchist approach to education. While an anarchist education does not imply any sort of dogmatic instruction, anarchist educators do view the open encouragement and practice of values, like solidarity, as a virtue. Further, and more distinctively, anarchist educators actively seek to engage with social and political questions, and to open for critique perceived repressive institutions and practices of wider society. True "neutrality" on the part of antiauthoritarian teachers in the face of an unjust and repressive social order is seen by anarchist educators as either impossible or "hypocrisy" (Ferrer, 1909, p. 6).

Desiring neither neutrality nor a dogmatic imposition of teachers' beliefs upon students, the role of an anarchist educator becomes that of a suggestive iconoclast and interlocutor with dominant social narratives. Going beyond a simple *laissez-faire* approach to learning, anarchist pedagogical practice, in seeking to encourage particular anarchist values (but not seeking to impose dogma, since this would be contrary to the values themselves) openly challenges the "sacred" institutions of the dominant social order by desanctifying their traditional justifications (Stirner, 2005, p. 19). The act of rendering the hegemonic or the sacred questionable and open to dissection, and extending to students an invitation to this sacrilege represents anarchism's primary pedagogical distinction. That it is an open *invitation*—rather than an ideological or dogmatic disciplining of students' minds, or a passive nonengagement with broader social contexts, roles, problems, and conflicts—allows anarchism to (at least partially) resolve the problematic paradox of attempting to develop free and critical minds without extensive coercion in instruction.

## Paulo Freire

Paulo Freire was a Brazilian educator whose work contributed to the development of a radical philosophy of education known as "critical pedagogy." While partially rooted in the ideas of "democratic education" as expounded by John Dewey (Dewey, 1916), and the theoretical framework of the Frankfurt School (Kanpol, 1999), critical pedagogy essentially began with Freire's publishing of *Pedagogy of the Oppressed* (1970). Freire's work laid the foundation for a host of subsequent advocates and expanders of the theory and practice of critical pedagogy (Apple, 1995; Kanpol, 1999; McLaren, 1989; Shapiro, 1990; Shor, 1992). Within *Pedagogy of the Oppressed*, Freire explores the relationships between oppressors and oppressed, and the manifestation and reproduction of these relationships within teacher-student power relations. In doing so he criticizes the elitist educational theories operating in traditional educational settings, such as the "banking theory" of education, which treats knowledge as something an authority figure deposits in the minds of pupils who do (and ought to) passively receive. Critical pedagogues argue against such theories, instead positing that students are individuals with their own minds, experiences and dignity, and they must be able to take an active role in their own process of liberation in *cooperation* with critical teachers (Freire, 1970; McLaren, 1989; Shor, 1992).

Along with emphasizing the dignity of students, and the need for nonoppressive teacher-student relationships, Critical pedagogy argues that critical educators must teach for social justice. For critical pedagogues, all education is necessarily political, and attempts at claiming neutrality or objectivity for education function as a de facto force for conservatism (Freire, 1970; Shor, 1987). The goal of critical pedagogy, then, is to develop an educational practice that can provide the necessary space and nonauthoritarian guidance for people to grow into their humanity, gain a critical analytical eye, and develop a compassionate and empathetic worldview that is capable of challenging the hegemonic order. This approach to education clearly shares much in common with the values of anarchist theorists. There remain, however, notable distinctions between the ideas of Freire and those of anarchist educators.

Richard Kahn poses a unique juxtaposition of the ideas of Freire and those of anarchist educator Ivan Illich. Kahn contrasts what he sees as the "promethean" attitude of Freire with the "epimethean" disposition of Illich. Prometheus represents, as in classic Greek myth, the "forethought" of planning and action. Prometheanism, Kahn argues, celebrates the "human potential for daring political deeds, technological ingenuity, and general rebellion against the powers that be to improve human life," but also represents the "industrial strivings of modernity" and "the ideology of progress" (Kahn, 2009, pp. 126–27). It is, then, a disposition toward active transformation and construction. Epimetheus, on the other hand, represents the "afterthought" to Prometheus's forethought. While Greek patriarchs viewed Epimetheus as "dull-witted" and weak, the epimetheanism of Illich offers a different interpretation, with Epimetheus representing a conservation of hope and an appreciation for what *is*, and a "convivial [relationship] with the world while the progenitor of the new world, Prometheus, remains bound and chained by his own creative deed" (ibid., pp. 127–28). Epimetheus's "afterthought" can then be interpreted not as a dull passivity, but rather as a disposition of reflection on the potentially harmful limits of transformation and appreciation for mutuality in the present (Kahn, 2010, p. 93). What is important for our understanding of this relationship, though, is that these attitudes need not be exclusive. After all, one cannot have an afterthought if there has not been a forethought.

The exchange between these two dispositions, then, provides a useful, process-oriented frame for understanding the role and method of education and pedagogy in anarchist thought, as does the distinction between Freire and the anarchists, and the ostensibly apolitical pedagogy of Neill. The anarchist approach to education is not accounted for entirely by a rigidly promethean or epimethean perspective, but is rather to be found in the experimental and dialectical tension between the two . . . much akin to the anarchist conception of a desirable and dynamic challenging and exchange between teachers and students.

## Anarchy, the State, and the Classroom

Usually developing in the interstices of dominant school systems, sustained anarchist schools have had an oft-troubled history of opposition and harassment from the powers-that-be. Often seen by states (even when not by the anarchist pedagogues themselves) as direct challenges to their organizational norms, social values, and principles of authority, anarchist schools have faced bureaucratic reaction, censure, and police suppression. We will look at a few examples of anarchist schools, specifically the Modern School of Francisco Ferrer and contemporary anarchist "free" schools and space, to see some of the general principles of anarchist education in practice.

### *Escuela Moderna*

The most prominent example of an overtly anarchist school would most likely be the Escuela Moderna (Modern School) movement that originated in Spain, as developed, operated and expounded by Francisco Ferrer. Ferrer was an anarchist and an educator, whose interest in experimental education grew alongside his disdain for the highly regimented and authoritarian school system of his home country. In the Modern School of Ferrer, children were allowed greater freedom of individual inquiry and spontaneity, time for personal reflection in the school or in the gardens surrounding, and were not treated as lesser beings to be commanded by a dogmatic authority, as in the dominant Catholic schools of Ferrer's native Spain (Goldman, 1911b). Children, thought Ferrer, ought to be able to develop the potentiality of their whole being, not simply the instrumental, vocational, or acontextually abstract, and thus were to be allowed to visit factories, museums, gardens, and other community locales in order to learn through practice (Ferrer, 1909, p. 2). Neither were they to be subjected to the nationalist messages of the state, impersonal and pedagogically inappropriate examinations, or the sexual segregation of the wider society. In his classic defense of these (still seemingly) radical practices, Ferrer (1913) declares that:

> Having admitted and practiced the coeducation of boys and girls, of rich and poor—having, that is to say, started from the principle of solidarity and equality—we are not prepared to create new inequality. Hence in the Modern School there will be no rewards and no punishments; there will be no examinations to puff up some children with the flattering title of "excellent," to give others the vulgar title of "good," and make others unhappy with a consciousness of incapacity and failure. (p. 55)

While eschewing dogma, Ferrer did not believe, like A.S. Neill, in the possibility or desirability of teaching from a stance of political or ethical neutrality. After searching in vain for textbooks he felt were appropriately nonauthoritarian for the school library, he eventually decided to install a printing press and commission works that addressed "the injustices connected with patriotism, the horrors of war, and the iniquity of conquest," things he viewed as brute facts obscured or hidden by the dogmas of the Catholic Church and the nationalism of the state (Avrich, 1980, p. 23).

Ferrer saw all of this as fitting rightly within the anarchist tradition of *prefiguration*, the development of a new society "in the shell of the old." As such, it shouldn't be a surprise that Spanish authorities reacted against this and closed down the school in 1906. What was a surprise to most, and the cause of an international outcry, was his subsequent execution resulting from bogus charges of "instigating uprising" following mass-protests and general strikes in the wake the Spanish war against Morocco (Goldman, 1911b).

*Free schools and free spaces*

Informed in many ways by Ferrer, education philosopher Ivan Illich criticized the notion that a formal school is *the* proper place where education happens, arguing in defense of education as a lifelong process, rather than something that you only go through while young. Taken together, these ideas could suggest a notion of a "school" that is a socially embedded and democratic institution, freely available to all age groups, with a far more interactive and cooperative role between teachers, students and parents in designing curriculum, allocating resources, and expanding education into experiences beyond the traditional schoolhouse and occasional field trip model. Especially important was Illich's insistence that sites of education remain open to the community, rather than rigidly institutionalized, in order to avoid monopolizations of informational/knowledge channels (Illich, 1971). This notion of open and free education fits well with Paul Goodman's (1977) belief that "in anarchist theory the world revolution means the process by which the grip of authority is loosed, so that the functions of life can regulate themselves, without top-down direction and coordination" (p. 215).

This notion seems to be demonstrated in the case of some recent Anarchist Free Schools. Allan Antliff provides an inspiring account of a Toronto Anarchist Free School, and its subsequent Internet counterpart Anarchist U. These schools were/are nonprofit, voluntarily operated and open-attendance schools run along anarchist organizational lines. Within them, classes are freely proposed and freely joined by anyone interested on any number of topics. Antliff (2007) describes the different attitude of participants: "Once education was made free and grading and other assorted punitive measures (degree denial) were set aside, people could learn without competing with one another or striving to satisfy authority figures in their midst" (pp. 248–60).

Such successful, open and community-embedded experiments can provide for a cornucopia of educational diversity, and stimulate interests beyond traditional subjects, while ensuring ready, open access to knowledge for those who desire it.

Anarchist schools and educational spaces have thus emphasized the free-flowing nature of learning, and abhorred intellectual regimentation, viewing this as the death-knell of independent thought. This notion of how a school can operate certainly appears radical when compared to the operation of contemporary public schools or universities. Both of the latter are usually managed in a top-down manner with little *direct* control over the meaningful operations of the institutions by teachers, students or parents, at least in the case of public schools. Academic departments within universities can have some degree of internal self-management, although this does not extend equally to graduate students, adjunct instructors, or other largely contingent university education workers who have little academic freedom or job security (AAUP, 2006).

## The State and the Classroom

> In our dreams, people yield themselves with perfect docility to our molding hands. The present education conventions of intellectual and character education fade from their minds, and, unhampered by tradition, we work our own good will upon a grateful and responsive folk.
> —John D. Rockefeller (1906)

The repression and marginalization experienced by many anarchist schools and experiments, among other obstacles, has historically made the operation of truly independent anarchist educational programs difficult. The implementation of anarchist educational and political ideals within the dominant state-run public school systems has had its own set of difficulties. The variety of critiques developed in response to this difficulty are diverse, but they are all rooted in the notion that various forms of state-run school organization, pedagogy, and practices violate the values and methods anarchists believe to be necessary to cultivate free and critical minds, and defend solidaristic and egalitarian social relations.

A principal critique from anarchist educators has been that the authority relations between students and teachers, teachers and administrators, and between schools and the state are part of a formidable hierarchy that seeks to instill and reproduce amenable attitudes toward institutional authorities and deference toward authority as such (Chomsky, 2000, p. 17). Rather than develop educational systems that gravitate around the needs of the individual child, children are molded to the goals and expectations of the state educational system. In a capitalist system, this manifests as publicly funded "apprentice-training for corporations, government" and the reproduction of the educational system itself, as well as "adjusting" students to their problems with authority (Goodman, 1964, p. 18). For Goodman, the bell-ringing, time-accounting, and hierarchical authority and disciplinary system of state schools function as a form of behavioral operant conditioning, developing obedience rather than spontaneity or initiative.

Voltairine de Cleyre, an American anarchist and teacher, criticized the school systems at the end of the nineteenth century for their authoritarian operations and the effects they had upon their unfortunate students. She decried how children were forced to sit silently and absolutely still for hours on end, while being "taught" material that had little relevance to their own lives and interests and usually sought to expound the virtues of the dominant political order through the guise of a benign claim to "truth." The effect of this, she noted, was to put "an iron mould upon the will of youth, destroying all spontaneity and freedom of expression" (de Cleyre, 2005, p. 260). Her most effective description of the absurdity of this system is encapsulated in a poignant, if lengthy (as was her style), metaphor:

> Any gardener who should attempt to raise healthy, beautiful, and fruitful plants by outraging all those plants' instinctive wants and searchings, would meet as his reward—sickly plants, ugly plants, sterile plants, dead plants. He will not do it; he will watch very carefully to see whether they like much sunlight, or considerable shade, whether they thrive on much water or get drowned in it . . . the plant itself indicate to him when he is doing the right thing . . . If he finds the plant revolts against his experiments, he will desist at once, and try something else; if he finds it thrives, he will emphasize the particular treatment so long as it seems beneficial. But what he will surely not do, will be to prepare a certain area of ground all just alike, with equal chances of sun and amount of moisture in every part, and then plant everything together without discrimination—mighty close together!—saying beforehand, "If plants don't want to thrive on this, they ought to want to; and if they are stubborn about it, they must be made to." (ibid., p. 255)

Anarchist educators would agree, then, with critical pedagogues in the judgment that the implementation of standardized testing regimes, a cornerstone of current policies like No Child Left Behind, renders pedagogical experimentation and potential challenges to this arrangement very difficult, even when a cantankerous or brave educator (anarchist or otherwise) does have the desire. Standardized tests are seen, in Fordist fashion, as imposing uniform performance expectations and methods upon students who have different learning styles, individual needs, and who may be at different places in their personal intellectual development. Further, rather than encouraging a curriculum oriented toward the development of critical analytical skills, or fulfilling personal curiosity, standardized tests encourage a shallow, bulimic approach to learning. This entails the rote consumption and regurgitation of contextually isolated facts and figures on command, with high performance on a test seen as an end in itself, and synonymous with having learned something. On top of it all, standardized tests serve as gatekeepers of educational advancement, threatening failure and halting further learning until "adequacy" is demonstrated (Kohn, 2000).

In the face of this sort of "education," some radical pedagogues have looked for inspirational educational alternatives in the ancient Athenian educational system and principles of paideia (Morrison, 1995; Fotopoulos,

2005; Shiva, 2005). The value of this system does have limits, given, among other things, the political limitations and prejudices of ancient Athens (Kahn, 2010, p. 38). However, in comparing broadly libertarian educational principles to the broad, civic-minded self-improvement goals of the ancient Athenian educational system of paideia we can find a useful epochal counterpart to relate to the modern state. The correlate "ideal" educational system of the modern state can, then, be understood as a combination of disciplinary market instrumentalism and agoge, the ancient Spartan disciplinary regimen. In the agoge regimen, youth (solely males then) were trained to value loyalty to the State over the self, military discipline, conformity, and competition among peers for the purposes of establishing dominance (Hodkinson, 1996). In creating more space within the modern educational system for alternatives to this disciplinarian and regimented pedagogy, alternatives like paideia or other models of inspiration, could certainly provide a welcome reprieve, and protect pockets of "spheres of free action," even if they are ephemeral (Ward, 1973, p. 18).

In comparing the structures and functional values of state schools in the United States with previous examples of anarchist schooling, and after elaborating on the values, organizational principles and understanding of human nature within anarchist thought, I hope that the differences in values instilled and desirable types of persons developed are made starkly apparent. Many of the critiques of state school systems offered by anarchist educators are over a century old, yet (unfortunately) sound incredibly contemporary.

## Conclusions

Ultimately, I hope to have demonstrated that understanding the relationship between anarchism and education is a worthwhile project. While sharing many commonalities with other radical traditions, I believe that anarchist theory provides an identifiably distinct perspective for understanding and approaching education as a political, prefigurative, and transformative encounter, regardless of one's politics. I hope to have also demonstrated the importance of education for anarchism as a political theory and emancipatory personal and social project. The implications of this appreciation for education and the importance of early prefigurative value-contestation and construction are two-fold, however. Gustav Landauer best summarized this conceptual problematic in this way: "The state is not something which can be destroyed by a revolution, but is a condition, a certain relationship between human beings, a mode of human behavior; we destroy it by contracting other behavior, by behaving differently" (Ward, 1973, p. 23).

Understanding oppressive institutions as not "things" to be destroyed, but relationships to remake and ideas to replace is a double-edged sword. It is frustrating in that it disperses the sites of critical social contestation against oppressive institutions and ideas to, literally, the minds of every individual (though this does not preclude traditional externalized social struggles for greater equity and liberty). It is encouraging, though, in that it reveals their nonmonolithic and mutable nature. Taking advantage of an anarchist approach to education, then, could, in terms of pedagogy and praxis, open up greater possibilities for imagining and cultivating alternative social relationships in the minds of those who would live them.

## References

AAUP. (2006). *American Association of University Professors Contingent Faculty Index 2006*. Retrieved from http://www.aaup.org/AAUP/pubsres/research/conind2006.htm.

Antliff, A. (2007). Breaking free: Anarchist pedagogy. In M. Cote, R. Day & G. de Peuter (Eds.), *Utopian pedagogy*, Toronto: University of Toronto Press.

Apple, M. (1995). *Democratic schools*. Alexandria, Virginia: Association for Supervision and Curriculum Development.

Avrich, P. (1980). *The modern school movement*. Princeton, NJ: Princeton University Press.

Bakunin, M. (1970). *God and the state*. New York: Dover.

Berkman, A. (2003). *What is anarchism?* Edinburgh/London/Oakland: AK Press.

Bookchin, M. (2005). *The ecology of freedom: The emergence and dissolution of hierarchy*. Edinburgh/Oakland: AK Press.

Chomsky, N. (2000). *Chomsky on miseducation*. New York: Rowman and Littlefield.

de Cleyre, V. (2005). Modern educational reform. In *Exquisite rebel: The essays of Voltairine de Cleyre*. Albany, NY: SUNY Press.

Dewey, J. (1916). *Democracy and education*. New York: The Free Press.

Ferrer, F. (1909). *The modern school*. New York: Mother Earth Publishing Association.

Ferrer, F. (1913). *The origins and ideals of the modern school*. London: Watts.

Fotopoulos, T. (2005). From (mis)education to Paideia. *International Journal of Inclusive Democracy*, 55(1) (September).

Freire, P. (1970). *Pedagogy of the oppressed*. New York: Continuum.

Goldman, E. (1911a). Anarchism: What it really stands for. In *Anarchism and other essays*. New York: Mother Earth Publishing Association.

Goldman, E. (1911b). Francisco Ferrer and the modern school. In *Anarchism and other essays*. New York: Mother Earth Publishing Association.

Goldman, E. (1940). *The place of the individual in society*. Garden City, NY: Doubleday.

Goldman, E. (1979). *Red Emma speaks*, A.K. Shulman (Ed.). London: Wildwood House.

Goodman, P. (1964). *Compulsory mis-education*. New York: Vintage Books.

Guérin, D. (1970). *Anarchism: From theory to practice*. New York: Monthly Review Press.

Hodkinson, S. (1996). Agoge. In S. Hornblower (Ed.), *Oxford classical dictionary*. Oxford: Oxford University Press.

Kahn, R. (2009). Anarchic epimetheanism: The pedagogy of Ivan Illich. In R. Amster, A. DeLeon, L. Fernandez, A. Nocella II & D Shannon (Eds.), *Contemporary anarchist studies: An introductory anthology of anarchy in the academy*. London, UK: Routledge.

Kahn, R. (2010). *Critical pedagogy, ecoliteracy, and planetary crisis*. New York: Peter Lang.

Kanpol, B. (1999). *Critical pedagogy: An introduction*, 2nd ed. Westport, Conn.: Bergan & Garvey.

Kohn, A. (1992). *No contest: The case against competition*. New York: Houghton Mifflin.

Kohn, A. (2000). *The case against standardized testing*. Portsmouth, NH: Heinemann.
Kropotkin, P. (1972). *Mutual aid: A factor of evolution*. London: Allen Lane.
Kropotkin, P. (1985). *The conquest of bread*. Catania: Elephant Editions.
Kropotkin, P. (1988). *Act for yourselves: Articles from Freedom 1886–1907*, N. Walter & H. Becker (Eds.). London: Freedom Press.
Malatesta, E. (1993). *Errico Malatesta: His life and ideas*, 3rd ed., V. Richards (Ed.). London: Freedom Press.
Marshall, P. (2010). *Demanding the impossible: A history of anarchism*. Oakland: PM Press.
Maximoff, G.P. (Ed.). (1953). *The political philosophy of Bakunin*. New York: The Free Press.
May, T. (1994). *The political philosophy of poststructuralist anarchism*. Philadelphia: Pennsylvania University Press.
McLaren, P. (1989). *Life in schools*. New York: Longman.
Morrison, R. (1995). *Ecological democracy*. Boston: South End Press.
Neill, A.S. (1977). *Summerhill: A radical approach to child rearing*. New York: Pocket Books.
Neill, A.S. (1992). *Summerhill school: A new view of childhood*. A. Lamb, (Ed.). New York: St. Martin's Griffin.
Shapiro, S. (1990). *Between capitalism and democracy*. New York: Bergin & Garvey.
Shiva, V. (2005). *Earth democracy: Justice, sustainability, and peace*. Boston: South End Press.
Shor, I. (1987). *Critical teaching and everyday life*. Chicago: University of Chicago Press.
Shor, I. (1992). *Empowering education*. Chicago: University of Chicago Press.
Spencer, H. (1993). *Spencer: Political writings*. J. Offer, (Ed.). Cambridge: Cambridge University Press.
Starr, A. (2000). *Naming the enemy: Anti-corporate movements confront globalization*. New York: Zed Books.
Stirner, M. (2005). False principles of our education. In D. Guérin (Ed.), *No gods, no masters*. Oakland: AK Press.
Suissa, J. (2010). *Anarchism and education: A philosophical perspective*. Oakland: PM Press.
Sylvan, R. (1993). Anarchism. In R.E. Goodin & P. Pettit (Eds.), *A companion to contemporary political philosophy*. Oxford: Blackwell.
Ward, C. (1973). *Anarchy in action*. London: Freedom Press.
Wolff, J. (1996). *An introduction to political philosophy*. Oxford: Oxford University Press.
Zimbardo, P. (2007). *The Lucifer effect: Understanding how good people turn evil*. New York: Random House.

CHAPTER 2

# Updating the Anarchist Forecast for Social Justice in Our Compulsory Schools

David Gabbard

Writing for Salon.com in 2007, Gary Kamiya pondered how George W. Bush, in light of his administration's incessant abuses of power, had managed to avoid impeachment. Bush's "problems go far beyond Iraq," Kamiya wrote. "His administration has been dogged by one massive scandal after the other, from the Katrina debacle, to Bush's approval of illegal wiretapping and torture, to his unparalleled use of 'signing statements' to disobey laws that he disagrees with, to the outrageous Gonzales and U.S. attorneys affair" (Kamiya, 2007). So, why hasn't he been impeached?

For Kamiya, "the main reason is obvious" when viewed from the perspective of realpolitik. The Democrats, with their narrow majority in Congress, did not have the political will to do so. In weighing the potential costs and benefits of such a move, they feared that impeachment could backfire on them. They preferred, it seemed, to give Bush enough rope to hang the Republican Party in the 2008 elections.

Kamiya, however, also identified a deeper and more troubling reason that Bush was not impeached. This reason had less to do with either Bush or the Democratic Party, and more with us—the American people. "Bush's warmongering," Kamiya contends,

> spoke to something deep in our national psyche. The emotional force behind America's support for the Iraq war, the molten core of an angry, resentful patriotism, is still too hot for Congress, the media and even many Americans who oppose the war, to confront directly. It's a national myth. It's John Wayne. *To impeach Bush would force us to directly confront our national core of violent self-righteousness—come*

> *to terms with it, understand it and reject it. And we're not ready to do that.* (Kamiya, 2007; emphasis added)

That national core of violent self-righteousness went on full public display the night of May 2, 2011, when President Barack Obama announced on national television that seventy-nine U.S. commandoes had raided a compound in Abbottabad, Pakistan and killed Osama bin Laden. Dozens of spontaneous celebrations erupted at a number of sites across the nation, including Times Square, a host of university campuses, as well as in front of the White House. Everywhere, the scene was the same. Hundreds, if not thousands, of flag-waving citizens, hyped up on the bloodlust of vengeance whooping and hollering beneath the moon, filled the streets and the night air with chants of "U.S.A.! U.S.A.! U.S.A.!" Had anyone stepped into any of those throngs to question a single element of the official version of the events of September 11, 2001, they'd have been torn to bits. The mob, inebriated on manifest destiny and other ideological elixirs, would tolerate no reflection, no questions, and no challenge to their God-given right to believe whatever the oligarchs had sanctioned them to know. It could have been a Super Bowl, Stanley Cup, NBA title, or World Series celebration. That's about the depth of understanding that most of our fellow citizens have of world affairs. America is "our team." And, as George Bush told us, "you're either with us, or you're against us." And that night in May, we scored a victory. It was time to *party*!

## Dare We Ever Grow Up?

If we'd ever find a way to collectively come to terms with our national core of violent self-righteousness, we would have to acknowledge what underlies it. We would have to recognize, as Cornel West argues in *Democracy Matters* (2004), that

> the American democratic experiment is unique in human history not because we are God's chosen people to lead the world, nor because we are always a force for good in the world, but because of our refusal to acknowledge the deeply racist and imperial roots of our democratic project. We are exceptional because of our denial of the antidemocratic foundation stones of American democracy. No other democratic nation revels so blatantly in such self-deceptive innocence, such self-paralyzing reluctance to confront the night-side of its own history. This sentimental flight from history—or adolescent escape from painful truths about ourselves—means that even as we grow old, grow big, and grow powerful, we have *yet* to grow up. (p. 41)

And whereas Kamiya simply asserts, "we need therapy," West offers a more specific prescription, calling for the enactment of a "democratic *paideia*—the cultivation of an active, informed citizenry—in order to preserve and deepen our democratic experiment," coupled with "*parrhesia*—frank and fearless speech—that is the lifeblood of any democracy" (ibid., pp. 41, 209). Such measures are necessary, he contends, if we are to escape "our self-deceptive innocence" and our "self-paralyzing reluctance to confront the night-side of [our] own history."

Educators committed to a pedagogy of social justice would eagerly answer West's call for fearless speech in service of what they hold to be one of the most important missions of America's schools: "the cultivation of an active, informed citizenry." Tragically, however, no one knows the sting of America's "violent self-righteousness" better than those same educators. Long before Bill O'Reilly of Fox News, the official network of violent self-righteousness, launched the national demonization campaign against University of Colorado professor Ward Churchill for disrupting the official narrative of September 11, the Monroe County Community Schools Corporation in Bloomington, Indiana, declined to renew the contract of Deborah Mayer, an elementary school teacher. Mayer's transgression occurred while discussing the December 13, 2002, issue *Time for Kids*, a children's version of *Time* magazine that was a regular part of the curriculum. That issue contained a story covering a peace march in Washington D.C. protesting the pending U.S. invasion of Iraq, which led a student to ask Mayer if she "would ever be in a peace march." Mayer informed the class that whenever she drove past marchers holding up signs asking motorists to "Honk For Peace" that she honked. She also told the children that she thought people "should seek peaceful solutions before going to war." The class then discussed a conflict resolution program at their own school, and they dropped the subject. Shortly afterward, however, a Bush-supporting parent brought a complaint against Mayer before the school principal, and the district later refused to renew her contract (Egelko, 2007).

Judge Sarah Evans Barker ruled against Mayer in her wrongful termination suit, arguing that "teachers, including Ms. Mayer, do not have a right under the First Amendment to express their opinions during the instructional period" (Global Research, 2006). Later, in the U.S. Court of Appeals for the Seventh Circuit, famed neoliberal jurist and Chief Judge Frank H. Easterbrook upheld Barker's ruling. "Expression," Easterbrook wrote, "is a teacher's stock in trade, *the commodity she sells to her employer in exchange for a salary*" (Egelko, 2007, emphasis added). Though she plans a further appeal, Mayer holds little optimism that the Supreme Court will take her case. If the decision stands, particularly in light of the neoliberal logic found in Easterbrook's ruling, we can abandon all but the slimmest of hopes that schools will ever become sites for pursuing social justice. In that case, perhaps the time has arrived for us to take the anarchist critique of education more seriously and recognize the futility of pushing for democratic educational reforms. Maybe we should begin considering the possibility that we might best pursue social justice, not by reforming schools but by resisting state-controlled systems of compulsory schooling altogether.

## The Anarchist Critique

When he published *What Is Property?* in 1840, Pierre-Joseph Proudhon became the first person to call himself an anarchist (Proudhon, 2003). He was not, however, the first person to call for the abolition of the state. For this reason, scholarship traces the anarchist tradition back to William Godwin. Credited with developing the first comprehensive anarchist critique of government schools in his *Enquiry Concerning Political Justice* in 1793, Godwin viewed freedom of thought as fundamental to political liberty (Godwin, 1796). As Joel Spring (1994) explains, Godwin believed that "since people constantly improve their reasoning power and their understanding of nature, their understanding of the best form of government is constantly changing" (p. 42). While he recognized that education was crucial toward the development of individuals' powers of rational thought that would guide them in self-government, Spring (1983) notes, Godwin also "considered national systems of education one of the foremost dangers to freedom and liberty" (p. 68). "Before we put so powerful a machine (education) under the direction of so ambiguous an agent (government)," Godwin warned, "it behooves us to consider well what it is we do. Government will not fail to employ it, to strengthen its hands, and perpetuate its institutions" (Spring, 1994, p. 42).

Indeed, Godwin's warning gives us good reason to question whether government-controlled schools can ever function as sites where students cultivate their powers of reasoning in the service of social justice. Furthermore, Godwin also provokes us to consider the extent to which schools, as instruments of state power, have contributed more to what Kamiya identifies as our "our national core of violent self-righteousness" than they have to cultivating the "active, informed citizenry" called for by Cornel West.

Echoing Godwin's concerns and armed with two hundred years of historical hindsight, contemporary anarchist scholar Noam Chomsky (2003) describes "the basic institutional role and function of the schools" as providing "an ideological service: there's a real selection for obedience and conformity" (pp. 27–28). In Chomsky's analysis, compulsory, government schooling brings children at a very early age into an indoctrination system "that works against independent thought in favor of obedience" with the goal of keeping people "from asking questions that matter about important issues that directly affect them and others" (Chomsky & Macedo, 2000, p. 24). In Deborah Mayer's case, of course, the important issue was the pending invasion of Iraq. Keep in mind that a *student* initiated the conversation concerning Mayer's participation in peace marches. Therefore, the decision of the school board and courts' rulings on that decision sent a clear message to students as well as teachers: "We don't discuss 'questions that matter' about issues that might interest *you*." That message, of course, underscores Chomsky's thesis that schools function to discourage independent inquiry and promote obedience and conformity.

Emma Goldman made similar observations early in the twentieth century. "What, then, is the school of today?" she asked. "It is for the child what the prison is for the convict and the barracks for the soldier—a place where everything is being used to break the will of the child, and then to pound, knead, and shape it into a being utterly foreign to itself. . . . It is but part of a system which can maintain itself only through absolute discipline and uniformity" (Goldman, 2007).

Goldman's description of schools receives considerable support in the more heavily analytic writings of Michel Foucault. In books such as *Madness and Civilization* (1988) and *Discipline and Punish* (1995), Foucault points out for us a very peculiar historical oddity. Systems of government-sponsored compulsory schooling did, in fact, begin to emerge at the same point in history as the modern prison, and each was modeled on the Army barracks. Compulsory schooling of the masses has always had less to do with education and more to do with discipline. By "discipline," Foucault refers to a form of treatment that

> increases the forces of the body (in economic terms of utility) and diminishes those same forces (in terms of political obedience). In short, it disassociates powers from the body; on the one hand it turns it into an "aptitude," a "capacity," which it seeks to increase; on the other hand, it reverses the course of the energy, the power that might result from it, and turns it into a relation of strict subjugation. If economic exploitation separates the force of and the product of labor, let us say that disciplinary coercion establishes in the body the constricting link between an increased aptitude and an increased domination. (ibid, p. 141)

Moreover, compulsory schooling functions to discipline individuals in a manner that increases the productive power that their bodies offer to the economic system while simultaneously diminishing their power to resist economic exploitation and the political system that initiates that exploitation by compelling students to attend school in the first place.

The writings of Benjamin Rush, a signer of the Declaration of Independence and recognized "father of American psychiatry," are particularly illuminative of how the early advocates of compulsory schooling viewed the importance of diminishing individuals' powers of resistance by building up their emotional attachments to the state. Rush wrote his "Thoughts upon the Mode of Education Proper in a Republic" in 1786—just seven years before Godwin wrote his *Enquiry Concerning Political Justice*. Rush declared "the principle of patriotism stands in need of the reinforcement of *prejudice*, and it is well known that our strongest prejudices in favor of our country are formed in the first one and twenty years of our lives. . . . Our schools of learning," he argued, "by producing one general and uniform system of education, will render the mass of the people more homogeneous and thereby fit them more easily for uniform and peaceable government" (Rush, 1786). The quotes below come from the same document:

> In order more effectually to secure to our youth the advantages of a religious education, it is necessary to impose upon them the doctrines and discipline of a particular church. Man is naturally an ungovernable animal, and observations on particular societies and countries will teach us that when we add the restraints of ecclesiastical to those of domestic and civil government, we produce in him the highest degrees of order and virtue. . . .
>
> Let our pupil be taught that he does not belong to himself, but that he is public property. Let him be taught to love his family, but let him be taught at the same time that he must forsake and even forget them when the welfare of his country requires it. . . .
>
> In the education of youth, let the authority of our masters be as *absolute* as possible. The government of schools like the government of private families should be *arbitrary*, that it may not be *severe*. By this mode of education, we prepare our youth for the subordination of laws and thereby qualify them for becoming good citizens of the republic. I am satisfied that the most useful citizens have been formed from those youth who have never known or felt their own wills till they were one and twenty years of age, and I have often thought that society owes a great deal of its order and happiness to the deficiencies of parental government being supplied by those habits of obedience and subordination which are contracted at schools. . . .
>
> From the observations that have been made it is plain that I consider it as possible to convert men into republican machines. This must be done if we expect them to perform their parts properly in the great machine of the government of the state. (ibid.)

Noah Webster, known as "the schoolmaster of America," could not have agreed more. "Good republicans," Webster wrote, "are formed by a singular machinery in the body politic, which takes the child as soon as he can speak, checks his natural independence and passions, makes him subordinate to superior age, to the laws of the state, to town and parochial institutions"

(Spring, 2005, pp. 48–49). Webster's real significance as a force in shaping the direction of American education and culture rests with his creation of a series of books that were the major school texts in nineteenth-century America, selling over a million and a half copies by 1801 and seventy-five million copies by 1875. As Webster's biographer, Harry Warfel, characterized them, "this series of unified textbooks effectually shaped the destiny of American education for a century. Imitators sprang up by the dozens, and each echoed the Websterian nationalism. The word 'American' became indispensable in all textbook titles; all vied in patriotic eloquence" (ibid., p 48)

We are able to trace, then, the roots of Kamiya's "national core of violent self-righteousness" right back to the very beginnings of America's experiment with compulsory schooling. "Our schools," wrote a veteran schoolteacher in 1910, "have failed because they rest on compulsion and constraint. . . . It is deemed possible and important that all should be interested in the same things, in the same sequence, and at the same time. . . . Under the circumstances (of 1910) teachers are mere tools, automatons who perpetuate a machine that turns out automatons" (Goldman, 2007).

Under the conditions of 2011, over a hundred years later, how little has changed. With Emma Goldman, we should recognize that under the enduring conditions of government-sponsored, compulsory schooling, "the child becomes stunted, that its mind is dulled, and that its very being is warped, thus making it unfit to take its place in the social struggle as an independent factor. Indeed, there is nothing so hated so much in the world today as independent factors in whatever line" (ibid.).

## The Permissible Purposes of Compulsory Schooling

I vividly recall the day my son Jackson came home from school when he was just in the first grade, complaining of a sore chin. "I get done with my work before everybody else," he told me. "And when I ask the teacher what to do next, she tells me to just sit there and put my head on my desk." Evidently, the weight of his head on his chin resting on his folded arms atop his desk caused the soreness. Then came the question I knew would one day come, "Why do I have to go to school, Dad?"

What was I to tell him, given all I know about the truth to that question? Of course, there are actually multiple truths that could be told in response to that question, and none of them, told honestly, are very gratifying. At the most basic level, kids have to go to school because the government says they must—an often forgotten, overlooked, or regularly ignored fact that ought to make each of us nervous about the enterprise of compulsory schooling from the start. It certainly explains why so many kids wind up hating school. Many, if not most of them aren't there because they want to be, but because they have to be. According to the Alliance for Excellent Education, seven thousand kids drop out of school *every day* (Alliance for Excellent Education, 2011). Who knows how many more *tune* out because they don't see any relevance in the curriculum?

Of course, I wasn't going to tell my own kid to drop out of first grade, but it's hard not to empathize with kids who make that decision at some point in their school career. At the same time, it's hard not to find sympathy for them, because we know what the consequences are for refusing the advertised beneficence of compulsory schooling. Or, at least, we used to.

One of the first lessons in most Foundations of American Education courses like the one I teach entails sharing Thomas Jefferson's belief that America should become a meritocratic society rather than an aristocratic society. In an aristocracy, one's position in a society stratified along economic and political lines was determined by one's birth. Economic and political power remained concentrated in the hands of just a few families and was passed on from generation to generation. The growth of the market and the rise of the new merchant class in the seventeenth and eighteenth centuries would challenge the aristocratic traditions of European feudalism. Eventually, that challenge would fuel the rhetoric of quasi-democratic revolutions such as ours in 1776.

For Jefferson, a system of public schools would help ensure that one's position in the new American society, which had, of course, remained highly stratified, both politically and economically, would be based on *merit* rather than birthright. So, if you went to school, worked hard, and demonstrated sufficient talent and ability, you could aspire to and achieve whatever position in society you wanted, or at least a position high enough to guarantee yourself and your family some measure of economic security.

These ideas helped form the basis of what we've come to know as the American Dream Ideology. Horace Mann would later borrow from Jefferson in formulating his arguments in favor a creating a tax-supported system of compulsory schools in the state of Massachusetts. To strengthen the persuasiveness of his rhetoric, Mann "framed" his proposal, not as government-mandated schools, but as "Common Schools." They would be "common" in three important ways. They would impart a "common" political philosophy to weaken political strife at a time when America's working classes were at deep odds with the ownership classes. They would also impart a common religious (Christian) doctrine to ameliorate the ongoing conflict among the various Christian sects at the time. Finally, and most importantly for our purposes here, Mann presented his system of schools as being "common" in the sense that children from all walks of life would attend the same schools and, therefore, have the same opportunity to demonstrate their talents and abilities and justify their future position in America's stratified social order. In theory, this meant that children from wealthy families who "failed" at school would end up as poor adults, while poor children who excelled at school would end up as wealthy adults. According to Mann's promise, and in keeping with Jefferson meritocratic vision, common schools would function as a great social equalizer.

That promise has yet to be fulfilled, because it's always been a false promise. Children of the most elite classes have, with rare exception, never attended public schools. So, those schools have never been truly "common." The state of Massachusetts alone is home to forty private boarding schools such as Groton, where the price of tuition for "boarders" is $48,895 and $37,020 for "day students." Interestingly, when we research the dates when those schools were founded, we find that most of them were established toward the end of the nineteenth century, just when larger numbers of children from lower-class families began being pushed into the public schools created in accordance with Mann's vision.

Comparably, here in North Carolina, where Jim Crow laws once segregated children into black schools and white schools, we have numerous so-called "Christian academies." When we research the dates of their founding, we find they were created in the early 1970s, shortly after the 1964 Civil Rights Act put teeth into the 1954 *Brown v. Board of Education* decision and ushered in a period of government mandated desegregation.

Elite and privileged groups have always had the financial and political means to pass their advantages on to their children. So, it becomes very hard to take someone like Bill Gates seriously when, in his teacher recruitment commercial for Teach.gov, he says, "My success came from how lucky I was to have some great teachers." Maybe so, but shouldn't he at least preface that with an acknowledgment that he was also "lucky" to have a father wealthy enough to pay $25,000 a year for his tuition at the Lakeside School, whose course catalog easily rivals most small private liberal arts colleges? For example, the history and social study curriculum at Lakeside's "Upper School" (high school) includes required courses in Modern World History, 1200–1870, Contemporary World History, 1870 to the Present, and United States History with electives in

- The Ancient Mediterranean World
- The Cold War
- After the Cold War, The World at the Turn of the Twenty-First Century
- Introduction to Philosophy
- Introduction to World Religions
- The Holocaust and Genocide Studies
- Leadership for the Modern Era
- Comparative Government and Politics
- Freedom, Crime, and the Law
- Africa Today

- Global Village
- Music of the African Diaspora
- Natives and Strangers: American Immigration
- Microeconomics
- Developing Economies
- Issues in the Contemporary Middle East and North Africa
- Race Matters: A (Fairly) Contemporary Intellectual History of African America, and
- Gender Studies

How many of us who attended public schools had those opportunities available to us? Perhaps more people would demand such a curriculum, but few of us have any awareness of the existence of places like Lakeside or Groton, let alone any knowledge of their curricula.

Nevertheless, if only because employers, primarily since the 1950s, began requiring educational credentials from their job candidates, the meritocratic argument for schooling did develop some measure of legitimacy over the years. Looking at Table 1 below, we find a very significant difference (18.6 percent) between the unemployment rates in 2008 for college graduates and high school graduates, and a nearly identical (17.9 percent) difference between those who earn a high school diploma and those who do not.

| Level of Educational Attainment | Unemployment Rate Among 16–24-Year-Old Out-of-School Youth in 2008 |
|---|---|
| College Graduates | 13.3% |
| 1–3 Years of College | 21.2% |
| H.S. Graduate | 31.9% |
| H.S. Dropouts | 54.0% |

Since the 1950s, then, most Americans learned to take the rules of the game for granted. If you work hard in school and graduate, you'll be able to find a job and establish some economic security for yourself. But that myth is quickly coming unraveled. In the words of a New Jersey man who lost his job in 2010, "I did everything right, I played by the rules, I got skills, I excelled in my job, all to no avail . . . I don't know what I'm going to do," he continued. "All the years of both parties talking about free trade agreements and how we will retrain America was just a bunch of BS; it was easy to say all that when times were good" (Delaney, 2011). As Arthur Delaney has so accurately pointed out, Barack Obama made these changes to what we used to take for granted as the "rules of the game" official, or at least publically acknowledgeable, in his 2011 State of the Union address:

> Many people watching tonight can probably remember a time when finding a good job meant showing up at a nearby factory or a business

> downtown. You didn't always need a degree, and your competition was pretty much limited to your neighbors. If you worked hard, chances are you'd have a job for life, with a decent paycheck and good benefits and the occasional promotion. Maybe you'd even have the pride of seeing your kids work at the same company.
>
> That world has changed. And for many, the change has been painful. I've seen it in the shuttered windows of once booming factories, and the vacant storefronts on once busy Main Streets. I've heard it in the frustrations of Americans who've seen their paychecks dwindle or their jobs disappear—proud men and women who feel like the rules have been changed in the middle of the game.
>
> They're right. The rules have changed. In a single generation, revolutions in technology have transformed the way we live, work and do business. Steel mills that once needed 1,000 workers can now do the same work with 100. Today, just about any company can set up shop, hire workers, and sell their products wherever there's an Internet connection.

Lest we be duped into renewing any faith in the "change" we were told we could "believe in," Obama has pledged to the U.S. Chamber of Commerce that he would pursue even more free trade agreements—this time with Panama, Colombia, and South Korea. With the North American Free Trade Agreement (NAFTA) having eliminated nearly eight hundred thousand U.S. jobs since 1991, it ought to strike us as highly unlikely that these pending new agreements will do anything but dim the economic prospects of America's youth, making it even harder for parents to point to a future economic payoff to motivate their children to stay in school.

According to an April 2011 report from the Economic Policy Institute, "the unemployment rate for workers aged sixteen to twenty-four was 18.4%—the worst on record in the sixty years that this data has been tracked" (Shierholz & Edwards, 2011). Even under the best of economic times, I couldn't honestly tell either of my sons that doing well in school and going on to earn a four-year degree would guarantee that they'd be able to find a job in their chosen fields. In today's economy, however, a four-year degree is even less certain to secure employment, as the unemployment rate for college grads in 2010 reached nearly 10 percent. With 85 percent of college graduates reporting that they are moving back home with mom and dad, we can expect that number for 2011 to climb even higher.

At least I can tell them that a college degree still improves their chances, because the unemployment rate among those with only a high school diploma or GED now stands at 22.5 percent. For dropouts, of course, the unemployment rates are even worse at 32.9 percent. For those closer to his age (those between the ages of sixteen and twenty-four), the figures and are far worse. According to a study conducted by the Center for Labor Market Studies at Northeastern University (2009), the jobless rate in 2008 for those with a four-year degree or higher was 13.3 percent, while it was 21.2 percent for those with one to three years of postsecondary education, 31.9 percent for high school graduates, and 54 percent for young high school dropouts. As reflected in the table below, the fewer number of years of schooling that one completes strongly correlates to both your risk of unemployment as well as your risk of incarceration.

| | **Unemployment Rate Among 16–24-Year-Old Out-of-School Youth in 2008** | **Incarceration Rate Among 16–24-Year-Old Out-of-School Youth 2006–2007** |
|---|---|---|
| College Graduates | 13.3% | 0.1% |
| 1–3 Years of College | 21.2% | 0.7% |
| H.S. Graduate | 31.9% | 1.0% |
| H.S. Dropouts | 54% | 6.3% |

At its core, the problem is this: the continued existence of compulsory schooling perpetuates the myth that people's success or failure hinges on their performance in school. In turn, this allows the state to blame schools for the larger problems in the economy that result in shrinking opportunities for people to find work. And this multitiered game of victim blaming drives the endless calls for school reform. The truth is that schools will never be reformed as long as they are made compulsory by the state. As documented by the Advancement Project (2010), in the the thirty years since the state launched its massive *A Nation At Risk* report and propaganda campaign that blamed schools for the alleged inability of U.S.-based corporations to compete in the global economy, the only meaningful changes we've witnessed in schools have been the implementation of high-stakes testing/accountability and zero-tolerance policies. Neither of those policies have changed the nature of compulsory schooling, but have only served to intensify its effects; namely, disciplining docile bodies to accept boring and monotonous work as an inevitable part of life while subjecting those who refuse to recognize the beneficence of this therapy to remedial discipline in prison.

The United States, which has less than 5 percent of the world's population, has 25 percent of the world's prisoners (Liptak, 2008). Figures range from between 1.6 million and 2.3 million Americans living behind bars. As the market economy continues its collapse, we should expect to see these numbers escalate, as globalization and domestic neoliberal policies continue to create a larger surplus population of people whom the market cannot absorb. State policy makers certainly do. As the National Association for the Advancement of Colored People (2011) points out in a report titled *Misplaced Priorities: Over Incarcerate, Under Educate*:

> Over the last two decades, as the criminal justice system came to assume a larger proportion of state discretionary dollars nationwide, state spending on prisons grew at six times the rate of state spending on higher education. In 2009, as the nation plummeted into the deepest recession in 30 years, funding for K–12 and higher education declined; however, in that same year, 33 states spent a larger proportion of their discretionary dollars on prisons than they had the year before.

Corporations and Wall Street investment firms also recognize and seek to capitalize on this same trend. The prison industry complex is one of the fastest-growing industries in the United States. Even the federal government and its defense contractors exploit the situation.

The anarchist critique of compulsory schooling leaves us little room for hope that our schools will ever be different. We are naïve to think that just because we are socialized to call them "public schools" that those schools are meant to *serve* the public. To the contrary, public schools exist to *target* the public. In keeping with the anarchist critique of the state, we need to recognize compulsory schooling as a technology of power, an instrument of statecraft, and the first line of domestic defense for the security state. Like the state itself, compulsory schooling serves the elite interests of our capitalist oligarchy over the public interests of the majority of citizens. Until state power is wrested from that oligarchy, we can't reasonably expect schools to function any differently. Indeed, current trends lead us to greater pessimism, not optimism, over the fate of schools, as the neoliberal assaults on schools and teachers' unions seek to remove the control of schools from the contested ground of the state and place them under the direct control of private corporations. Sooner or later, people will have to recognize that compulsory schools are part of the problem. Eliminating them is part of the solution.

## References

Advancement Project (2010). *Test, punish, and push out: How "zero tolerance" and high-stakes testing funnel youth into the school-to-prison pipeline*. Retrieved from http://www.advancementproject.org/digital-library/publications/test-punish-and-push-out-how-zero-tolerance-and-high-stakes-testing-fu (accessed June 9, 2011).

Alliance for Excellent Education (2011, June 9). About the crisis. Retrieved from http://www.all4ed.org/about_the_crisis.

Center for Labor Market Studies, Northeastern University (2009). *Joblessness and jailing for high school dropouts and the high cost for taxpayers*. Retrieved from http://www.northeastern.edu/clms/wp-content/uploads/The_Consequences_of_Dropping_Out_of_High_School.pdf (accessed June 9, 2011).

Chomsky, N. (2003). The function of schools: Subtler and cruder methods of control. In K.J. Saltman & D.A. Gabbard (Eds.), *Education as enforcement: The militarization and corporatization of schools*. New York: Routledge.

Chomsky, N. & Macedo, D. (2000). Beyond a domesticating education: A dialogue. In D. Macedo (Ed.), *Chomsky on miseducation*. Lanham, MD: Rowman & Litttlefield.

Delaney, A. (2011, May 23). "I played by the rules"—"The rules have changed," *Huffington Post*. Retrieved from http://www.huffingtonpost.com/2011/05/23/long-term-unemployment_n_864873.html (accessed June 9, 2011).

Egelko, B. (2007, May 14). "Honk for peace" case tests limits on free speech. *San Francisco Chronicle*. Retrieved from http://www.sfgate.com/cgi-bin/article.cgi?file=/c/a/2007/05/14/MNG9PPQGVV1.DTL (accessed June 17, 2007).

Emptywheel (2011, March 8). They won't even create jobs in the military-industrial complex anymore. Retrieved from http://emptywheel.firedoglake.com/2011/03/08/they-wont-even-create-jobs-in-the-military-industrial-complex-anymore/ (accessed June 9, 2011).

Foucault, M. (1988). *Madness and civilization: A history of insanity in the age of reason*. New York: Vintage.

Foucault, M. (1995). *Discipline and punish: The birth of the prison*. New York: Vintage.

Global Research (2006, October 20), Judge rules teachers have no free speech rights in class. Center for Research on Globalization. Retrieved from http://www.globalresearch.ca/index.php?context=viewArticle&code=20061020&articleId=3551 (accessed June 17, 2007).

Godwin, W. (1796). *An enquiry concerning political justice*. Charlottesville, VA: Electronic Text Center, University of Virginia Library. Retrieved from http://etext.virginia.edu/toc/modeng/public/GodJust.html (accessed June 17, 2007).

Goldman, E. (2007, June 17). The social importance of the modern school. Emma Goldman Papers, Manuscripts and Archives Division, The New York Public Library, Astor, Lenox and Tilden Foundations. Retrieved from http://dwardmac.pitzer.edu/anarchist_archives/goldman/socimportms.html.

Kamiya, G. (2007, May 22). Why Bush hasn't been impeached. Salon.com. Retrieved from http://www.salon.com/opinion/kamiya/2007/05/22/impeachment/ (accessed June 17, 2007).

Liptak, A. (2008, April 23). U.S. prison population dwarfs that of other nations. *New York Times*. Retrieved from http://www.nytimes.com/2008/04/23/world/americas/23iht-23prison.12253738.html (accessed June 9, 2011).

National Association for the Advancement of Colored People (2011, April 7). *Misplaced priorities: Over incarcerate, under educate*. Retrieved from http://www.naacp.org/pages/misplaced-priorities (accessed June 9, 2011).

Proudhon, P.-J. (2003). *What is property; or, An inquiry into the principle of right and of government*. Oshawa, Ontario: Mondo Politico. Retrieved from http://www.mondopolitico.com/library/pjproudhon/whatisproperty/toc.htm (accessed June 17, 2007).

Rohrlich, J. (2011). Why are prisoners building patriot missiles? Minyanville. Retrieved from http://www.minyanville.com/businessmarkets/articles/defense-industrial-base-defense-budget-defense/3/7/2011/id/33198? (accessed June 9, 2011).

Rush, B. (1786) Thoughts upon the mode of education proper in a republic. In *A plan for the establishment of public schools and the diffusion of knowledge in pennsylvania; to which are added, thoughts upon the mode of education proper in a republic*. Retrieved from http://www.schoolchoices.org/roo/rush.htm (accessed June 17, 2007).

Shierholz H. & Edwards, K.A. (2011, April 11). *The class of 2011: Young workers face a dire labor market without a safety net*. Economic Policy Institute Briefing Paper #306. Retrieved from http://www.epi.org/latest_research/ (accessed June 9, 2011).

Spring, J. (1983). The public school movement vs. the libertarian tradition. *The Journal of Libertarian Studies, 7*(1). Retrieved from http://www.mises.org/journals/jls/7_1/7_1_3.pdf (accessed June 17, 2007).

Spring, J. (1994). *Wheels in the head: Educational philosophies of authority, freedom, and culture from Socrates to Paulo Freire.* New York: McGraw Hill.

Spring, J. (2005). *The American school, 1642–2004.* New York: McGraw Hill.

West, C. (2004). *Democracy matters: Winning the fight against imperialism.* New York: Penguin.

CHAPTER 3

# Educate, Organize, Emancipate: The Work People's College and The Industrial Workers of the World[1]

**Saku Pinta**

## Introduction

Education has always been central to the Industrial Workers of the World (IWW) union's vision of working-class liberation. In an April 1927 article published in the Finnish-language IWW periodical *Tie Vapauteen* (Road to Freedom) the author, William Ranta, noted that "The first star in the I.W.W. emblem means working-class 'education,' the second 'organization,' and the third 'emancipation,'" continuing, "An enlightened group organizes itself and an organized group liberates itself." ("*Valistustyöhön*," p. 7)[2]

Founded in Chicago in 1905, the "Wobblies," as members of the IWW were known, fashioned a conception of "revolutionary industrial unionism" both as an alternative to the dominant union formations organized around trades or crafts and as an organizational form that would prefigure the desired self-managed economic arrangements of a post-capitalist society. Trade or craft forms of union organization were regarded by the IWW not only as being exclusionary, divisive, and conservative, but also as organizational forms rendered ineffective and outdated in challenging the power of employers due, in part, to technological changes in the labor process and the resultant "deskilling" of the workforce. Workers in the same industry, they asserted, ought to belong to the same union regardless of ethnicity, gender, or their particular roles in production. By organizing industrially, workers could increase their collective power and leverage in day-to-day struggles with the increasingly concentrated power of employers over wages, hours, and working conditions, while building the capacity of the working class to abolish capitalism. Direct economic action, as opposed to a reliance on "official" bureaucratic channels to settle grievances, was the preferred tactic (Kornbluh, 2011, pp. 35–64).

While direct action could serve to radicalize workers, forge solidarities on the shop floor, and increase the confidence and capacity for collective struggle—simultaneously, through these actions, laying the libertarian and democratic foundations for a new society structured from below—the importance of theory and of spreading of revolutionary ideas was routinely emphasized within the union as a crucial, complementary element. This was positioned alongside a critique of traditional education as promoting bourgeois values such as patriotism and uniformity in a system which, as one Wobbly argued, sought to "adapt one to the social order and teach respect for the class division of society into masters and wage slaves" (quoted in Kornbluh, 2011, p. 366). Workers' education, then, should augment the class-consciousness generated by direct class conflict experienced at work, but it could not imitate the methods of the traditional education system as this would simply recreate the undesirable hierarchies associated with capitalist institutions. Consequently, strict divisions between leaders and led were eschewed, as were rote or authoritarian methods of instruction that discouraged critical, independent thinking.

One fairly well-known dimension of this commitment to radical working-class education was described in Salerno's 1989 *Red November, Black November*, a work focused on the culture of the IWW. Salerno argued that "cultural expressions such as songs, cartoons, and poetry became a critical form and means of communication between the I.W.W. and its members" (p. 149). In print since 1909 and now in its thirty-eighth edition, the famous IWW *Little Red Songbook*—featuring "songs to fan the flames of discontent"—is but one well-known example of the union's cultural approach to disseminating revolutionary ideas. In addition to the transmission of ideas through cultural means, the IWW press and enormous pamphlet literature played a key role in working-class self-education, as did two collective spaces—the union hall and the "hobo jungle." These served as spaces for learning, critical reflection, and debate, particularly through the first three decades of the twentieth century. Rosemont (2003) writes that the union hall functioned as a radical cultural center, "meeting place, reading room, and hangout . . . the union's alternative to such conservative institutions as church, tavern, gambling parlor, race-track, and men's club" (p. 33). The hobo jungles "served a similar function" as the union hall, namely, as subversive spaces "in which the most down-and-out wage-slaves could express themselves openly" (ibid., p. 33).

The most significant and sustained achievement by the IWW in the area of workers' education was the Työväen Opisto (Work People's College; hereafter WPC), an immigrant institution very closely tied to Finnish working-class communities in the Upper Midwest. The WPC, however, did not begin as an IWW school. Founded as the Suomalainen Kansan Opisto ja Teologinen Seminaari (Finnish People's College and Theological Seminary) in Minneapolis in 1903, the aims of the college were to provide religious instruction, promote Finnish language and culture, and address the growing need for a formal liberal education among new immigrants. A lack of enrollment prompted a move the following year, in 1904, to Smithville, a suburb of Duluth, Minnesota, where it was hoped that the school could draw on the support of the substantially larger Finnish communities in that region. By 1907, the year that the Western Federation of Miners led a mass strike in the mines of Northern Minnesota's Mesabi Range, tensions surrounding the college's religious curriculum had caused a rift between the radicalized Finnish working class and many of the institution's officials. These divisions would ultimately culminate in the *Suomalainen Sosialisti Järjestö* (Finnish Socialist Federation; FSF)[3] legally gaining ownership of the college through the purchase of stock, changing the name of the school from the People's College to the WPC in 1908. All religious instruction was now jettisoned in favor of courses on topics such as the history of socialism, Darwinian evolution, and Marxist economics. Ideological harmony at the WPC, however, would not prevail. In 1914, the FSF underwent a major split which pitted a radical Left faction, supporting the IWW and industrial unionism, against a more moderate, social democratic faction backing the American Federation of Labor (AFL) and embracing a gradual, parliamentary vision toward achieving socialism.[4] Many of the midwestern locals of the FSF, including those grouped around the WPC, had sided with the radicals. In fact, the WPC had been a major center of IWW support in the years leading up to the split, and for this reason had long been considered a nuisance by some of the more moderate eastern-based leadership of the FSF. Radical students at the school were pejoratively labeled *tussarit* (meaning "gunslingers" or "gunhawks") by their opponents—a term which was irreverently reclaimed and proudly adopted by pro-IWW WPC students as their own. With the organizational split, the FSF withdrew its financial backing from the WPC and the now independent pro-IWW faction promptly gained stock ownership of the school.

For over twenty-five years (between 1914 and 1941), the WPC served as a residential labor college tied to the IWW and sustained by the Finnish membership of that union. The main three-story building featured classrooms, student dormitories, a drama room, gymnasium, and library with a smaller adjacent building holding a fully staffed kitchen and dining room. For a tuition fee of $39 a month (the equivalent of about $500 today)—a price which included meals and accommodations—students were provided with instruction in the skills necessary for union organizing, administering IWW union infrastructure, and staffing the large network of consumer cooperatives in the Upper Midwest, operating their own press, and ultimately, for self-managing a postcapitalist society. Instruction was carried out over the course of a five-month term, which typically stretched from December to April. The school also featured a small number of correspondence courses for students unable to take up residence at the WPC. Altogether, an estimated 1,600 to 2,000 students had studied at the school throughout the nearly four decades it was in operation and through its various transitions (Altenbaugh, 1990, p. 136).

Although the WPC represents the most outstanding historical contribution of the IWW to the area of workers' education, it has received relatively little in the way of attention from historians, remaining largely unknown outside of a specialist audience. In terms of the existing literature, Ollila (1977) and Heinilä (1995) provide excellent general historical accounts of the WPC while Kostiainen (1980) concentrates on some of the major debates and controversies generated over the course in the school's early years. The WPC is also mentioned in several accounts of the Finnish-American Left (Wasatjerna, 1957; Karni, 1975a; Ross, 1977; Kivisto, 1984). By far the most in-depth analysis of the WPC is Altenbaugh's well-documented book *Education as Struggle* (1990), in which the WPC is examined through the lens of Gramscian social theory—alongside the Brookwood Labor College (Katonah, New York, 1921–1937) and Commonwealth College (Mena, Arkansas, 1923–1940)—as "institutions clearly formulated to serve a counter-hegemonic function, promot[ing] proletarian culture, and train[ing] a working-class cadre" (p. 8).

A comprehensive history of the WPC has yet to be written, but such a task goes well beyond the scope of this study. The purpose of this chapter is to provide an historical account of the WPC through its years as an IWW labor college, focusing on the years 1920–1941, and in so doing shed some light on some of the largely overlooked aspects of the school during this period. The first section will provide necessary background and context by discussing the institutions and ideology of the Finnish North American membership of the IWW—the ethnic contingent that established, supported, and sustained the WPC. The succeeding sections will cover WPC curriculum, students, and faculty. Beyond historical interest, there is further reason to revisit the WPC and its contributions to libertarian education. In 2006, the WPC was revived as a free educational project of the IWW Twin Cities General Membership Branch. The conclusion shall be devoted to an assessment of the legacy and impact of this working-class institution along with a discussion of the renewed WPC. If the historical WPC provides a glimpse at how a fairly large-scale self-managed working-class educational institute functioned, its current revival suggests the urgency of developing such emancipatory spaces and the contemporary relevance of these endeavors.

## Background and Context: The Work People's College and the Finnish Wobblies

From 1914 onward, with the split in the FSF, it becomes possible to speak of an organized Finnish presence in the IWW. At this stage, the WPC was politically positioned, in effect, as a kind of "Left-socialist" institution, openly advocating the revolutionary industrial unionism of the IWW but also accepting the necessity of a working-class political party. It was not long before the Finnish supporters of the IWW would adopt an explicitly anti-parliamentary Left outlook, rapidly becoming the largest foreign-language contingent in the union. Kostiainen estimated Finnish membership in the IWW to be somewhere between five and ten thousand through the first two decades of the twentieth century (Kostianen, 1976, section 5, para. 1), however, no systematic analysis of Finnish IWW membership numbers currently exists.

During the 1916 IWW convention in Chicago, a motion to create formal ties between the union and the WPC was presented by representatives of the school, although no arrangement was reached. However, the 1916 convention was also notable for fulfilling the last wishes of the famous IWW labor martyr Joe Hill, namely, that his body be cremated and his ashes spread around the globe. In February 1917, a packet of Hill's ashes was spread to the winds at the WPC, symbolically cementing the relationship between the union and the school from that point onward. Four years later, a May 28, 1921, report in *Industrialisti* (Industrialist) on the IWW convention in Chicago carried the news that the union would formally adopt the WPC as its school, ratifying an earlier decision made at the Lumber Workers Industrial Union convention to forge official ties ("*Tietoja I.W.W. Liiton 13:sta Koventsionista*," p. 1).

An account of Finnish IWW print media gives some indication as to the size of the Finnish membership in the union and the vibrant working-class culture of which it was a part. The two most important Finnish IWW publications were *Industrialisti* and *Tie Vapauteen*. *Industrialisti* was the daily IWW Finnish-language newspaper from 1917 to 1950, appearing five days a week in the 1950s, and later, published as a weekly until it ceased publication in October 1975.[5] *Industrialisti* was the only daily newspaper in the history of the IWW and the last of the surviving foreign-language IWW papers from the early days of the union.[6] At its peak in the early 1920s, *Industrialisti* had a distribution of over 10,000 copies and a readership spread throughout the United States and Canada, laying claim to be the largest circulating Finnish-language newspaper in America during this period. *Tie Vapauteen* was a monthly periodical published first in New York, and later, in Chicago, between 1918 and 1937, with a distribution fluctuating somewhere between 2,500 and 6,000 copies. *Industrialisti* along with a small number of annual Finnish IWW publications were published by the Workers' Socialist Publishing Company in Duluth, a cooperative owned by IWW locals.

The September 28, 1927, *Industrialisti* directory still listed contact addresses for no less than seventy-eight Finnish IWW associations or groups ("*Yhdistysten ja Rhymien Osotteita*," p. 3) and in 1930, *Industrialisti* held a readership of approximately 9,000 (Karni, 1975a, p. 222). By the early 1940s, the number of affiliated groups had fallen to less than forty and the distribution of *Industrialisti* to 6,000 (ibid., p. 222). Outside of the Upper Midwest, significant pockets of IWW support were to be found in Finnish communities in various locations throughout North America. Examples include the Detroit Finnish Marxian Club, the Butte Finnish Workers Club, the Chicago Finnish IWW Agitation Committee, and the Aberdeen Finnish Workers Association. In Canada, from the mid-1920s onward, Finnish Wobblies organized the *Canadan Teollisuusunionistien Kannatus Liitto* (CTKL; Canadian Industrial Unionist Support League). The CTKL was an IWW auxiliary organization with a cultural orientation. It was composed mainly of radical-minded small farmers (many of whom were blacklisted miners or lumber workers) who supported the aims of the union but were ineligible for membership as they owned productive property and were not wageworkers. Formed in the mid-1920s, the CTKL grew to include no less than twenty-three halls spread throughout Ontario, Alberta, and British Columbia and regularly provided support for IWW strikes and other activities (Radforth, 1987, pp. 119–20). Students of the WPC were drawn from all of these areas, with the region around the Western Great Lakes as the main stronghold of Finnish IWW support. It is in this cultural and associational context that we must place the WPC.

Many locals held regular fundraisers, organized WPC support circles, and purchased stock to support the school. Gust Aakula, a former instructor, recalled "Over 30,000 shares had been sold, and as soon as some chapter had purchased a minimum of 1,000 shares it was granted a vote in the annual meetings of the Institute stockholders" (quoted in Wasatjerna, 1957, p. 230). A board of directors was elected yearly from the ranks of the stockholders. Aside from the purchase of stock, one unique example of the support for the WPC was the stipend program. "Two- or four-month stipends were issued by the school, and tickets were sold as either raffle tickets for donations to the school or as admission tickets to social events, where drawings were held. Winners could use the stipends, sell them to someone else, or give them away to friends" (Altenbaugh, 1990, p. 141). Another method to raise funds for the school was through the activity of the WPC drama troupe, which regularly toured Finnish communities in the United States and Canada during the spring and summer months performing plays, in later years, helping "to raise perhaps a third or half of the school's annual deficit" (Roediger, 1993, p. 68).

Ideologically, Finnish Wobblies differed little from their organizational comrades, accepting Marxist class analysis and the materialist conception of history along with a deep distrust of parliamentary politics and the strategy of capturing state power. The revolutionary interpretation of Marxism preferred by the IWW was guided by a vision of communism, sometimes referred to as industrial democracy or the cooperative commonwealth, defined as "a form of economic organization in which private and state ownership of the means of production has ceased and replaced with social ownership; in which wage labour, economic exploitation, and all privileges and special powers have been abolished" ("*Väärä Tulkinta*," p. 2). Inspiration was also drawn from anarchist-communist theoretician Peter Kropotkin, the most widely read anarchist among the Finnish Wobblies. Kropotkin's *Conquest of Bread* was translated into Finnish in 1906,[7] and excerpts from his writings regularly appeared in the Finnish IWW press, particularly in *Tie Vapauteen*, the annual winter magazine *Industrialistin Joulu* (Industrialist's Christmas), and the summer publication *Punainen Soihtu* (Red Torch). Of note is Kropotkin's 1880 pamphlet *An Appeal to the Young*, which was distributed by the Workers' Socialist Publishing Company. In this work Kropotkin succinctly outlined the role of intellectuals and libertarian educational work in terms that apply to the approach adopted by the WPC. Kropotkin urged those who possess skills and knowledge to offer their services to the oppressed asserting "remember, if you do come, that you come not as masters, but as comrades in the struggle; that you come not to govern but to gain strength for yourselves in a new life which sweeps upward to the conquest of the future" (Kropotkin, 1880, para. 79).

## Knowledge Is Power: WPC Curriculum, 1920–1941

The WPC, during its period as an IWW school, did not require entrance examinations, and only one course was compulsory: Essentials of the Labor Movement (Altenbaugh, 1990, p. 99). One student gave the following description of a typical day at the WPC.

> In the mornings, after having first gone to the dining area to fill our stomachs with a bit of porridge, we go off to digest in three different classes by playing with numbers. After this we get a good portion of nominatives and verbs in English and Finnish, twisting and turning the English-language into Finnish and vice versa. Now we are in the condition that we can digest a portion of Wobbly-ism [*tuplajuulaisuutta*]. On other days this is taken under the name of American working-class research which began with Columbus and went up to the Wobbly cooperative commonwealth. On other days we investigate currents in international social affairs, beginning with old-time Greek philosophy up to Wilson and Lenin via Martin Luther and "Kalle" Marx. Then we'll chew on some hardstack and inflect our voices by reading the American language. After this we rest for an hour chatting with Bogdanoff and "Kalle" Marx. The afternoons get debit and credit for aspiring boarding and rooming house [*poikatalo*] managers, and those

> enthusiastic about public speaking and poetry reading get an opportunity to show their skills. ("*Opiston Toverikunnan Vaiheista Lukuvuotena 1920–1921*," pp. 39–42)

All courses, at least up until the mid to late 1930s, were available in both Finnish and English, typically in elementary and advanced levels. In total, one week of study generally included around seventy hours of class time in various courses conducted by four full-time instructors. Aside from core courses (working-class history, Marxist economics, sociology, journalism, industrial unionism, IWW delegate duties, commercial studies, and languages) topics fluctuated somewhat, depending on the expertise of the faculty. English as a second-language satisfied the needs of a large segment of the Finnish student body early on, many of whom were first-generation immigrants, while courses in Finnish demonstrated the commitment to helping retain Finnish-language and culture among second and third-generation Finns. Esperanto was also taught for at least one term, in 1928–1929, by Hjalmar Reinikainen, and German was offered in earlier years. The emphasis on language training also included courses on translation. During the 1922–1923 term, for instance, Justus Ebert's *The Evolution of Industrial Democracy* was chosen as the text to be translated by students from English to Finnish.

Practical courses in accounting, bookkeeping, and business mathematics were offered at the WPC. These courses were arranged primarily for the purpose of training and staffing the large network of cooperatives in the Upper Midwest, but also in order to train competent organizational business managers. In 1927, the Central Cooperative Exchange, a network of cooperatives located in the Upper Midwest, boasted a membership of 16,595 members in sixty member societies, "fifty-four of the sixty societies were either exclusively Finnish or mixed with Finns predominating. Only two of the societies were purely 'American'" (Karni, 1975a, p. 280). Through the 1920s and 1930s, these cooperatives became a major site of political contestation as concerted, and ultimately unsuccessful, efforts were made by the Communist Party to control them (Karni, 1975b, pp. 186–211). Although the Finnish sections of the IWW did not officially regard consumer cooperatives as revolutionary institutions, large numbers of prominent Finnish cooperative movement members in the 1930s had nonetheless been trained at the WPC and came to constitute a radical faction (Karni, 1975a, p. 223).

Labor history courses generally used John R. Commons et al. *History of Labor in the United States* as a standard text along with various IWW publications and other materials, frequently discussing in detail such pivotal episodes as the 1871 Paris Commune and the Haymarket Affair. Marx's *Capital* was, throughout the history of the WPC, the standard text used in courses discussing economic theory. Sessions on public speaking were designed to train effective agitators for union "soapboxing" and faculty with union organizing experience taught regular courses on the tasks associated with carrying out delegate and administrative duties as well as signing up new members.

Among the most innovative and participatory lessons at the WPC were the student-guided "tactical sessions," organized Friday afternoons, which appear to have been tremendously popular among the student body. One student provided the following description: "During these sessions students in turn present an issue which is then discussed. The issues have always related to class struggle and industrial unionism, so everyone has had something to say about them. Discussions often become very lively and many-sided. Matters have come to be considered in detail and from a variety of perspectives. Students have learned a great deal as a result of these sessions" ("*Työväen-Opiston Lukukausi, 1923–1924*," p. 26). Summaries of the issues discussed during the tactical sessions routinely appeared in *Industrialisti*, as did other student writings. The offices of the newspaper, located in Duluth, were also utilized by the WPC for the benefit of students who had an interest in gaining hands on experience in the various tasks associated with running a daily paper.

## The Toverikunta: WPC Students

The tactical sessions are one indication of both the WPCs antiauthoritarian pedagogy and the student direction of WPC affairs. Students were organized into a student union, the *toverikunta* (literally, "comrade community"). The *toverikunta* held its meetings on Friday nights and had considerable input into the day-to-day functioning of the WPC. "By and large, the students," observed one historian, "planned the program themselves and were free to choose their own courses," with the *toverikunta* self-managing all matters relating to student conflicts and disciplinary issues, and "although its decisions could be appealed to the school's board of directors, not much use was made of this right" (Wasastjerna, 1957, p. 228). The *toverikunta* was also responsible for organizing dances, social events, plays, and athletics. On the topic of extracurricular activities, a former student and faculty member Taisto Luoma noted "No, you don't have to comb Marx's whiskers all winter long, not by a long shot" ("The Wobbly Way," p. 3). Sports and athletics were central to student life. An oft-repeated slogan among the *toverikunta* was "a healthy mind in a healthy body."

Between 1920 and 1930, average yearly total enrollment[8] at the WPC hovered around fifty-nine students a year, with a high of ninety-four students during the 1920–1921 term and a low of forty during over the 1929–1930 school year, with return students generally representing around a third of the student body year-to-year. Over this ten-year span, lumber workers, miners, and construction workers were by far the largest occupational groups represented in the student body. Based on available statistical data provided in the director's annual report to the shareholders and published in *Industrialisti*[9] (no detailed occupational breakdown was given for 1923, 1926, or 1928), we may surmise that lumber workers and miners together represented approximately half of all students (about 25 percent each), while construction workers made up about 16 percent of the student body. The remainder was composed of a variety of occupations, with workers in the foodstuffs, agricultural, and marine transport industries being among the more prominent occupational groups. Unsurprisingly, around 75 percent of the students during this decade belonged to the IWW, with small numbers coming from the Canadian One Big Union,[10] AFL unions, and "unaffiliated" workers.

Between 1931 and 1941 there was a gradual decline in numbers, with total enrollment averaging thirty-four students a year and only thirty registered over the final 1940–1941 term. Organizational affiliations were not discussed in director's annual reports during this period, apparently due to requests from students to omit them. However, one of the notable trends during this decade was that, while the WPC had continued to be closely tied with Finnish working-class communities, significant numbers of U.S.-born or raised Finns began enrolling. The 1932 report notes that of the thirty-six students enrolled, twenty spoke English as their first language. In 1934, director Antti Vitikainen's report noted that out of forty-three students, thirty-seven had been born in the U.S. and of these only two were non-Finns. Similarly, director Carl Keller's 1937 report suggested that the need for basic-level English-language courses had almost totally disappeared. One year later, for the first time in the history of the WPC, no social science courses were taught in the Finnish language.

Although statistical information published in the annual director's reports in *Industrialisti* did not always discuss gender, based on available numbers it is reasonable to assume that less than a quarter of the students were female—a shockingly small number for a segment of the union which had a strong reputation for gender equality (Campbell, 1998). The best known female student, and non-Finnish college alumnus, was Amelia Milka Sablich, popularly known as "Flaming Milka." Sablich, the daughter of a striking coal miner and of Croatian parentage, at nineteen years old became one of the most prominent figures in the IWW-led coal miners' strike in Colorado in 1927; a conflict now remembered as the "first Columbine massacre" after police opened fire on striking workers in Serene killing six and wounding dozens (May and Myers, 2005). "The Colorado coal strike," writes Kornbluh (2011), "introduced innovations in strike technique" (p. 353). Sablich, and other youth and women, helped to maintain picket lines and organize the strike as union miners were arrested and deported, using "car caravans to carry their message to other communities to persuade workers to come off their jobs" (ibid.). Her determination, charisma, and leadership during the strike—as well as her fights with company thugs and her five-week imprisonment—garnered national attention and the adoration of the labor movement. Following a national speaking in support of the striking miners, in February 1928, Sablich became a student at the WPC. In a letter at the end of the term, in April 1928, Sablich wrote an open letter in *Industrialisti* praising the school and connecting the need for workers' education with her own direct experience in class struggle:

> When I was in jail for five weeks in Trinidad [Colorado] I found out that most of our fellow workers there spent most of the time studying and discussing the strike, the I.W.W. etc. I found out that the experience of former strikes and the labor movement was put in books from which we could learn much about what to do in any given situation.
>
> After I got out of jail and went on a speaking tour in the east it became clearer to me that if I wanted to be a real wobbly I would have to do quite a bit of studying. That it was not everything to have a little experience of strikes, but that I should have to study quite a few books as well, and under the guidance of somebody that understood the connection between them and the labor movement of today. ("There are some deep-rooted questions to be understood in the industrial unionism," p. 4)

Ollila (1977) lists such figures as August Wesley, Gust Aakula, Ivar Vapaa, George Humon, Fred Jaakkola, Matti Kainu, and Jack Ujanen as key members of the IWW who had studied at the WPC (p. 107). Jack Ujanen, for instance—editor of *Industrialisti* for that paper's final twenty-two years (1953–1977), retiring at age eighty-five—received his only formal education at the WPC ("Editor's Tribute to Jack Ujanen," pp. 23–25). Nick Viita, one of the leading members of the Finnish-Canadian IWW and CTKL for over five decades, is also included as WPC alumni, having studied there in 1919. Some former WPC students, such as John Wiita, drifted into the orbit of both the Canadian and American Workers (Communist) Parties in the 1920s, becoming a leading figure (Wilson, 1986). Other former students and faculty built on the skills and experiences gained at the WPC, pursuing university education. Walfrid Jokinen, for example, a student and teacher at the WPC, in later years went on to successfully complete postgraduate studies, becoming the chair of the Louisiana State University Sociology Department. Another former Wobbly and WPC faculty member, John Olli, also went on to earn a doctorate, at the University of Wisconsin, and taught at the City College of New York for thirty-six years (Kivisto, 1984, p. 193).

The most prominent Finnish labor movement figure and former WPC student was Niilo Wälläri. Wälläri, a sailor, came to the United States in 1916 after jumping ship in Boston. He joined the IWW in Seattle in 1918, attended classes at the WPC, and became active as a union organizer and agitator in the Great Lakes region. Arrested in 1919 as an illegal alien and radical, and deported back to Finland the following year, Wälläri later assumed the role of chairman of the militant Finnish Seamen's Union (*Suomen Merimies-Unioni*; SMU) from 1938 until his death in 1967. Adopting a staunch anti-Stalinist Left position in the 1920s, his contributions to the Finnish labor movement include successfully winning the first labor agreement in coastal and inland waters shipping and the eight-hour day in 1946. The militancy and political autonomy of the union, as well as the industrial structure of the SMU, demonstrates IWW influence. Wälläri and the SMU maintained independence from the left-wing parties in Finland and included all maritime workers regardless of trade in the union. Furthermore, the commitment by Wälläri and the SMU to social justice was evidenced by the support for the antifascist cause during the Spanish Civil War, 1936–1939. SMU members helped to smuggled arms to Spain and contributed volunteers, and later, assisted Jews in escaping to Sweden from Nazi Germany ("*Mailman Teollisuustyöläisten Litto 100 vuotta*," p. 10; notes from Harry Siitonen, 1999 Seattle FinnFest lecture).

## Junior Wobblies

Another key segment of the WPC student body over the final decade of its operations, often neglected in the historical literature on the school, were the Junior Wobblies. The Junior Wobblies' Union was another innovation connected to the 1927 Colorado miners' strike, formed for the purpose of "class education of workers' children to prepare them for the organized labor movement in industry" (Rein, 1929, p. 126). To facilitate the growth of the Junior Wobblies the WPC began to organize summer youth courses for children and teenagers aged twelve to eighteen. These courses ran for four to six weeks between the months June and July for a fee of twelve dollars. The WPC summer youth courses proved to be fairly successful through the 1930s. Ollila (1975) reported that in 1929, the first year that a youth program was introduced, 130 students enrolled, eventually dropping to forty-two students a decade later (p. 112). In 1941, the final year of adult and youth courses at the WPC, seventeen students attended the summer sessions ("*Uutisia Opistolta*," p. 3). Aside from courses on natural history and the history of the working-class movement, the summer youth program included activities such as swimming and sports. Baseball appears to have been one of the more popular sports.

In 1929, the Workers' Socialist Publishing Company produced a textbook geared for IWW youth attending summer courses: *Nuoriso, Oppi ja Työ* (Youth, Learning, and Labor). The book, written by W.M. Rein, was explicitly aimed at a Finnish-American working-class youth audience. The text's foreword further reveals the libertarian pedagogy adopted by the WPC. Instructors, it noted, should ask, and be asked questions, rather than encouraging memorization, as rote methods of learning would merely result in dogmatism and fail to fully develop the student's ability to think critically (Rein, 1929, p. 2).

Divided into two sections, the book's first part was written entirely in Finnish and intended for younger children, given that "the children of Finnish-speaking parents may preserve their ability to speak Finnish with relative ease" (ibid., p. 2). This section, written in the form of a story, follows the adventures of Arvo and Irma as they learn about the natural world, class society, and the working-class movement. The first section closes with the question, "where is the worker's homeland?" The internationalist, antiracist conclusions were that, despite the fact that patriotism and the superiority of the white race were taught in most schools, all people are equal regardless of skin color, ethnicity, or culture. The workers' homeland, it goes on to state, is "nowhere or everywhere" since workers will go where they are best able to earn a living, and thus, their "homeland" may change very quickly and often (ibid., pp. 79–80). The second part, written in English, was designed for older children and teenagers. It covered such topics as the evolution of human beings and early human history, the shift from feudalism to capitalism, the history of the American labor movement, industrial unionism (including the IWW Industrial Union Manifesto in full as well as the Preamble), an introduction to socialist theory (focusing on the Marx and the "materialist conception of history" and anarchist theory), and a detailed discussion of the history of the Finnish people and language.

## Faculty and Staff

Over its years as an IWW school, the WPC generally employed no less than four full-time faculty during the course of its five-month term. Leo Laukki and Yrjö Sirola were two of the best-known instructors at the WPC as towering intellectual figures in the Finnish-American Left and direct participants in the revolutionary movement in Finland.[11] Their tenures at the school overlap during the period between the WPC as a school of the FSF to its leftward drift to the IWW: indeed both Laukki and Sirola were integral in instigating the radical left orientation of the college. Laukki became the chief theorist of the pro-IWW radical faction in the Finnish left, and under his directorship, the WPC curriculum changed to reflect the ideas and practices of revolutionary industrial unionism over that of parliamentary socialism. Sirola supported these views as well, but as Campbell (1998) notes, "Industrial unionism, the general strike, and basing anticapitalist struggles in the union, rather than the party, made sense to Sirola and other Finnish leftists in a North American context, but not so in a Finnish context" (p. 124).

The same perspective might equally apply to Laukki, who enthusiastically supported the Bolsheviks after October 1917.

Indeed, both Laukki and Sirola eventually ended up in the Soviet Union, although under different circumstances. Sirola left for Finland under his own volition in 1917 after revolution had broken out in Tsarist Russia, participating in the short-lived Finnish Socialist Workers' Republic in the capacity of minister of foreign affairs. Following the defeat of the revolutionary forces in the Finnish Civil War, Sirola fled to the Soviet Union, acting as a leading figure in the Finnish Communist Party in exile, Bolshevik government, and Communist International until his death in 1936. Laukki, on the other hand, was arrested along with 166 other IWW members during the wave of mass arrests in 1917 on charges related to newly created Espionage Act (covering sedition and interference with American military operations) during a period of intense government repression.[12] Laukki was sentenced to a twenty-year prison term, but fled to Moscow along with William Haywood while out on bail pending their appeal—a bitter experience for many in the IWW, as thousands of dollars had been collected for costs associated with the trial and bail (Kivisto, 1984, p. 157). Laukki later disappeared during Stalin's purges in the 1930s.

George Humon was among the most prominent WPC faculty members during its period as an IWW institute. Humon served as the school's director for no less than seven terms. His contributions include an original Finnish IWW text, *Uusi Yhteiskunta Ja Sen Rakentajat* (The New Society and its Builders) and the translation of several IWW pamphlets, including Abner E. Woodruff's 1919 IWW pamphlet *The Advancing Proletariat: A Study of the Movement of the Working Class from Wage Slavery to Freedom*. Taisto Luoma is also notable as he went on to become one of the IWW's most celebrated cartoonists in the 1930s; "most were done in a sullen, grim style, full of dark foreboding" (Rosemont, 1998, p. 433). Luoma taught a course on graphic design at the WPC during the 1938–1939 term. Other long-time faculty included Otto W. Oksanen, Aku Rissanen, Antti Vitikainen, and August Angervo.

Fred Thompson is among the best-known of the English-language faculty members. Thompson began teaching at the WPC in 1927, and continued as an instructor for seven nonconsecutive terms (including as a teacher for five summer youth sessions), ending his career as the school's last director in 1940–1941. Covington Hall, a celebrated IWW organizer from the U.S. South, described by Kornbluh (2011) as "one of the most prolific of the I.W.W. writers," (p. 259) taught labor history and industrial unionism at the WPC during the 1937–1938 term. Carl Keller, a leading member of the Chicago IWW for decades, serving as the union's General-Secretary Treasurer in the late 1960s, was the only other non-Finnish WPC director (in 1933–1934 and 1936–1937).

Of course the WPC, nor any other educational institution for that matter, could not function without the many key tasks carried out by a support staff. In addition to faculty, the WPC also employed a business manager, responsible for the organization's accounting, bookkeeping, and preparing annual financial reports to shareholders; kitchen staff; and a caretaker. A September 16, 1927, *Industrialisti* job advertisement for a head cook, two kitchen helpers, and a caretaker for the upcoming WPC school term notes that successful candidates must be members of the IWW or be prepared to join. Responsibilities of the head cook included preparing meals for the *toverikunta* and baking. It states that the WPC possessed both a gas and a coal oven [*kooliuuni*]. Kitchen helpers were tasked with cleaning, dishwashing, serving, and general duties as required, while the caretaker's position mainly centered around the cleaning, upkeep, and heating of the building.

## Conclusion: Evaluating the Impact and Legacy of the Work People's College

At the close of the 1940–1941 term, the decision was made by the WPC shareholders to suspend courses for the upcoming year. Falling enrollment contributed to the decision, but the writing was clearly on the wall when, during the final term, several student stipends had remained unused. The property was leased and eventually sold, in 1962. One of the original WPC buildings still stands and now functions as an apartment building.

How might the experience of the WPC as an IWW labor college be evaluated? During the polarizing period of the Cold War and an era of government sanctioned social democratic labor relations—the era when much of the literature on the WPC was written—many previous commentators on the school's history may be forgiven for attributing the school's decline on the staunch and "sectarian" adherence to Wobbly precepts, which were argued to have alienated more moderate potential supporters, and the resultant failure of the school to shift to more "realistic" Communist or social democratic-oriented alternatives. How distant this all now seems with the collapse of the Soviet Union, the centrist political trajectory of modern social democracy, declining union membership numbers, and the global resurgence of an antistatist Left libertarian alternative. To be sure, the strong ties between the WPC and its radical Finnish support base, that are frequently cited in the historical literature, served as both a major strength and a weakness. In failing to penetrate more deeply into the broader North American working class, the ethnic ties and solidarities that helped sustain the WPC gradually unraveled as the second, third, and fourth generations of the Finnish immigrant population gradually assimilated into the dominant culture, often abandoning not only the language and culture of their predecessors, but also their associational, radical, and egalitarian commitments. In contrast, and by way of conclusion, the WPC and its impact on labor organizing, its contributions to the radical counterculture on the Finnish membership of the IWW, and its broader legacy will be examined. That the decline of the IWW approximately mirrors that of the WPC is evident, however, it is in the context of the specifically Finnish contingent of the union that the lasting contributions and achievements of this institute, and the culture of which is was part, must be assessed.

Aside from the role of a few individuals, as noted above, it is somewhat difficult to accurately assess the impact that the WPC had in the field of industrial conflict, given the absence of documentation directly linking students to union organizing and strike activity. This in itself is a task that requires a much longer and more in-depth study. However, since a significant proportion of the student body were drawn from the mining industry, it is reasonable to assume that the IWW-led mass strike of miners on Minnesota's Mesabi Range in 1916 included the contributions of WPC trained organizers and agitators. The same assumption might also be applied to industrial actions carried out in the logging industries in Northern Minnesota and Northern Ontario in the 1920s. At least one former WPC faculty member, Kristen Svanum, an instructor during the 1924–1925 term, was identified in the reports of company-hired labor spies as a leading organizer in the 1927 Colorado miners strike (Rees, 2004, pp. 32–35). Fred Thompson held a more cynical outlook on the effectiveness of WPC organizer training, stating that his major criticism of the school was that "I.W.W. unions should have arranged to make more systematic use of it" and that he felt fortunate "if among the sixty or so students, there were a dozen who came there with the idea of increasing their capacity as organizers or labor educators" (Roediger, 1993, p. 67). It should be noted that Thompson's comments may more accurately reflect the period of the institute's general decline during his time there in the 1930s, rather than the WPC as a whole. His reflections, however, also hold invaluable insights. Thompson suggested, in retrospect, that the WPC should have sent "organizer-students" to places where organizing campaigns were happening at the time (namely, Detroit and Cleveland in the 1930s), where they could concentrate "partly on organizing chores, partly in systematic study and always trying to relate one to the other" (ibid., p. 69).

The tenacity of the Finnish Wobblies, however, most certainly owed much to the training and sense of camaraderie that the WPC provided. *Industrialisti*, with former WPC student Jack Ujanen as editor, as mentioned above, survived until 1975—a remarkable feat for a foreign-language radical newspaper in North America—as did the CTKL and several IWW-supported halls and cooperatives in the United States and Canada. Even as IWW unions began a sharp decline through the 1930s, Wobbly methods, ideas, and organizers remained devoted to the principles of direct action, solidarity, and labor militancy in the broader working-class movement. In the late 1930s, Wobblies or former members in Northern Minnesota and Northern Ontario actively participated in strikes in the lumber industry through "mainstream" unions—their inclination to rank-and-file control and direct action, instead of negotiating binding collective agreements, often aggravating union bureaucrats (Hudelson and Ross, 2006, pp. 190–92; Campbell, 1998, pp. 118–19).

At a later stage, the WPC and the militants it trained served as an important generational link between the "old guard" of the IWW and the New Left radicals of the 1960s who began the task of rebuilding the IWW. When Franklin Rosemont joined the union in 1962 in Chicago, establishing the Rebel Worker group and journal, he fondly recalled meeting former WPC students and faculty like Carl Keller, Aino Thompson (Fred Thompson's wife—the two met at the college), and Jenny Lahti Velsek (Rosemont and Radcliffe, 2006, p. 19). Rosemont also noted that the Solidarity bookshop in Chicago, included "a couple thousand old books from the IWW's Work People's College" (ibid., p. 30).

Fittingly, the latest incarnation of the WPC is in Minneapolis, the city in which the original People's College was established over a century ago. In 2006, a decision was made by the IWW Twin Cities General Membership Branch to begin providing "free, radical, and practical education to the working women and men of our communities, education that will further the aims of the working class revolution that we advocate as a union" (WPC Mission Statement). Jeff Pilacinski, one of the leading figures behind the WPC revival, explains that the historical WPC was chosen as the model for this project for several reasons:

> One, the obvious historical connection between the school and the I.W.W. was important to maintain. Second, as a self-managed working-class institution, the historical WPC offered educational opportunities whereby workers were teaching workers in an organized, yet loosely-structured environment. This is something that branch members wanted to replicate given the fact that there were few if no other opportunities of this kind available at the time. Third, we took inspiration from the school's core curriculum and structured our offerings around working-class culture/history, sociology, Marxist economics, and industrial unionism.[13]

Courses, which began in mid-October 2006, have typically been organized during evenings for six to eight weeks at an accessible venue, such as a meeting room in a public library, usually for two hours sessions. Facilitators are responsible for creating a course framework and a list suggested readings combined with a strong participatory focus. Students largely guide the direction of each course with instructional methods varying widely course-to-course from group discussions and lectures to role-plays and media presentations. The revived WPC, like its historical namesake, is open to all workers and the occupational backgrounds of both its facilitators and study body are reflective of the working class in contemporary capitalism—the miners and lumberjacks of the historical WPC have now been replaced with workers from the service, education, and telecommunications industries.

To date five courses have been offered: Lessons of the Spanish Revolution, Imagination and Social Liberation (the thought of Cornelius Castoriadis), Political Economy in Karl Marx's *Capital*, Chomsky 101: An Introduction to Noam Chomsky's Life and Political Thought, and Coup de Sabots and the Creativity of Direct Action. The flier for one course offering stylishly asserted that "credit for participation in this class is not transferrable to any state or private institution, but only to the daily struggle for the emancipation of the working class."[14] Currently, the branch educational committee responsible for organizing logistics (room bookings, photocopies, child care, etc.) for the WPC is aiming to structure the WPC as a quarterly series of weekend sessions composed of workshops, panels, speakers, films, debates, and trainings.[15]

In considering the importance of, and relationship between, theory and working place organizing, Pilacinski observes:

> Each course included components that developed I.W.W. members and non-members' abilities to situate themselves in and further understand the history and dynamics of their class—these developments fundamentally bolster the I.W.W. and its members capacities to organize where they work.[16]

He also notes that "the union also has a dedicated and successful workplace organizer training program that the Twin Cities runs several times throughout the year, including times when WPC courses are offered."[17] These efforts have contributed to some of the most innovative and pioneering workplace-organizing campaigns in Minnesota and beyond. Recent campaigns initiated by the Twin Cities IWW include substantial work in the poorly paid, notoriously difficult, and almost totally unorganized fast-food industry.

If the best and most sincere tribute to the working-class militants of the historical WPC is to carry on their work, then certainly the revival of the school in the Twin Cities must be considered as the most important and critical component of the school's legacy.

## Notes

1 The author would like to extend his thanks all those who supported the writing and research of this essay: the friendly and helpful staff at the Northern Studies Resource Centre at Lakehead University; Gary Kaunonen, who took the time to

give a number of insightful comments and suggestions on an earlier draft, helping to greatly improve the rigour and quality of this work; and Harry Siitonen, who generously provided his personal lecture notes, a number of difficult-to-find sources on the Work People's College, and his encyclopedic knowledge of the IWW and Finnish North American labor movements. Last, but not least, the author would like to thank the Twin Cities General Membership Branch of the IWW, and specifically, Jeff Pilacinski, Erik W. Davis, and Kieran Knutson for their support and the information they gave about their efforts to revive the Work People's College.

2 All translations from original Finnish sources in this chapter are by the author.

3 During this period, the FSF was the largest foreign-language federation in the Socialist Party of America, with an influence and membership disproportionate to the relatively small number of Finnish immigrants in the United States. In 1912 the FSF was composed of over eleven thousand members in 225 local chapters. "At that date," writes Ollila (1975), "the organization included four newspapers, the Work People's College with 123 students, seventy-six club houses, eighty libraries, and a combined income $184,128.83, coupled with an overall valuation of $558,201.14" (p. 156).

4 The split in the FSF mirrored a similar division in the ranks of the English-speaking sections of the Socialist Party of America in 1912, when IWW members including William Haywood were expelled from the National Executive of the party. This also presaged a second split in the FSF in the early 1920s that witnessed the exit of Communist Party supporters. We might consider, perhaps somewhat schematically, the Finnish left in North America as more or less crystallizing into three distinct currents in the years following the First World War: 1) a social democratic tendency, with *Raivaaja* (The Pioneer) in the United States and *Vapaa Sana* (The Free Word) in Canada as representative newspapers; 2) a Leninist tendency, represented by the Workers (Communist) Party in the United States and Canada and their newspapers *Työmies* (Working Man) and *Vapaus* (Freedom), respectively; and 3) an antistatist, libertarian socialist tendency represented by the IWW, auxiliary organizations, and their newspaper *Industrialisti* (Industrialist).

5 The newspaper began as *Sosialisti* (Socialist) in June 1914, changing to *Teollisuustyöläinen* (Industrial Worker) in December 1916, and finally to *Industrialisti* in March 1917. For an excellent account of the early years of the paper, see A. Kostiainen, A dissenting voice of Finnish radicals in America: The formative years of *Sosialisti-Industrialisti* in the 1910s. *American Studies in Scandinavia*, 23, 1991 (pp. 83–94). Retrieved from http://www.genealogia.fi/emi/art/article256e.htm.

6 In 1920, the IWW had no fewer than thirteen foreign-language publications.

7 Translated by Kaapo Murros (born David Gabriel Ahlqvist, an early Finnish advocate of industrial unionism in the United States) as *Taistelu Leivästä* (Tampere: Työväen Osuuskirjapaino) who, that same year, also provided the first Finnish translation of Marx and Engels's *Communist Manifesto.*

8 Total yearly enrollment represents the total number of students enrolled over the course of an entire term. Some students were not able to study for an entire term due to financial constraints or left when employment opportunities arose. Interestingly, the very low cost of attending the WPC was argued, in school's advertisements and outreach material, to be an ideal way for seasonal workers to *save money* as it was a cheaper alternative to staying in boarding houses or arranging other temporary accomodations during the off-season.

9 Compiled from director's reports through the years 1920–1941. See references below for a complete listing.

10 Not to be confused with the IWW, the Canadian One Big Union (OBU) was formed in 1919 as a Western alternative to the Trades and Labour Congress. See D. Bercuson (1990), Syndicalism sidetracked: Canada's One Big Union" (pp. 221–36) in M. van der Linden and W. Thorpe (eds.) *Revolutionary Syndicalism: An International Perspective*, Aldershot: Scolar Press. Finnish-Canadian OBU members, particularly lumber workers, switched organizational affiliation to the IWW in large numbers in the early 1920s.

11 Laukki, as a young lieutenant, fled to the United States in 1907 after his participation in the Sveaborg (now *Suomenlinna*) military fortress rebellion against Tsarist rule. Sirola, on the other hand, was a well known Finnish socialist politician, who also fled after Tsarist repression of the revolutionary movement in Finland.

12 Four additional Finnish Wobblies were among the 166 arrestees: Fred Jaakkola, Frank Westerlund, William Tanner, and Charles Jacobson. During this period, IWW union offices in Duluth were raided and destroyed by the National Guard and a newly constructed WPC building burned to the ground amid widespread rumors that vigilantes were responsible. In 1918, Olli Kinkkonen, a Duluth longshoreman and vocal opponent of the war, was forcibly removed from his boarding house lodgings by vigilantes, tarred, feathered, and hanged. The official explanation for Kinkkonen's death was suicide.

13 Correspondence with Jeff Pilacinski, January 11, 2011.

14 Correspondence with Eric W. Davis, December 6, 2010.

15 Correspondence with Kieran Knutson, January 11, 2011.

16 Correspondence with Jeff Pilacinski, January 11, 2011.

17 Ibid.

## References

"Tietoja I.W.W. Liiton 13:sta Koventsionista" (1921, May 28) *Industrialisti*, 1.

"Työväen-Opiston Johtajan Tomintakertomus," (WPC Director's Activity Report, 1921–1941, *Industrialisti*): 1921, May 21, G. Humon; 1922, April 24, G. Humon; 1923, May 10, A. Vitikainen; 1924, April 22, A. Vitikainen; 1925, May 7, G. Humon; 1926, May 12, G. Humon; 1927, May 3, G. Humon; 1928, May 11, J. Kiviniemi; 1929, April 20, J. Kiviniemi; 1930, May 21, G. Humon; 1931, April 16, A. Rissanen; 1932, May 9, G. Humon; 1933, May 15, I. Vapaa; 1934, April 21, C. Keller; 1935, April 25, A. Vitikainen; 1936, May 16, F. Thompson; 1937, May 3, C. Keller; 1938, May 2, F. Thompson; 1939, April 22, G. Humon; 1940, May 24, F. Thompson; 1941, May 2, F. Thompson.

"Väärä Tulkinta" (1936, October 10) *Industrialisti*, 2.

Work People's College Mission Statement. Retrieved from http://www.iww.org/en/branches/US/MN/twincities/wpc.

"Yhdistysten ja Ryhmien Osotteita" (1927, September 28) *Industrialisti*, 3.

Altenbaugh, R. (1990). *Education for struggle: The American labor colleges of the 1920s and 1930s*. Philadelphia: Temple University Press.

Campbell, J. The cult of spontaneity: Finnish-Canadian bushworkers and the Industrial Workers of the world in Northern Ontario, 1919–1934. *Labour/Le Travail*, *41* (Spring 1998), 117–46.

Etholén, K. Mailman Teollisuustyöläisten Litto 100 vuotta. *Merimies-Sjömannen* 2, 2006, 10.

Hannula, R. Editor's tribute to Jack Ujanen. *Finn Heritage*, 5(2) 1988, 23–25.

Heinilä, H. (1995). Work People's College. *Finnish Americana: A Journal of Finnish American History and Culture, 11*, 22–31.

Hudelson, R. & Ross, C. (2006). *By the ore docks: A working people's history of Duluth*. Minneapolis: University of Minnesota Press.

Jaska. (1924, April). Työväen-Opiston Lukukausi, 1923–1924. *Tie Vapauteen, 4*(6), 23–27.

Karni, M. (1975a). *Yhteishyvä—or, for the common good: Finnish radicalism in the western Great Lakes region, 1900–1940* (Doctoral dissertation). Minneapolis: University of Minnesota.

Karni, M. (1975b). Struggle on the cooperative front: The separation of central cooperative wholesale from communism, 1929–1930. In M. Karni, M. Kaups & D. Ollila Jr. (Eds.), *The Finnish experience in the western Great Lakes region: New perspectives*, 186–201. Turku, Finland: Institute for Migration.

Kivisto, P. (1984). *Immigrant socialists in the United States: The case of Finns and the left*. Cranbury/London/Mississauga: Associated University Presses.

Kornbluh, J. (Ed.). (2011). *Rebel voices: An IWW anthology*. Oakland: PM Press.

Kostiainen, A. (1976). Finnish-American Workmen's Associations. In V. Niitemaa, J. Saukkonen, T. Aaltio & O. Koivukangas (Eds.), *Old friends—strong ties: The Finnish contribution to the growth of the USA*, 205–34. Vaasa. Retrieved from http://www.genealogia.fi/emi/art/article257e.htm.

Kostiainen, A. (1980). Work People's College: An American immigrant institution. *Scandinavian Journal of History, 5*, 295–309. Retrieved from http://www.genealogia.org/emi/art/article243e.htm#Alku.

Kostiainen, A. (1991). A dissenting voice of Finnish radicals in America: The formative years of *Sosialisti-Industrialisti* in the 1910s. *American Studies in Scandinavia, 23*, 83–94. Retrieved from http://www.genealogia.fi/emi/art/article256e.htm#a15.

Kropotkin, P. (1880). *An appeal to the young*. Retrieved from http://flag.blackened.net/daver/anarchism/kropotkin/atty.html.

Luoma, T. "The Wobbly Way" (1938, September 6) *Industrialisti*, 3.

May L. & Myers, R. (Eds.). *Slaughter in Serene: The Columbine coal strike reader*. Denver: Bread and Roses Workers' Cultural Center.

Mukana ollut. (1921, May). Opiston Toverikunnan Vaiheista Lukuvuotena 1920–1921. *Ahjo*, 39–42.

Ollila, D. (1975). From socialism to industrial unionism (IWW): Social factors in the emergence of left-labor radicalism among Finnish workers on the Mesabi, 1911–19. In M. Karni, M. Kaups & D. Ollila Jr. (Eds.), *The Finnish experience in the western Great Lakes region: New perspectives*, 156–71. Turku, Finland: Institute for Migration.

Ollila, D. (1977). The Work People's College: Immigrant education for adjustment and solidarity. In M. Karni & D. Ollila Jr. (Eds.), *For the common good: Finnish immigrants and the radical response to industrial America*, 87–118. Superior, WI: Työmies Society.

Oppilas. "Uutisia Opistolta" (1941, June 20) *Industrialisti*, p.3.

Radforth, I. (1987). *Bushworkers and bosses: Logging in northern Ontario, 1900–1980*. Toronto/Buffalo/London: University of Toronto Press.

Ranta, W. Valistustyöhön. (1927 April) *Tie Vapauteen* (4) 9, 7.

Rees, J. "X," "XX" and "X-3": Labor spy reports from the Colorado Fuel and Iron Company archives. *Colorado Heritage* (Winter) 2004, 28–41.

Rein, W. (1929). *Nuoriso, Oppi ja Työ (Youth, Learning and Labor)*. Duluth: Workers' Socialist Publishing Company.

Roediger, D. (Ed.). (1993). *Fellow worker: The life of Fred Thompson*. Chicago: Charles H. Kerr Publishing Co.

Rosemont, F. (2003). *Joe Hill: The IWW & the making of a revolutionary working-class counterculture.* Chicago: Charles H. Kerr Publishing Co.

Rosemont, F. (2011). A short treatise on Wobbly cartoons. In J. Kornbluh (Ed.), *Rebel voices: An IWW anthology*, 425–43. Oakland: PM Press.

Rosemont, F. & Radcliffe, C. (2006). *Dancin' in the streets! Anarchists, IWWs, surrealists, situationists & provos in the 1960s as recorded in the pages of Rebel Worker and Heatwave.* Chicago: Charles H. Kerr Publishing Co.

Ross, C. (1977). *The Finn factor in American labor, culture and society.* New York Mills, MN: Parta Printers Inc.

Sablich, M. (1928, April 15). There are some deep-rooted questions to be understood in the industrial unionism. *Industrialisti*, 4.

Salerno, S. (1989). *Red November, black November: Culture and community in the Industrial Workers of the World.* New York: State University of New York Press.

Wasastjerna, H. (1957). *History of Finns in Minnesota.* Duluth: Minnesota Finnish-American Historical Society.

Wilson, J. (1986). John Wiita: A Finnish-American in Canada, 1918–1923. *Finnish American: A Journal of Finnish American history and culture, 7*, 19–23.

CHAPTER 4

# From Deschooling to Unschooling: Rethinking Anarchopedagogy after Ivan Illich

**Joseph Todd**

> When we call ourselves anarchists, that is, people who advocate the principle of autonomy as opposed to authority in every field of personal and social life, we are constantly reminded of the apparent failure of anarchism to exercise any perceptible influence on the course of political events, and as a result we tend to overlook the unconscious adoption of anarchist ideas in a variety of other spheres of life. (Ward, 1966, p. 397)

Colin Ward establishes a point of origin for anarchist theory, situating it within autonomy and individual freedom. Although he is optimistic about spaces where anarchic projects may be carried out, he is deeply aware of the marginalized nature of anarchy as a political movement. We can see the tension that Ward highlights in anarchism itself in the antagonistic relationship between schooling and deschooling. Schools are one of the institutions where the State sustains its stronghold, creating an institutionalized form of authority over the nature of education, while deschooling may be one of these spheres that might be anarchic without explicitly stating so or even consciously attempting to be. Although deschooling might remain highly marginal in practice and theory, as Ward suggests, it may also gain enough strength to mobilize influence on policy and act against the institution of compulsory schooling. Ivan Illich, the major philosopher of deschooling, may have added an important dimension for anarchist theorists in his insistence of including education in revolutionary frameworks. However, we must be equally critical of these alternative sites in hopes of creating diversity among anarchic possibilities and experiments.

Contemporary compulsory public education is understood only through public and private conceptions, which are increasingly narrowed by trends in reform, while Illich is representative of a third, anarchic model that is beyond this dichotomy. For this reason the focus of this chapter will be on spaces of alternative education that emerge beyond or between the public/private distinction. Illich provides a model of what this might look like in theory, but it is not without its own limitations and will need to be updated to account for changes in technology, social relations, and globalization since 1970. The criteria he devised are as follows: *reference service to educational objects, skill exchanges, peer-matching, and professional educators*. Homeschooling practices demonstrate certain aspects of Illich's theory and could present possible resources for furthering an anarchist project of social reconstruction, albeit from outside the anarchic tradition. Some homeschoolers, who typically define themselves as unschoolers, radical unschoolers, deschoolers, or no-schoolers accomplish aspects of Illich's model. For the time being, we will conflate these groups, but as the movements expands it may be necessary to draw distinctions between them to determine which, if any, approximate an Illichean anarchopedagogy and which reproduce a public mode. By examining these spaces critically we'll find that some homeschoolers may not be questioning the hidden curriculum at all and are creating explicitly private educational models, albeit with alternative values and goals, but private nonetheless, that does not challenge institutional learning and cannot be perceived as a counterpublic.

## Politics of Homeschooling

> Educational publics are sites where parents and educators can resist or reconstruct the state's goals for education and schooling, debate and agree upon various shared educational needs and visions, and hold the state accountable for helping them to implement these visions. (Abowitz, p. 87)

In this section I will begin navigating the homeschooling landscape and also test the political climate that homeschoolers are facing. Data on homeschooling have been compiled by the National Center of Education Statistics, a research extension of the U.S. Department of Education, which has provided information exposing the growth homeschooling has experienced in recent decades. There were an estimated 1.5 million homeschooled students in the United States in 2007 (NCES, 2008, p. 1). Since 2003 this signifies an increase from 1.1 million homeschooled students. More specifically this represents a "74 percent relative increase over the 8-year period [since 1999] and a 36 percent relative increase since 2003" (NCES, 2008, p. 2). However, this rise in homeschooling does not exclusively signify an increase in deschooling. "From 2003 to 2007, the percentage of students whose parents reported homeschooling to provide religious or moral instruction increased from 72 percent to 83 percent [an increase of 11 percent]" (NCES, 2008, p. 2). Whereas "interest in a nontraditional approach to education, [increased only] 7 percent" (NCES, 2008, p. 3). However, there is a chance we can be more optimistic about this because Grace Llewellyn finds that "[most] people who do fantastic unschoolish things with their time *call* themselves homeschoolers, because it keeps them out of trouble and it doesn't freak out the neighbors" (Llewellyn, 1998, p. 27). For our purposes we must remain aware that "schooling can still take place outside schools themselves, and clearly that is what many homeschooling families do; they are *schooling* their kids at home" (Hern, 1996, p. 2). Obviously this includes homeschoolers who choose to opt out of public school for religious reasons, but it also includes homeschoolers who are not making the choice to leave *public* education (Abowitz, 2003, p. 77). The percentage might in fact be much higher but is represented lower because deschoolers could be intentionally trying to avoid attracting attention. One thing that becomes clear is that deschoolers, that is, homeschoolers of a particular variety, are a minority within the minority. Regardless of the form homeschoolers are assuming, this overall increase is significant because it may indicate a rise in private models of schooling, not counterpublic models of deschooling that entreats research into the public dimension of homeschooling.

Internationally, homeschooling has seen similar trends as in the United States. In Germany for instance, the implementation of an educational policy against homeschooling can be rather accepting or perceive homeschooling as "deviant behavior" and a severe transgression of the school law with sanctions to follow (Spiegler, 2009, p. 297). In Sweden the practices of implementing the law against homeschooling is becoming strictly regulated and institutionalized (Villalba, 2009). We again find the distinction between religious homeschoolers "who considered the public schools as too liberal and antiauthoritarian" and deschoolers who are "liberal supporters of children's rights for whom the school was still too authoritarian and rigid" (Spiegler, 2009, p. 299). What we find however, and this gives hopes to deschoolers in the United States, that "the idea that it is adequate and helpful to sanction home educators with high fines or imprisonment does not have much more acceptance than homeschooling itself" (Spiegler, 2009, p. 302). Germany itself is conflicted about homeschooling, illustrated by the contradictions in sanctions and the inconsistencies between cases. Also of importance for anarchic theorists is the fact that "home educators do not consider their own behavior as deviant, rather the German law is seen as deviant" (Spiegler, 2009, p. 304). This is a fundamental distinction of anarchists; that they are willing to dispute the laws of the state they deem to be unjust or reproduce inequality.

Domestically, homeschooling has met increasing opposition as the trend toward deschooling and unschooling gains momentum. "Critics contend the HSLDA [Home School Legal Defense Association] supports a conservative political agenda as well and that the group has helped pass legislation that hurts more relaxed home-schoolers—like new regulations in New York that require standardized tests and official oversight." (Kleiner & Lord, 2000, p. 52). The source of this opposition originates within the group of homeschoolers representing the majority of homeschoolers. We find that "[in] recent decades, home schooling has come to be closely associated with religious conservatives and a Bible-based curriculum. This school-at-home approach allows families to avoid a secular take on subjects like evolution and to provide moral and ethical training according to their own religious values" (Kleiner & Lord, 2000, p. 52). It is one thing to face opposition from outside of the homeschooling movement and another entirely to have to deal with it internally. Because of the extreme diversity, conservative versus liberal, deschoolers now seem to be facing more opposition from religious homeschoolers.

On February 28, 2008, judges in California "found that parents without a teachers' credential who educate their children at home could be criminally liable under California law" (*California Catholic Daily*, 2008). Pat Farenga (1998), an associate of John Holt's, recognizes that "[parents] who wish to teach their own children are not required to have a teaching credential in any state" (p. 128). This important observation is the first step that removes power from teachers and schools as the only place professionals can educate, nullifying the teaching profession. Threatening the profession will lead to stronger opposition against homeschooling because it threatens the institution itself from compulsory schooling, to teacher education programs, to private professional development companies, and teachers unions. In this case we find that "among those filing briefs opposed to homeschooling were the California Teachers Association, which warned the court that allowing parents without credentials to teach children would lead to 'educational anarchy'" (*California Catholic Daily*, 2008). In response to this accusation, profamily attorney and president of the Pacific Justice Institute, Brad Dacus had this to say, "[this] is ignoring the facts that home schooling is widespread in California. Over 200,000 children are being home schooled right now in California—and they score higher academically than not only public school children, but also children in traditional private schools. If there is anarchy, the anarchy is in the public schools" (Johnson, 2008). The term "anarchy" is used sensationally and represents a misunderstanding about anarchist theory by both parties; those opposed and those in support of homeschooling. Also inherent in this squabble is the fact that the Teachers' Union seems to be threatened by homeschoolers because they represent a political, ideological movement that undermines professional certification of teachers and charts new educational terrain.

For Illich, "[citizens] conceive the inconceivable and thereby create a world free from social inequity. Illich felt that change is a process of demystification, the eradication of false ideologies imposed by a hegemon, and in order to find those boundaries, citizens must create alternatives to the status quo" (Sewell, 2005, pp. 11–12). What are the boundaries of educational change and how do we know when we're approaching them? In light of the opposition to homeschooling and deschooling, both domestically and globally, we find it likely that when the State reacts to these educational alternatives with counterinsurgency tactics, we are tiptoeing near the boundary and may even be stepping across, enabling us to look back from the other side. Judging by the reception of homeschooling by the State, teachers' unions, the public, the media, etc, deschoolers are on the right track because the institution is threatened and actively trying to subvert deschooling projects and silence the movement (Lugg & Rorrer, 2009).

Overall, homeschooling faces predictable challenges. As has been shown, there are separate battles being waged against different factions; some external, such as the State and policymakers, and others internal, such as other homeschoolers and conservative homeschooling advocacy groups. This situation illustrates how we have confined our thinking about education exclusively through public and private lenses. Consequently, anarchist theory linked with education has been villainized by the Right and the Left, with the effect that each misses the true political potential of homeschooling, that of authentic freedom and autonomy. Borrowing from Nancy Fraser's model of the public sphere, Kathleen Abowitz helps to identify a third model of social identity, in this case educational counterpublics, but does not go far enough in suggesting how homeschooling and other educational alternatives can nurture this new identity and engage in collective struggles.

## Anarchic Educational Counterpublics

> A political program which does not explicitly recognize the need for deschooling is not revolutionary. (Illich, 1970, p. 75)

Any anarchist struggle must be critically analyzed for its inclusion and reconstruction of education, particularly alternative deinstitutionalized learning, within the community as it exists and as it strives to become. Anarchist theory and practice must account for deschooling in more direct and explicit ways in order to rekindle its own revolutionary potential which has waned but is seeing a strong resurgence and rearticulation that focuses on liberty, active student-directed learning, and political participation (Godwin, 1966, p. 424). Revolutionary struggles must actively and consciously avoid reproducing the inculcating tendencies of the hidden curriculum, less they compromise their project for social change in the name of freedom and justice. In addition to analyzing anarchist struggles and their articulation of deschooling as it relates to political and social subjectivity, we can also examine spaces where deschooling may be happening but not articulated as part of a larger anarchist tradition of struggles.

In tracing this demarcated line of schooling on one side and deschooling on the other, we find descriptions that help to make the path more discernible. Multiple homeschooling, deschooling, and unschooling advocates put forward the negative goals of compulsory education such as coercion into capitalistic hierarchies and unquestioning obedience, as opposed to equality and community that are the targeted ideals of anarchists and deschoolers (Hern, 1996; DeLeon, 2006; DeLeon, 2008; Wheatley, 2009). These aspects of schools that are anything but empowering take shape through the hidden curriculum and operate through mechanisms designed for conformity and normalization. These techniques rely on shame, guilt, ridicule, and peer pressure to reinforce and maintain the hidden curriculum. Institutionalizing dependency on the State produces individuals that are virtual wards of the State, incapable of inspiring any community action toward social justice on a local level, and beneficiaries of the structure in which they were produced and left forever with the impression that things could not carry on or get done without the institution. If "schools teach children to rely on teachers, instruction, and methodologies for their learning rather than their own experience, self-reliance, and individual abilities," then this is where the project of anarchopedagogues and deschoolers begins (Peretti & Jones, 2001, p. 377).

Deschooling itself requires a different structure and different relationship to learning, but getting there requires a different kind of social movement, bent on creating the alternative form of activism in the present, instead of attempt to influence policy and wait for the effects to trickle down. Anarchists argue for a different structure not reliant on the institutions of the State, otherwise the hidden curriculum remains unchanged and intact and will reproduce a similar State in the generation to follow the revolution (Illich, 1970; Suissa, 2001; DeLeon, 2006). This feature of Illich's thought makes it possible to position him in anarchic theory as it relates to education, the State, and institutions and an individual's relationship to each. Deschoolers confront, attack, and sabotage the hidden curriculum.

In direct opposition to these debilitating practices, anarchopedagogy stands to reimagine education, building it on principles of freedom, equality, and community. For Illich a "renewal of education [requires] an institutional framework which constantly educates for action, participation, and self-help" (Illich, 1970, p. 64). Illich himself did not articulate his project as anarchic but the similarities cannot be ignored. Perhaps he moved through anarchy unconsciously as Ward suggested in the beginning. The features that we must be aware of and actively seek out and plan for in any educational alternatives are stated repeatedly by anarchist theorists and deschooling advocates (Godwin, 1966; Ward, 1966; Watt, 1981; Hern, 1996; Farenga, 1998; Llewellyn, 1998; Suissa, 2001; Holt & Farenga, 2003; DeLeon, 2006; Morrison, 2007; DeLeon, 2008; Kahn, 2009). These include:

1 at the level of the individual: autonomy, student-directed learning or self-help, and active learning;
2 at the level of the community: participation, mutual aid, social/political action, and participation;
3 and lastly at the structural level: decentralized management and non-hierarchical relationships.

Illich advanced that "the way ahead will be found by those unwilling to be constrained by the apparently all-determining forces and structures of the industrial age" (Illich, 1969, p. 17). Imagining alternatives and creatively inventing and constructing these alternatives is profoundly anarchic. As an anarchic technique "[direct action] is most viable when communities decide that institutional structures can no longer serve them and actions must be done *now* to alleviate the problem" (DeLeon, 2006, p. 133). Homeschooling can be viewed as direct action of the family against the institutional structure of school and deschooling, in its most overtly political and activist-oriented manifestation, could even be viewed as a form of institutional sabotage, another anarchic technique to use against compulsory schooling.

The process begins politically as parents and students choose to defy the expectations of compulsory schooling and instead invent their alternative. Illich maintained that "[only] disenchantment with and detachment from the central social ritual and reform of that ritual can bring about radical change" (Illich, 1970, 38). In regard to this concern, there seems to be a need for rigorous and sustained opposition to the social ritual and reflective/creative efforts to overcome schooling, outside of the institution of schools. The institution is not only abusive to the rights and freedoms of children and schools us to internalize this politically desirable silence, but is equally oppressive to parents and even teachers, the community, and society at large. John Holt doubted whether the public would ever question and divert public school funding and, for this reason, worked to provide alternatives outside of schools (Farenga, 1998, p. 127). In order to challenge the funding one would already need to be deschooled to an extent. In this way Holt might be right; we need a space to deschool as individuals, families, and communities before the entire institution of compulsory schooling can be combated.

There may come a time when the homeschooling movement will not encompass a diverse array of religious homeschoolers, unschoolers, deschoolers, etc. It may become more fractured and dislocated as each grows more incompatible with the other. The consequences of this cannot be seen from our vantage point but it may create less diversity within homeschooling networks, revitalizing some of the concerns of Abowitz, and it may also weaken each movement individually making them more susceptible to political opposition. Homeschooling in general is challenged by public school institutions, and deschooling in particular is facing opposition internally from homeschoolers following a private notion of education, suggesting that, deschooling does in fact represent a new social identity.

## Homeschooling and Deschooling

Homeschooling may be able to cultivate this new identity, but it will need to be cautious when interacting with other educational counterpublics. Abowitz (2003) recognizes the problem of inequalities among publics that could arise from the binary homeschooling counterpublic (p. 90). Inequality is the pivot point for anarcho-pedagogues in that any educational counterpublic that can be considered anarchic must avoid being reabsorbed into either a public or a private model, rife with inequality. Deschoolers are in a position to create this anarchic social identity but will need to counter any efforts to define the movement in public or private conceptions. She also acknowledges that "[thanks] to the works of feminist scholars and activists, it is possible here to discuss public spheres without automatically invoking the public/private dualism" because these separate realms are no longer isolated and definitive (Abowitz, 2003, p. 78). However, the fact that a counterpublic can evade this public/private distinction does not necessarily mean that it is representative of an anarchic identity. Although counterpublics are seeking alternatives to compulsory public education, Abowitz's examples of educational counterpublics suggest a State-oriented or privatized models of educational reform, reverting back into public/private dualism. According to Abowitz, the counterpublics that avoid this relapse are those whose practices can be defined as democratic, which deschooling may embody, but is not typically the case with homeschooling generally because of the internal opposition.

As the movement expands, the homeschooling counterpublics must address deschooling on its own terms, but for now we can use models such as Illich's to measure the amount of freedom, autonomy, and trust they have reclaimed from practices of schooling. "What prevents [the counterculture's or insurgency's] frustration from shaping new institutions is a lack not only of imagination but frequently also of appropriate language and of enlightened self-interest" (Illich, 1970, p. 73). Anarchist theory can provide some of this vocabulary and conceptualization, but also Abowitz's suggestions for counterpublics will provide a more robust definition of education. Abowitz suggests using advancements made by contemporary critical theorists. The feminist "counter public has, among other achievements, produced and introduced a new lexicon into larger society, emblematic of the larger ideological and legal changes it has brought about in the last century. [Terms like date rape and sexual harassment] symbolize the feminist counter public's engagement with wider publics, with the effect of influencing the prevailing understanding and notion about gender and power in American life" (Abowitz, 2003, p. 81).

In effect this counterpublic then becomes institutionalized by infiltrating public policy and carving out a space for their unique identity. In doing so, the anarchic vision is limited, as the identity—in this case, women—is reinserted back into the State. By using a model such as Illich's, the process of evaluating educational counterpublics, in the most general sense of the term, can begin, with a focus on education and power. As it gains confidence and variety, moving beyond Illich's model will result in a more complex model for which to base practice and innovation. Illich's model provides an immediate foundation that may be in need of urgent revision considering the time the model was proposed, but nonetheless imparts a vocabulary to begin experiments in deschooling. His model may help anarchopedagogues suggest a model of learning that can maintain its anarchic origins.

## Learning Webs

Illich's criteria help measure deschooling practices for their commitment to "support personal growth rather than addiction" (Illich, 1970, p. 53). To reiterate, his criteria are, *reference service to educational objects, skill exchanges, peer-matching, and professional educators*. Based on what has been discussed thus far about deschooling we find the presence of these features in deschooling and can also see how blatantly some homeschoolers maintain *schooling*. Deschooling has the potential to instill a different ethics of self, identity, freedom, spontaneity, discovery, curiosity, etc., thus creating arrangements of power that are productive, not oppressive, and preserve individual freedom and autonomy. These arrangements or relationships must be considered not only on the level of individual-to-individual or individual-to-community, but also individual-to-content and individual-to-structure. This is central for Hern who suggests:

> . . . deschooling is about relationships, and is the antithesis of professionalism. Genuine relationships are exactly what teachers are looking to avoid. It is what they call "unprofessional." But if adults are willing to take the time to get to know the kids they are around really well, to spend large amounts of time with their daughters and sons, to listen carefully to their needs and wants, and to understand what they are capable of, then trust can't be far behind. (Hern, 1996, p. 62)

Basing his model of relationships on trust implies that there is no inherent hierarchy in education, and can only be attained through nonhierarchical relationships.

## Homeschooling Networks

Anarchists and deschoolers, as well as educational theorists, argue for the creation of networks, as opposed to institutions, that are temporary, autonomous, and nonhierarchical, and facilitate a variety of diverse modes of learning and community interaction (Ward, 1966; Llewellyn, 1998; Abowitz, 2003; Holt & Ferenga, 2003; DeLeon, 2006; Morrison; 2007; Olsen, 2009). Abowitz (2003) recognizes how "homeschoolers are forming informal networks for specialized study and activities—like writing groups or math clubs and forming associations, support groups, legal aid societies, publishing networks, and Internet sites to support homeschooling families and connect them with one another" (p. 89). This is reiterated by Olsen (2009) who adds that "homeschooling networks are becoming increasingly sophisticated and self-sustaining" (p. 201). She goes on to illustrate how "many more mainstream, middle-class American parents and students themselves are beginning to see homeschooling as a way of conscientiously objecting to the wounding culture of schools. More and more people are opting out of school, and finding the alternative viable, attractive, and very rich socially, academically, and economically" (p. 198). In a similar thread, John Taylor Gatto (2003) wants parents and students to address their own needs, focusing on the needs that are not met or even addressed by schooling such as leadership and adventure, critical thinking and independence, and lastly self-initiative and creativity (p. 38). Illich's criteria may set us on our way, but the need to include new characteristics of deschooling will become evident.

The first of Illich's criteria is *reference service to educational objects*. The resources he is referring to include the materials in libraries, museums, and theaters, as well as opening the local community industries and services to individuals seeking to learn about things or processes in factories and farms (Illich, 1970, p. 78). This represents Illich at his most prophetic, foreseeing the possibility that technology, in a similar way to telephones, can connect not only people but also people and resources. The Internet is a virtual library that allows for access to countless materials, not censored by public schools or the State, at least in its most ideal form. This converges with Holt's and Farenga's conception of technology and education. Farenga (1998) states that "homeschooling can be seen as the logical destination for the convergence of education and technology customizable curricula, seminars in new educational techniques, educational TV, video-taped classes and lectures, Internet, CD ROMs, are all touted by some educators and homeschoolers alike as being more efficient education delivery systems than schools" (p. 132). This, combined with autonomy, enables self-disciplined students to learn independently yet effectively and meaningfully. Having a robust structure that allows for this type of learning is paramount for the proliferation of other freedom-based educational alternatives.

Illich's second criterion is relationships that allow for *skill exchanges.* The network will provide a database of individuals that are willing to demonstrate their skills to others, the skills these individuals are associated with, and the conditions these individuals are able to share their skills. In some ways this is already happening in an organic way but needs to be developed further to create larger networks, allowing for a more diverse set of skills and a wider pool of individuals sharing and learning skills. Many homeschool networks provide these services internally to members of their networks or sister networks and center around parents or community members who are willing to share a set of skills. Morrison (2007) has also taken note of this characteristic, finding that families participate in the "4-H club, and they are also active in doing service projects, such as taking care of preschoolers, serving food at soup kitchens, and helping out at the animal shelter" (p. 46).

The third criteria of Illich's model concerns *peer-matching* or locating like-minded individuals interested in coinquiring into a specific skill or topic. By finding a cohort of individuals, the skills available in the *skill-exchange* network increases because *any* individual can serve as a potential skill-bearer or skill-seeker. The network has the potential to increase and amplify; however, Illich (1970) is aware of the tendency that the poor, the group who needs peer-matching the most will unlikely take advantage of such a practice (p. 95). This might become irrelevant for deschoolers who make conscious efforts to diversify their homeschooling network or learning web taking a more inclusive approach and averting any homogenizing effects. There is recognition of increasing diversity, both racially and economically, within deschooling networks (Nichols-White, 1996; Kleiner and Lord, 2000).

In addition, hierarchies begin to be dismantled, a benefit for challenging the hidden curriculum, because we find that "other adults, and/or children who become 'teachers' of [homeschooled] children are not just planners of activities for the children (although they can be). Rather, they are resources, facilitators, 'mid-wives' for children's learning" (Morrison, 2007, p. 47). Peretti and Jones (2001) recognize that "[schools] provide a functional environment where youngsters can associate on many different levels with equals, as opposed to teachers, parents, and other adults" (p. 379). It is interesting that Peretti and Jones express that only peers can be viewed as equals and, intentionally or not, reinforce educational hierarchies. This is an aspect of the hidden curriculum that is reproduced in schools, positioning children at the bottom and requiring them to blindly accept their status, or lack thereof. What is needed is a reconstruction of the teacher-student relationship, which *skill-exchanges* and *peer-matching* touches upon. Hern (1996) addresses this through the typical rhetoric of teaching and parenting styles, supporting "approaches to parenting which are neither authoritarian nor permissive nor authoritative, but egalitarian" (p. 61). Llewellyn (1998) shares this sentiment of equality between teacher and student or child and parent, fostering relationships built on trust. In addition to nurturing the direct relationships between individuals, the larger picture of this criterion demands rediscovering one's local community to uncover peers and available skills.

The final criterion of the deschooling model is access to *professional educators*. This may be the most problematic of Illich's features because in some ways it reintroduces teaching as a profession. He puts forward that the rise of the professional educator will coincide with the elimination of schoolmasters (Illich, 1970, p. 97). Illich does not equate professionalism with attaining degrees and certifications and instead suggests a more pragmatic structure where professional educators are identified by the niche they fill. Illich identifies two areas in which professional educators could prosper. The first concerns assisting parents with understanding and contributing to their children's learning experiences (Illich, 1970, p. 97). The focus here is on having knowledge of human learning, in a form that allows for freedom and autonomy to flourish, not perish. For the most part, parents themselves are assuming this role and using the standard homeschooling texts of Holt, Farenga, Llewellyn, Hern, etc., as their professional guides. The second concerns the learners themselves and the need for guides that will help to introduce educational encounters and offer a critical model of understanding and making meaning of these experiences (Illich, 1970, p. 97). The type of experiences and the disposition desired is determined by the individual learner who then tries to find professional educators who match their descriptions.

It is within the criteria of *professional educators* that we might find permissible levels of inequality but only in the sense that the relationship is such that one individual serves as a temporary guide who can encourage and facilitate learning that might not be achieved by an isolated individual. Llewellyn (1998) classifies these "adults" as teachers and tutors, role models, mentors, or other less concrete, more ambiguous relationships that, without compromising egalitarian ideals, still maintain a degree of hierarchy; a non-oppressive power relationship. Most importantly about these professional educators is the nature of the relationships they build with learners that can be traced back to philosophical traditions in Ancient Greece. Citing Aristotle, Illich (1970) defines how these learning experiences are based on friendship, trust, and leisure (p. 101). Todd May (2009) offers concerns for radical politics that apply to models of deschooling by "[looking] at an arrangement of power, [and asking] whether it is creating something bad for those who are subject to it" (p. 14). This suggests that the power relationship that is present in any educational encounter carries with it an opportunity for the hidden curriculum to reemerge and taint such an encounter.

After reviewing the previous criteria there are at least two concerns that are brought to light. Using the model loosely, not dogmatically, will allow for the tampering of the model and usher in improvements to the deschooling model. The first criticism involves the myopic focus on schools. Although Illich argues for the centrality of public schools as the dominant manipulative institution, we now have other equally manipulative institutions. It may also be the case that schools do not hold this unique totalitarian power. Instead the power may have been redistributed to other institutions. Deschooling must take on the project of deschooling these other manipulative institutions and create convivial alternatives within them. The second concern is a way for parents and learners to maintain the suspicion of and participate in the deconstruction of the hidden curriculum.

George Wood (1982) finds it "unreasonable for schools to be singled out as central among such socializing institutions as the family, the media, the church, and other ideological apparatus" (p. 367). Schools are not solely responsible for maintaining the social order as there have emerged new institutions that reify the hidden curriculum which must be considered and included in deschooling practices. These new institutions include mass media, the workplace, the home, the family, marriage, democracy, parenting, etc. (Falbel, 1996; Hern, 1996; Llewellyn, 1998; DeLeon, 2006). Other institutions are present and critical homeschoolers, aside from using a new model of teaching and learning will also need to establish ways to critique media, marketing, politics, technology, etc. Critical homeschoolers must be wary of all institutions and evaluate their manipulability or conviviality. Hern (1996) wants "to encourage deschoolers at every level to take the analysis and impulses that led them to reject traditional schools and apply them to the wider community. I want people to look at hospitals and cities and eating and houses and sex and city halls and shopping malls and community centers and everything else with the same critical eye they bring to bear upon school" (p. 6). He is pushing it into all institutions physical/conceptual, explicit/implicit and asking for the same rigorous critique, rejection, and renewal. Parents, with the help of professional educators, will need to develop strategies that enable deschooling these other institutions in the same way that homeschooling can challenge compulsory schooling.

In addition to opposing new trajectories of oppression we also need more rigorous practices to finding our way out of schooling. We may need new tools and structures that will allow for a more complete deschooling of all manipulative institutions, in particular, the hidden curriculum. The new social identity requires new skills which must be distilled into deschooling practice. Within the unchallenged hidden curriculum we find patterns of "[capitalism], racism, sexism, patriarchy, heterosexism, and classism [which are] systems of oppression that anarchists resist" (DeLeon, 2006, p. 3). All of these are a deep part of schooling and to such an extent define the experience in schools. For this reason, it is not enough to homeschool or even to unschool. An anarchic deschooler must dismantle these systems of oppression; these manipulative institutions and "pay much more attention to 'missing standards' such as positive emotions, love of learning, initiative, creativity, and persistence" (Wheatley, 2009, p. 27).

Deschoolers require and are advancing a different set of skills and resources than their schooled counterparts. The difference lies in the ideals of freedom and autonomy, but more specifically, on self-discipline, motivation, and persistence that are inherent in the deschooling model. As Illich suggests, "[the] ideal way of life would obviously be to a much greater degree a do-it-yourself life, in which, individuals and small groups took more responsibility for meeting a much wider range of their own needs, rather than concentrating on one specialty and depending on a wide range of other specialists" (Watt, 1980, p. 8).

## Creating Autonomy

Homeschooling and deschooling, although not directly located within the anarchy discourse, represent a way that anarchy might make some progress while nobody is looking, so to speak. This may be a positive thing, given the current global hostility toward homeschooling and the complete lack of understanding and sensationalism surrounding anarchy. If deschooling were to intentionally define itself as anarchic, deschooling youth, deinstitutionalizing mandatory education, and deinculcating neoliberal hidden curriculum, it would be viewed as far more radical and would warrant accusations of corrupting the youth, unraveling the social fabric of democracy, and possibly even be categorized as an insurgency, or worse, terrorism.

Deschooling faces similar misunderstandings and resistance as anarchy. The positive definition of anarchy, "a society based on cooperation, social justice, community participation, and mutual aid," resembles the positive definition of deschooling which focuses on an individual's relationship to the knowledge she actively acquires and to the local community, with a propensity for creativity and self-discipline (DeLeon, 2008, p. 123). More simply, in deschooling, learning is without the imposition of the authority of the master or the hidden curriculum of the State or the market (i.e., the public or the private). However, just as with the volatility of the term anarchy, and the negative definition that follows, that of "lawless disorder, violence, oppressive individualism, and chaos," deschooling too can be perceived with similar fear and hostility, from the individual who has embraced the hidden curriculum as the means to happiness and achievement, to special interest groups who have much at stake with institutionalized education and the current trends of charter schools, vouchers, and for-profit schools, and finally the state, which in many ways education reifies (DeLeon, 2008, p. 123). The fear stems from the desire to remove authority from the public or private definition of education and recover a third option to pursue more autonomous learning experiences, overcoming public and private rhetoric.

Illich was aware of the controversy surrounding *any* discussion of "radical alternatives to school-centered formal education," just as any serious, informed argument in favor of anarchy is represented sensationally by the media (Illich, 1969, p. 116). In this respect, anarchy and deschooling couple together nicely because they are up against the same misunderstandings and resistance but also share a radically humanizing potential. If, as Ward suggested, there might be unconscious efforts toward anarchy, and unschoolers are unconsciously manifesting these anarchic tendencies, the cause might be better served if we are patient and allow for the movement to become self-aware and find its own social identity and anarchic voice to announce its arrival into radical politics, social change, and education revolution. Abowitz (2003) recognizes that "[on] the one hand [counterpublics] function as spaces of withdrawal and regroupment; on the other hand, they also function as bases and training grounds for agitational activities directed toward wider publics" (p. 82). This is something that will define the future of the homeschooling movement and whether the deschooling fringe can make its unique voice audible in wider and wider circles; first, other homeschoolers, then educational policy makers and beyond. Abowitz (2003) suggests that the educational counterpublics will be defined by its fractured overlapping structure, and to some extent this will represent the topology of deschooling, but more important is not the structure of the counterpublic itself, but its structure as it relates to wider and wider publics. Deschoolers are able to elude the dichotomy of public or private and are able to avoid being reabsorbed into broader publics as long as they stay true to their origin of disenchantment and desire to create a new social reality. However, an anarchistic interpretation of deschooling allows us to see the features that prevent it from being classified as public or private and also suggests a distinct form of a counterpublic that Abowitz proposes. The anarchist capacity of deschooling may lie, as Richard Kahn (2009) suggests, "in our scholarly capacity to opt-out of the excited drive to reconstruct education once again in the hope of a better world and to recognize the programmatic suffering of our institutionalized existence as students and teachers" (p. 133). We cannot theorize and design for humanity, we can only practice humanity. And if humanity is not present in obligatory schooling then the only places it has potential to creep up is in deschooled learning spaces.

> We can only live these changes: we cannot think our way to humanity. . . . The many models which will develop should give each one of us an environment in which we can celebrate our potential—and discover the way into a more humane world. . . . We must build in hope and joy and celebration. (Illich, 1969, pp. 15–16)

## References

Abowitz, K.K. (2003). Civil society and educational publics: Possibilities and problems. In G. Dimitriadis & D. Carlson (Eds.), *Promises to keep: Cultural studies, democratic education, and public life*. New York: Routledge Falmer.

*California Catholic Daily*. (2008, June 25). Educational anarchy? Retrieved from http://calcatholic.com/news/newsArticle.aspx?id=44eadbfe-925a-41f3-b64a-e61609b214b8 (accessed March 17, 2010).

DeLeon, A. (2006). The time for action is now!: Anarchist theory, critical pedagogy, and radical possibilities. *Journal for Critical Education Policy Studies*. 4(2).

DeLeon, A. (2008). Oh no, not the "a" word!: Proposing an "anarchism" for education. *Educational Studies*, 44, 122–41.

Falbel, A. (1996). Learning? Yes, of course. Education? No, thanks. In M. Hern (Ed.), *Deschooling our lives*, 64–68. Philadelphia: New Society Publishers.

Farenga, P. (1998). Homeschooling: Creating alternatives to education. *Bulletin of Science, Technology, and Society* 18(2), 127–33.

Gatto, J.T. (2003). Against school: How public education cripples our kids and why. *Harper's Magazine*, 307(1840), 33–38.

Godwin, W. (1966). How should knowledge be communicated? In L. Krimmerman & L. Perry (Eds.), *Patterns of anarchy: A collection of writings on the anarchist tradition*. New York: Doubleday, 421–25.

Holt, J. & Farenga, P. (2003). *Teach your own: The John Holt book of homeschooling*. Cambridge: Da Capo Press.

Hern, M. (1998). *Deschooling our lives*. Philadelphia: New Society Publishers.

Illich, I. (1969). *Celebration of awareness: A call for institutional revolution*. New York: Doubleday.

Illich. I. (1970). *Deschooling society*. New York: Marion Boyars.

Johnson, J. (2008, June 5). "Home schooling labeled 'anarchy.'" OneNewsNow.com. Retrieved from http://www.onenewsnow.com/Education/Default.aspx?id=129886 (accessed March 17, 2010).

Kahn, R. (2009). "Anarchic epimetheanism: The pedagogy of Ivan Illich." In R. Amster, A. DeLeon, L. Fernandez, A. Nocella II & D, Shannon (Eds.), *Contemporary anarchist studies: An introduction of anarchy in the academy*, 125–35. NY: Routledge.

Kleiner, C. & Lord, M. (2000). "Home school comes of age." *U.S. News & World Report*. 129(15), 52–54.

Llewellyn, G. (1998). *The teenage liberation handbook: How to quit school and get a real life and education*. 3rd ed. Eugene, OR: Lowry House.

Lugg, C.A. & Rorrer, A.K. (2009). The politics of (im)prudent state-level homeschooling policies. In G. Sykes, B. Schneider & D.N. Plank (Eds.), *Handbook of education policy research*, 805–18. NY: AERA/Routledge.

May, T. (2009). Anarchism from Foucault to Rancière. In R. Amster, A. DeLeon, L. Fernandez, A. Nocella II & D. Shannon (Eds.), *Contemporary anarchist studies: An introduction of anarchy in the academy*, 125–35. New York: Routledge.

Morrison, K.A. (2007). Unschooling: Homeschooling can provide the freedom to learn. *Encounter: Education for Meaning and Social Justice*. 20(2), 42–49.

National Center for Educational Statistics (NCES). (2008, December). 1.5 Million homeschooled students in the United States in 2007. (NCES 2009–030). Retrieved from http://nces.ed.gov/pubs2009/2009030.pdf (accessed March 17, 2010).

Nichols-White, D. (1996). Dinosaur homeschool. In M. Hern (Ed.), *Deschooling our lives*, 72–75. Philadelphia: New Society Publishers.

Olson, K. (2009). *Wounded by school: Recapturing the joy in learning and standing up to old school culture*. New York: Teacher's College Press.

Peretti, P.O. & Jones, E.L. (2001). Limitations of deschooling as a viable model. *Education*. 102(4), 377–80.

Sewell, W.C. (2005). Affecting social change: The struggle for educators to transform society. *Educational Foundations*. 19(3–4), 5–14.

Spiegler, T. (2009). Why state sanctions fail to deter home education: An analysis of home education in Germany and its implications for home education policy. *Theory and Research in Education*. 7(3), 297–309.

Suissa, J. (2001). Anarchism, utopias, and philosophy of education. *Journal of Philosophy of Education*, 35(4), 627–46.

Villalba, C.M. (2009). Home-based education in Sweden: Local variations in forms of regulation. *Theory and Research in Education*, 7(3), 277–96.

Ward, C. (1966). Adventure playground: A parable of anarchy. In L. Krimmerman & L. Perry (Eds.), *Patterns of Anarchy: A collection of writings on the anarchist tradition*, 397–402. New York: Doubleday.

Watt, A.J. (1981). Illich and anarchism. *Educational Philosophy and Theory*, 13(2), 1–15.

Wheatley, K.F. (2009). Unschooling: An oasis for development and democracy. *Encounter: Education for Meaning and Social Justice*, 22(2), 27–32.

Wood, G.H. (1982). The theoretical and political limitations of deschooling. *Journal of Education* 164(4), 360–77.

**SECTION II**

# Anarchist Pedagogies in the "Here and Now"

# DIALOGUE 2

## *(In a crowded place, between strangers)*

**Alejandro de Acosta**

**A:** Do you, stranger, have the sense that what is foremost in your concerns is echoed in an experiment that is unfolding right now? An experiment in freedom?

**B:** In this crowd, everyone speaks at once, stories cross, become confused. It is difficult to stay focused on you, stranger, let alone my own concerns. But, yes, it is as if I had heard a tale of origins, forgotten, then remembered. If we grasp this experiment from the story of its origin…

**A:** …or any other story about it with sufficient curiosity…

**B:** … if we accept the challenge of a new problem under exploration…

**A:** …we see that it could expand in every direction. This crowded place we have traversed so as to meet suggests that to me.

**B:** It could invent new directions in which to expand. I struggle to recall the details of the tale. Was it not a question of freedom? Of the will, at least?

**A:** The will? New directions? Where have you come from? Where are you going? After all, in a calm pause…

**B:** …in the chaos of a street fight… this crowd…

**A:** …in intimate moments…

**B:** …in foreign and unfamiliar settings… this crowd again…

**A:** …there is some delicate opening for a new sort of experience. This crowd, its murmur, deceives in a way that your words do not, stranger. We need many names for what we are discussing… someone said: heteroglossia… Any story will do so long as we can live with the consequences.

**B:** We risk not being able to live with the consequences.

**A:** We will call it science or ciencia…

**B:** …knowledge or savoir…

**A:** …its only test will be that of experience.

**B:** But we are not all pragmatists, especially not here. Look around, stranger, who are you, so far from what is familiar in this hubbub?

**A:** Where else would such an attitude truly make sense? I like to suppose that we share this idea: a discussion, even one as distracted as ours, has its own concrescence before and beyond what is under supposedly discussion.

**B:** As you say, we need many names...

**A:** As though we could take this crowded place, subtract the crowd, and be witness to a clearing... do you not hear, in the murmur, talk of destruction? Some no-, un-, de-, an-... seeking to make room for... someone said: heterotopias.

**B:** But even given the prehistory of destruction and its clearing, the transmission of these names is obviously delicate, face-to-face, intimate...

**A:** ...which is why I said that intimacy is a time of experimentation.

**B:** ...

**A:** Well, then, humor this as the hypothesis: The lesson is not like money.

**B:** I accept it immediately. Look around. It is local, and its transmission is fragile indeed.

**A:** *That* lesson is to be learned one thousand times... we have the time, stranger, in our wanderings through this crowded place...

**B:** and one thousand times again... we have the space, stranger, having imagined the clearing.

CHAPTER 5

# Street Medicine, Anarchism, and *Ciencia Popular*

Matthew Weinstein

## Introduction

This chapter describes the network of medical personnel organized to support protesters, most notably at meetings of G8, Free Trade Area of the Americas (FTAA), the Republican and Democratic Parties, but also more general protests against the war, against immigration policy, and in support of the homeless, and communities in general when states of emergency are declared. This network is known as the street medics and consists of people carrying a wide variety of medical credentials: doctors, nurses, wilderness first responders (WFR), and people having no more than first aid or street medic specific training.

The relationship of the street medics to anarchism is complex. Certainly many of the medics are themselves anarchists. However, often medic collectives declare themselves to be nonpolitical. One of my trainers described the role as being "Switzerland," nonaligned in the factional battles that are frequent in coalition work. This neutrality leaves the medics free to assist anyone, independent of politics. At the same time the medics exist to enable a politics. They came about (along with legal observers and peace keepers) from within the community of protesters to provide support that is legally denied protesters: traditional emergency medical personnel are barred from entering zones of civil conflict (which in addition to protests includes natural disasters—street medics set up the first clinic in New Orleans after hurricane Katrina (DeRose, 2005). Since the medics derive from these communities, the medics embody the culture of the protesters and practice forms of democracy and practice with deep roots in anarchist struggles including consensus processes such as the spokes council model and more generally a strong emphasis on individual ethical decision-making, for example, as to whether to provide medical assistance to the police or counter protesters that the protesters face.

I will first describe the history, social structures, and practices of the street medics (hereafter, just the medics). Next I look at the educational work of the medics. To understand the medics as education workers I locate their efforts within the work of popular education movements in South America and Africa. Within this descriptive material I explore the politics of the medics, briefly noting how their politics have changed over time. I specifically explore the ways that the medics, even when denying explicit connections to anarchism, adopt much of its ethos. Street medicine is as much an educational effort as it is a therapeutic one. Finally, I conclude by building on this theorizing of street medicine as education, by contrasting the kind of educational work the medics do with other efforts to articulate science and lay publics: school science, popular science, etc. I call the particular approach that the street medics take, in contrast, *ciencia popular*, a Spanish phrase meaning "science of the people." These different projects position knowledge and expertise in very different ways, and I end the paper by exploring these differences.

This chapter is part of my work trying to map the possibilities for a science education that supports radical visions of social justice, what I term a science education of love and rage (Weinstein, 2010a). For the last three years I have focused on the work of the street medics. I have ethnographically studied one street medic collective; I have attended a twenty-hour street medic training, as well as other street medic educational outreach efforts. I have also collected material from a wide variety of street medic collectives that are available through the web and through zine archives and anarchist bookfairs. This chapter draws generally from this archive of material as well as from the historical work of John Dittmer (2009b) and Malika McCay (2007).

## Making Waves over Time

Street medics trace their roots to the organization of doctors and other medical personnel to support Freedom Summer and the March on Selma in 1965. This began a sustained effort to provide medical support to protesters of, first, the civil rights movement, and, later, protesters more generally. This was done under the umbrella of the Medical Committee on Human Rights that also took on the integration of the American Medical Association (AMA) and proxy battles to challenge the military industrial complex (Dittmer, 2009b) in the 1960s. Their support of protesters, sometimes termed action medicine, included, in addition to support for the civil rights movement in the U.S. South, medical support at the Chicago 1968 Democratic Convention, and the battle at Wounded Knee, South Dakota, in 1973 (Dittmer, 2009b; Manriquez, ND; Street Medic Wikia, 2007).

According to Dittmer the MCHR was taken over by radical parties and factions at different times over its organizational life (Dittmer, 2009a). The Maoist Revolutionary Communist Party, for instance seized control of the group in the 1970s. In the early 1980s the organization disbanded, though its member medics remained active through the 1980s and 1990s (Street Medic Wikia, 2007). The end of the MCHR marks symbolically the end of the first wave of organized street medicine.

Reflecting the radical political spectrum of the New Left, the medics of the 1960s and 1970s focused both on action medicine, establishing the basic protocols that define modern (i.e., current) street medicine, and on policy concerns regarding the organization of medicine as an institution, especially its racial politics and its collaborations with industry in the Vietnam War, and worked to reframe the war as a medical issue (Dittmer, 2009b; McCay, 2007). It is the action medicine dimension of the MCHR that reemerges as a second wave in the wake of the 1999 World Trade Organization Ministerial Meetings in Seattle. According to the Medic Wikia, which is as much a defining text as exists in the street medic community,

> The contemporary incarnation of the street medic movement traces its inception/revival to the 1999 World Trade Organization (WTO) protests in Seattle, Washington. During those protests, small cadres of street medics were highly visible and very helpful when police used tear gas and pepper spray against protesters. This alerted activists of the necessity of acquiring training to deal with protest-related injuries. Thousands of street medics were trained in preparation for further anti-globalization protests. Street medic training became more standardized and specialized—they learned how to care for pepper spray, tear gas, and taser injuries, as well as hypothermia, dehydration and other likely complications of protests. (Street Medic Wikia, 2007)

While this origin narrative downplays the continuity of medical practice with the earlier MCHR, it is widely shared in the medic community, and clearly, after Seattle there was a wide spread blossoming of street medic collectives in the U.S., Canada, and Europe. This continuity includes the education of medics on the legal framework that allows them to operate, the limitations of their legal ability to practice, and general standards for care such as the now discontinued use of a protocol called MOFIBA (mineral oil followed immediately by oil) for exposure to pepper spray on the skin.

The continuity was established through the training of younger medics by experienced MCHR action medics, most notably Doc Ron Rosen, a doctor of Chinese medicine, who served at the March on Selma, the Democratic

Convention of 1968 in Chicago, and at the siege at Wounded Knee. He founded the Colorado Street Medics and trained many other collectives, including the Seaview Street Medic Collective (SSMC) that I studied. His training program included a variety of standard emergency medical operating procedures, a combination of allopathic and Chinese medical treatments, and a set of ethics and standards for both trainings and practice.

Medics primarily recall the history of the second wave of street medicine as a sequence of traumas, as the medics became exposed to the worst violence and harm at national and local encounters between police and demonstrators. After the Seattle WTO meeting, the Quebec City and Miami meetings (2001 and 2003 respectively) of the Free Trade Area of the Americas meeting seemed to be moments of remarkable violence and trauma for the medics I have spoken too. The Republican National Committee meetings of 2004 and 2008 are also critical time markers as they were times when medics gathered nationally to support protesters and faced escalated police response in the form of tear gas and pepper spray, batons, and other weapons. PTSD is an ongoing point of discussion and concern among medics, and many collectives are focusing more energy on what is termed "self care" and "after care," that is, physical and emotional healing after the excitement and distress of mass demonstrations.

In 2001, medics held their first national conference in Athens, Ohio. This meeting resulted in the Athens Manifesto (2001), a one-page document that collectives generally recognize as important, especially in managing the coordination of care between collectives and noncollective medics. The document is divided in four parts: proposals, rights, responsibilities, and a second proposals section. In the first proposals section medics agreed on a number of critical points. First, they agreed to incorporate antioppression work into their own trainings. Second, they agreed that democratic coordination was just as important a skill as medical technique. In the words of the manifesto: "Oppressive behavior has happened in trainings and on the streets and in the clinics coming from action medical/1st Aid people. We want to prevent it from happening again. You can be a neurosurgeon or the most experienced trainer around, but if you don't know how to facilitate or are oppressive in your behavior, you are doing more harm than good."

Third, authority has to be yielded to local medics, since they will be most familiar with the geographic and political history of the site/situation. The rest of the document, a series of bullet points, covers a wide variety of issues: the right to disagree, the right to check medical "references" (more on this below), the value of multiple medical traditions including Chinese, Wiccan, allopathic (a.k.a. Western medicine), and herbalism, and the management of "clinic" areas, that is, relatively safe stable locations at the margins of demonstrations where higher levels of medical care can be delivered.

In the collective I studied, the Manifesto was a point of ongoing conversations in 2008. The collective operated in a relatively isolated rural community. The community formed a street medic collective because materiel for the Iraq War moved through the town. Tear gas and pepper spray (chemical weapons) had been used to squelch peace demonstrations that included the blocking of roads. For the collective, addressing the Manifesto had meant, in their eyes, becoming a part of a larger "national scene." (Collective Interview, 10/17/2008) While the Manifesto does have suggestions for specific collectives, its primary focus is on how to coordinate between medic organizations when they must work together at larger events. I should note that even in local protests in the immediate area of the Seaview Street Medics, they were often only one of several medic collectives offering support, so that the issues addressed by the Manifesto were certainly relevant to them.

In 2010, medics met for a second time nationally in Conneaut, Ohio. This meeting resulted in a review of the Manifesto. While the changes in language are just now circulating back to collectives, the modifications seem to serve to (1) provide more concrete procedures for resolving disputes, verifying references, etc. and (2) emphasize collective as well as individual responsibilities (e.g., in resolving differences).

Finally, while protests and meetings define time and history in many ways for medics, some singular events also mark time in their history. In particular, one collective famously (within the tightly knit medic community) conducted its own blinded randomized trials to find treatments for tear gas and pepper spray exposure on both skin and eyes. The story and results of the Black Cross Collective trials are preserved on a web site, though the collective no longer exists (Black Cross Health Collective, 2003b). Conducted in 2001, the trials verified the effectiveness of MOFIBA (mineral oil followed immediately by alcohol—now agreed upon as too dangerous to perform in the context of protests) for exposure of skin to chemical weapons such as tear gas and pepper spray and identified new effective treatments for eye exposure to chemical weapons: liquid antacid and water (LAW). (The practice of reducing treatments and protocols to short abbreviations comes from emergency medicine, which uses short mnemonics to try to help responders work systematically in chaotic situations). Subjects were exposed to pepper spray and then treated with a variety of items claimed effective by street medics. Many treatments washed out. LAW was quickly established as the gold standard for chemical weapon treatment of the eyes. The trials were not unproblematic. Nonsubjects became exposed to the chemical weapons, including at least one with allergies. However, the trials represent a high level of ownership of one of the specific skills of first- and second-wave street medicine and the development of a science for social justice, what I will later discuss as *ciencia popular* (people's science) or as the Black Cross Collective terms it "activist science" (Black Cross Health Collective, 2003b).

## Fighting the Power, Doing No Harm

The structure and practice of second wave (or current) street medicine reflects a combination of the legacy of first wave street medical practice and the politics of twenty-first-century radical activism in which anarchism has played a central role. Much of the essential practice of street medicine, especially "running as a medic" (i.e., serving as a medic in a protest context) remains unchanged from the 1960s. The focus on treatment of chemical weapons as a defining skill of street medicine, the ethic of doing no harm, and rules for who can and cannot train others are inherited from the first wave.

The medics also inherit from the first wave the legal structure that allows them to act. Street medicine has always been necessitated by limits in the geography of medical practice. In the first wave this meant that southern Black activists and their northern allies could not expect medical assistance (clinics were segregated in the South) when shots were fired, bombs thrown, or clubs swung. Furthermore, because of the state system of licensure, doctors who traveled south could not operate as doctors. Instead the Good Samaritan laws, which allow people to come to others' aid with some legal protection, shielded them. The same applies to second-wave medics. EMTs are barred from entering zones of civil unrest, which characterizes many of the current peace and anticorporate globalization protests as well as natural disasters (street medics have provided care in New Orleans after Katrina, in Haiti after the 2010 earthquake, and in Texas after Galveston suffered a hurricane). It is only under the cover of the Good Samaritan laws that street medics operate. The conditions of the laws (which vary by state) determine much of what medics are allowed to do and how they operate. Specifically consent has to be obtained in most states and the care cannot be reckless or grossly negligent. Much of initial street medic training is about meeting these conditions: continuously obtaining consent (including discussions of why people may refuse) and trainings of a specific set of skills. In my own training it was repeatedly stressed the limits of our training and who could provide and what constituted higher levels of treatment, that is, the limits beyond which our actions could be taken as reckless.

The street medics ideally operate in pairs when running as medics. The fact is that the chaos of protests and the need to treat many people simultaneously often divides "buddies." The primary protocols that street medics use are just those of emergency medicine in general, and would be familiar to any emergency responder. These protocols, as I have noted, are taught along with mnemonics so that medics can recall them in the chaos of the field, such as ABC (airways, breathing, circulation) or LOC (levels of consciousness). Bandaging, splinting, maintaining biological cleanliness, and carrying patients are also in the rudimentary skill set that medics learn. Beyond allopathic (Western) medical protocols, we also learned Chinese medical treatments for asthma and hypothermia. A particular training, organized by the Seaview Medics included an herbalist; others included allopathic doctors who support the medics. The medics take a distinctly pragmatic view toward medical practice and combine medical systems based on the recommendations of other medics they trust. Elsewhere I have referred to this as medical heteroglossia, the ability to speak multiple medical languages at the same time and to bricolage their practices together (Weinstein, 2010a, 2010b).

The allopathic medical tradition, which at least partially informs street medicine, includes a deep commitment to doing no harm. The Black Cross Collective famously adopted the slogan "fight the power; do no harm." This clearly involves tensions, given the danger that protesters and radical communities inherently face. The specific nuances given to the Hippocratic oath are discussed at length on the Medic Wikia:

> ... The guiding principle—"the only bit of street medicine ideology that is consistent" according to one person interviewed—is "do no harm." This is also the guiding principle of the Hippocratic oath, but it has a specific interpretation among street medics. It means "in the theaters of street medicine ... the person you are treating, if you do anything to [harm them] you put that person into immanent danger, more than they were before." Street medics work under the assumption that their patients might not be willing to seek care in a hospital—because they can't afford it, fear legal ramifications, and so on—so if there is a possibility that a street medic's treatment will make someone sicker, they will not do it. Street medicine's emphasis on prevention and wellness rather than treatment also results from the "do no harm" ethic. Street medic protocols emphasize preventative measures such as "dress[ing] warmly, eat[ing] protein," and debriefing afterwards if something emotionally stressful occurs. There is also a sense of crisis in the way "do no harm" is described. Street medics see their work—when it is responding to medical problems rather than preventing them—as occurring in dangerous of high-pressure situations. They lack the privilege of "back-up" from police or hospitals that a paramedic enjoys. Thus, they see an increased potential for them to commit harm with no additional resources to repair it. (Street Medic Wikia, 2007)

In my interviews with the medics of the Seaview Street Medic Collective, they repeatedly pointed to "do no harm" as a guiding principle. When pressed to explain what this meant to them, they first identified procedures they would not use because of risks (such as MOFIBA) and then they pointed to another regional medic collective that they felt embraced a contrasting philosophy of "do least harm" which meant that they were willing to do some procedures that might be riskier than the ones the SSMC were willing to teach and to use. Do no harm is also tightly connected to preserving the reputation of the medics, not just beneficence. In my training, the "Do no harm" section of the training began with an emphasis that when things go wrong it tarnishes the reputation of medics in general. This theme was picked up in medic interviews in our discussions of the collective that used "least harm" as its standard. The two collectives had different standards for what constituted a legitimate training, the SSMC felt that the shorter training that the other collective used could lead to problems and ultimately harm the reputation of street medics in general (Interview 9/18/2008). As it is, the SSMC has had to deal with people claiming medic status that were clearly unskilled and causing harm at demonstrations in Seaview—medics not trained by them.

Medics tend to serve in two types of social structures. My focus here has been primarily on what might be called "collective medics," that is, medics who have organized to support protesters through collectives dedicated to street medicine. The collectives necessarily must maintain a degree of political autonomy from the groups that form the coalition of protesters. Their obligation is to serve protesters whatever their ideologies. Medics might even disagree with the protest itself, but feel that the safety of the protesters trump the protesters' agenda and still serve. Affinity group medics, by contrast, serve a specific group of protesters and come from the affinity group itself. Affinity groups form a basic social structure of modern anarchist politics—and broader radical politics as well, though the origin of the concept of the affinity group is in nineteenth-century anarchism. The affinity group medic has a primary responsibility to their group and not to the protest as a whole. It is too easy to become separated from their group if they choose to assist others, and so they may have to choose to ignore people needing assistance to support their group. Talking to the Seaview collective medics, I however got the sense that the group was grateful to those who they train and ultimately serve as affinity group medics rather than becoming part the collective. Since the affinity groups might engage in riskier behaviors associated with direct action, having their own medic freed the collective medics to serve the main body of protesters rather than having to shadow black bloc groups, for instance. To be clear, it is not that they objected to the black bloc group's actions (which have included smashing chain store or bank windows), some of the collective might even be part of such groups, but that by having their own medic the SSMC could focus their energies elsewhere.

It should be clear that there is a critical division is between running as a medic and being a protester, and that the two roles are distinct, though the line between them is a fragile one, and the cause of much consternation in the SSMC. They have had to deal with people changing roles without warning, leaving medic buddies stranded, and on occasion being marked (having crosses, etc.) as a medic:

> Bonnie: [A medic] at the last protest, he threw off his medic gear; threw it at another medic and went and got into the blockade and got arrested. You know, he made the decision to become a protester. But he did the right thing; he unmarked it, he gave away his gear. Now we have so many medics that we have medics that are like "okay, well I know there's going to be, you know, 10 other medic pairs there so why don't I do this instead?"
>
> Amy: And that's a nice comparison. [Another medic] a little while ago did the exact opposite. He decided he just wanted to go--he was a medic; he was wearing my backpack at the time. So I remember this very well. And he got it cut (B: He got cut) because he wanted to join a line of blockaders with a medic backpack on, it turns out it's just a black backpack. It doesn't have any medical signs on it or anything. But if you were to open it all it has gauze and stuff inside.
>
> Bonnie: You can get in trouble for the scissors.
>
> Amy: They didn't have scissors at the time, but they just cut the straps and removed the bag, you know. He didn't think about it. He didn't even hand it off to like a friend or somebody, like, "hey, get this back to Amy" or whatever.
>
> Bonnie: That's why you have a buddy.
>
> Amy: No, no, he just went right in. And that, you know, we've had some difficulty with that kind of activity. (Interview, 9/18/2008)

Many medics of the SSMC felt loss about running as medics. They felt that the neutral position of the medic meant there were ways they could not participate in the protest. One medic who decided to switch roles for a particular protest captured this position:

> Carin: Well that changes too, because for example now, after the last Anchor City protest we ran as medics, I ended up basically deciding that my presence at this protest was needed more for organization than for medics.
>
> Me: So you switched hats.
>
> Carin: Yeah, so I decided that that I've been a medic for every protest since I became a medic and I realize that I really thought that they needed my help with organizing. And I had ideas that as a medic you just—it's not appropriate. For you to say, like, I don't think you guys should be doing this. And I've always had a really hard time if I go to organizational meetings because they'll like want the medics

> to represent and we'll be like, "hey, we're your medics." But then it's hard because you can't organize, you can't be a part of that decision-making . . . (Interview, 9/18/2008)

Carin admitted to feeling "weird" about not being in the fray, but other medics like Bonnie and Amy have no such loss. Bonnie loved the simple service the role provided, "It's really nice. It's really nice to be able to grab the people who are running out but you can see they're, 'waaa waaa,' and you just grab them, eye wash them" (Interview, 9/18/2008). For Carin, part of becoming a medic was to keep her out of harm's way, to thwart her own risky impulses:

> For example, myself, part of my impetus for joining it was as a way of stopping myself from getting arrested, because I can't help but throw myself in front of a military vehicle. I can't help—like, I will throw myself—I can't do anything (laughs). If I'm a medic, at least I'm doing something else and I have a good reason not to throw myself in front of a military vehicle, because I cannot get arrested. (9/18/2008)

The street medics, in short, have developed a distinct role and distinct politics within the structure of modern radical movements. Their power comes from both distinction from the coalitions that make up modern movements of resistance and empowering those very same movements through their service. But the structure and activity I have described here, associated with running as medics is a small part of the work medics do, and it is to this other part of their activities that I wish to turn.

## Street Medicine as Popular Education

> This is what schools should be teaching —Street Medic Trainer

Much of the work of street medics is reactive: responding to the needs of protesters. At the same time the street medic movement is just as much about education as it is about post-hoc patching up and eye-washing protesters. This is glossed over in the Medic Wikia overview of "do no harm" in its emphasis on prevention. Prevention is one of several projects medics engage in to, not just to heal, but educate. In general medic collectives are involved in multiple kinds of education projects. Of course, all collectives are involved in getting new members, which is done through formal trainings. They also brief protesters in what the SSMC calls health and safety workshops. Finally, collectives engage in a wide variety of education programs to empower the communities they serve. The SSMC, for instance, created a zine for the nearby college most of the medics were associated with about consent and date rape. Another collective has conducted workshops on "travelers' troubles" to help disease prevention among community members who are nomadic (or even or those who are just traveling).

Much of the work of collectives is involved in organizing trainings. Most collectives seem to train new medics once or twice a year. When national/international-scale protests happen, additional trainings will be done prior to the event to help medics anticipate specific issues (new weapons they anticipate seeing, specific logistical problems of the protest site, etc.) as well as to increase the number who can provide medical support. The SSMC defines a training as twenty hours, and is part of a network of collectives that use specific outlines to provide a curriculum. The trainings involve briefings that cover specific topics such as obtaining consent, bandaging, dealing with common medical issues (hypothermia, dehydration, allergies, bee stings, etc.), issues specific to police violence including treating the effects of chemical weapons, dress, what to pack in a medical kit, and a review of police weaponry. Between briefings there is usually time to practice with a buddy—someone paired with the student at the start of the training. In addition, trainers usually stage a series of scenarios to give medics a taste of the chaos, danger, and logistical nightmares of protest situations. In my own training, scenarios included fake tear gas, working in the dark, and carrying wounded through mobs of both protesters and police.

At the SSMC training students came for a variety of reasons. Many planned to try to join the collective; others were there to be trained as affinity medics; but some were people seeking a kind of community and personal self-sufficiency. The SSMC medics seemed to find all of these reasons congruent with their purposes. This indexes a much larger mission of the street medic network—to raise the medical capacities of the communities they serve. It is only in the light of this larger purpose that strong links can be made between the structure of second wave street medicine and anarchist politics/philosophy. The street medic movement is establishing networks of medical care and educating people in general to manage a wide variety of illness and injury. As the Medic Wikia notes:

> Running parallel to "do no harm" as a recognition of their limitations, street medics also believe that basic healthcare is not overly difficult to teach or learn. This tenet hearkens back to the Black Panther Party's emphasis on demystifying healthcare. Many believe that the bureaucracy and rules currently associated with both the training for and implementation of medical care in the United States are excessive and at times counter-productive. One long-term Clinic volunteer and street medic described this as approaching medicine "without all the anxiousness and all that bureaucracy." Street medics view street medicine as portable, because it is neither bureaucratic nor difficult. (Street Medic Wikia, 2007)

The training I went to reflected this popular vision of medical know-how. People were there to achieve individual and collective "sovereignty" (a term used by one of my fellow students). While street medics are definitely engaging in popular health education in ways congruent with health and literacy campaigns in Latin America and Africa, there is also always an understanding that their own knowledge and skills are limited. As a result the medics I have known both respect degree and length of training and acknowledge broad spectrums of medical know-how. This includes recognizing that some designations (doctor, nurse, paramedic) represent levels of skill and knowledge. In the same training I heard our educators at times condemn the medical system and acknowledge it: through reminders, for instance, that only a doctor could do this or that procedure (dispense medicine or suture, for instance). Also, a great deal of time was spent teaching us to work and communicate with the traditional EMT/medical system. In this sense the medical capacity that the medics are seeking to build cannot be read as radically "other" to the extant medical structure. They know it needs the extant system as a safety net for cases beyond the medics' abilities (which may not mean knowledge, but the conditions to do medicine in a safe, sterile area).

Beyond the trainings, the SSMC was constantly being booked to provide workshops for protesters, and this much more than the medic trainings was their venue for popular education. In these workshops medics advised protesters what to look for in police behavior, how to dress to prevent exposure, hypothermia, and to minimize the pain and injury of chemical weapons. It provided guidance on what to bring, what to eat, and how to care for one's belongings and self before, during, and after a demonstration. In these ways the medics have actually shaped demonstrations in subtle ways, changing the behaviors (choice of dress and choice of location) to increase the safety of protesters. This education, along with their running as medics measurably increased the capacity of protesters to resist the police. This is what the SSMC medics were most proud of: clear evidence that they had enabled more enduring resistance. As Bonnie explained to me:

> If you look at like videos from the last Seaview protest you see the people who have the whites around their eyes and running down. You see multiple lines; they're different colors. That's because they were eye-washed multiple times from being pepper sprayed multiple times. And it's amazing when I watched the news after that how many people I saw. I cured that guy! I cured that guy! (Interview, 9/18/2008)

By eye-washing and preparing protesters (wearing the right clothes, for instance), the medics were able to somewhat neutralize what the police had counted on, to scatter demonstrators.

But, the medics push beyond the world of protesters and try to identify medical issues within their communities that they can address through education and medical action. The tackling date rape on the Oceanview College campus most clearly illustrated this, to me. Viewing the medics as merely action medics (i.e., as merely the medical back-up for demonstrators) misses a larger and community level politics. Through their short (eight-page) zine the medics addressed issues such as how to get consent, what to consent over (everything), and where to go for local support, all while trying to retain sex-positive culture in the community. This as much as action medicine illustrates the basic level at which the medics have tried to empower their immediate communities.

This politics of medically informing their communities reflects the distinctly anarchist turn of the second street medic wave. The first wave echoed, first, the civil rights movement and, later, the New Left. In its early days the MCHR pioneered the integration of the American Medical Association (AMA) and medical services in general; by the late 1960s the organization was taking part in proxy struggles at Dow Chemical and other military industrial complex industries. In the second wave there has not been examples of policy oriented reform directed action. Instead the politics of their educational activities seem focused on building an alternative community within extant capitalist society, a politics commensurate with a certain postinsurrectionist anarchist approach of creating an alternative culture within capitalism while simultaneously resisting capitalism (in the case of medics through action medicine). It should be clear that such locally oriented, institution-building practices do not mean that the medics lack a structural analysis of health. The Medic Wikia (2007) explains: "[A] commonality between anarchists and street medics is a "structural determinacy" approach to health. Both groups believe that "oppression" (racism, sexism, economic deprivation, etc.) causes poor health, rather than genetics, biology, or personal choice. To this extent, street medicine is political, because it implies that social change will go further to improve health than individual healthcare."

There is a largely undeveloped critique of health systems common in street medic culture. The Black Cross website (2003a), for instance, states:

> We believe that health care is political. The kind of care we do or don't receive, where and how we receive that care, who provides that care, who has access to training to provide care, and what kinds of trainings are smiled or frowned upon, all involve inherently political issues. We believe the system needs to be changed . . . the health care system right along with all the others.

However, the site does not elaborate, that is, describe, how systematic exclusion happens. Their own actual activities reflect the second wave dual practices of action/crisis medicine and medical training. I suspect to the extent there is analysis it is similar to Paul Farmer's concept of structural violence (2003). Farmer examines how systems of medical practice work to deny health care for the poor and oppressed. Farmer's organization in Haiti, Partners in Health, actually brought in teams of street medics to help after the Haiti Earthquake of 2010. Farmer's work, like the medics', juxtaposes structural analysis and pragmatic action (direct delivery of care).

## *Ciencia Popular*

To understand street medicine as an educational project, one committed to putting medical knowledge directly in the hands of people, one has to analyze their work in contrast to other parallel projects. Street Medicine-As-Education is an effort to articulate (literally connect) technical knowledge and expertise and consuming publics. It can be contrasted in this sense with science and health schooling as well as with contrasting projects like citizen science.

In school science and health, students are taught to objectify their body, to learn the language of scientists, but ultimately to defer to scientific authority for solutions. In other words, school science is about the production of a consumer class—the development of a bioscientific market for expertise. Morris Shamos (1995) makes this explicit in his book *The Myth of Scientific Literacy*, arguing that disinterest in science and technology should be taken as axiomatic in school populations; that the purpose of science education should merely be educating people in the processes of science and the knowledge of how to find experts when needed. It should also be clear that science, as embodied by school science, references a standard set of facts, concepts, and technical procedures as canonized in texts like the National Science Education Standards (NRC, 1996). It is a systematic way of knowing that excludes practices like Chinese medicine and herbalism.

Similarly, citizen science projects—that is, projects in which scientists recruit nonscientists to participate with them in research, most famously in bird counts in which birders across North America contribute data about the bird populations of their communities—often are set up to reaffirm the role of the scientist as expert and the public is a resource or source of labor. Even online efforts such as SETI which farms out calculations in the search or extraterrestrial life—or Folding@Home which does the same for calculations of protein folding—follow this hierarchical model. Ironically, citizen science projects often reveal the fragility of this hierarchy. In many environmental citizen science projects there emerge real tensions between local knowledge of the data gatherers and the scientists' expert knowledge (Brandt, Shirk, Jordan, Ballard & Tomasek, 2010).

School and citizen science attempt to develop or reinforce hierarchies of authority, knowledge, labor, and consumption. Both have specific visions of democracies as informed publics, but those publics are not self-sufficient communities, but publics that have simultaneously internalized the worldview of the expert and acquiescence to the expert.

Street medics acknowledge that there are hierarchies of knowledge and skill, but have no system of certification beyond an oral culture. A street medic's authority is verified by the word of her or his trainers and her/his experience with other medics. Furthermore, street medics in a variety of forums try to share knowledge, make available what they know, and to develop and circulate knowledge intentionally shaped for communities of which they are part of, that is, to make knowledge public. Expertise is not something to be held onto but to be circulated. Knowledge follows the needs of the community rather representing an abstract worldview. This pragmatism allows street medics, in creating a popular health science, to bricolage medical traditions. This bricolage is positively encouraged through documents like the Athens Manifesto. In this way street medicine's project is to develop and disperse knowledge that serves social justice communities both in and out of protests. It is in this sense that street medicine is a people's knowledge, captured by the Spanish phrase *ciencia popular* (science of the people), a science whose questions, networks, practices, and ethos serve people in democratic struggle.

*Ciencia popular* implies that knowledge is not just applied to people's struggles, but developed to advance them, that knowledge, research, and dissemination are organized around the needs of people. As others have pointed out, allopathic medicine has often been organized to answer not the questions of the colonized but the colonizers, and this continues to be a dominant pattern in neocolonial geopolitics, tropical medicine being just the most blatant example (Bass, 1990; Farley, 1991; Goonitalke, 1993). School science draws from the same standpoint of the powerful (Weinstein & Makki, 2009). Street medicine exemplifies a counterpractice, a differently organized science within but not of the capitalist healthscape.

## Notes

1 The Good Samaritan laws have recently been contested. In California a judge recently ruled that good Samaritans can be sued (Williams, 2008).

2 The medics have expertly refused the media's attempts to paint black blocs as the criminals and street medics as heroes (e.g., Kielburger, 2010). For instance, after the 2010 G20 meeting in Toronto, the Toronto Streets released a statement condemning the media focus on property damage while ignoring the real injuries to people caused by police violence (JoyInc30, 2010; Toronto Street Medics, 2010).

3 My use of "project" comes from the sociological sense of the term, as a shared socially organized effort to articulate people and social ends (Omi & Winant, 1986).

## References

Athens Manifesto. (2001). Athens Manifesto. Retrieved from http://www.bostoncoop.net/balm/training/athens_manifesto.pdf (accessed July 23, 2010).

Bass, T. A. (1990). *Camping with the prince and other tales of science in Africa*. New York: Penguin.

Black Cross Health Collective. (2003a, September 4). About Black Cross Health Collective. Retrieved from http://blackcrosscollective.org/about (accessed February 2, 2009).

Black Cross Health Collective. (2003b, November 24). Brave? Crazy? Black Cross' pepper spray trials. Retrieved from http://blackcrosscollective.org/OCTrials (accessed January 29, 2009).

Brandt, C., Shirk, J., Jordan, R., Ballard, H. & Tomasek, T. (2010, March 23). *Symposium: Beyond citizen science: Science learning and public participation in environmental research.* Paper presented at the meeting of the National Association of Research on Science Teaching (NARST), Philadelphia.

DeRose, J. (2005, September 23). Anarchists providing medical aid in New Orleans Retrieved from http://www.npr.org/templates/story/story.php?storyId=4860770 (accessed January 29, 2009).

Dittmer, J. (2009a, February 9). [Personal conversation].

Dittmer, J. (2009b). *The good doctors: The Medical Committee for Human Rights and the struggle for social justice in health care*. New York: Bloomsbury Press.

Farley, J. (1991). *Bilharzia: A history of imperial tropical medicine*. Cambridge, New York: Cambridge University Press.

Farmer, P. (2003). *Pathologies of power: Health, human rights, and the new war on the poor*. Berkeley, CA: University of California Press.

Goonitalke, S. (1993). Modern science and the periphery: The characteristics of dependent knowledge. In S. Harding (Ed.), *The racial economy of science*. Bloomington: Indiana University.

JoyInc30. (2010, July 3). A Toronto Street Medic talks about her experience at the G20 protests Retrieved from http://www.youtube.com/watch?v=Es7BC7q0RV0 (accessed September 17, 2010).

Kielburger, C. (2010, June 27). Global voices at G20: Violence steals the day's message Retrieved from http://www.thestar.com/news/globalvoices/article/829262--global-voices-at-g20-violence-steals-the-day-s-message (accessed September 17, 2010).

Manriquez, L. (ND). *Street medic* [Film].

McCay, M. A. (2007). *Radical health activism: The Boston chapter of the Medical Committee for Human Rights, 1964–1981*. MH Masters, Tufts, Boston.

NRC. (1996). *National science education standards*. Washington, DC: National Academy Press.

Omi, M. & Winant, H. (1986). *Racial formation in the United States: From the 1960s to the 1980s*. New York: Routledge & Kegan Paul.

Shamos, M. H. (1995). *The myth of scientific literacy*. New Brunswick, N.J.: Rutgers University Press.

Street Medic Wikia. (2007). Street medic history and philosophy. Retrieved from http://medic.wikia.com/wiki/Street_medic_history_and_philosophyw (accessed September 13, 2010).

Toronto Street Medics. (2010, June 28). Street Medics call for independent investigation into injuries caused by police. Retrieved from http://toronto.mediacoop.ca/newsrelease/3926 (accessed September 17, 2010).

Weinstein, M. (2010a). A science literacy of love and rage: Identifying science inscription in lives of resistance. *Canadian Journal of Science, Mathematics and Technology Education, 10*(3), 267–77.

Weinstein, M. (2010b, March 23). *Science education, radical social justice, and scientific heteroglossia: An ethnographic examination of the street medic movement.* Paper presented at the meeting of the National Association of Research on Science Teaching, Philadelphia, PA.

Weinstein, M. & Makki, N. (2009). *Bodies out of control.* New York: Peter Lang.

Williams, C. J. (2008, December 19). California Supreme Court allows good samaritans to be sued for nonmedical care. Retrieved from http://www.latimes.com/news/local/la-me-good-samaritan19-2008dec19,0,4033454.story (accessed January 29, 2009).

CHAPTER 6

# Anarchist Pedagogy in Action: Paideia, *Escuela Libre*

**Isabelle Fremeaux and John Jordan**

For twenty-nine years, the city of Mérida, in Southwest Spain, has hosted what is probably the only anarchist school left in Spain: Paideia. The school is named after the classical Greek concept of civic education involving the process of personal and social training toward active citizenship, aiming not to teach "stuff" but to create a working community of learning. Broader than mere education, Paideia was conceived of as a lifelong process of character building in preparation for direct democracy. It involved the absorption of knowledge and skills, but most importantly, it was about creating a living practice of participatory self-managed citizenship. Through a unique pedagogical methodology profoundly rooted in anarchist values and principles, the small Spanish school has been facilitating such a practice with and by children.

This chapter is based on a three-day-long participant observation at Paideia, during which we shared the life of the children and the adults that constitute it. Even though this is a short period to carry out in-depth critical ethnography and, admittedly, did not offer us sufficient time to, for instance, ascertain potential discrepancies between discourses and specific practices, our sojourn in the school, during which we had unsupervised access to all students, classes, and activities, remains a good starting point for the description and analysis of anarchist pedagogy in action. Indeed it is notoriously difficult to obtain permission to visit the school, let alone undertake participant observation there and we were thoroughly vetted by the pedagogic team before being granted access in September 2007.

The chapter will describe and analyze the main pedagogical precepts that regulate the school, as well as explain how these are implemented in every aspect of the school life. Indeed, Paideia is fundamentally rooted in the notion that anarchism must be *experienced*, and it thus seemed crucial to communicate this through a form of reflexive storytelling. Our findings will thus be presented in the form of a narrative of our life on site.

## Freedom as Responsibility

Located in an old two-storey pastel yellow farmhouse on what was once the edge of the city, Paideia used to be surrounded by fields and lush olive groves. Today, every single tree has been bulldozed and the school sits in a desolate landscape of churned up brown mud and partially built roads, which make it feel like a threatened oasis stuck in the hell of urban sprawl. Enormous bulldozers roam around its edges, the old walls and floors shudder with every scoop of broken earth. When the bulldozers are gone, 1,500 brand new identical suburban homes will surround the school. "We are making the future," declare the developers' colorful billboards.

Term has begun a few days before our arrival and we have been asked to meet with the staff collective on the evening before we actually come to observe the daily activities of the school. The fifty-eight children have all gone home and despite the long days, from 10 a.m. till 6 p.m. with students and then admin till 9 p.m., the collective of pedagogues greet us with warmth and numerous kisses. We sit down at a large round table surrounded by messy shelves of books and towering piles of paper. Everyone introduces themselves. Josefa Martín Luengo, whom all here call "Pepa," is one of Paideia's founders and its main theorist; she has just published her sixth book on libertarian pedagogy, a reflection on the methodology developed at the school: *Paideia, 25 años de educación libertarian* (2006). All seven female and one male teachers are adamant that they are not "teachers," they are facilitators of experience and processes, rather than transmitters of knowledge. Most of the students call them by their first name or simply "the adults."

Unlike "free schools" such as A.S Neill's Summerhill in the UK (Neill, 1960; Miller, 2002), Paideia does not see the process of growing up free as something passive. It is not a relaxed *laissez-faire* attitude where children can simply do whatever they want while the educators remain impassive and value free. It is instead a dynamic exercise, which involves creating a working community that is held by a set of clear values and where the rights of educators and students are acknowledged as equal. Central to the life and learning of the school are seven values derived from anarchist philosophy: equality, justice, solidarity, freedom, nonviolence, culture, and most importantly happiness. More than maths and languages, science and history, these are the real subjects. But *how* these values are learnt is as important as what they represent.

"The first few weeks of term after summer are always different from the normal way the school runs," Martín Luengo explains during this first meeting. "Returning from the summer holidays is always a problem, because for two whole months the kids live with their parents and their grandparents, who do everything for them, they watch a lot of TV, get influenced by consumerism and competitiveness. The children lose their autonomy. Thus, when they come back they forget how to do things: if they need to cut carrots, for example, they look at us with imploring eyes, they have forgotten what needs doing . . . Their minds aren't free when they have to ask what to do!"

### Practicing Self-Management in the Everyday

At the core of Paideia's practice is enabling the children to take charge of their autonomy and practice self-management (Martín Luengo, 2006). From as young as eighteen months until they leave at sixteen years old, the students run the entire school in collaboration with the adults. Every aspect of school life is decided through assemblies attended by all. From organizing the lunchtime menu to planning the timetables, resolving personal conflicts to choosing what academic subjects to study, every detail is discussed and managed collectively without coercion or authority. As Martín Luengo explains: "They are free when they know what they want. It is so much simpler to be told what to do than being free. Passing on your responsibility to others is easy."

Due to the number of students who have returned from summer holidays with "tendencies toward dependence," as the adults call it, the school is temporarily under what is known as *Mandado*—which roughly translates as "to be ordered." It is a state of exception, sometimes applied to individual students but in this case applied to the entire school. As the students are seen to no longer be able take the initiative to do things themselves and are asking the authority figures (the adults) what to do, they are *mandado-ed*, told what to do by the staff. This state of exception remains until the students decide to call for an assembly where they will discuss collectively whether they have returned to a state of freedom and responsibility. If there is consensus for the *Mandado* to be lifted, then the school will return to normal and no one will be told what to do anymore. "They need to re-find their anarchist values," concludes Martín Luengo. "It doesn't take long. No one likes being told what to do all the time. But if they want to be free they have to fight for it."

The morning after, we go to the school for 9:30 a.m. and wait for the children. The school bus arrives, a long sleek brand new white coach. Children pour out. The older ones hold hands with the little ones guiding them down the steps and into the school grounds where they pat the two lounging school dogs and are kissed by the waiting adults. The smaller children, eighteen months to five years old, peel off to the kindergarten annex; we stay with the older ones in and around the main building.

There is a flurry of activity as the children scatter in every direction to join their different "collective working groups." We follow the cooking group: seven children in mixed ages from five to sixteen go into the kitchen put on white aprons and start preparing the day's meals. Outside, a couple of children are swinging on the trapeze attached to an old crooked Cypress tree but the rest are busy, some weeding the garden, some tidying the classrooms, and a few sweeping floors with brooms that are nearly twice as tall as them. Despite the state of *Mandado*, no one seems to tell anybody what to do. There is a constant flow and movement of energized children throughout the building, getting on with things without being managed by teachers or even a school bell. In fact the school has no bells, and the only clock visible seems to be a tiny plastic one tucked away in the corner of the kitchen where the cooking group are chatting away as they prepare breakfast. All take part: the older children and one adult look after the younger ones as even five-year-olds wield large knives, diligently cut up tomatoes, and stir the industrial cauldrons.

Every Friday, a working group in charge of the week's daily meals meets to organize cooking for sixty people. Spanning from six to thirteen years old and chaired by one of the children but with an educator present to guide them on issues such as nutrition and balanced diets, the group decides a daily menu. Each child proposes an idea for a dish, which is debated and agreed upon. If it happens to be one of their birthdays, they have the right to choose the day's menu without debate. Once the week's menus are set, the children check what food is left in the store cupboards. Lists are made, the children, armed with specially devised forms, decide who will telephone the wholesale suppliers to place the weekly provisions order, and then cooking begins. Next week another group will take over.

"Come on, it's time to work, Manu," calls Carlos from the kitchen. Although he is only seven, and not the official coordinator of the cooking group, who is thirteen-year-old Arai, Carlos is able to see what needs doing and can gently wheel his friend away from playing and back in the kitchen. Meanwhile, three other children, who can't be older than nine, are going around the entire school with a pen and paper, asking everyone how many fried eggs they want for lunch. They skip up the wooden stairs, past a 1930s framed poster declaring: "If the tyrant doesn't grow the wheat; why do you demand bread?"

Food is seen as a key aspect of the socialization process at Paideia: not only is it a simple way of coming together and building relationships, but by giving the children the opportunity to choose their own food and cook, they learn to be much more independent and self-reliant. The nursery children are the first to eat in the morning. They arrive holding each other's hands, accompanied by an adult. A five-year-old and two three-year-olds begin to set the tables for the twenty-three children of the nursery.

### Values as Pedagogical Framework

The white walls of the dining room next door are plastered with colored pieces of paper each printed with a different quote, including Joseph Proudhon's famous tirade: "To be governed is to be watched over, inspected, spied on, directed, legislated, regimented, closed in, indoctrinated, preached at, controlled, assessed, evaluated, censured, commanded" (1851).

No school is value free, state or otherwise. State schools are potent vehicles for replicating the values of capitalism (Giroux, 1984, 1987). For eighteenth-century philosopher William Godwin, there were two axes of power: government and education (Pollin, 1962). Godwin argued that since government depended on the consent of the governed, the most important area for political struggle was education, because it was there that people's thinking was formed. In 1783, as the public debate over the implementation of mass state education was taking place, he published a prospectus for a school that abolished authority and valued the autonomy of the child, in which he expressed his fear that if education fell into the hands of the state, "governments [would] not fail to employ it, to strengthen its hands, and perpetuate its institutions" (1783).

His vision was prescient: individualism, competitiveness and the acceptance of hierarchical authority, the dominant values of our culture, are subtly encouraged through schooling to this day (Whitty and Young, 1976; Giroux, 1988). Although not necessarily part of the openly designed public curriculum, these values are transmitted through the conditions of learning and the way the school operates. It is a form of "hidden curriculum" where implicit values and priorities are picked up at an unconscious level. It is not blatant indoctrination but insidious influences that emanate from the everyday climate and structures of the school; the relationship between teacher and pupil, the layout of the classroom, the way the school is managed, the system of rewards and punishments, and so on. Added to this are the unexamined and unspoken assumptions of the teachers who send messages out daily: only certain kinds of achievements count, bookish learning is more valuable than practical skills, middle-class values are more worthwhile than working-class ones, obedience to law is good, disobedience is bad, certain career choices are more worthy than others, contributing to society is honored, criticizing is discouraged (Postman & Weingartner, 1969). Despite a long tradition of anarchist educational ideas and practices (Bakunin, 1969; Suissa, 2010), many which eventually percolated into mainstream education, there is rarely any mention of it in histories of education and pedagogical theory.

"Children must be accustomed to obey, to think, according to the social dogmas which govern us" wrote Spanish anarchist and educator Francisco Ferrer (Spring, 1998, p. 23) describing church-run Spanish state schools in the first decade of the twentieth century. Freed from religion, his *Escuela Moderna* (Modern School) was about "a drawing out rather than a driving in" (Avrich, 2006, p. 192). It was a process of self-development where the child's unique spirit could be nurtured rather than shaped or suppressed. His ideas spread following the global condemnation of his mock trial and execution after the bloody suppression of a Catalan antiwar uprising in 1909. As a result forty-eight schools inspired by his ideas sprang up in Spain and many more across the world (Avrich, 2006). The notion that education could be for emancipation rather than subservience began to gain ground. Ferrer had been inspired himself by earlier anarchist experiments in France, first at Cempuis (Brémand, 1992), a state school where Paul Robin's ideas of *integral education* aimed to develop every aspect of the child's potential—physical, intellectual and moral and where sexes were mixed, something unheard of at the time (Demeulenaere-Douyère, 2003)—and later at La Ruche, which merged an independent school, with a cooperative farm funded by the production of honey.

To anarchists, the whole idea of teachers imposing authority on children and there being a hierarchical learning relationship where knowledge is poured into the silent, obedient heads of students, is an anathema (Avrich, 2006). Despite the evolution of teaching methodologies in the twentieth century and the recent trend of "student-centered learning" (Rogers, 1983a and 1983b), the underlying structures of most schools remain the same. It is still the teacher who decides *when* the "student-centered learning" takes place, *where* it will happen and *what* the student will learn. The student is certainly not the center of decision-making but a passive recipient of decisions made from "above." They don't learn to own themselves but to obey others. They have been ingrained with what primitivist author Derrick Jensen (2000) says is our culture's central belief, "that it is not only acceptable but desirable and necessary to bend others to our own will" (p. 242). Spending six hours a day for twelve years in a place where they have virtually no say in anything, where being governed is all they know, a profound passivity becomes normalized, the hopelessness of submission becomes fixed deep below the child's skin. It is a perfect preparation for the consumerist future that awaits them (Giroux, 2000).

## *Asambleas:* The Core of Self-Management at Paideia

"Religion *fuera de la escuela*!" (Kick religion out of schools!) reads a red and black sticker stuck on the large oak double doors that open to reveal the main entrance hall. Children are running up and down the wooden staircase, the noise resonates through the building. A tall, skinny sixteen-year-old, her freckled heart shaped face framed by enormous jangling hooped earrings, bounds up to us. Everyone kisses and she introduces herself as Jara. "That was our collective work session," she tells us breathlessly. "It is when we all do the cooking, cleaning, etc. Let me explain our timetable to you." She leads us to a cork notice board at the back of the hall. Sepia postcards of the CNT anarchist-run tram system during the 1936 revolution are pinned beside colorful lists of workshop groups and numerous timetables decorated with children's crayon drawings.

"After the collective work we have breakfast. Then from 11:15 a.m. to 2 p.m., we either have an assembly or attend a workshop, after that we have free time till lunch at three, unless we are in the cooking group that week. After lunch it's collective work again till four, followed by an hour-and-a-quarter-long workshop and finally afternoon tea at five before we head home." Jara realizes that she is dominating the conversation and turns to Manuel, a shy, spotty classmate of hers. She encourages him to continue the explanation. The timetables are decided by *asambleas*. Before each term starts, a general *asamblea* takes place in order to analyze how the last term went, decide what subjects pupils want to study in the workshops (the preferred term to "lesson"), what working groups they want to be in and how the timetable should be organized. There are four age groups in the upper school, each with a self-assigned name and their own classroom: five-to-seven-year olds' "cool group," the seven–to-eight-year-olds' "tornado," the nine-to-eleven "group one," and twelve-to-fifteen "group two."

When we ask Lali, one of the adults, if it is OK for us to attend a workshop, she retorts sternly: "Don't ask me, ask the children." Feeling rather embarrassed at our faux pas, we get to the door of a classroom full of ten-year-olds. One of them stands out from the other distinctly Latin children, with his blonde hair and blue eyes. He invites us in, in an English rounded by a strong Yorkshire accent. He has been living in Mérida for two years. At first he went to state school, but learnt little Spanish since the only time he could practice speaking was in the playground: most of the school day was spent sitting silently in class listening to unrecognizable words. In Paideia, he quickly became bilingual: the school not only thrives on children's conversations, but is run by them, through the debates at the *asamblea*.

The general *asamblea* is the main organ of school life, attended by both children and adults, and facilitated by the former; it is where every decision that affects the whole school is taken. Even in the nursery, the day starts with one, facilitated by four- and five-year-olds. Seeing our astonished looks, Augosto, the only male adult of the school, explains: "They do it really, almost better than older children because they take it really seriously. The small ones who cannot yet speak obviously don't take part in the decision-making, but they know that the *asamblea* is where one sits quietly and listens." In the primary and secondary school, *asambleas* are fed by a series of "commissions," which give feedback about what is happening in the school. Made up of groups of two to four children, armed with complex tables to fill in, the commissions are mirrors to reflect the workings of the school back to itself. They relate information and analysis to the general *asamblea*, and rotate every fortnight. Chris explains that he is in the "solution makers commission": "I have to be on the look out for problems and conflicts that arise . . . if there is a problem we go and try to help out, if we can't find a solution there and then, we call an *asamblea*." There are commissions to observe the school bus, manage the teaching materials, and even a "values commission," whose members observe how the values of equality, justice, solidarity, freedom, nonviolence, culture, and happiness are being practiced.

## Nonviolent Conflict Resolution

A dozen children walk purposefully through the open door of the classroom, none of them are older than seven. "Pablo bit me, we have to have an *asamblea*!" declares Miguel as they shepherd Pablo, a new boy, out into the main hall. They find a corner and sit in a circle on the floor. Everyone is talking. Hands are flailing passionately. Adriane, a supremely confident seven-year-old takes a piece of paper from her notebook and draws two columns on it: one for stacking the speakers, the other for the proposals. She begins to facilitate. A hush descends on the gaggle. One by one the children put up their hands to speak. Miguel calmly explains the situation: "Pablo snatched my workbook and then bit me." The other children describe their version of events. Most of them seem totally relaxed, it is clearly a normal part of conflict resolution at Paideia. Pablo, however, is reacting differently: he is tense, frustrated and fidgeting nervously. "Why did Miguel call for an assembly when I didn't do anything?" he shouts. He doesn't wait for the facilitator to take his turn speaking. This is hardly surprising: while most of the children have been attending assemblies since they started school at eighteen months old, Pablo arrived here two weeks ago. The resolution of conflicts through nonviolent methods is a crucial part of the curriculum at Paideia (Martín Luengo, 2006, p. 96) and one that the children learn through practice rather than abstractly in "citizenship classes."

Eventually an adult, Lali, arrives: she has heard Pablo speaking out of turn and decided to come and see if she could help out. "I wanted to see Miguel's drawing . . . he wouldn't let me. But I didn't bite him," Pablo remonstrates. Miguel shows everyone the bite mark on his arm. The children study it carefully, then one of them realizes one can tell who bit whom by looking at the shape of the bite marks and relating it to the tooth pattern. Suddenly they are all biting their own arms to see what marks they leave. But the bite marks on Miguel don't seem to match Pablo's. "Did you bite yourself?" Lali quizzes Miguel, who shakes his head blamelessly. Lali calmly mediates between the two children: "Pablo, you cannot force someone to show you their drawing.

If your friend says he doesn't want you to do something, you don't do it." She turns to Miguel: "And you have to help Pablo if you see him doing things in a violent way." However, she lets Adriane play her role of facilitator of the spontaneous *asamblea*. The latter suggests that it is time to make some proposals. "My proposal is that Pablo should not be in the Tornado group," suggests Carlos. Another proposal is that he is sent out from communal life for a bit. "I have another one," says Lali, "Pablo is new and has to learn to behave in a different way. How can he learn to be different without being in a group? His problem is not the group he is in, but himself. The group has to help him and he has to respect the group." Adriane summarizes the proposals, a vote is taken on each one, the kids raise their hands, Adriane counts and notes the results. Lali's proposal gains unanimous support, apart from Miguel who abstains.

Learning at Paideia is thus not simply about acquiring abstract knowledge—dates, facts, and arithmetic—but about encouraging a different way of being in the world, evolving the senses and deepening the capacity to connect with one's own potentiality and that of others. By instilling the seven values the school sets a clear and dynamic direction. Unlike the "hidden curriculum" of state schools, these profoundly human principles are the visible anchors of the curriculum. Constantly referred to, analyzed and reflected upon, they are the center of gravity of the school's culture (Martín Luengo, 2006, p. 96).

The values of solidarity, justice, freedom and nonviolence all aim to resolving conflict through dialogue, which is one of the keys to the school's culture (Martín Luengo, 2006, p. 122). The only time that a child has been expelled was when they were repeatedly violent. The value entitled "culture" is about acquiring the skills so that others don't interpret the world for the children. As for "happiness," it is seen as more than a value, rather it is the sum of all the values. However, as Martín Luengo had explained to us: "It is not about getting everything you want, it is about attaining emotional maturity and stability. It's about being not having."

The educators were candid about the fact the hardest value to attain was "equality," which is a fundamental objective of Paideia (Martín Luengo, 2006, p. 111). This difficulty has actually resulted in one of the most controversial practices of the school: to alleviate social privileges and the acquisition of cultural capital (Bourdieu, 1990), students are not allowed to follow any extracurricular activities.

## Open Classroom

The history workshop is in full swing. "I like history," Chris tells us, "especially the Napoleonic period, we should learn from the mistakes of the past so we don't repeat them." He chose to do the subject at the general *asamblea* where the staff suggest a dozen different workshops and the class groups collectively decided five that they want to do. Chris's group chose: History, English, Global Economy, Grammar, and Art.

The classroom windows are wide open and the smell of cooking drifts up the stairs. Although a blackboard covers the back wall, there is no teacher standing in front of it lecturing. In fact there is no adult to be seen anywhere. The half a dozen students sit facing each other in a circle of desks each one getting on with their own work. Some are diligently writing notes or filling in workbooks while others are leaning back on their chairs chatting. Every now and then Chris gets up to pick a book off the shelves lining the wall. Anton has just aimed a rubber at a classmate, it ricochets off the side of his head. Iban asks Miguel if he can help: "I can't do this. I don't understand." Miguel leans over to explain. Iban starts scribbling in his book, but it doesn't take it long before he is distracted again. "Give me your pencil, Miguel." He reaches across the desk. "No, I'm working," Miguel replies, annoyed. "Oh, be quiet, Iban," Anton pleads.

Despite the appearance of mild chaos, academic learning must be taking place: the school boasts excellent end-of-compulsory-education exam results. The school has not been properly legalized by the state, and consequently the students cannot take their final exams here. They must therefore finish their schooling in the local college.

Pepa walks casually into the classroom. "If your work is ready I can correct it," she says. Iban trots out of the door, but Anton produces his workbook. "Hmm . . . there is a lack of good grammar, just like last year," she says and strolls into another classroom. "Shit," grumbles Anton, screwing up his sheet of paper, "I have to start all over again."

We ask the children what motivates them to study in the absence of coercion. Chris and Anton explain that all students fill in and sign "commitment" forms, which list the personal commitments they have decided to make and a date by which they commit to have completed them (see examples Martín Luengo, 2006, p. 509). Commitments range from how many projects and workbooks they are going to complete, to how they are going practice the anarchist values, what collective work they will do, to what they commit to on an affective level. At the end of the term they collectively assess each other's commitments. If the *asamblea* thinks that someone has not fulfilled them properly, they can be *mandadoed* for a while. They also make a commitment to do what is called "intellectual work." This is a totally self-determined project, on a subject of their choice. Chris has decided to do a project on the Roman Empire. In a fortnight he will stand in front of his group and present it. He won't be given any mark since there is no form of summative assessment. However he will have to take part in "La Prueba Larga" (i.e., the big test) at the end of term, an in-depth formative assessment that takes place one to one with an educator in Martín Luengo's study. A holistic appraisal observing the development of the child, it looks at everything from motor coordination to numeracy, character traits to the way they engage with *asambleas*, energetic temperament to diction, artistic proclivity to relationship to food, emotional qualities to social skills, grasp of history to connection with their own bodies. All these traits are recorded on complex psychopedagogic tables (see templates in Martín Luengo, 2006, 366–508), which are evidence of the rigor of Paideia's pedagogic methodology.

## Punishments and Uprisings

Jara takes us into Pepa's office. It is covered with political posters, including one that proclaims: "If fighting for a better world means being a terrorist; then I am a terrorist." The lanky teenager plunks herself on the large, paper-strewn desk. "This is the headmistress' office," she smiles cheekily. "It is funny, most people in Mérida don't understand this place, they think it's a boarding school or somewhere for people with mental illness. They don't believe anyone learns anything. But a lot of our friends are jealous that we don't have any exams and so never fail anything." We ask if there is any form of punishment. "The main punishment is to be taken out of the collective life, to do things on your own, to eat and study without your friends. Sometimes you have to spend all day cooking. Once I spent two weeks in this office, no one was allowed to come and see me, but they did anyway!" she grins. "When you decide that you are ready to go back, then you go to the *asamblea* and explain that you have realized why you were punished and have reflected on what you did." She looks up to the ceiling thoughtfully. "You know, you can tell when people have changed. In the *asamblea* you can see when people have really thought through their behavior. Then everyone decides whether you should return from exclusion or not, sometimes there is a trial period . . . I think it's a just form of punishment."

At first, it reminded us of Maoist self-criticisms and confession rituals. Yet emphasis on the notion of responsibility as a collective as well as individual value, and constantly trying to eliminate all forms of authoritarianism quickly changed our opinion. Moreover an anecdote pointed to the coherence of the antiauthoritarian approach at Paideia. Indeed, as one would expect from an anarchist school, there have been student uprisings. The most serious one was five years ago when the children excluded all the adults from school and ran it themselves. It began, as it should, during an *asamblea*. Most of the time everyone moves about the school freely, weaving in and out of classrooms at will. There is hardly a closed door in sight. But there is a strict rule stating that no one is allowed to walk out of an *asamblea* without asking the facilitator first.

"One day," Jara enthusiastically recounts, "we were all screaming and shouting at each other during the *asamblea*. Pepa got really annoyed, and walked out in a huff. The rest of the adults followed. So the children decided that as they hadn't asked the facilitator, they should all be excluded. The adults agreed and went away. They spent their days reading and playing cards, only looking after the little ones. All the older children had to take on the adult roles, correcting each others' work and so on, but this meant they did not have time to do any of their own stuff. After a week we realized it wasn't working." The children called the adults into an *asamblea*, apologized and asked them to come back: running the school without the adults was proving too much work! "Whenever I tell the story of our 'occupation' to my friends from 'outside,' they don't believe me," says Jara.

### Constant Evolution and Experimentation

Schools most often seem suffused with a rigid sense of stillness, places where not much changed, where each term looked very much like the next, where bodies were tense and timetables static. Very occasionally a cathartic outburst would disturb the icy routine, but the authorities would soon repress it. The atmosphere at Paideia could not be more different. There is constant movement, not just the physical motion of the children's bodies through the building, but the whole structure of the school is organically evolving and adapting. Timetables, subject matters, working groups; everything is always being carefully considered, revised, adjusted, and tailored to the specific students and situation. The only things that remain constant are the anarchist values, the moral foundations, everything else is up for amendment via the *asambleas*. Some might see this constant fluctuation as destabilizing and counterproductive to learning. But for anarchist educators, encouraging interactive experimentations is one of the linchpins of their pedagogy. Learning is a continuous feedback process fuelled by free will. The role of anarchist education is to reclaim free will, not simply for the sake of practicing freedom but because free will is seen as the catalyst of qualitative learning, and learning to learn is a big step toward autonomy.

Yet it has not always been a smooth ride and Paideia has had a stormy history: it was founded in 1978 after a similar experiment in *Fregenal de la Sierra* (started by the same group of three women) was shut down by the right-wing authorities. It has always been run as a cooperative, made up of parents and supporters of the project and the adult collective of educators. Over the years there have been internal splits and parental coups, including attempts to abandon the principle of self-management. The main tension has been with parents who don't understand the difference between a progressive school and a truly free school. For the founders, Paideia is not simply an alternative to mainstream schooling, in fact it is a radical critique of everything a school normally stands for. Some parents wanted to turn Paideia into what Martín Luengo describes as "a school for the bourgeoisie." "They wanted the pedagogy but not the ideology," she told us indignantly.

The school has survived the crises by constantly changing, evolving and responding to the problems over the years. Very little seems immutable here and anarchism's emphasis on permanent experimentation is the key to its longevity. There is however a constant lack of money, illustrated by the slightly shabby feel of the buildings and decor. A monthly fee of 545 euros per student pays for the upkeep of the school, the rent, school bus, all meals and materials; what is left goes to the collective. If parents cannot afford the fee, arrangements are made to pay in installments and there is a solidarity fund for parents who can afford to pay more to help families who find the fees difficult.

The lack of money however means that salaries are very low, which forces Gloria, one of the teachers, to also teach in the local state school. This gives her an invaluable perspective on Paideia's pedagogical approach. When we ask her if she thinks that the anarchist school is an island, her answer is a resolute "no." "It's the opposite of an island," she tells us, "because people leave here with skills for critical analysis, they can engage and challenge the world. In the state system there is no critique of anything. The whole thing is based on domination and authority, between staff and pupils but also between older and younger pupils, heads and teachers. There are so many levels of authority and no love. That's the island: kids who are little individualistic islands."

The notion of love is primordial to Gloria. "In the state school the children are not loved by the teachers, in fact the students become an enemy and the whole idea is to domesticate them." She also thinks that the whole experience of early schooling is deeply confusing for children. "At five or six years old, when the children move to primary school, they go from a situation where learning is about talking to each other and playing, to one where suddenly everything changes: they have to sit and be silent. The only way this can be achieved is by bringing in fear, punishment and authority."

She tries to apply some of Paideia's pedagogy to the state system, but it is complex: "The children get confused: suddenly they are allowed to talk, to have *asambleas*, to criticize. I use *asambleas* in my classes, but the other teachers are completely against it, they feel personally threatened. The parents at first thought it was a waste of time, especially when the children felt it was more important to resolve conflicts than to do maths or languages, but now they have come to understand that it was worthwhile."

## Life after Paideia

The afternoon sun beats down, we retreat to the shade on the edge of the playground. We are chatting to ex-students Laura and Johanna. Eighteen years old, both dressed in tight white jeans and belly tops, they give off an air of relaxed self-confidence. "I come back here after college, sometimes every day," Laura tells us, her big chocolate eyes framed by a mass of dark tangled hair. Both her and Johanna are at the local *instituto* (high school) preparing for their final exams, yet they are still deeply committed to the longevity of Paideia. "It is not like a school here, more like a family," Laura explains. "People have their responsibilities and commitments to each other; everyone helps one another."

"The hardest thing here," Johanna chips in, "is the work one does on oneself, pushing oneself. In the end it's worth it for the satisfaction of getting somewhere. But the other hard thing," she says with a hint of sadness in her voice, "is leaving this place."

We are intrigued at how it must feel to go from the freedom of Paideia to the rigidity of the state institute. One of the questions often leveled at alternative education is whether it can prepare students adequately for the "real" world. "The first thing I noticed was that we had to sit in rows instead of circles," Laura gestures in disbelief. "I was shocked that I had to have my back towards my friends . . . Also the relationships between teachers and pupils, and between pupils themselves is so different, in many ways it feels ultra-masculine. There seemed to be men shouting and telling others to do things all the time. And they use the grammatical masculine everywhere, instead of @!"[1] Despite these elements of disruption, both teenagers insist that schooling at Paideia have given them a strong grounding, in that they have been taught *how* to learn and so has given them a huge advantage over the other college students who don't seem to have the ability or the motivation unless they obliged and directed.

We are impressed by the maturity of Laura and Johanna, but cannot help wondering why did so few of the ex-students become "activists"; in fact we haven't heard of any and this seems almost counterintuitive to us. Is the school really embedded in social movements or is it just creating free children, who would end up working in capitalist society as atomized individuals? Do these young adults schooled in anarchism really want radical change? Or, as political philosopher and social ecologist Murray Bookchin wrote in his abrasive critique of contemporary anarchism, did they "eschew any serious commitment to an organized, programmatically coherent social confrontation with the existing order" (1995, p. 58). They certainly are not what he calls "Lifestyle Anarchists," wallowing in subcultures, celebrating "latter day anarcho-individualism . . . with polymorphous concepts of resistance . . . disconnected with the public sphere" (1995, p. 10).

Maybe what the school has taught them is a trick: to mask their anarchism, to work embedded in their communities and become anarchists "disguised" as hairdressers and postmen, psychologists and teachers, lawyers and nurses. In doing so, they refuse the division of labor that occurs when activists take on the role of social change expert. As Andrew X pointed out in his seminal essay "Give Up Activism": "To think of yourself as being an activist means to think of yourself as being somehow privileged or more advanced than others in your appreciation of the need for social change, in the knowledge of how to achieve it and as leading or being in the forefront of the practical struggle to create this change" (2001). Activism, he explains, not only reproduces capitalism's divisions of labor but it encourages hierarchies, fetishizes action, self-sacrifice, and isolates the "activist" from "normal people." More often than not, he writes, "activism" gets in the way of real change. In the end it is not what we call ourselves that matters but the way we behave. This approach was confirmed by Martín Luengo herself: "We don't want to produce conveyor belt anarchists, each student has to choose their own way," she explained. For her, the ideal student is one that, "practices anarchy and anarchist values where ever they go." "In Spain," she continued, "many of the youth who gravitate towards Anarchism don't really understand its core ideas—they are attracted to violence and rebellion without embodying the real values. In fact they embody the very things that the state identifies with anarchism: disorder and dirtiness. If you can't change the way you think then you don't change anything. In Mérida, students transmit their values to others, there is more free thinking locally, more libertarian unions, and a strong alternative culture. And . . ." she pauses, to allow a mischievous grin to spread across her face, "no student ever got married."

## Conclusions

At Paideia, the theory is that freedom and autonomy cannot be taught, only experienced. Its pedagogy is based on the conviction that when freedom is merely given, it tends to create a distorted individualistic concept of freedom, common within capitalist culture. For the pedagogues of Paideia, freedom is an active process, it is the art of developing personalities who have an uninhibited sense of volition embedded within acute consciousness of self and connection to the other. Only a transformed selfhood can display the attentive self-consciousness needed to engage in self-management and prepare us for living in a community of other self-realizing beings (Clark, 1984). The students learn to be free by working together to create the collective *conditions* for freedom; from which emerges not unlimited freedom but what political philosopher Alan Ritter (1980) calls "communal individuality." Through a rigorous and highly theorized and reflexive pedagogical practice (Martín Luengo, 1978, 1990, 1993, 2006), the school enables a kind of direct feedback mechanism to occur, where individual freedom and collective responsibility go hand in hand and encourage each other toward ever-greater autonomy.

## Note

This is an edited version of a chapter in Fremeaux, I. & Jordan, J. (2011) *Les Sentiers de l'Utopie*. Paris: Zones (a book/film available in French on www.editions-zones.fr from February 2011).

1 In Spanish, like in most Indo-European languages, the masculine is usually employed by default to refer to persons of unknown gender and, in the plural, to refer to a mixed group of people. Those willing to distance themselves from this sexist practice replace the letter signifying the masculine by the gender-neutral inverted symbol @.

## References


Andrew X. (2001). Give up activism. In *Do or Die: Voices from the Ecological Resistance*, 9. Also available at http://www.eco-action.org/dod/no9/activism.htm

Avrich, P. (2006). *The modern school movement: Anarchism and education in the United States*, Oakland: AK Press.

Bakunin, M. (1869). Les endormeurs. In *L'Égalité*, 26, June & 3, 10, 17, 24 July.

Bookchin, M. (1995) Social anarchism or lifestyle anarchism: An unbridgeable chasm. In *Social Anarchism or Lifestyle Anarchism: An Unbridgeable Chasm.* Oakland: A.K. Press.

Bourdieu, P. & Passeron, J.C. (1977). *La reproduction*. Paris: Ed. De Minuit. Brémand, N (1992) *Cempuis: Une expérience d'éducation libertaire à l'époque de Jules Ferry*, 1880–1894, Paris: ed. du ML.

Clark, J. (1984). *The anarchist moment: Reflections on culture, nature, and power*, Montreal: Black Rose Books.

Demeulenaere-Douyère, C. (2003). Un précurseur de la mixité: Paul Robin et la coéducation des sexes. *Clio* 18. Retrieved from http://clio.revues.org/index615.html.

Giroux, H. (1988). *Schooling and the struggle for public life: Critical pedagogy in the modern age*. Minneapolis: University of Minnesota Press.

Giroux, H. (2000). *Stealing innocence: Youth, corporate power, and the politics of culture.* New York: Palgrave.

Godwin, W. (1783). *An account of the seminary that will be opened on Monday the fourth day of August, at Epsom in Surrey, for the instruction of twelve pupils*. London: T. Cadell.

Jensen, D. (2004). *A language older than words*. Vermont: Chelsea Green.

Martín Luengo, J. (1978). *Fregenal de la Sierra: Una experiencia de escuela en libertad.* Madrid: Campo Abierto.

Martín Luengo, J. (1990). *Desde nuestra escuela Paideia*. Móstoles: Madre Tierra.

Martín Luengo, J. (1993). *La escuela de la anarquía*. Móstoles, Madre Tierra.

Martín Luengo, J. (2006). *Paideia: 25 años de educación libertaria. Manual teórico-práctico.* Madrid: Ediciones Villakañeras-Colectivo Paideia.

Martín Luengo, J. (1981). *Intento de educación antiautoritaria y psicomotriz en preescolar.* Mérida: S.I.

Miller, R. (2002). *Free schools, free people: Education and democracy after the 1960s*. New York: SUNY Press.

Neill, A. (1960). *Summerhill: A radical approach to child rearing*. New York: Hart Publishing Company.

Pollin, B.R. (1962). *Education and enlightenment in the works of William Godwin*. New York: Las Americas.

Postman, N. & Weingartner, C (1969) *Teaching as a subversive activity.* New York: Dell.

Proudhon, P.J. (2004 [1851]). *General idea of the revolution in the nineteenth century.* Courier Dover Publications.

Ritter, A. (1980) *Anarchism: A theoretical analysis*. Cambridge: Cambridge University Press.
Rogers, C. (1983a). As a teacher, can I be myself? In *Freedom to learn for the '80s*. Ohio: Charles E. Merrill Publishing Company.
Rogers, C. (1983b). The politics of education. In *Freedom to Learn for the '80s*. Ohio: Charles E. Merrill Publishing Company.
Smith, M. (1983). *The libertarians and education*. London: George Allen and Goodwin.
Spring, J. (1998). *A primer on libertarian education*. Montreal: Black Rose Books.
Suissa, J. (2010). *Anarchism and education: A philosophical perspective*. Oakland: PM Press, 2010.
Whitty, G. & Young, M. (Eds.). (1976). *Explorations in the politics of school knowledge*. Driffield: Nafferton Books.

**CHAPTER 7**

# Spaces of Learning: The Anarchist Free Skool

**Jeffery Shantz**

Social theorist Michel Foucault used the occasion of his 1967 lecture, "Of Other Spaces," to introduce a term that would remain generally overlooked within his expansive body of work, the notion of the "heterotopia," by which he meant a countersite or alternative space, something of an actually existing utopia. In contrast to the nowhere lands of utopias, heterotopias are located in the here-and-now of present-day reality, though they challenge and subvert that reality. The heterotopias are spaces of difference. Among the examples Foucault noted were sacred and forbidden spaces which are sites of personal transition.

Decades later, Foucault's notion of heterotopias would be echoed by the anarchist writer Peter Lamborn Wilson. Published in 1985 under the pen name Hakim Bey, the book *T.A.Z.: The Temporary Autonomous Zone, Ontological Anarchy, Poetic Terrorism* would become an almost instant contemporary anarchist classic. In *T.A.Z.* Wilson/Bey outlines, in often exhilarating flourishes, a lively version of anarchist heterotopias. These anarchist heterotopias, now called TAZ, are the anarchist society in miniature. In them structures of authority are suspended, replaced by relations of conviviality, gift-sharing, and celebration. They are living embodiments of what the anarchist Peter Kropotkin termed "mutual aid." And they exist, not in a postrevolutionary future of in the distance, but right here, right now.

While Bey's work put forward some unique visions, and did so in often-provocative language engendering a fair bit of controversy within anarchist circles, what he calls TAZ, or something very close to them, have always been part of anarchist culture and politics, as well as the culture and politics of the working classes and oppressed more generally. These have been, in other contexts, infrastructures of resistance (Shantz, 2009). To mention only a few examples, one might make note of the culturally vital and politically raucous Wobbly union halls of the 1910s and 1920s, the revolutionary community centers of Barcelona during the Spanish Revolution in the 1930s and the variety of squatted cultural centers of Europe from the 1960s to the present. Indeed Wilson/Bey's inspiration is drawn explicitly from the diversity of heterotopias and intentional communities of history, including pirate utopias, the Munich Soviet of 1919, Paris 1968, autonomist uprisings in Italy during the 1970s, and the radical ecology camps of the 1980s and 1990s.

Over the last two decades, whether aware of this history or not, many young anarchists, punks and artists took Bey's message to heart, building a host of community centers, infoshops, and free spaces in cities across North America, including Toronto. These spaces were intended as something a bit more permanent than the temporary autonomous zone. Envisioned as permanent autonomous zones, or at least potentially durable ones, these anarchist spaces have provided support structures for oppositional cultures, infrastructures of resistance. They have formed crucial aspects of the broader do-it-yourself (DIY) movements which provide alternative cultural and economic infrastructures in music, publishing, video, radio, food, and, significantly, education. Anarchist heterotopias provide important sites for skills development, for learning and practicing those skills which are undeveloped in authoritarian social relations.

Their existence allows for some autonomy from the markets of capital, some freedom from the restrictions of mainstream education. Their *ethos* runs counter to capitalist consumerism: play rather than work, gifts rather than commodities, needs rather than profits. For participants, they provide the imaginal, if not the material, means for undermining state and capital relations and authorities both ideological and structural. Practice often settles for something much less than that.

Contemporary anarchist heterotopias are not to be confused with the intentional or "drop-out" communities that have emerged at various points in North America, most recently the countercultural communes in the 1960s and 1970s. Contemporary anarchists are less interested in dropping out, preferring to build alternatives in alliance with people involved in more mainstream projects rooted in the day-to-day experiences of poor and working-class people. Anarchist heterotopias today are most likely to be located in urban neighborhoods and open and accessible to community involvement, rather than the arcadian spaces of isolated rural communes.

The following provides a glimpse into one such heterotopia, the Anarchist Free Space and Free Skool (AFS). Hopefully the images reveal both the promise and problems that people face while trying to create room for education outside of the confining structures of the permitted. These are experiences of collaborative learning over several years bridging classrooms and communities, particularly marginalized communities, to highlight opportunities for critically engaged teaching and learning. Through participatory approaches bringing students and street involved people together in contexts in which people are simultaneously teachers and learners these efforts contributed to a teaching/learning praxis informed by critical pedagogy and antiauthoritarian social perspectives contributing to empowerment for learners and communities. Along the way participants tried to effect positive changes in themselves, the skool, and the community.

## Anarchy and Education

For anarchists, learning should help people to free themselves and encourage them to change the world in which they live. As Joel Spring (1998, p. 145) suggests: "[E]ducation can mean gaining knowledge and ability by which one can transform the world and maximize individual autonomy." Anarchist pedagogy aims toward developing and encouraging new forms of socialization, social interaction, and the sharing of ideas in ways that might initiate and sustain nonauthoritarian practices and ways of relating. At the same time it is hoped that such pedagogical practices might contribute to revolutionary changes in people's perspectives on society, encouraging broader social changes.

Anarchists seek freedom from internalized authority and ideological domination. "In the modern state, laws were internalized within the individual, so that 'freedom' merely meant the freedom to obey the laws that one had been taught to believe" (Spring, 1998, p. 40). Internalization of the laws through socialization in school has been viewed as a means to end disobedience and rebellion. Freedom is freedom from *direct* control of the state but only if one acts according to the laws of the state (Spring, 1998).

The protoanarchist Max Stirner referred to the thought that one could not get rid of, the thought that owned the individual, as "wheels in the head." Such thought controlled the will and used the individual, rather than being used by the individual (Stirner). What Stirner called "the ownership of the self" meant the elimination of wheels in the head. Stirner distinguished between the educated and the free. For the educated person, knowledge shaped character. It was a wheel in the head that allowed the individual to be possessed by the authority of the church or the state. For the free one, on the other hand, knowledge facilitated choice, awakened freedom. With the idea of freedom awakened within them: "the freemen will incessantly go on to free themselves; if on the contrary, one only educates them, then they will at all times accommodate themselves to circumstances in the most highly educated and elegant manner and degenerate into subservient, cringing souls" (Stirner, 1967, p. 23). For the free, knowledge is a source of greater choice rather than a *determiner* of choice (Spring, 1998, p. 39). Ideas, as wheels in the head, subject people to the ideas themselves. Domination does not refer only to the internalization of ideologies that refer to sacrifice for supposed needs of society, external to the individual. It also refers to moral imperatives that capture a person's creative capacities.

> There were two levels of wheels in the head. The first levelled people through everyday life. One went to church and paid taxes because that was what one was taught; that was the way one lived. On the second level were *ideals*—ideals that move people to sacrifice themselves for the good of the fatherland, that made them try to be Christ-like, ideals that led them to give up what they were for some unrealizable goal. It was this realm of ideals upon which the strength of the Church and State was built. Patriotism and religious fervor were the results of people being possessed by ideals. (Spring, 1998, pp. 40–41)

Stirner objected to notions of "political liberty" because it only spoke of the freedom of institutions and of ideology. Political liberty "means that the polis, the State, is free; freedom of religion that religion is free, as freedom of conscience signifies that conscience is free; not therefore that I am free from the State, from religion, from conscience, or that I am rid of them" (Stirner, 1963, pp. 106–7). This perspective proved profoundly influential for a range of Free Skool participants, as it has for anarchist educators for decades.

The free school movement finds its inspiration in the anarchist Modern School movement begun by Francisco Ferrer in Spain. The free school movement emerged in the 1950s and spread through the 1960s as an effort to develop alternative forms of education and self-development in a context that was considered increasingly alienating, rationalized, and industrial. Anarchists were actively involved in the free school movement and their involvement is seen as crucial to the antiauthoritarian character and direction of the movement. Free schools were viewed as "an oasis from authoritarian control and as a means of passing on the knowledge to be free" (Spring, 1998, p. 55). Indeed, one of the principle proponents of the free school movement was the best-known anarchist in the United States, Paul Goodman, whose works were widely read and discussed during the 1960s and 1970s. Notably, contemporary anarchist activists have rediscovered Goodman's works through recent emerging movements. Free schools were, for Goodman, part of a broader decentralization and de-bureaucratization of social institutions. Goodman argued that schooling had become a process of grading and certification that largely benefited industrial elites who gained trained, and largely obedient, personnel. Education had become more and more geared toward perceived labor market demands. For Goodman (1966, p. 57): "This means, in effect that a few great corporations are getting the benefit of an enormous weeding out and selective process—all children are fed into the mill and everybody pays for it." In response Goodman argued for the development of small-scale schools or minischools in urban centers. Through participatory involvement and decentralization, these minischools could allow for direction according to the needs and desires of students and the communities and neighborhoods in which the schools were situated. Goodman also suggested that "in some cases schools could dispense with their classes and use streets, stores, museums, movies and factories as places of learning" (Spring, 1998, p. 56). Indeed Anarchist Free Skool participants pursued such an approach regularly holding classes on the sidewalks in Kensington Market. On other occasions classes were held in laundromats, nearby parks, and at picket lines where workers were on strike.

### The Anarchist Free Skool

The Anarchist Free Space and Free Skool (AFS) was begun in April 1999 by artists and activists who had organized a fairly lively freeskool at a soon-to-be-closed hangout, the Community Cafe. When the Cafe shut down some of the freeskool participants, looking to keep things going, set up shop in a roomy storefront location in Kensington Market, a multicultural, historically working-class neighborhood in downtown Toronto.

The Free Space was intended as a venue for committed anarchists, novices, and nonanarchists alike to come together and share ideas about the prospects, difficulties, and strategies for creating new, antiauthoritarian social relations. The primary vehicle for this was an ambitious schedule of classes on diverse issues. The hopefulness of the new collective was expressed in a statement on the front page of its course calendar.

> Education is a political act. By deepening our knowledge of ourselves and the world around us, sharing skills and exchanging experiences in an egalitarian, non-hierarchical setting free of prejudice, we challenge disempowering habits and broaden our awareness of alternatives to the inequalities of a capitalist society. The Anarchist Free School is a counter-community dedicated to effecting social change through the application of anarchist principles in every sphere of life. This Space represents and opportunity for the community at large to come together and explore these alternatives. The Anarchist Free Space welcomes all applications for use of the Space.

Courses reflected the desire for openness—they weren't all about anarchists talking to anarchists about anarchy (though a few of them were just that). Some of the courses included "Love Songs of the 20s and 30s," "Street Art," "Understanding Violence Against Women" and "Alternative Economics." Not just the mind but the body was taken care of in a yoga class and in shiatsu workshops. For most of the year at least one class was running every weekday evening. Far and away the most successful and long-running were "Introduction to Anarchism" and "Class Struggle Anarchism, Syndicalism and Libertarian Socialism" (See Appendix).

For me, some of the most interesting courses weren't courses at all but more like events. Every Tuesday at 9:23 p.m. sharp the International Bureau of Recordist Investigation gathered for excursions in their particular type of mayhem. The Recordists promised and often delivered "A weekly meeting, open to those with an interest in Recordism, Surrealism, and other currents of the Fantastic and the Absurd in contemporary art and culture (and spirituality, and politics, etc., etc.), for the exploration of those topics via discussion, presentations, game-playing and other collective activities, and general nonsense and tom-foolery." One Recordist evening consisted entirely of a fellow cutting his way out of a cardboard box. Eyebrows were raised throughout the space when one of the Recordists' mummies turned up in the basement. The mummy proved popular, however, eventually garnering its own wardrobe and securing a privileged place in the front window.

Another interesting event-class was the ponderously titled and sadly short-lived "Drifting as Foundation for a Unitary Urbanism." Inspired by the Situationists' dérive (or creating spontaneous pathways through the city), "The Drift," as it became known, brought people together to wander through the nighttime city exploring the hidden, unseen, out-of-the-way places of an alter-Toronto.

In addition to classes the AFS tried to revive the anarchist salon tradition. As the course booklet noted: "Salons have a colourful history throughout the world and in particular within Anarchist Communities. Salons are intentional conversational forums where people engage in passionate discourse about what they think is important." At the AFS the third Friday of every month was reserved for lively discussions on various topics decided upon by participants. Often the salons included a potluck dinner and performance. By all accounts the salons were enjoyable and engaging affairs drawing upwards of forty people.

Other memorable happenings ranging from the wacky to the profound included the infamous Satanic Ritual Party which brought the cops and almost made one of our pagan members quit; the Go Guerrila performances and zine launch; a couple afternoon punk shows organized after Emma closed; and (on the profound side) the Books to Prisoners poetry readings by ex-lifer John Rives.

Some projects never did come together and others suffered a lack of attention. The lending library suffered regular neglect as no one seemed interested in taking care of it. Eventually it fell into complete disrepair. A proposed free table for used goods never really got started. Neither did the

Revolutionary Anarchist Bowling League (RABL). More positively Anti-Racist Action and the Toronto Video Activist Collective (TVAC) continue to make use of the space for meetings and video showings. Others such as Food Not Bombs and the Recordists pulled out before dissolving completely.

Free Skool participants openly acknowledged the example of the anarchist educator Francisco Ferrer who suggested that radical pedagogy should question and challenge the traditional or habitual practices that sustain existing social structures (Ferrer, 1913). Courses emphasized the capacities of people to act and shape society's direction, starting with local environs in which they lived, worked and learned. The anarchist Paul Goodman argued that, within free schools, "The use of certified teachers could be dispensed with and people like the druggist, the storekeeper, and the factory worker could be used as teachers" (Spring, 1998, p. 56). The participants at the Anarchist Free Skool pursued such an approach. In place of instructors who presented information in a unilateral fashion, with a dominant voice, classes involved AFS members who acted as facilitators, taking responsibility to photocopy and make readings available, and ensuring that the space was available and open and people welcomed. Given their initial familiarity with anarchist ideas and texts they helped to fill gaps in knowledge, particularly about specific practices, theories, or histories, where possible and necessary or to suggest texts for future reading. Often new students would ask specific questions about how anarchists had handled particular issues, such as justice or punishment, historically. Typically, responsibility for introducing a topic rotated through the class participants according to their personal interests or availability as they volunteered to take responsibility for specific readings or weekly topics. Following a brief introduction to the readings or cases, classes were opened up to a loosely structured discussion based on individual and collective readings of the topic.

Even more, within Free Skool classes and meetings, anarchists tried to develop active listening, respectful debate and productive disagreement, in a context that recognizes the harm done to many "students" by their previous negative experiences in mainstream schools. Punctuality, passivity, and obedience were in no way promoted at the AFS. Emphasis was on training for community action and the development of critical social consciousness. Some even identified the structures and pace of modern urban environments themselves as barriers to learning.

Organizers realized that there are many barriers people face to free and independent learning. They emphasized efforts to break dependency and inhibition within the learning process. The anarchist Emma Goldman criticized approaches to learning that emphasized the actions of rulers, elites, and governments. Such an approach, still too common today, conditions people to accept a society in which the majority of people are passive, expecting groups of leaders to direct events. Such approaches typically reinforce authoritarian institutions. Anarchist Free Skool participants saw the impacts of such teaching first-hand. In initial meetings of classes nonanarchist participants often expressed an acceptance of social stratification or presented a view that elites were entitled to the unequal social rewards they received. One of the common responses was that they had "more important jobs" or "greater responsibilities." The Anarchist Free Skool classes provided an important opportunity to discuss such questions in a constructive and respectful manner. Anarchists noted that often the most important jobs, such as garbage pickup, were least rewarded. Similarly, work with the most responsibility, such as mothering, was not rewarded monetarily at all. Caring work, such as early childhood education and nursing, was not rewarded in terms of status and was often underrewarded monetarily, relative to the work's importance.

For anarchists, learning should contribute to independence of thought and action and contribute to capacities for self-determination. In the view of Free Skool participants, it is always important to avoid ideological approaches to learning. Anarchist ideas should be subjected to lively criticism and revision like any other ideas. Debate should always be open and welcomed within anarchist spaces. Dogmatic insistence on the rightness of particular theories or ideas must be avoided and tendencies to dogma actively undermined.

Anarchists at the Free Skool did not view the space as a place to indoctrinate or spread a particular ideology. Such an approach would be bound to fail anyway, and furthermore it would contravene participants' principles of anarchism and antiauthoritarianism. Education should support people in freeing themselves from social dogma and encourage their efforts to change social structures and social relations positively. Rather different varieties of anarchism and other steams of radical thought were presented for debate, discussion and appraisal. Hidden histories of resistance and alternative social organizations were explored.

Classes enjoyed participation from around five to thirty people. Gender was mixed with the proportion of men, women, and transgender participants varying by class. Similarly classes were facilitated by men and women in roughly equal proportion. The AFS was quite successful in overcoming the generational divisions that afflict many activist groups, particularly some of the direct action groups of the alternative globalization movement. The Free Skool provided a space in which children as young as a few months old played while folks in their eighties debated and shared jokes. Participants in classes ranged widely in age, with classes generally enjoying involvement from a range including late teenagers to sixty- and seventy-year olds.

In addition to classes, the Free Skool also served as an information center in which books and other media were available on loan to community members. More than simply offering courses on alternative and independent media, the Free Skool made cameras and movie-editing equipment available for community movie making. Experimental filmmaker Kika Thorne brought equipment for editing Super 8 film and showed anyone who was interested how to use it.

This was all part of the broader emphasis on skill-sharing. People registered their various skills with the Free Skool so those seeking to learn specific skills could easily contact someone willing to share information and experiences. Larger workshops were regularly held on specific topics, skills, and activities including zine-making, guitar, art, knitting, cooking, and gardening. Sessions were also provided on self-defense. Reflecting holistic approaches to health, classes, and workshops were provided on nutrition, first aid, and basic health care.

## "Class" Organizing

Libertarian or anarchist approaches to education emphasize participatory involvement, consensual practices and relations and the limiting of stratifications based on expertise or experience (Spring, 1998). At the Free Skool the educational emphasis was on learning for social justice, learning as social justice. This was not an academic or even purely intellectual pursuit but rather a holistic approach to education in and as practice. For participants learning was geared toward positive social as well as personal transformation. Learners who were also teachers had a commitment to use their opportunities and resources, collective practice, knowledge, to contribute to the betterment of particularly poor communities. The Free Skool encouragement of social justice was not limited to the radical content of courses but as expressed as much in the structure and practice of courses and the space more broadly. In particular this included consensus-based decision-making processes and participatory practices in which learners guided the direction of courses and the space itself.

Anarchists emphasize the school as a site of political, cultural, social, and economic power. Schooling instills a respect for authority and builds a habitual deference and adherence to the laws of the land. In the words of one of the directors of the anarchist Modern School movement in New Jersey in the 1920s, "From the moment the child enters the public school he is trained to submit to authority, to do the will of others as a matter of course, until the result that habits of mind are formed which in adult life are all to the advantage of the ruling class" (Kelly, 1925, p. 115). Criticisms of the government-based public school system include its nationalistic emphasis (with anthems to start school days and flags on buildings and images of presidents or monarchs in every room. Also of concern is training for the demands of the labor market and industrial system rather than for critical analysis or engaged "citizenship." It is part of organizing more broadly against patriotism and moral regulation within society as well as school systems.

Anarchists, like other radical education theorists, raise concerns about ways in which traditional schooling trains people to accept work that is monotonous, boring, or without personal satisfaction (Spring, 1998, p. 14). There is great, and growing, pressure from policymakers, government officials, bureaucrats, and corporate leaders to direct all education toward the fulfillment of perceived or anticipated demands of the labor market. Education is viewed primarily, or even solely, as career preparation. Learning s placed in the service of a future social role and preparation for that role. As Spring (1998, p. 146) notes: "Knowledge is not presented as a means of understanding and critically analysing social and economic forces but as a means of subservience to the social structure."

Not simply an abstract or philosophical concern, Free Skool participants were critical of the neoliberal education policies of their own province, which shifted the emphasis of education toward training geared to the labor market almost exclusively. The Ontario government at the time the Free Skool opened had recently legislated the requirement that university programs justify funding on the basis of the employment success of graduates. It forced programs to justify their existence on the basis of vague references to employability. This employability proof shifted emphasis in programs away from critical analysis toward supposedly practical considerations. Sociology programs, for example, shifted from critical theory or social movement studies toward supposedly more marketable areas such as criminology and family studies.

Another concern of anarchists is the contribution of educational discourses to the myth of social mobility within stratified capitalist social relations. Within these popular discourses, educational credentials are uncritically accepted as a basis, even *the* basis, for social rewards, or more as a measure of social worth or standing (Wotherspoon, 2009; McLaren, 2005, 2006). Unfortunately, such credentials are largely distributed along existing lines of inequality and reflect ongoing divisions of class and status. Rather than increasing mobility, education, and the focus on credentials, prestige, and reward reinforces social class divisions (Spring, 1998; McLaren, 2005; 2006). As Spring (1998, p. 29) notes:

> The poor are led to believe that schools will provide them with the opportunity for social advancement, and that advancement within the process of schooling is the result of personal merit. The poor are willing to support schooling on the basis of this faith. But since the rich will always have more years of schooling that the poor, schooling becomes just a new way of measuring social distances. Because

> the poor themselves believe in the rightness of the school standard, the school becomes an even more powerful means of social division. The poor are taught to believe that they are poor because they did not make it through school. The poor are told that they were given the opportunity for advancement, and they believe it. Social position is translated through schooling into achievement and underachievement. Within the school the social and economic disadvantages of the poor are termed underachievement. Without school there would be no dropouts.

The anarchist approach aims at radically transforming society rather than reforming it. As Joel Spring (1998, pp. 9–10) suggests, while reformist approaches to education try to eliminate poverty by educating the children of the poor to function within existing social structures, radical education tries to change the social structures that support and perpetuate unequal social relations. Reformist approaches can certainly make improvements, and these improvements are not to be dismissed, but they do not make the thoroughgoing sociostructural changes needed to address poverty and inequality. In Spring's (1998, p. 10) words: "The first approach would emphasize changing behaviour to fit into the existing social structure while the second would try to identify those psychological characteristics of the social structure which keep poor people under control." For Free Skool participants, education should be part of processes of social transformation and human emancipation. Individual efforts to succeed within existing structures tend not to end inequality and injustice. Schools should not reinforce the social organization of society. They should challenge and change it.

> What must be sought in the future is a system of education which raises the level of individual consciousness to an understanding of the social and historical forces that have created the existing society and determined an individual's place in that society. This must occur through a combination of theory and practice in which both change as all people work for a liberated society. There should not be a blueprint for future change but, rather, a constant dialogue about means and ends. Education should be at the heart of such a revolutionary endeavor. (Spring, 1998, p. 146)

For anarchists, educational alternatives are situated as part of overall attempts, within collective movements, to change broader systems of power, including but not limited to those of education. Anarchists seek a de-institutionalization of the socialization process. For anarchists, schools teach people to trust the judgment of the educator while developing distrust for their own judgment (Spring, 1998; McLaren, 2005; 2006).

> Implied in the concept of a society without schools is the end of all other institutions which are breeding grounds for dogma and moral imperatives. In a sense the church and state are themselves schools, with ideas of how people should act and what they ought to be. A society without schools would be one without institutions of mysticism and authority. It would be a society of *self-regulation* where institutions would be a product of personal need and usefulness and not sources of power. (Spring, 1998, pp. 52–53)

For anarchists at the AFS, working toward a new society depends, in part, upon changes in ideas and attitudes. New social relations do not spring into being fully formed from nothing. They must be taught, learned, played with, experienced, revised, and relearned. At the same time, less acceptable or less desirable practices must be unlearned or discarded. This is not done immediately, the outcome of an act of will. Even more, people who are raised in authoritarian contexts, socialized within authoritarian assumptions, will understandably need to learn new ways of acting. They will need to adjust, through trial and error, to new ways of relating to one another. Yet there are relatively few accessible spaces available in which such practices can be engaged. The anarchist Max Stirner (1967, p. 23) was drawn to ask: "Where will a creative person be educated instead of a learning one, where does the teacher turn into a fellow worker, where does he recognize knowledge as turning into will, where does the free man count as a goal and not merely the educated?" The AFS anarchists tried to provide opportunities for people to experiment and struggle with creating new forms of relationship, interaction and understanding one another.

Most Free Skool members struggled under public schooling regimes, finding their education to be constraining, restrictive, and lacking in venues for the expression of creativity. Many of the people who participated in Free Skool classes were decades removed from formal schooling. For them, the Free Skool provided a welcome alternative to their generally unsatisfactory and unsatisfying educational experiences. Many were thankful for the presence of the Free Skool, suggesting that they had searched a lifetime for such engaging learning experiences.

For Free Skool anarchists, the question of content is not the only one. Anarchists also stress the importance of methods. As in other areas of activity, anarchists stress the importance of a correspondence between means and ends, form and content. For anarchists, antiauthoritarian relations and practices cannot come from authoritarian methods. In education there is a link between methods and approaches to learning and the organization of the classroom and the character of the development of relations among participants. Learning can be an end in and of itself and should be an enriching process that allows for the rewarding experience of nonauthoritarianism in practice.

Concerns over the types of methods pursued in the classroom involve the nature and extent of control and authority (Spring, 1998, p. 26). Radical education critics suggest that classroom techniques have been related to shaping a character that fits within and functions according to existing institutions of authority outside the school (in government or corporations). Modern mass consumer societies, according to critical theorist Ivan Illich, require a citizen character that relies upon, or is dependent upon, the advice of experts, which can be broadly integrated within decision-making processes (see Hardt and Negri, 2009). The society depends upon the consumption of packages expertly planned and circulated according to marketing strategies. For radical critics, schooling prepares the individual by assuming responsibility for "the whole child" (Spring, 1998, p. 26).

> By attempting to teach automobile driving, sex education, dressing, adjustment to personality problems and a host of related topics, the school also teaches that there is an expert and correct way of doing all of these things and that one should depend on the expertise of others. Students in the school ask for freedom and what they receive is the lesson that freedom is only conferred by authorities and must be used "expertly." This dependency creates a form of alienation which destroys people's ability to act. Activity no longer belongs to the individual but to the expert and the institution. (Spring, 1998, pp. 26–27)

Indeed Free Skool participants were explicitly working to overcome the dominance of experts in social life. This is not to say they reject the knowledge developed by some people in specific areas, such as computers, health care, nutrition, or woodworking, based on experience and training. Rather it is the dominance of broad spheres of social life by experts and the frame of mind that suggests an uncritical deference to authorities. It also speaks against the proprietary character of much expert knowledge, as privileged possession or competitive advantage, within capitalist societies. More specifically, the Free Skool anarchists sought to allow everyone opportunities to develop their own expertise and confidence. This was part of an overall emphasis on do-it-yourself (DIY) or do-it-ourselves (DIO) practices. People were encouraged to formulate answers and develop solutions to problems in a participatory and collective way, brainstorming, experimenting, practicing, and reworking with fellow participants.

Anarchist critics argue that poor people learn in school that they should submit to the leadership or authority of those with more schooling. Those with more schooling, in terms of years and grade levels, tend to be those from more privileged class backgrounds who complete postsecondary education and graduate school. Thus anarchists seek to subvert this relationship of education and leadership or authority, particularly on the basis of class.

> Here the concern is not with order and efficiency but with increasing individual autonomy. The goal of social change is increased individual participation and control of the social system. This model rests on the conviction that a great deal of the power of modern social institutions depends on the willingness of the people to accept the authority and legitimacy of these institutions. In this context the question becomes, not how to fit the individual into the social machine, but *why* people are willing to accept work without personal satisfaction and authority which limits freedom. (Spring, 1998, p. 131)

Anarchists attempt to overcome traditional teacher/student relationships which can inhibit students and reinforce authority structures of command ad obedience. For Stirner, education should assist individuals to be creative persons rather than learners. Learners lose their freedom if will in becoming increasingly dependent upon experts and institutions for instruction on how to act. Rather than learning how to act they might determine for themselves how to act.

Anarchists seek educational practices and relations that will contribute to the nurturance of nonauthoritarian people "who will not obediently accept the dictates of the political and social system and who will demand greater personal control and choice" (Spring, 1998, p. 14). This includes experience in the development of collaborative practices, knowledge sharing and mutual aid, rather than the competition, for grades or status, or emphasis on individual knowledge possession, intellectual property, and "originality" that marks much of mainstream, particularly postsecondary, education.

For anarchists, methods of discipline and reward in mainstream teaching undermine freedom and self-determination (Spring, 1998, p. 25). Too often teachers use extrinsic motivation, through grades, threats of punishment, or promises of promotion (Spring, 1998, p. 25). The focus can readily be displaced onto the extrinsic motive, such as grades. This is a common feature of the neoliberal classroom, as grades, a surrogate for wages, become a primary concern of students seeking a specific credential, which can be converted to a job on the labor market. This is similar to the process by which satisfaction in the intrinsic qualities of labor has been displaced toward satisfaction in the wage, even where the work itself is despised or debilitating.

Part of the modern state's power rests in its awareness of the significance of the "domination of the mind" (Spring, 1998, p. 40). For anarchists, freedom must extend beyond political liberty and equality before the law, to emphasize self-control over one's perspectives, beliefs, and practices. Most educational systems have been geared toward the internalization of values and beliefs or the development of a conscience that favors support of existing social structures and relations (Spring, 1998; McLaren, 2005; 2006). Nonauthoritarian practices of education seek to encourage this broader approach to freedom, through people's own efforts and experimentation, successes and failures. Anarchists do not claim to have perfect pedagogical practices or ready-made answers to difficult questions. They recognize that they themselves have much to learn about practices of freedom and radical transformation, socialized within authoritarian systems as they have been.

Anarchist Colin Ward suggests that one of the tragedies of social struggle is that people do not know immediately how to deal with freedom. We all need to learn through experience practices of consensus, direct action, mutual aid, solidarity, and restorative justice. Education is a key aspect in organizing any society, whatever its scale. The goal of libertarian approaches "is therefore an educational method which will encourage and support non-authoritarian individuals who are unwilling to bow to authority and who demand a social organization which provides them with maximum individual control and freedom" (Spring, 1998, p. 131). The DIO approach to education pursued by Free Skool anarchists was driven by a belief that "no social change is meaningful unless people participate in its formulation" (Spring, 1998, p. 132). This convergence of revolutionary organizing and radical education is a key aspect of working to develop infrastructures of resistance. Thus it is an area of some emphasis for anarchists. For anarchists the failure of previous revolutions and their development in conservative directions, relates to the lack of "radically new means of education and socialization by which all people could be brought into the revolutionary movement and become *acting members* of it rather than its objects" (Spring, 1998, p. 133). Anarchist Free Skool members were clear that a nonauthoritarian society could not be wished into existence and it would not happen without organizing, discussion, and engagement. The Free Skool was part of those broader processes. At the same time Free Skool organizers were conscious not to become a therapeutic space and not produce dependency on the Free Skool as an institution.

In social and political terms the AFS was at its liveliest, and indeed its most relevant, during its second spring and summer when a number of members managed to bring a community organizing perspective to the space. Tired of the seemingly endless drift into pedantic debates and mystical dreaming the community activists tried to develop the AFS as a useful community resource. Importantly, unlike others in the collective, the community organizers had a clear vision and strategies they wanted to pursue. Taking the view that the AFS could (and should) be a worthwhile organizing and education center they reached out to serious activists in the city. The Ontario Coalition Against Poverty (OCAP) was invited to hold their movie nights at the space every Saturday and held several successful large "screenings."

The anarchist zine *Sabcat* was produced out of the AFS and since its first appearance has met with tremendous enthusiasm locally and abroad. *Sabcat* has presented original artwork, reviews, and articles on such topics as "green syndicalism," "OCAP," and "alternative education."

Trying to overcome the educational divide that separates "citizens" and prisoners AFS members initiated a Books to Prisoners program which became quite successful. Poetry readings and hardcore punk shows brought in hundreds of book donations along with the help of some independent publishers and distributors. Before long the first shipments went out from the Free Skool to inmates in both women's and men's prisons.

## Whose Market? Against Poor Bashing

Almost everything I've ever read about such alternative spaces raises the business of gentrification in North American cities. This story is no exception. At the same time, the educational approach of the Free Skool maintained that members develop a commitment to social justice and community involvement in support of those lacking resources. Putting their education to work members of the Free Skool collectives took leading parts in the battle against gentrification in the Kensington Market neighborhood.

During a general meeting in May of 2000 a member alerted Free Skool participants to a petition which had begun circulation against plans by St. Stephen's Community House for a soup kitchen and hostel for homeless people to be opened on Augusta Avenue just north of the Free Space. The rather viciously worded petition openly attacked poor people saying they were unwelcome in the Market. This was viewed by Free Skool members as an act of what antipoverty organizer Jean Swanson (2001) calls poor bashing. At the same meeting the collective decided without delay to interview every storeowner or manager in the Market to see who was carrying the petition and who supported the attacks on homeless people and the poor. Enlisting support from the AFS, teams of two spent the next few days talking to people throughout the Market. Where petitions were found, and thankfully very few places had accepted them, it was made clear that such antipoor propaganda was unacceptable. A boycott of a trendy cafe previously frequented by activists was begun, and perhaps coincidentally it closed by the end of the summer.

At the end of June a leaflet was distributed in the Market which asked, "Do you want Kensington Market to become just one more rundown neighborhood with no hope for its future?" A second leaflet, circulated by the Kensington Market Working Group hysterically raged against the planned soup kitchen suggesting that feeding and sheltering homeless people was simply cover for the real "goal of destroying the family shopping atmosphere that is Kensington." Members of the AFS organized a campaign to attend the City's Committee of Adjustment hearing and brought letters of support for the soup kitchen. Eventually the plans were approved though the Kensington business association has promised to keep up the attacks.

Later in the summer another more directly aggressive battle developed over harassment by the City of Toronto of a few homeless men living in the Market. The situation came to a head when one of the men asked several of us at the Free Skool for help in keeping city workers from taking his stuff to the dump. When we approached the workers they refused to tell us which bylaw they were citing when removing the stuff but implied that they were under pressure from the business association. After some debate we worked out a deal where the city workers promised not to touch anything left in the area fronting the Free Space. The guys hung out at the space and sold their wonderful array of used goods in front of and alongside the Free Space. For a couple of months it was like a real street bazaar. Shoppers loved the piles of stuff and there was always serious bargaining going on. They sold more in those two months than the AFS ever did.

## Vision Trouble

The Anarchist Free Skool was open for participation by anyone who had a general agreement with nonauthoritarian and nonoppressive perspectives and practices. Anyone who agreed to these basic principles could take part in membership meetings and involve themselves in the decision-making process. The egalitarianism and participatory democracy of the relatively small collective should allow developing inequalities and grievances to be more readily identified and more immediately dealt with, as many anarchists historically have argued (Hartung, 1983, p. 96). At the Free Skool this was generally, if imperfectly, the case.

At times the Free Skool found it difficult to develop ongoing political projects. Even agreement on short-term actions was difficult to come by. The Free Skool vision, as reproduced above, was a rather vague commitment to "deepening our knowledge of ourselves and the world around us, sharing skills and exchanging experiences." While promising a dedication "to effecting social change through the application of anarchist principles in every sphere of life" there was little agreement on what these principles were and even less sense of what strategies might be necessary to "effect social change" or even to "challenge disempowering habits."

The collective took as its model of decision-making process the consensus approach outlined by the Public Interest Research Groups. Consensus, whereby decisions are based upon lengthy discussions and much compromise of positions, is an article of faith for many anarchist groups who believe it to be more participatory, more open, and more likely to lead to better and more satisfactory decisions. It was also viewed as an important part of participatory pedagogy.

Despite the commitment to consensus as a pedagogical tool, there were difficulties with the process. First, the Free Skool was sometimes fractious throughout its history, never quite sure if it was a countercultural "hangout," an artist colony, or an activist resource center; never certain whether its politics were "lifestylist," petty bourgeois market socialist or class war anarchist. Art, theory, practice education, or activism? The AFS suffered from a failure to bring these approaches together

Secondly, consensus, because of the long time involved in making decisions and because it always tends toward compromise answers, is in many ways unsuited to a lively activist group which must take quick decisions and may not be able to compromise on principles. Diverse groups with vastly divergent notions of what anarchism is about require a process which allows each vision to be expressed without either limiting or implicating the other members of the larger group. In practice this is very difficult to negotiate and to realize. Free Skool meetings often bogged down in hours of heated discussion over whether activist posters could be placed in the windows because some of the artists found the postings to be unsightly and aesthetically displeasing. Needless to say the activists thought it more important to publicize important events regardless of aesthetic considerations.

The persistent lack of analysis and vision along with a failure to assess the political context for action and develop useful strategies for meeting stated goals consistently undermined the collectives' capacities to do political work. Clearly good intentions were not enough.

## Conclusion

Projects such as the Anarchist Free Skool emerge to meet specific needs, transform as priorities and interests shift and eventually dissolve only to emerge elsewhere as the Anarchist Free Skool has morphed to become the Anarchist University. I prefer autonomist Marxist Harry Cleaver's suggestion that such spaces are acts of "self-valorization" which can mess with the circuits of capitalist re/production. Certainly they represent places in which people have the time to value themselves and their relationships with each other beyond the commodified time in which much of our lives are contained. Following Cleaver we might understand temporary autonomous zones (TAZ) both as aspects of a refusal of domination and as creative attempts to fill the time, space and resources thus liberated.

One must be careful not to underestimate the rather large amounts of real labor required to keep a TAZ running. While Bey often portrays TAZ as profoundly mystical moments, it is important to remember that they have a substantial materiality. TAZ are constructed of the mundane, the everyday. As a sign in the Free Space proclaims, "Anarchy doesn't mean dirty dishes." (Although a glance at the Free Space sink too often suggested otherwise.) In the end its how well the demands of the everyday are met that can determine the success or failure of autonomous zones.

Still there is always an aspect of the carnivalesque in spaces like the AFS. Whether it be the lively conversations, crass hardcore music, the quirky zines, humorous buttons, joyful camaraderie, or the clarion of agit-prop, the spaces signal their difference from their surroundings, their "otherness." As liminal sites they are places of transformation from present to future—glimpses of the "new world in the shell of the old."

Autonomous zones are hubs of do-it-yourself (DIY) culture and politics. In scenes where transience and the ephemeral often predominate free spaces offer some permanence, some rootedness. They provide a space where the underground can move above ground and engage in an everyday discussion with nonactivists, with people who want to find out what this anarchy stuff is all about.

The Free Skool participants were successful at taking anarchist ideas beyond the confines of anarchist subcultures and radical political "scenes." Unlike many other infoshops and free spaces the Free Skool did manage to bring people from the neighborhood into the spaces. Most just dropped by to chat but many took part in classes and a few even joined the collective. The Free Skool provided a venue, within a working-class neighborhood, for nonanarchists to inquire about anarchism, ask tough questions, and have discussions about anarchist theory and practice. It also provided a community center, a space in which community members could come together to discuss neighborhood issues and organize to address community needs, both through developing their own self-directed activities, but also by preparing collective approaches to local government authorities around aspects of city planning and policy. Without the Free Skool it is certain that the homeless shelter and soup kitchen would have been defeated and an important resource for poor people would not have been available in the neighborhood. It is also certain that homeless people would have faced greater harassment and criminalization.

That the Anarchist Free Skool was able to extend its reach beyond current students to bring in nonstudents, particularly individuals from poor and working-class backgrounds, and those who had long ago left school behind, stands as a testament to the promise of the participants' commitment to open and engaged learning. It also showed the significant work done by Free Skool members in doing outreach into the local neighborhoods and communities, actively working to build bridges and take anarchism outside of any preexisting subcultural comfort zones. A promising beginning though it still has not grown in the way needed to forge an organic connection with other communities.

This is by no means the final paragraph in this story. New ones are being written at this very moment. Already a number of people involved in the

AFS have worked to start up a new space, an activist resource center geared toward political projects and solidarity work. Rather than simply affirming a commitment to some nebulous notion of anarchy these folks are developing the basis for shared principles and shared work as part of the preparation for opening new projects.

Intended as something a bit more permanent than the temporary autonomous zone, these anarchist spaces provide the support structures for oppositional cultures. They are parts of the broader do-it-yourself (DIY) movements that provide alternative community and economic infrastructures in music, publishing, video, radio, food, and education. Anarchist heterotopias are places for skills development, for learning those skills that are undeveloped in authoritarian social relations.

The existence of TAZ allows for some autonomy from the markets of capital. Their *ethos* is counter to capitalist consumerism: play rather than work, gifts rather than commodities, needs rather than profits. In theory, they offer means for undermining state and capital relations and authorities both ideological and material. Practice often settles for something much less than that.

As always, the challenge is to maintain openness and inclusion while actually working to create "the new world in the shell of the old." Many at the Free Skool struggled to show that freedom is not some fanciful idea, something for philosophers and mystics to ponder. It only has meaning when it is lived.

## Appendix

Course descriptions for the most popular courses at the Anarchist Free Skool:

**CLASS STRUGGLE ANARCHISM, SYNDICALISM AND LIBERTARIAN SOCIALISM**

Anarchism, as a political movement, emerged as part of broader workers' struggles for socialism and communism and contributed greatly to those struggles. Contemporary anarchists in North America, however, have generally forgotten this important connection, as anarchism has become a largely subcultural phenomenon. Similarly distinctions between authoritarian and antiauthoritarian traditions within the diverse history of socialism have been obliterated by the horrors of state capitalist regimes calling themselves "socialist." This course seeks to reconnect anarchism with the struggles of working people to build a better world beyond capitalism of any type. The course is initiated by activists concerned with class analysis and day-to-day organizing and is not intended simply as a study group.

**INTRODUCTION TO ANARCHISM**

This course will be a broad introduction to anarchist theory and practice, as well as a look at the history of anarchism and anarchist struggles. There will be readings taken from some of the major anarchist thinkers such as: Bakunin, Kropotkin, Goldman and others. Also, the class will be structured in such a way that the participants may suggest the focus and direction of the readings and discussion topics.

## References


Bey, H. (1985). *T.A.Z.: The temporary autonomous zone, ontological anarchy, poetic terrorism*. New York: Autonomedia.

Bookchin, M. (1995). *Social anarchism or lifestyle anarchism: An unbridgeable chasm*. Edinburgh: AK Press.

Cleaver, H. (1992). The inversion of class perspective in Marxian theory: From valorisation to self-valorisation. In W. Bonefeld, R. Gunn & K. Psychopedis (Eds.), *Open Marxism: Volume II, theory and practice*. London: Pluto Press, 106–44.

Ferrer, F. (1913). *The origin and ideals of the modern school*. London: Watts and Company.

Foucault, M. (1986). Of other spaces. *Diacritics, 16*(1), 22–27

Hartung, B. (1983). Anarchism and the problem of order. *Mid-American Review of Sociology, 8*(1), 83–101.

Shantz, J. (2009). Re-building infrastructures of resistance. *Socialism and Democracy, 23*(2): 102–109.

Spring, J. (1998). *A primer of libertarian education*. Montreal: Black Rose.

Stirner, M. (1963). *The ego and his own: The case of the individual against authority*. New York: Libertarian Book Club.

Stirner, M. (1967). *The false principle of our education*. Colorado Springs: Ralph Myles.

Swanson, J. (2001). *Poor bashing: The politics of exclusion*. Toronto: Between the Lines.

**CHAPTER 8**

# The Nottingham Free School: Notes Toward a Systemization of Praxis

**Sara C. Motta**

Nottingham Free School was formed in the summer of 2009 as a space to develop nonhierarchical and noninstitutionalized processes and practices of radical education. The members of the original group shared a reaction against experiences of alienation, exclusion, and oppression from within formal institutions of education. To differing degrees we sought to develop an educational practice that was against and beyond formal education. Fundamentally this would be based on principles of openness, collaboration, egalitarianism, and relevance for activist and broader community needs and desires. We wished, as a collective working with and in community organizations and activist communities, to take control of the process and outcomes of learning in a creative and constructive way.

We shared a commitment to education as a means of resistance, creation, and fundamentally as a way of constructing the types of horizontal postrepresentational communities that create worlds beyond capitalism to which we aspired. We hoped to gain inspiration from past and current examples of education being used as part of a process of liberation and emancipation, and hope to do what we can to continue that legacy in Nottingham. In terms of theoretical-practical inspirations particularly influential have been Paulo Freire's *Pedagogy of the Oppressed* (1970), Ivan Illich's *Deschooling Society* (1971), and experiences with the ideas of Open Spaces of Dialogue and Enquiry (OSDE, http://www.osdemethodology.org.uk/). Empirically the group had different experiences with radical education from the coordination of skill-shares in Nottingham based on the idea of mutual aid and horizontal learning processes, coordinating activist networks, and consensus decision-making to working with popular education with autonomous social movements in Latin America.

We therefore spent our first few meetings discussing how we should begin to work and with whom. While we wanted to work with working-class communities in Nottingham it was agreed after much discussion that we couldn't inorganically create relationships with these communities if they weren't existent at present. We therefore focused on the communities that we did have relationships with and participated in autonomous activist groups and communities in and around Nottingham. Our entire process has been experimental, very much making the road by walking, influenced by our traditions, experiences, and commitments but not preplanned, predictable, or necessarily successful. The process has not merely involved the development of workshops, skill- shares, and discussion groups but has also begun to forge a collective of radical educators in Nottingham. This process of construction has demonstrated to us that radical education and its role in the construction of autonomous anticapitalist communities, subjectivities, and social relationships combines the intellectual, affective, political, personal, and cultural. Learning to know and trust each other, understanding the particular exclusions experienced and lived by fellow collective members, drinking together, looking after each other's kids, crying together, cooking together, and thinking together. All these are part and parcel of breaking down the divisions between the intellectual and the emotional, between imagination and theorizing, between mind and body, and between teachers and learners that characterize institutionalized and alienated educational practices.

To facilitate a process of reflection and beginnings of systematization of our practice to date I will focus on two workshops that we developed, a series of skill-shares and the process of the development of a collective of radical educators. I hope to reflect in relation to a number of elements: their ability to open up spaces of dialogue and reflection; their ability to contribute to the development and practice of autonomous anticapitalist communities; and their contribution to praxis of horizontalism and postrepresentational knowledge production. The forms of systematization developed are firstly an evaluation of the lived experience of the project in relation to predetermined frameworks of analysis based in Freirian, Illichian, and OSDE-inspired conceptualizations of radical education. This evaluation links the theoretical with the practical and contextual as a means of creating new theoretical practical insights. Secondly, this is combined with a dialectical systematization, which seeks to create new theoretical and practical knowledge as a means of contributing to transformations in reality and social and political change (for further conceptualization of types of systematization see Mejía, 2010).[1] This is not a final end product but rather a contribution to our ongoing process of learning. As we state, "We don't pretend to have all the answers, and are committed to a continuously evolving process in which those participating have ample opportunity to evaluate, challenge and contribute to the running of the project."

## Nottingham Free School Workshops

We developed a workshop called Radical Education. This workshop sought to explore the nature of radical and alternative education and its use for the construction of the communities and relationships we desire. We explored how and if it was desirable to move completely away from institutional education. We ran the workshop perhaps seven to eight times over a period of about a year in different activist and community settings. After each session we discussed what we thought had worked and what not and adapted the workshop accordingly. As a group we were also open to a facilitator changing the workshop and experimenting with different structures and methods. The first structure was envisaged as a four-hour-long session to which we invited individuals and groups that we thought might be interested in participating in the Nottingham Free School. The workshop was framed as part of the development of identity or identities of the Free School, which was trying to get a sense of its objectives and forge a community of radical educators. This workshop was organized as part of this process and its main objectives were: i) get to know each other's backgrounds, interest in radical education, and understanding of radical education; ii) problematize terms like "radical," "education," and "learning" in order to help make explicit our assumptions about education, learning, teaching, the nature of knowledge, what knowledge is for and how it is created, etc. in order to iii) make clearer resonances and dissonances/similarities and differences between us and build on these constructively and creatively.

It began with a reflection upon one's life history of education. In which we asked participants a number of questions: note down experiences of education (formal and informal) where they remember learning something; what it was they learnt, how they learnt it and what it had felt like. We gave participants a sheet of paper and asked them to answer these questions in any way they wanted: drawing, text, and image. We then asked participants to put their paper up on the wall and organized a break where people could get tea, coffee, etc. and also look at each other's education life stories noting anything that struck them as interesting, they wanted to learn more about or they were puzzled or intrigued by. We began from the experiences of participants in the workshops as we believed, following our experiences but also the ideas of Freire and Illich that transformatory education has to be relevant and meaningful. It needs to be embedded within the experiences, histories, and cultures of individuals and communities in this way turning on their head the assumptions of traditional education in which the teacher is the knower and the student an empty vessel to be filled with knowledge (Freire,

1970; Illich, 1971, pp. 30–35). As Freire argues this type of dialogical learning is designed to make people "feel like masters of their thinking rather than passive learners" (1970, p. 95). Fundamentally it needs to recognize the validity of the experiences and knowledges of participants and be premised in the rejection of the self-sufficiency and privilege of the educator (Freire, 1970, pp. 62–63). Therefore we thought that to make this discussion meaningful and relevant and to bring in the knowledges of participants, we needed to pull out those elements which had been enjoyable in learning that we could link to forms of radical education and help participants to systematize and name these experiences in relation to traditions and practices of radical education.

Therefore our next step was to begin to pull out generative themes from the educational timelines that participants had made (Freire, 1970, p. 69). This was done as a group in which each individual was asked about any issues or questions they had in relation to the education timelines they had looked at and their own. The facilitator tried to bring out key themes and issues from the discussion which she began to note on the wall. This was a means of beginning to make our own concepts and lines of investigation and exploration into radical and alternative education. From this basis we wished to move onto a next step. This we called "naming/making assumptions explicit." On the basis of the themes and issues identified we aimed to split participants into groups and assign them a particular reading[2] with questions but also leaving the group open to come up with their own questions. The next step was to return to the broader group and discuss the answers the groups came up with. If a group didn't come up with an answer to a question then we encouraged the group as a whole to work through an answer(s). The penultimate step, "working through what different conceptualizations of radical education might look like in practice," involved participants returning to their small groups and developing a miniworkshop based on the tenets of radical education fleshed out in section 2. Each group would then run a minisession for the entire group for about ten minutes. Finally the session would end with a short summary by the facilitators of their understanding and experiences of radical education and why they were interested in running this type of workshop and then a group evaluation of the workshop.

When we tried to run the workshop we reached stage two at which point we needed to end the workshop as some participants felt emotionally upset and uncomfortable. When bringing out generative themes tensions had arisen in relation to different understandings of the nature of authoritarianism in education and what a liberatory education should and should not include. These tensions had been intensified due to the personal nature of the reflections. The breakdown in the workshop threw up some important questions for us as a collective. We had planned the workshop as a space to bring out resonances and dissonances and to question what we mean by radical and alternative education. We had purposefully made individual experiences and histories central to this collective reflection and process of knowledge construction. However by bringing together a disparate group of people, some with knowledge of each other, others without, who vaguely shared an identification or interest in radical education we had created an open space but not necessarily a safe space (Andreotti, n.d.). We had brought to the fore the individual, the subjective, and the emotional in a situation in which people did not have the bonds of struggle, experience, or history between them to have created trust and a shared understanding of limits and norms of respectful dialogue. The inevitable conflict that would arise when breaking down consensus and assumptions and bringing out difference and variety was something we were not ready to deal with. We were unable to transform this conflict into productive grounds for dialogue and further engagement and instead were faced with the breakdown of the workshop. This raised important questions for us about the nature of openness. We had assumed a setting as found by Freirian popular educators working with exploited and excluded communities whose territorially close-knit communities often give a commonality of experiences and struggles in which bonds of trust, reciprocity, and norms of dialogue have been and are being formed (Freire, 1970, pp. 52, 66). However, this was not the setting we were in. So the questions we asked where whether the openness we were looking for in the spaces we were creating needed to be defined by more grounds of commonality: that is, should we actively only invite people who shared some close political and social principles; or whether if we continued to have very diverse groups with little knowledge of each other should we not focus so much on the individual and perhaps focus on different concepts of radical education as is done in OSDE settings. OSDE is a critical literacy approach which in many ways is a development of the Freirian model as it also draws on dialogical and perspectivist concerns. It connects in particular to the idea of critical literacy: the ability to make sense of radically different perspectives and to situate these perspectives within relations of power-knowledge. The purpose is not to change people's orientations on the issues under discussion, but to make them aware of the constructedness and perspective-relativity of their own knowledge, and hence to acquire critical literacy. Thus in OSDE workshops different assumptions about a topic are the building blocks of discussion and questioning taken-for-granted assumptions. These are then used as a means to think about one's individual assumptions. However these individual reflections are not necessarily a point of general discussion, providing a kind of protection to individuals and a level of safety and security to groups who are not groups or collectivities outside of the learning space (Andreotti, n.d.). It also brought to the fore how openness which lacks community and collectivity can be highly exclusionary to vulnerable participants whose experiences of trauma and exclusion can be triggered unintentionally by different norms and understandings of respect, dialogue, and education.

We didn't come up with any definitive answers to these questions. However, we did respond by organizing workshops about radical education with diverse groups and individuals in the university for example using a more OSDE methodology so scrapping step one and focusing instead on what participants associated with formal education and radical education and then moving on to step three in relation to traditions and experiences of radical education. We were also careful to bring in the personal to settings of distinct activist communities such as the Rossport Campaign, Radical Roots Gathering, and the Earth First Gathering where we assumed that a level of commonality and experiences of struggle together would create levels of trust, respect, and understanding to enable the possibility of a constructive transformation of conflict via facilitators and the group. We also immediately after the breakdown of the first workshop realized that a four-hour workshop was much too long and that therefore we needed a two-hour workshop at most, perhaps with an idea of developing a second sister workshop if desired. This meant that the radical education workshops tended to either focus on part one and two or a variation on these, or an adaption of the groups' ideas about radical and traditional education and then discussion about how and where we might develop elements of radical education identified.

An issue that we found with the workshop was that at gatherings and activist events, to which we were lucky in Nottingham to have a number scheduled through the spring of 2010 that we were often timetabled at the beginning or end of gatherings as the timetables were full with meetings/discussion more directly related to the campaign/project. Additionally we were often unable to attract significant numbers to the workshops. After informal reflection and discussions with participants at the gatherings and other activist and educator friends we began to think about how education and radical pedagogies form in relation to movements and communities historically and contemporarily in the global south for example. We used the experiences of one of the collective with autonomous social movements in Latin America as a basis of informal reflections. Often what is found is that communities begin to organize around a particular issue like land or water rights or education and it is during the process of trying to consolidate their struggle and deepen their communities of resistance that questions of pedagogy become more important. However, this often happens as a result of key members of the community having a history and experience with popular and radical education (see for example Motta, 2009). While members of the collective participated in many of the activist communities that had gatherings in Nottingham these gatherings were not merely local communities but large national and at time international meetings. Thus there was something external to the relationship between movement and workshop (Free School). In many ways discussion and practices about the use of radical education and pedagogy for the building of the objectives of activist groups and movements and for building autonomous anticapitalist communities hadn't taken place. This meant that for many there was perhaps little motivation or relevance in the workshop. This didn't imply that the workshop was a failure rather perhaps that it was a contribution to an opening toward these types of discussions, reflections, and practices. The process of constructing communities and the organicity of radical education as a part of this is a process that becomes embedded in concrete struggles and communities. Through these experiences we began to learn about the possibilities and limits of particular workshops; what they could and couldn't achieve. We also began to discuss the need to perhaps develop a NFS pamphlet which is interactive and dialogical as a means of deepening the discussion of radical education and its role in anticapitalist struggles with activist communities in and around Nottingham. This we hope will plant further seeds for the continued development of a collective of radical educators who are also activists in different movements thereby opening space to develop a praxis of radical education in Nottingham's anticapitalist movements, networks, and communities of resistance and creation.

Finally we held a relatively large workshop at the Earth First Summer Gathering of 2010. There were participants from activist movements, individuals interested in radical education, and participants from other radical education collectives. The workshop went well in terms of personal reflection and developing generative themes. The final part was how and where we imagined we could be able to develop the practices of radical education identified. It was here that the workshop broke down somewhat and returned to general discussion about the different forms of radical education. On reflection with participants and other members of the Free School, we again thought about the limits and possibilities of workshops in different contexts. This time the problematic was not so much questions of trust and some sense of collective cultural norms (however exclusionary and problematic these implicit norms themselves can be as one participant commented) but rather a common political project, experiences, or objectives. This meant that we went from the concrete experiential to the generic but were unable to move back the complex concrete in terms of developing particular strategies, theorizations, and methodologies for moving forward with a political project or objective, as is assumed in Freirian praxis. This left some participants feeling frustrated at the level of generality of the workshop. However again this was a process of realizing possibilities and coming to an understanding and an opening toward the different types of openings and possibilities from our practices. It was a realization of the process like nature of all that we are involved in and that we cannot always look for concrete outputs and outcomes (as in capitalist understandings of success and failure) but rather move with the movement of creating and exploring different ways to engage and create collectively, or creating our own concepts of politics and praxis. Thus as a group of radical educators we were also involved in a process of learning to name the world and develop our own concepts (Freire, 1970).

## Trauma and Privilege

The second workshop I would like to explore in these reflections was entitled Trauma and Privilege. This workshop developed out of a desire to explore the hierarchies, exclusions, and assumptions within activist communities. This desire was generated by participants' experiences of these often-silent exclusions and power over, whether that is in terms of gender, class, race and, other contexts such as childcare responsibilities or histories of trauma and abuse. We discussed how it was often assumed how power, exploitation, and alienation was out there and that we as activists in autonomous social movements, communities, and relationships were immune to these alienating and alienated practices that reproduce hierarchies. When developing the workshop we knew that this was going to be a highly emotional and potentially explosive space; a space that actively looked to create ruptures and create productive uncomfortableness. In this sense we built on Freirian pedagogies desire to challenge common sense and taken-for-granted ideas and practices about and in the world, to create limit situations that push us out of the taken-for-granted (Freire, 1970, p. 16). However in many ways we stepped away from OSDE with its focus on external reflection as a prompt to internal reflection and action. For this we agreed, on the basis of previous experiences, that it would be run with consolidated activist communities and perhaps among ourselves as a means of engaging with each other and our experiences and histories. In this way, processes that were emotional and personal could not be respectfully developed with groups of individuals who shared no common experience, history, struggle, or knowledge of each other. The workshop aimed to open up a discussion around the issues of trauma and privilege, and their interconnectivity. Asking questions such as, How does our own psychological experience affect the ways in which we are able to act in radical social change? and How do we negotiate the social, cultural, or economic capital we have (or lack) as we experience radical political action and the traumatic events it can often cause? How does our social change work relate to trauma we have experienced?

The basic outline of the workshop was for participants as a group to talk about the type of privileges and hierarchies they had experienced in activist circles. We wrote these up into categories. We then asked participants to think about a trauma they had experienced in their life, break down into small groups, and discuss the trauma with others in their group. We also all agreed (three of us facilitating the workshop) that we would participate in this and be willing to use our experience in a small group if others didn't feel they could. We then asked those in the group who had heard the trauma to think about if this trauma had happened to them how their situation might have differed from the person who experienced the trauma, not in a judgmental way but to think about how the types of privileges they had might change the experience. We aimed to encourage participants in their reflections to refer back to the hierarchies and exclusions noted in the first exercise. Our aim was to bring the emotionality of trauma and experience to the heart of collective thinking and feeling, to break down taken-for-granted barriers of norms and limits of dialogue. We aimed to challenge individuals to recognise and think about potential privileges that they have and how these might impact upon their behaviors and relationships in activist communities.

We experimented with this workshop at the Rossport Gathering. The first part went relatively smoothly and a number of exclusions along age, gender, knowledge, class, and race were noted and discussed. But when we went on to discuss trauma, participants began to question the relevance and necessity of this process. They were understandably uncomfortable at being asked to reveal highly traumatic experiences in their lives and didn't see the direct links with understanding privilege and hierarchy in activist communities. We therefore had to have time for this discussion in the workshop. We came to an agreement that this section was optional and that only those who wanted to participate would. However, the actual process of individuals talking about traumas and then others attempting to reflect on how their experience might have been different in relation to privileges was traumatic to say the least. There were three groups. In one group the conversation broke down and there was active resistance to the facilitator with the facilitator feeling unable to negotiate and transform the situation productively. In the second a facilitator and other participant shared their trauma. Those participating in the group engaged very powerfully and emotionally with the experiences of the individuals and engaged in a process of reflection in relation to potential privileges. In the final group there was a lot of discussion about the usefulness and relevance of a practice such as this, how it potentially opened up people who were vulnerable to more pain, and how there seemed to be no direct link with expressing and discussing trauma and thinking creatively and constructively about privilege and our role in reproducing unequal power relations and exclusions. Two people discussed their traumas in this group: a facilitator and a participant. The experience of discussing trauma was highly emotional and created an intense linkage and recognition among the two who shared their trauma and some reflections about privilege within individual histories and contexts and how this might affect dynamics within activist circles.

Our reflections about the workshop, its success and its productiveness were also relatively conflictual. One facilitator didn't want to be involved in the running of this workshop again because the experience had been traumatic. This brought to the fore the importance of taking each other seriously as not external facilitators but internal participants in the workshops; how the experience of facilitating was also an emotional, effective, and intellectual process that challenged ourselves and put us potentially into uncomfortable situations or situations we felt we lacked the experience to deal with. This was a learning experience that profoundly impacted upon our relationships as a collective in the sense that it was a point of recognition of ourselves as embedded individuals and not merely as people working abstractly on a workshop to be delivered the following week. It raised the question of how we develop practices of care and support. It also made clear our lack of experience in dealing with such emotional reactions. It brought to the fore (often implicitly) the necessity of having tightly organized, intensely thought out, and highly trained facilitators to work in situations and workshops related to trauma and other emotional issues affecting workshop participants (including the facilitator).

Others differed on the extent to which the rupture and uncomfortableness created was productive, whether it actually helped to systematize and make explicit the hierarchies and privileges in activist communities. There were questions about whether there was a useful link between trauma and privilege. Nevertheless it was agreed that it had been a powerful experience which had broken down taken-for-granted norms of dialogue and opened a space of knowing each other which pushed boundaries of collectivity and understanding. For one facilitator the chance to make visible and give voice to an experience of trauma was a release and a part of healing. It had a testimonial element as found in much collective healing processes associated with feminist and indigenous political practices (Restrepo, 1998; Robinson, 2010). Yet these practices are generally collective whereas this was individual. However she also felt that she was ready to do this and that the process of healing from trauma is a long one with many different stages many of which are not about articulating publically or to others your experience. The impact however demonstrated the powerful emotions and consequences of the workshop, even if they differed somewhat from the stated objectives of the workshop. They did bring in to the open people's traumas and the intensity of their lived experiences and emotions. While many participants' feedback was focused around feeling uncomfortable or not seeing the relevance of the workshop there was a minority who found the workshop extremely powerful and able to create an opening to a different level of understanding of self and other in their community.

On reflection there was a tension between the different objectives of the workshop. On one hand we hoped to facilitate a space which made visible and gave validity to people's traumas and their personal context in the tradition of feminist and indigenous political practices. On the other we wished to open up a space of reflection about informal and often invisible hierarchies and exclusions in activist communities. By attempting to facilitate two very different objectives we perhaps confused two different processes and ended up potentially opening up a situation which could have caused harm and reproduced (unwittingly and naïvely) emotional and psychological violence against participants and ourselves.

These two processes—a kind of collective therapy, an attempt at emotional bonding as a form of community building, and an attempt to challenge privilege in the activist movement—seem to require different methodologies and pedagogies. The first, as practiced by feminist groups, indigenous communities, and black groups have developed nuanced and complex forms of collective grieving and visibilization of trauma that are acutely political. They avoid the potential trap of our workshop that could easily lead to self-blame by its individual focus. The work of La Mascara feminist theatre of the oppressed group in Cali, Colombia, is an example of such collective healing and visibilization. It uses popular education methodologies combined with theatre techniques to make visible and contextualize the multilevel experiences of violence of displaced women and children. They contain a strong testimonial content. Yet individual reconstruction and understanding are embedded within transformative collective practices and contextualization realized through theatre work (Medina and Teatro La Mascara, 2010; Motta, 2010). These processes are often embedded in intensely spiritual practices and rituals. The second objective of challenging privileges could perhaps be productively explored by the use of a framework closer to OSDE, which seeks to explore different understandings of a particular topic—be that privilege and hierarchy and their nature—from a number of different perspectives as a means of opening up processes of revealing personal and collective assumptions. This aims to create dissonances and uncomfortableness which are productive and achieved in a safe setting.

The combination of two very different processes into one workshop was unable to facilitate collective healing or collective reflection about internal practices of power and hierarchy. For me it intensely brought to the fore our responsibility as facilitators to each other and to the participants in workshops and the importance of continual individual and collective reflection of our experiences and experiments in radical education.

## Sumac Skill-Shares

The Sumac skill-shares have been running for a number of years. They have been premised on Illich's idea that to break down formal institutionalized education we need to take education into our streets, communities, and homes. Education needs to be horizontally organized and around knowledge that is needed by a particular individual or community (Illich, 1971, p. 80). It is assumed, as in Freirian philosophy of education, that all have knowledge and can participate as learner and teacher in the experiences developed. The skill-share approach is also similar to approaches found in indigenous education, where skills are learnt mainly through activity (Ingold, 2000). The approach consists mainly in the transmission of skills through skill-modeling and learning by doing, with practitioners acting as instructors, demonstrating techniques and then overseeing learners who attempt to copy the techniques. However, in contrast to Illichian and indigenous learning, it is typically very short-term with a skill-share (treated as a complete teaching-learning relation) lasting usually a few hours. It is mainly used to disseminate practical knowledge. Therefore the skill-shares have traditionally kept to a format of someone learning and someone teaching in a particular skill-share, even if the following week the teacher would become the learner and the learner a teacher.

As one of our collective was a coordinator of the skill-shares since 2009 we decided in discussion with the other coordinator of the skill-shares to experiment with the format and content that had been developed up until then. Our orientation was to emphasize a praxis based on the idea that we

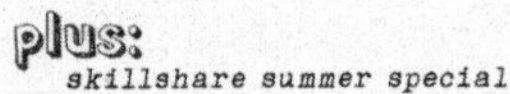


THE OUTDOORS SKILLSHARE

18th - 21st June

A weekend of workshops and skillsharing in rural Scotland.

Climbing and rope access // building tree houses // tunnelling // cooking for the masses // knot-tying // fire-lighting // wild foods // and more!

At Mainshill Solidarity Camp people occupied land facing destruction. They lived outside, grew as a community and took continuous targeted action.

They want to focus on the skills needed to occupy and defend land with a weekend-long event bringing people together to learn and share the skills for living outdoors as a community, building defences, resisting evictions and thinking about strategies for action.

These are transferable skills that can be taken away and used in a wide range of campaigns and actions.

This skillshare will be a safe, inclusive and participatory environment for learning new practical skills and is open to people of all abilities and experiences. If you have any queries or special requirements, please let them know - they will do their best to accommodate everyone's needs.

They will be asking for donations toward food and other costs from those that can afford it.

If you want to find out more, or if you have skills you want to share then please contact them at:

outdoorskillshare@riseup.net

http://outdoorskillshare.noflag.org.uk

/// Spring Term ///

/// skills for autonomous living ///

are all skill-sharers and all have dormant skills and knowledges that we have developed throughout our life experiences more in line with the Illichian approach. As our pamphlet stated,

> If communities are going to strive and flourish outside of the states control and influence then we must break down the current paradigm of learning and knowledge. There can no longer be a dependence on what has been established, but development of what is hidden and kept silent. In order to do this we must bring together all our existing understandings and create new ways of doing, learning and sharing. We must no longer reach to the outside for expertise, as there will come a time when that reach is slapped back and we will be left to fend for ourselves as a community.

Accordingly we developed a series of two weekly workshops around key themes and issues: housing, health, education, culture and media, and food sustainability. The basic organizing idea was that individuals would spend two consecutive Saturdays engaged in skill-sharing around one of these topics. We would facilitate the discussion not as teacher but rather as a participant facilitating questions, identifying themes and issues for further exploration, and pulling out resonances and dissonances. The premise was that all who participated had skills and knowledge in relation to the topic. We envisaged that the first half of the first day would be about discussing our understanding and pulling out our knowledge about the topic. The second half would be exploring and developing one of the themes or issues discussed and high-

## Summer 2010
### programme of workshops

*This term, the Sumac Skillshare is going to be experimenting with format. We will be seeking to facilitate the sharing of skills that skillshare participants already have, skills derived from our own experiences of life.*

*We can't rely on the knowledge taught to us by those in authority. In order to live autonomously, we need to create and develop our skills and abilities autonomously.*

*This term's workshops have been put together to create an opportunity for everyone to share and collectively develop the skills for living which we already possess.*

### FOOD
Saturday 8th & Saturday 15th May

Previous skillshares have looked at attempts to recreate skills to feed ourselves autonomously, and enable us to go beyond capitalist food-production methods. We have discussed thingas like how to grow food, preserving food, mass catering, and creaming off the waste produced by capitalism. This skillshare will discuss all these skills, as well as broader issues around feedingourselves autonomously. How can the ability to produce food collectively and autonomously be accessible to everyone, no matter where they live and whether or not they have access to land? Can we provide food for large numbers of people without conflict over resources? How can we defend the resources we claim for ourselves from authorities who might wish to dispossess us? How might we go about feeding ourselves in a post-capitalist society?

### EDUCATION
Saturday 5th & Saturday 12th June

What exactly did we learn in school? What do those lessons enable us to do - and how do they limit us? What other ways can we share knowledge and ideas? The skillshare is maybe one alternative, but what are the others? As with all / any of the other workshops, these discussions will help to inform practical action we could take; from these discussions, we might decide to draw up a participatory workshop and go on tour, set up a literacy group, squat an infoshop, occupy a university buildingand establish a freeschool, or make a film about the autonomous future of education.

### HEALTH
Saturday 22nd & Saturday 29th May

How can we decentralise knowledge about medicine? What medical skills do we already have? How can we liberate ourselves from having to work and suffer work-related illnesses? Can we reduce our dependency on psychiatric drugs - and develop alternatives to them for maintaining our mental health? What importance does our mental health and social situation have for our physical wellbeing? How can we create a society which nurtures our mental and physical wellbeing?

### CULTURE
Saturday 19th & Saturday 26th June

What can we do to create culture that represents who, what and where we are as well as where, what and who we want to be? How might we subvert and go beyond the stories the culture industry tells us about what people are and what life is? What cheaply- or freely-available tools are there for creating our own music, art, films, television, plays, radio, computer games, comic books, artcitecture? How can we create a news media which communicates what we see in the world? What outlets for our music, films and news are there, and where can we access those that others have made? How can we change the urban environment so we find it more aesthetically pleasing?

### SHELTER
Saturday 3rd & Saturday 10th July

What are the different ways of housing ourselves? What state benefits are there which we can use to help us house ourselves, and how can we claim themwhile maintaining our autonomy? How can we organise rent strikes? How can we liberate ourselves from landlords and rent altogether? How do we go about setting up squats, housing co-ops, building our own houses or making old ones habitable? What effect do the environments we live in have on us - and how can we create housing that enables us to flourish?

### 11am-5pm Sumac Centre
245 Gladstone Street, Forest Fields, NG7 6HX

Lunch: provided for a donation // People's kitchen in evening from 6.30pm
Creche: can be organised if it's needed. Please email nottinghamfreeschool@riseup.net or phone 07947671182
General info: email nottinghamfreeschool@riseup.net or phone 07947671182

lighted in a more practical way. We originally had the idea of two training sessions for a group of facilitators who would coordinate the skill-shares and would ideally enter into a reflexive process about their facilitation that would help to systematize the methodology we were trying to develop. However, due to issues of time, this didn't happen between regular Free School participants. It also didn't happen with those we had hoped would join a facilitator team. To some extent this raised questions about the inclusiveness of our collective. Paradoxically the process of building group solidarity and understanding throughout the previous nine months while creating connections, collective learning, and relationships also potentially excluded others who had not been part of this process and made them feel that they were not equal participants or that this was not their project. The problematic remains, particularly how to expand and deepen the collective outside of a group of people who have built a deep level of trust or already knew each other politically and socially.

We framed the skill-shares with questions such as these. In the housing workshops, for example, we asked:

> When exploring how we will create and maintain shelter for ourselves and one another, as individuals we already have life times of experience in doing this in a variety of ways, if we bring these experiences together what will we be able to create? What new knowledges will come forth? And will we make these knowledges both sustainable and flexible? These are the questions we'll be asking in the first two weekends, where discussions will encourage us into action. Actions which will be determined by those who attend. Whether those practicalities are the setting up of a new co-op, squatting a new building, improving an old house or creating a shanty town.

And in the health workshops, for example, we asked:

> In the third fortnight the attention falls on health. We all fall prey to sickness, whether that be a common cold or something more serious. But do we really need to be so reliant on the National Health Service and the medical industry? Which aim for quick fixes and quick profits, and are intrinsically tied up with the various causes for the illnesses that may come our way. What other options are there? What other options have people being used for centuries? How can we produce and share new models for maintaining our physical and mental health? What importance does our mental health and social situation play in our physical well being? What effect does child care have on the health of the child as they become an adult? As individuals we may have our own answers to these questions, but if we combine our knowledges and resources what can develop from that?

The skill-shares had very low turnouts with some having to be cancelled. However, there were some productive discussions at the education and health workshops. At the education skill-share participants in the Really Open University (http://reallyopenuniversity.wordpress.com/) came up from Leeds and a long set of discussions about radical education, strategies for developing radical education, and potentials for linkages between the groups discussed. This has since been followed up by collaboration between participants in both radical education collectives. Three women participated in the health discussions, one as the facilitator. A huge amount of critique of current health systems and mental health systems was developed. This was built on by explored alternatives which potentially combined elements of dominant health systems with practices of indigenous communities and practices that have been lost and buried from previous groups of women midwifes and healers. We spent the second half of the day exploring lost traditions and alternative traditions as a way to begin to think about how we might use these in our everyday practices of health and healing. Since then, ideas about a mental health and trauma collective have been discussed with the idea of developing a network in and around Nottingham.

These were important moments of openings and connections which created resonances and recognitions building the grounds for collective praxis and creating. However, the low turnouts and subsequent cancellation of sessions opened up a series of discussions about the reasons for the lack of interest in the workshops as structured in this way. Previously skill-shares had been organized around the sharing of a specific skill. This has acted as a motivation of participation, which in many ways replicated the practice of learning as an instrumental process of attaining a particular skill or knowledge as a thing. Our rupturing radically that premise and opening up daylong workshops around a general theme without any immediately identifiable concrete skill or outcome was unable to reach out to people's motivations and desires. To some extent, we put the cart before the horse. It is important to connect to where people are at, to their everyday concrete needs, desires, and interests. To sidetrack this is to miss one of the basic premises of Freirian popular education and Illich's emphasis in deschooling society: that education to be liberatory and transformative must be relevant and context-specific. Disrupting traditional ways of learning and knowledge construction is a process. It takes a slow opening to learning that gradually breaks down fixed subjectivities and understandings of ourselves as learners (but not as teachers unless trained to do so) and of knowledge as a thing as opposed to a creative process. These reflections led us to agree that future skill-shares needed to combine the concrete needs and desires of potential participants with the development of a dialogical methodology that pushed to breaking down the divisions between skill sharer (practitioner/teacher) and learner in the skill-share space.

## Conclusion

This piece has attempted to begin a process of systematization of the praxis of the first eighteen months of the Nottingham Free School. It has used the Freirian, Illichian, and OSDE philosophies and methodologies of radical education and the experiences of the facilitators to evaluate some of the practices and projects of the collective. It has done so in relation to whether they manage to facilitate open and dialogical spaces, help to construct postrepresentational and horizontal anticapitalist communities, and forge horizontal and participatory processes of collective knowledge construction. It has also reflected on the process of building a collective of radical educators.

Perhaps one of the most significant elements of the theory and practice that emerge from this systematization is the importance of taking into consideration the context and nature of the community that one is working with. There are distinct differences between working with organized political groups and varied groups of individuals and collectives that may or may not share common objectives and principles. This recognition implies the adaptation and transformation of methodologies and pedagogies from a range of radical education traditions. It also enables recognition of the limits and possibilities of working within different contexts. This lends itself to the development of a different conceptualization of success and politics, away from the output/object orientation of capitalism and toward and open and processal understanding of success and a multifaceted understanding of the construction of anticapitalist communities, which includes the affective, symbolic, spiritual, intellectual, institutional, and cultural. Fundamentally it also highlights the processal like nature of developing a collective of radical educators that are prepared and able to work in diverse settings. This is a long-term process with no shortcuts, which must be necessarily embedded in ongoing individual and collective reflection and systematization. The process of forming this collective is itself not merely about learning different methodologies and pedagogies but also learning to relate to each other in postrepresentational ways and unlearning our learnt subjectivities which embed us in relations of power-over.

I hope with this piece to have contributed to this process of continual individual and collective reflection of the Nottingham Free School and to have provided some useful notes toward the problems, possibilities, and potentialities of constructing an educational praxis beyond capitalism.

## Notes

1 Ideally this should be carried out as a collective. However due to time and political pressures we were not able to undertake the systematization in this way,

2 Excerpts from Freire's *Pedagogy of the Oppressed*, Illich's *Deschooling Society*, and Postman and Weingartner's *Teaching as a Subversive Activity* are examples of the readings we give.

## References

Andreotti, V. (n.d.). Soft versus critical global citizenship education. Retrieved from http://www.osdemethodology.org.uk/texts/softcriticalvan.pdf.

Freire, P. (1970). *Pedagogy of the oppressed*. Harmondsworth: Penguin.

Gadgil, M., F. Berkes, F. & Folks, C. (1993). Indigenous knowledge for biodiversity conservation. *Ambio, 22*, 151–56.

Illich, I. (1971). *Deschooling society*. Harmondsworth: Penguin.

Ingold, T. (2000). *The perception of the environment: Essays on livelihood, dwelling and skill*. London: Routledge.

Medina and Teatro La Máscara (2010). *El teatro de género: Memoria del proceso*. Medellín: Editorial Lealon.

Mejía, M.R. (2010). *La sistematización: Empodera y produce saber y conocimiento*. Bogotá: Ediciones desde abajo.

Motta, S. (2009). Old tools and new movements: Political science as gatekeeper or intellectual illumination. *Latin American Politics and* Society, 51(1).

Motta, S. (2010). Aves de paraiso: Theatre of the oppressed, Cali, Colombia. *Nottingham Critical Pedagogy*. Retrieved from: http://nottinghamcriticalpedagogy.wordpress.com/2010/12/26/aves-de-paraiso-theatre-of-the-oppressed-in-cali-colombia/

Postman, N. & Weingartner, C. (1969), *Teaching as a subversive activity*. Harmondsworth: Penguin.

Restrepo, P (1998) *La máscara, la mariposa y la metáfora: Creación teatral de mujeres*. Santiago de Cali: Teatro La Máscara.

Robinson, A. (2010). Anarchism, war and the state. *Ceasefire*. Retrieved from http://ceasefiremagazine.co.uk/anarchism-war-and-the-state/.

**CHAPTER 9**

# Learning to Win: Anarchist Infrastructures of Resistance

**Jeffery Shantz**

Activists, ensconced in familiar, even comfortable, spaces that are inhabited by other activists, can too readily forget that the activities in which they are engaged each day—whether meetings, organizing, or debates—do not come naturally. They have to be learned through practice and shared labors. Similarly, the actions that are undertaken less frequently, irregularly—such as pickets, occupations, and demonstrations—also have to be learned and relearned through direct experience in order to be carried out effectively. Even more, do activists and organizers have to learn and revise specific theoretical positions and perspectives? In societies in which we are set up to lose, we all need to learn to win and what winning might mean in specific contexts.

Typically the learning involved in these varied activities, and reflections upon them, are nurtured in specific collective spaces. These spaces, from community centers to might be understood as infrastructures of resistance, resources that support organizing among the working classes and oppressed and provide some transfer of knowledge over time and space. For working-class people in Canada and the United States the primary spaces for learning have been associated historically with unions and workers associations. Yet over the last thirty years, with the decline of unionization rates and the transfer of unions into primarily bargaining agents, the spaces of learning, particularly radical or activist learning, have eroded or even disappeared. This has deprived rank-and-file workers of opportunities to learn about the histories of working-class struggle, even of their own unions and locals. It has also deprived workers of resources to learn, create, and debate strategies, tactics, practices, and ideas of struggle, whether historic or more recent.

This chapter examines attempts by anarchist workers to restore, revive, and maintain spaces of learning and infrastructures of resistance. It discusses, in particular, efforts of anarchist workers to build radical rank-and-file networks and resources through workers centers. Specifically it details the work of the coalition of anarchists, employed, and unemployed workers that has formed to develop a workers action center in Windsor, Ontario. Beyond the immediate outcome of each particular occupation or struggle, the turn to more militant and direct action tactics poses a rethinking of the avenues available to workers. The projects and alliances, networks, and experiences forged within them provide the foundations for new infrastructures of resistance. They also serve to stir memories of working-class struggles, practices, and visions that had seemingly been forgotten, lost to time.

## Rebuilding Infrastructures of Resistance

As my colleague Alan Sears (2008, p. 8) notes, the habitat in which twentieth-century working-class radicalism, such as anarchism, could thrive no longer exists in the twenty-first century in the form that previously sustained radical movements and ideas. The forms of political radicalism that animated much resistance of the working classes, poor, and oppressed, were vital as components of broader infrastructures of resistance (Shantz, 2009c). The infrastructures of resistance included a range of institutions, venues, organizations, and practices. Some important examples included free schools, alternative media and publishing, shared spaces such as social centers bookstores, union halls, and bars, and workers' campgrounds and medical clinics. These infrastructures developed within contexts of particular organizations of life and work. Through struggle and the pressing realities of meeting material, cultural, personal, and social needs and desires, people and their communities developed infrastructures of resistance to sustain themselves and provide the necessary supports to sustain ongoing struggles and the inspiration of the new world they sought to make. The last few decades have ushered in significant changes in the organization of social relations and conditions of production, which have transformed the possibilities for specific political projects (Sears, 2008, p. 8). Emerging movements need to focus on the reemergence of infrastructures of resistance if they are to be relevant parts of contributions to the development and growth of new waves of radical renewal and resistance.

As the anarchist labor organizer Sam Dolgoff often stressed, the labor movement once put a great deal of energy into building more permanent forms of alternative institutions. An expanding variety of mutual aid functions were provided through unions in the early days of labor.

> They created a network of cooperative institutions of all kinds: schools, summer camps for children and adults, homes for the aged, health and

> cultural centers, insurance plans, technical education, housing, credit associations, et cetera. All these, and many other essential services were provided by the people themselves, long before the government monopolized social services wasting untold billions on a top-heavy bureaucratic parasitical apparatus; long before the labor movement was corrupted by "business unionism". (1990, p. 31)

Infrastructures of resistance also included practices such as rank-and-file networks, flying squads and working groups and opposition movements within unions (see Shantz, 2009d). The infrastructures of resistance also included, notably, anarchist and socialist groups and organizations themselves. Key here were the informal networks of workers and community members inside and outside official union structures. These varying infrastructures of resistance provided, allowed for, and encouraged a range of material and imaginal supports within communities of working-class, poor, and oppressed people. Indeed it is within these infrastructures of resistance that community became possible and practiced in real ways. As Sears (2008, p. 8) notes, these infrastructures of resistance "cultivated collective capacities for memory (reflections on past experiences and struggles), analysis (discussion and debate about theory and change), communication (outside of official or commercial media channels) and action (networks of formal and informal solidarity."

Over the last half century, many of these infrastructures of resistance have severely eroded within working-class communities across North America. The erosion of infrastructures of resistance has resulted from a series of significant transformations in work and social life. It has also been impacted by shifts in the reorganization of political and social priorities and opportunities of official institutions within communities of the working class and oppressed. Most of the changes have been effected by defeats suffered through offensives of states and capital. At the same time, others have resulted from seeming working-class victories, including the legalization of unions themselves (Sears, 2008, p. 8). For all of their potential power, the trade unions in Ontario are restricted by a leadership that cannot allow decisive force to be unleashed.

This has meant that over the past few decades working-class opposition in North America has been contained largely within official, typically legalistic channels. Most common among these have been established bargaining and grievance procedures via union representatives in economic matters. This has been accompanied by a containment of political action within the official channels of party politics and elections. Indeed the separation between economic and political spheres (and the relegation of unions to the limited terrain of economic management) is a reflection, and result of, the collapse of infrastructures of resistance that expressed the connections, even unity, of economic and political action, and the need for organizations that recognized the connections between struggles in these areas. Activities such as occupations, blockades, wildcat strikes, and sabotage have been dismissed or diminished within unionized workplaces in which unions act as a level of surveillance and regulation of workers, attempting to contain their actions within the framework of contracts with employers.

Indeed the main role of the unions became supervision of the contract during periods between bargaining and symbolic mobilization to support official union negotiations during legal bargaining. Rank-and-file militants have faced disciplinary actions, lack of support, or outright shunning by union officials. Contracts include provisions that prohibit wildcats, as agreed to by the union representatives.

In Canada, the institutionalization of unions as economic managers has been accompanied by the institutionalization of working-class politics within electoral politics in campaigns of the New Democratic Party federally and provincially, at national and local levels. Politics has been reduced to party campaigns and lobbying for legislative reform as proposed and channeled through NDP caucuses (Shantz, 2009b).

In the current period these institutional pressures and habits have constrained working-class responses to structural transformations of neoliberalism and economic crisis. Unions have sought to limit losses rather than make gains. The approach has been to negotiate severance deals that limit the harm done to former employees (and members) rather than contest the rights of employers and governments to determine the future of workplaces and workers' livelihoods.

These arrangements have also engendered a certain faith in or reliance upon the system among the working classes. Rather than seeking new relations, a new society, the institutions of the working class presented and replayed the message that working-class desires and needs could not only be met within capitalist society, but, even more, depended upon capitalism for their realization.

Such a notion played into the "trickle-down" fantasies of neoliberal Reaganomics, which insisted that policies and practices that benefited business should be pursued as some of the gains made by capital would eventually find their way to the working class and the poor. Such was the justification for the massive multi-million-dollar bailouts handed to corporations as part of the economic crisis of 2008 and 2009.

Infrastructures of resistance provided the imaginal universe in which alternatives could be thought, pursued and even, if in part, implemented and realized. The decline of infrastructures of resistance left communities without alternatives or the possibility of alternatives, consigned to the sense that capitalism was the only option. This sense of resignation was reinforced by official institutions (unions and labor parties) that, in their rhetoric and actions suggested that another world was not possible and all desires had to be met or discarded within the context of capitalist social relations. Relations of exploitation.

There has also been a decline in working-class institutions such as the working-class social centers, "labor temples," or union halls as centers of cultural life and activity. Cultural activities have been reduced to the occasional union barbecue or pub night. Shared spaces for discussion, debate strategizing and developing collective visions and practices have eroded. So too have opportunities to nurture connections across generations of workers.

The cultural activities of working-class elders and youth have been separated, and even segregated. Great distances obtain between the so-called "youth subcultures" and the touchstones of adult cultures, themselves divided along a range of consumer preferences.

All of this has meant that more militant responses, possibilities of occupation, factory recuperation, or wildcats, have not been raised as reasonable responses to capitalist crisis or restructuring. Now as the previous gains made by workers and social movements are being, or have been, erased under neoliberal regimes, the working class, poor, and oppressed are left alone to face precarious existence and exploitation without the necessary infrastructures that might sustain them or offer a basis for renewed struggle. This is true in terms of the loss of autonomous institutions of the working class and poor, but also in terms of the loss of public institutions (the reified outcomes of struggle reflected in the welfare state and various social services), which have been privatized, turned over to the market and its cold profit logic.

These memories are often buried beneath layers of bureaucracy, legal procedure, and parliamentary process. The stirring of rank-and-file initiatives and the lessons learned in practice energize a militant hope that poses new questions and new opportunities. They can change the context in which workers' expectations develop. They can also change the context in which the rights of workers, capital, and even the meaning of property itself are understood. They offer wonderful opportunities for workers to gain a powerful sense of their own strength and shows fairly clearly the sort of impact they can have beyond the typical confines of legal negotiations and bargaining.

Anarchists have always emphasized people's capacities for spontaneous organization, but they also recognize that what appears to be "spontaneous" develops from an often-extensive groundwork of preexisting radical practices. Without such preexisting practices and relationships, people are left to patch things together in the heat of social upheaval or to defer to previously organized and disciplined vanguards. Preexisting infrastructures, or transfer cultures, are necessary components of popular, participatory, and liberatory social reorganization. A liberatory social transformation requires experiences of active involvement in radical change, prior to any insurrection, and the development of prior structures for constructing a new society within the shell of the old society.

Various alternative institutions, whether free schools or squats or countermedia, form networks as means for developing alternative social infrastructures. Where free schools join up with worker cooperatives and collective social centers, alternative social infrastructures become visible at least at the community level. Contemporary projects are still quite new. None have approached the scale that would suggest they pose practical alternatives, except perhaps in the case of new media activities and Internet networks. Yet all are putting together the building blocks that might promote practical alternatives extending well beyond the projects from which they originated.

## Toward the Rebuilding of Infrastructures of Resistance in a Blue-Collar Town

The infrastructures of resistance help people and communities to develop the capacities to sustain human struggles over time and place. They provide a basis for self-directing these struggles strategically. They also allow for the crucial connection between local and immediate struggles and campaigns and broader and more thoroughgoing projects of contesting and even overthrowing the existing social structures (Sears, 2008, p. 10).

Windsor, like many working-class centers, is certainly a community that would benefit from a renewal of rank-and-file direct action. As Ross and Drouillard note (2009), between 2002 and 2006, secure, well-paying, and unionized manufacturing jobs in Windsor declined by 28 percent. The loss of jobs has devastated the community, with people losing homes, leaving the community, or turning to food banks, soup kitchens, and shelters to get by. The city's downtown has become abandoned in certain areas, the boarded up storefronts a ghostly reminder of the city that once was. While there have been outward signs of opposition, such as the forty-thousand-strong community demonstration in 2007 calling for government support for unemployed workers and those facing job loss, the overarching sense has been one of resignation and hopelessness (Ross and Drouillard, 2009). Such has been the impact of ongoing and deepening experiences of unemployment, marginalization, and poverty across the community (Ross and Drouillard, 2009).

In Windsor many of the organizations and institutions that had recently provided infrastructures of resistance, such as the Windsor Coalition for Social Justice and the Anarchist Working Group, had disappeared. Central spaces in which activists had gathered, met, and organized, such as the Eclectic Cafe, which had provided something of an organizing nerve center during the demonstrations against the meetings of the Organization of American States (OAS), had folded. The roving Coffeehouse 36 weekly anarchist gatherings had faded away after providing lively venues for discussion, debate, and organizing. As Ross and Drouillard (2009) note:

> The CAW's strategy of using buyouts as a way to mitigate layoffs (while allowing employers to permanently reduce the workforce) has generated a growing number of ex-union members in the community, some of whom were local union activists. As these workers drift away into other workplaces or struggle to find new jobs, and with nothing to connect them to their former union or workplace community, they experience isolation and the dissipation of their activist knowledge, experience and capacities.

One interesting attempt initiated by anarchists to rebuild working-class infrastructures of resistance emerged in Windsor at the end of 2008. On November 1, 2008, the Windsor Workers' Action Centre (WWAC) threw open its door with a celebration attended by a standing-room-only crowd (Ross and Drouillard, 2009). Participants view the WWAC as a venue for developing new strategies for collective struggle and for providing resources, material and imaginal, that will contribute to new types of worker's organization and action. The concern is not solely with helping people survive the crisis but, even more, to forge the solidarity and support that might build the capacity to raise seriously workers' alternatives to capitalism (Ross and Drouillard, 2009). One key challenge is to make connections between unemployed workers and those who still have jobs. Similarly there is the need to build solidarity between unionized workers trying to hold onto relatively decent paying jobs and nonunionized workers, many of whom have never enjoyed such jobs in the first place.

The initiative comes out of a growing sense that working-class organizations, and community advocacy groups, are not capable of confronting, let alone overcoming, the issues and difficulties facing the working class and oppressed in twenty-first-century capitalism. The WWAC is a material manifestation of working-class and poor people to develop and share resources among themselves in a way that will forge durable relationships within or between individuals and groups while helping to overcome the sense of isolation and defeatism that often impedes struggles. It is a space of mutual aid and solidarity, an infrastructure of resistance in the making.

In other contexts and eras, infrastructures of dissent provided venues and resources through which workers and community activists could come together and collaborate on shared projects, making connections between seemingly distinct issues and concerns and creating a critical mass for dealing with them effectively. As Ross and Drouillard (2009) remind us, "workers' independent social and cultural spaces outside the workplace . . . allowed workers to gather, socialize, debate and argue, develop their own forms of cultural expression as well as bonds of friendship and solidarity that could underpin difficult struggles as well as generate alternative perspectives." Initial meetings thus emphasized building opportunities for bridging gaps, bringing movements, groups, and activists together to find common cause and common ground.

Contemporary infrastructures of resistance must be places that recognize and are open to the diversity of working-class experience. They must be spaces in which people from different workplace and community backgrounds can feel comfortable and welcome. This marks them as distinct from union halls, church basements, and university campuses, spaces that have often been used for organizing. As WWAC participants are aware, union halls can be difficult spaces to enter for nonunionized workers "given the broader cultural atmosphere of antiunionism, the resentment fostered against unionized workers, and the fear of reprisal from employers if seen associating with the movement" (Ross and Drouillard, 2009). Similarly many working-class people still feel uncomfortable or unwelcome on university campuses, spaces that are viewed as the domain of elites who do not or cannot relate to working-class people or, worse, who look down on them. I still have vivid memories of being physically assaulted my first week as an undergraduate simply for wearing my union jacket on campus, the student assailants repeatedly asking why I was wearing a union jacket on *their* campus. In other cases community organizers sometimes fail to recognize cultural diversity. I recall an antipoverty group holding a welfare clinic in a church basement only to find that some Muslim people, who were among the groups to whom outreach was being directed, would not enter the building.

For the founders of the WWAC, it was essential that the space they created be open to any working-class people who wanted to participate, from a broad diversity of backgrounds and experiences. The gathering space should be free from direction by any particular group, organization, or workplace (such as the university). Its focus must be straightforwardly to provide a free space, both in terms of openness but literally free in terms of cost, in which people can meet to pursue their own organizing needs. Additionally this space should allow for people to meet others, unfamiliar to them, who might have similar interests, experiences, concerns, and intentions. These opportunities and encounters, it is hoped, will lead to new forms of interconnected struggle and even allow people "to develop broader forms of consciousness" (Ross and Drouillard, 2009).

A key goal that motivated the creation of the WWAC space was challenging and overcoming the false divide that too often separates community and workplace struggles, as if they were somehow separate spheres

(Ross and Drouillard, 2009). Indeed, the organizational structures, activities, and membership of social justice groups often (re)produce that divide. Antipoverty groups, housing advocates, injured workers groups, migrant workers' organizations too often have limited aims, scopes, and activities related to specific concerns of a particular working-class constituency with too little interaction between them, shared memberships or mutually engaged strategies and tactics. Precisely because such divides are false, in many ways the outcome of previous struggles and defeats, and even victories (see Sears, 2008), "activists needed to better understand and organize around the *intersections* between work-based inequalities and injustices and those experienced in the family, in schools, in the grocery store, in neighbourhoods, and in the city" (Ross and Drouillard, 2009). Participants in the WWAC were aware and concerned that unions have still not made organizing around working-class issues beyond the workplace a real priority. This situation has only gotten worse as unions retreat and retrench around a limited defense against demands for concessions (Sears, 2008; Ross and Drouillard, 2009).

In January 2009, the WWAC set up a phone line to assist workers in dealing with current employers or to help unemployed workers and community members deal with government agencies and programs such as Employment Insurance (EI) or Workers' Compensation claims (Ross and Drouillard, 2009). WWAC participants have also developed and hosted workshops on employment standards to the Windsor Unemployed Help Centre and Windsor Women Working With Immigrant Women (an organization that helps immigrant women secure employment), and has developed workshops on EI and the Workplace Safety and Insurance Board (WSIB). At present, the work of the WWAC is focused on service provision, in a context in which many people are without adequate support in dealing with government systems that are not accessible or easy to navigate (Ross and Drouillard, 2009). Notably people often lack the knowledge required to navigate such institutions of authority effectively in ways that meet their own specific needs. Assistance is offered for anything from filling out government forms properly to taking direct action against an employer or landlord who is ripping people off. Those affected decide the best approach to deal with their situation and the WWAC helps with resources and people to get it done. Recognizing that "established channels" rarely work in favor of poor people the working group is committed to developing the skills and resources necessary so that people can take whatever action is necessary to get what they need. This is an example of an infrastructure of resistance, one in which skill-sharing and learning occurs collectively to help people meet rather essential needs.

One of the central, essential infrastructures lacking for a variety of organizations of the working-class and poor is simply space to meet and gather safely and securely. Addressing this ongoing need, the WWAC makes available free meeting space for several community organizing groups, including the FedUp Community Gardening Network, the Windsor Peace Coalition, and the Windsor Fair Trade group, a group devoted to making Windsor a fair trade city (Ross and Drouillard, 2009). The center also holds a number of free school classes, including classes on anarchist economics and theory.

The availability of a common organizing space allows a diversity of social justice groups and organizers to meet, talk, and build relationships. This provides opportunities to move beyond the fragmentation and isolation that often mark struggles and issues and allows organizers to make connections that would otherwise not emerge. Indeed participants in the WWAC note the numbers of people who have remarked that before spending time at the center they did not know about a range of other projects underway in the city (Ross and Drouillard, 2009). This is clearly a case in which involvement or interest in a specific group or event can, through the presence of a shared space, lead to contact and involvement with other groups and issues, contributing to the expansion of group participation and the forging of relationships of mutual aid and solidarity (Ross and Drouillard, 2009).

Developing practices for overcoming barriers between people and movements and moving past the fragmentation and isolation that are part of relations of exploitation and oppression remain key challenges to be addressed in building and nurturing infrastructures of resistance. Ross and Drouillard (2009) note that most workers' centers have been geared toward more clearly defined or specific constituencies, typically around particular industries, workers, citizenship status, or employment status. In their view, organizing workers as a class is a difficult task, particularly as it must avoid the pitfalls of traditional labor organizations and movements.

The type of service provision that unions and community organizations are typically involved in, such as accessing government, contractually affirmed or legal resources does not entail much risk, either for recipients or providers (Ross and Drouillard, 2009). Various limited resources exist to support individual workers, as long as it remains within a context that reintegrates them into the system of waged labor. Collective organizing for more than this is both more difficult and more risky, in material and emotional terms. Before people are willing or ready to engage in such collective actions they must experience or see examples of success. As Ross and Drouillard (2009) note: "Many people, whether unionized or not, are well aware of the pervasive injustice of the current state of affairs, but are skeptical that collective action can change these circumstances. If the CAW, the most powerful union in Windsor, must take major concessions to preserve jobs, what can other organizations do?"

Infrastructures of resistance, like the WWAC, must crucially develop and maintain capacities for making and securing real victories that are meaningful in people's lives. At the same time this requires that people develop the confidence to struggle further (Ross and Drouillard, 2009). Even so-called minor victories, such as securing proper severance or benefits or delaying a plant closure, can be essential. People, in a context of too many, often ongoing, losses, need to win to experience what winning feels like. As Ross and Drouillard (2009) note, in the current context, even addressing the question of making real gains and attempting to develop new ways of answering it can be a real contribution to the regeneration of workers' resistance.

## Reflections

We need to be prepared not just intellectually but organizationally for radical struggles and transformation. Infrastructures of resistance serve as means by which people can sustain radical social change before, during, and after insurrectionary periods.

As a child growing up in a union family in Windsor I can remember many occasions in which members came together to share good times, discussion, play, and friendship—parties at the union hall, picnics, sports clubs, etc. These events provided spaces in which members and their families could benefit culturally and materially from a shared community and culture, from mutual aid in practice. By the time I went to work in the plant and became a member of the local myself, most of these activities and spaces were things of the past. My fellow workers on the line were finding support and solidarity not within the shared spaces of the local, but often, instead, in born-again religions and reactionary clubs.

Indeed this is perhaps one of the lessons to be learned from the successful organizing done by the Right in the 1980s and 1990s. In times of need and crisis, the evangelical churches provided institutional support and emotional defense against capitalist alienation (though not necessarily in ways that the Left should emulate). Many evangelical communities provide food, clothing, and shelter for members. Many can mobilize hundreds to build a house for someone in their community. The Left has been less active in developing these infrastructural capacities, though these are things we could be doing in our own neighborhoods.

Infrastructures of resistance encourage people to create alternative social spaces within which liberatory institutions, practices, and relationships can be nurtured. They include the beginnings of economic and political self-management through the creation of institutions which can encourage a broader social transformation while also providing some of the conditions for personal and collective sustenance and growth in the present. This is about changing the world, not by taking control of the state, but by creating opportunities for people to develop their personal and collective power.

Infrastructures of resistance create situations in which specific communities build economic and social systems that operate, as much as possible, as working alternatives to the dominant state capitalist structures. They are organized around alternative institutions that offer at least a starting point for meeting community needs such as education, food, housing, communications, energy, transportation, child care, and so on. These institutions are autonomous from, and indeed opposed to, dominant relations and institutions of the state and capital. They may also contest "official" organs of the working class such as bureaucratic unions or political parties. In the short term these institutions contest official structures, with an eye toward, in the longer term, replacing them. The creation of alternative institutions and relationships, which express our more far-reaching visions, can be desirable in and of itself. It is important to liberate or create space within which we might live more free and secure lives today, as we work to build a new society.

Superseding the status quo requires, in part, a refusal to participate in dominant social relations. Communities might seek to reorganize social institutions in such a way as to reclaim social and economic power and exercise it in their own collective interests. They might seek an alternative social infrastructure that is responsive to people's needs because it is developed and controlled directly by them. Such an approach takes a firm stand against the authority vested in politicians and their corporate masters. It might also speak against the hierarchical arrangements that exemplify major institutions such as workplaces, schools, churches, and even the family. It is important to develop the skills and resources, some forgotten or overlooked, that might contribute to this.

The perspectives and practices of our movements, in addressing immediate day-to-day concerns, remind us that we must offer examples that resonate with people's experiences and needs. Additionally, any movement that fails to offer alternative and reliable organizational spaces and practices will be doomed to marginalization and failure. Or as Herzen has remarked, "A goal which is infinitely remote is not a goal at all, it is a deception" (quoted in Ward, 2004, p. 32). These practices could point the way toward the development of real world alternatives to capitalism. The challenge remains how such activities might allow for the creation of greater spaces for their autonomous development and extension. There is an ongoing push and pull between forces driving toward dis/valorization into capitalism and forces working for autonomous development.

Such projects as the workers center together are showing the reasonableness and promise of workers control as meaningful responses and alternatives to the failures of capitalism. Examples like the WWAC suggest that where these reemerging infrastructures of resistance become able to reinforce and encourage each other, new contexts for struggles might emerge.

## References

Babbage, M. (2009). Ontario job losses mean bleaker times ahead: Opposition. *Toronto Star*. March 13. Retrieved from http://www.thestar.com/News/Ontario/article/602005, (accessed October 21, 2009).

Bell, K. (2009). Canadian workers occupy auto parts factory. Retrieved from http://www.marxist.com/canadian-workers-occupy-auto-factory.htm, (accessed October 21, 2009).

Beltrame, J. (2008). Job losses worst in Ontario. *Toronto Star*. July 11. Retrieved from http://www.thestar.com/Business/article/458479 (accessed October 21, 2009).

Dolgoff, S. (1990). *The American labor movement: A new beginning*. Champaign: Libertarian Labor Review.

Eley, T. (2009). Autoworkers end factory occupation in Windsor, Ontario. *World Socialist*, March 20.

Ross, S. & Drouillard, R. (2009). Renewing workers' struggles in the crisis: The Windsor Workers' Action Centre. *The Bullet E-Journal*. Toronto: Socialist Project

Sears, A. (2008). Habitats for socialism. *Relay*, 23, 8–10.

Shantz, J. (2009a). *Living anarchy: Theory and practice in anarchist movements*. Palo Alto: Academica Press.

Shantz, J. (2009b). The limits of social unionism in Canada. *WorkingUSA: The Journal of Labor and Society*, 12(1): 113–30.

Shantz, J. (2009c). Re-building infrastructures of resistance. *Socialism and Democracy*, 23(2), 102–9.

Shantz, J. (2009d). Anarchy at work: Contemporary anarchism and unions. *WorkingUSA: The Journal of Labor and Society*, 12(3), 371–85.

Ward, C. (1973). *Anarchy in action*. New York: Harper Torchbooks

CHAPTER 10

# Inside, Outside, and on the Edge of the Academy: Experiments in Radical Pedagogies[1]

Elsa Noterman and Andre Pusey

## Introduction

Universities, as well as other educational institutions, are currently facing economic instability, debt, and an uncertain future. The squeeze on higher education is like the crisis of capital: global. But so too is the emergent resistance. People around the world are challenging the neoliberal model of the university, which produces "skilled" workers to be put to use for the (re)production of capital.

The "double crisis" of the economy and the university has made campuses once again sites of resistance, and the "new student movement can be seen as the main organized response to the global financial crisis" (Caffentzis, 2010). These struggles have not only formed spaces for opposition—to budget cuts, the increasing precarity of labor, rising education costs—but have also featured calls for new models for education to "transform the campus into a base for alternative knowledge production that is accessible to those outside its 'walls'" (Caffentzis, 2010). In this chapter we will investigate recent attempts to create alternative spaces for radical pedagogy and knowledge commons inside, outside, and on the periphery of the academy, exploring several spaces of pedagogical praxis and to reflect on the potential for radical pedagogy and knowledge production.

First we look at attempts to open autonomous spaces within the neoliberal university, including the MA in Activism and Social Change at the University of Leeds (UK) that attempts to reconcile radical scholarship and activism. We also look at a project called "Student as Producer," which aims to transform the form that teaching takes across the undergraduate syllabus, at the University of Lincoln (UK).

We then engage with "Free School" and "Free University" projects as instances of pedagogical spaces outside the academy—specifically those organized in places such as autonomous social centers and explicitly rooted in the anarchist tradition of collectivism, autonomy, and self-management.

Finally we reflect on a group attempting to place itself in what we term "creative cramped space" on the edge of the university. The Really Open University (ROU), which we are both involved with, is working to develop a collective critique of the current university system, and develop experimental and participatory interventions.

The refrain of the ROU is "strike, occupy, transform." To our mind it is this transformative politics of antagonistic affirmation that offers us hope at creating open and nonhierarchical institutions of research and learning, based on what have long been anarchist principles of creating prefigurative examples in the here and now. This transformative space on the edge of the academy can perhaps provide a place for the merging of critical pedagogy with anarchist theory—prefigurative education (DeLeon, 2006). Expanding on the Zapatista saying, "*Preguntando caminamos*" (asking, we walk) (Holloway, 2005), we seek to examine spaces where as researchers, asking we *struggle*.

## Experiments Inside the Academy

In this section we wish to look at experiments in opening radical educational spaces within the academy. We focus mainly on the course we have most experience of, the MA in Activism and Social Change, run from the School of Geography at the University of Leeds in the UK.[2]

Stevphen Shukaitis (2009) notes that "anarchism has always had an ambivalent relationship to the academy." Indeed, from an anarchist perspective, critical of universities as hierarchical and exclusionary institutions, it is easy to see an array of problems arising from attempts to experiment with radical education within the bounded and striated space of the academy. The course fees alone mean that any attempt at running a radical course will only attract those who are able to afford to pay tuition or willing to go into debt for the purpose of further study. Within the current point in the edu-crisis this situation looks like it will only intensify, with a recent UK government report (Browne, 2010) recommending the doubling of undergraduate university fees to around £7,000 to £10,000 a year for "home students"[3] in the United Kingdom. Course fees globally are skyrocketing, along with student debt. In the United States, the average debt for students who graduated in 2009 was $24,000 (up 6 percent from the previous year) (The Project on Student Debt, 2010).

In addition to the financial issues, there is the recurrent accusation that the academy "recuperates" radical struggles and ideas, thereby rendering them harmless and capitalizing off them for its own ends (Vaneigem, 1972).

To some extent, academic courses with a specific focus on gender, class, and race, among others, have only been granted space within the academy as part of wider social struggles outside (as well as within) university space (although we concede that the university as often as not acts as a machine that captures and recuperates these "minor knowledges") (Thorburn, 2003). Indeed, as Shukaitis (2009) states, "anarchism . . . cannot find a home in such a space without betraying itself."

In the UK, as elsewhere, students and teachers are currently facing an all-out attack on whole sections of knowledge production and education, especially within the humanities and social sciences, which are deemed less important than subjects more explicitly tied to the generation of profit. It is therefore difficult to see much of a future for courses in the current university system whose subject matter is overtly "radical" or even "critical." The criticisms outlined above, and many more, have been leveled at the masters program in activism and social change, developed, and currently taught, within the Geography Department at the University of Leeds (UK).[4] The MA in Activism and Social Change (hereafter MAASC) was established in 2007 and is now in its fourth year. The FAQ for the MA states that the course "is not about a detached study of activism, activists, or social change. Rather, it aims to promote free and critical thinking about the challenges we face, how we can develop tactics and strategies and skills to respond to them, as well as creative alternatives to life under capitalism" (MAASC FAQ).

The program covers a range of topics from anarchist, Marxist, and ecological ideas to radical research methods such as Participatory Action Research and Militant Inquiry. At the end of the course students embark on an "action dissertation," connecting their training in progressive research methods and radical theory with their campaigning and activism. This aims to be a form of assessment, which is radically different to conventional dissertations.

Discussing the reasons he and Chatterton devised the course Hodkinson (2009) states, "We saw a real and urgent need for undergraduate and postgraduate courses that would reopen educational spaces for students to develop their own ideas and thinking *per se*, challenge the neoliberal direction of our own workplaces, and at the same time, create new learning opportunities for those who clearly wanted to take action to make the world a fairer and sustainable place to live in." Here we can see that the MAASC is identified as having a dual role, as a form of what bell hooks (1994) has described as "teaching to transgress," as well as comprising a part of the struggle against the further neoliberalization of higher education. Hodkinson (2009), again highlighting the link between resisting neoliberal reforms and the practice of teaching, states that "one of the main ways in which we can resist corporate takeover and the neoliberal agenda is through our teaching." He has conceded, however, that "there have, understandably, been plenty of criticisms from activist quarters of our decision to put on this particular Masters course," continuing that "a common reaction is that the very essence of an elite-level university degree in 'radical activism' is a contradiction in terms as universities are 'part of the problem' and the course will inevitably be exclusive to white middle class kids who will go on to become a 'professional elite' of 'career activists' and 'social movement managers'" (Hodkinson, 2009).

Academics, like those in any other profession, are challenged by the fact that they are involved in the reproduction of capital, regardless of the content of their lectures. However, as John Holloway (2005, p. 235) reflects in *Change the World Without Taking Power*, "[l]iving in capital means that we live in the midst of contradiction." Therefore, "in spite" (Holloway, 2005) of this, many academics have a long involvement in activism from stopping road building and airport expansion, to squatting and fighting gentrification (Chatterton, 2002; Maxey, 2004; Plows, 1998 and Wall, 1999). Academics are also involved in struggles closer to home, for example the Royal Geographical Societies sponsorship by Shell and academic complicity in the arms trade (Chatterton and Featherstone, 2007; Chatterton and Maxey, 2009; Gilbert, 2009).

The academics who established the MAASC, Paul Chatterton and Stuart Hodkinson, as well as others involved in the course, are themselves engaged in movements and struggles that are critical of capitalism and the state form. This work informs not only their research, but also their teaching on the MA. Chatterton, for example, worked with the Zapatistas before taking his lecturer's post at Leeds and has also been active in a variety of radical projects, from helping to establish an autonomous social center called The Common Place to being arrested for occupying a coal train as part of a struggle against the causes of climate change. He is also involved with a popular education collective called TRAPESE[5] and interested in using teaching as a way of generating critical and defiant subjects (Chatterton, 2008). Among other projects, Hodkinson is engaged in an ongoing campaign against the gentrification of Leeds's Kirkgate Market, is active in housing struggles, and was also involved in the establishment of The Common Place (Hodkinson and Chatterton, 2006; Hodkinson, 2010).

There has been a range of debates within radical academic literature on the relative merits of "scholar-activism" (Chatterton, 2008). There have also been many discussions—in and out of academia—around whether an academic's activism should take place inside or outside the academy, or whether this is a false binary (Castree, 2002). It is sometimes difficult for those outside of formal education to see education itself as a site of contestation and political struggle—especially because of the privileged position university education occupies in society. As we have illustrated, this course is viewed as part of the fight against neoliberal education, but it is also a site of struggle in and of itself. The first year the course was held, for example, the fees were lowered for asylum seekers (the course organizers were, however, quickly reprimanded by the university administration for doing so) (Hodkinson, 2009). We feel that the course name—masters in activism and social change—needlessly courts criticism. Using the term "activism" is highly contentious to many people, leading some to view the course as a form of "professionalization" of struggle. It is also a term that is very open to (mis)interpretation, raising many questions, including: "What forms of activism are actually represented on the course?" It fails to take into consideration many of the debates within movements about the role of activism and activists as being exclusionary and elitist, especially where activists themselves become a form of specialists in struggle (Andrew X, 1999).

Beyond the content of the course and some experimentation with alternative pedagogical practice, it is hard at times to discern how this course varies from other academic courses. Assessment, for example, takes fairly traditional forms for the most part (essays, reports, individual assessment, etc). There is more emphasis on seminar, discussion-based learning, rather than lectures, and the course aims at a participatory approach, but this is perhaps is not as radical as the scope of the course suggests. It also fails to fundamentally change the traditional relationship between student and teacher. Of course there are a variety of difficulties in running the course within the current neoliberal university and therefore its existence maintains a precarity which many courses face today. But this once again suggests the limitations of organizing and maintaining radical courses within the university system, as it exists today.

There have been, of course, many limitations that the university placed directly on the program. Hodkinson (2009) discusses how one senior manager told him and the other organizers of the course that the MA was "very controversial" and was being "closely watched in higher places." Nothing has come of these comments, and indeed the main threats to the course have come from the pressure for it to be "profitable" rather than because of ideological arguments around the course content or assessment. At the end of the day, to some extent, you can teach what you like within the neoliberal university, as long as people are paying enough for it!

So how does the MAASC "market" itself? In terms of future "employability," it aims its publicity fairly explicitly at the NGO sector, with supportive statements from organizations such as the World Development Movement (WDM) on its literature and websites. This would seem to confirm activist fears that the course contributes to the proliferation of "experts" in social change and professionalization of activism. Of course, we recognize that graduates may go on to a variety of other, unrelated jobs (or maybe more likely none at all) but in terms of those outside the academy looking in, this may further agitate those who are critical of NGOs and other "professional" activists.

It has, however, not been our experience over the four years that the course has been running that most students have decided to take the course simply as a stepping-stone to a job within an NGO or similar organization. Most seek an engaging and educational experience, in which they can learn new skills, uncover new literatures and partake in a participatory pedagogical experience where they can learn from others while sharing their own experiences. As expressed by a former student:

> In our opinion the MA should attempt to tackle a number of challenges. It should attempt to bring more activism into the academy by directly studying the academy as a major social institution and by seeking to engage students in the politics of that institution. Secondly, the MA must work to take itself outside the academy by organizing activities or forms of activity that can be utilized by all campaigners not just the ones privileged enough to afford the luxury of joining the course. In so doing the MA could help contribute to a culture of reflexive activism, that is critical and strategic thinking amongst radical social movements. (MAASC program participant, 2008–2009)

All this is what we feel education should be about, not merely the cynical "employability" so favored by today's education system—and certainly some people are attracted to the course because they seek something different from the status quo. However, one must be able to afford the fees with which to embark on this individual/collective learning adventure!

This leads us to the problem of institutions. The university as it currently exists, is clearly not an institution of our own making. When we work within it, as students and academics, we are grappling with it as a messy and contested space of, often contradictory, values and ethics. On the one hand the role of the university is (increasingly) about social reproduction: creating docile, debt-ridden workers for capital. On the other hand, the university is a potential space of community and commons (Harvie, 2004), a "crack in capitalism" (Holloway, 2010)—a place where students can discover radical ideas and develop critical thought, often engaging in their first forms of activism. Nonetheless, the university is becoming ever more "closed." The massive increase in fees, in both the UK and United States, is leading to a staggering amount of graduate debt. A recent survey shows that graduates from the "Class of 2010" in UK universities expect to owe an average of £17,900, up from an average of £11,600 in 2008 (High Fliers Research Limited, 2010). Therefore is it possible that this course is just perpetuating the elitism and privilege of university education? Once again, the spiraling costs of gaining a university education exacerbate this dilemma. Debt, in this case student debt, acts as a disciplining mechanism. The actions one takes and opportunities open to us are affected by the debts we have.

In our examination of the MAASC, we hope to highlight some of the opportunities, challenges, and questions raised by attempts to open up spaces for radical pedagogy within a neoliberal educational institution—in this case the university. Ultimately we are left with more questions—How can the course remain in the university without becoming *Institutionalized* or simply a mechanism for capitalistic production? Are efforts at placing radicalism as the object of academic inquiry useful and necessary within a larger context of struggle against neoliberal capitalism? To perhaps shine some light on these questions by virtue of comparison, we now turn to a project where radicalism takes the form of teaching and research.

## Student as Producer Project

At the University of Lincoln a project called "student as producer" has been launched.[6] The initiative aims to make a break with the logic, increasingly taking ground within Higher Education, which positions students as consumers. Instead, the goal of the "student as producer" model is to place the student, not as the passive recipient of knowledge transmitted though the "teacher" but as an active participant. The project recognizes students' capacity to take part in a process of research activity that produces knowledge while engaging the participants in an active process of learning. As the project states, "The Student as Producer project develops this connection by re-engineering the relationship between research and teaching. This involves a reappraisal of the relationship between academics and students, with students becoming part of the academic project of universities rather than consumers of knowledge" (Student as Producer Project Proposal: http://studentasproducer.lincoln.ac.uk/project-proposal/).

The concept of "Student as Producer" is informed by the work of Walter Benjamin (1934), in particular his lecture, "Author as Producer," which focused on the question of how radical intellectuals intervene in moments of crisis. Another intellectual who had a significant impact on the idea of Student as Producer is Lev Vygotsky who suggested that the teacher must arrange the social context so that the students teach themselves (Neary, 2010a). The instance of its practice at the University of Lincoln is the result of a £200,000 grant from the Higher Education Academy (through the National Teaching Fellowship Project Scheme 2010–2013) to initiate a three-year project that aims to transform teaching across the entire undergraduate curriculum. The project will mean that all teaching across the entire undergraduate curriculum is based on research, or research-like activity (Neary and Winn, 2009). This may include collaborations between students and academics, students writing journal articles or some other form of research-based knowledge production.

In contrast to the MA in Activism and Social Change discussed earlier, the subject of study is not specifically "radical," but the *form* of pedagogical approach looks to be both radical and wide-ranging in its reach. Rather than radicalism being isolated to a handful of courses where the object of study is radical ideas and movements, this project attempts to challenge the instrumentalization of education across the entire curriculum, with a radically different form of teaching approach. As Mike Neary (2010a) from the University of Lincoln states, "A key issue for Student as Producer is that social learning is more than the individual learning in a social context, and includes the way in which the social context itself is transformed through progressive pedagogic practice."

It is too early to evaluate this project in practice, but we look forward to discovering more about its development and impact. The extent to which the transformation of the pedagogical experience this project entails will in turn transform the university may prove interesting—as will its potential impact on other institutions of learning. We are also curious to see to what extent this form of learning could spread to other institutions. There are of course risks associated with this project, ranging from academics exploiting students for research work, to recuperation. Mike Neary (2010b) has already attempted a form of autocritique, titled the "Pedagogy of Excess," and acknowledges these risks.

In this section we have focused on projects almost entirely bounded within the university as it is, despite some radical differences to the way we may experience the subjects and styles of the pedagogical approach of many courses and institutions. In the next section we look at experimental educational projects on the "outside" of the universities walls, which often intentionally posit themselves against traditional hierarchical educational institutions.

## Outside the Academy

Below we focus mainly on the proliferation of anarchist(ic) Free Skools both in the UK and the United States as well as the "Free University" projects that are scattered across Europe.

### *From Free Skools...*

There is a long history of autonomous alternative education efforts. By abandoning or rejecting the normative educational system, people have sought to organize new spaces for the exchange of ideas and skills. Free skools,[7] the anarchist manifestation of this trend, are based on principles of horizontality, autonomy, self-reliance, equality, and collective organizing. These skools create educational opportunities and encourage skill-sharing in their communities while functioning outside the market economy, in favor of a gift economy. Ardently student-centered, many of these skools call into question the traditional dichotomy between "student" and "teacher." Held in autonomous social centers, church basements or other public spaces, they seek to maintain openness and a lack of entrance requirements.

Free skools have their roots in the anarchist Escuela Moderna (Modern School) of Spain, established in the early twentieth century. This period of history was a zenith of libertarian schools and pedagogical projects—the best known of which was Francisco Ferrer's Escuela Moderna, where classes were guided by "the principle of solidarity and equity" (Bookchin, 1998, p. 117).

Popular education projects were also a major characteristic of 1960s and '70s, including the establishment of the University of Paris VIII–Vicennes in 1969. An "Experimental University Center," *Pedagogy of the Oppressed*, written by the Brazilian educator Paulo Freire in 1970 also proposed a new relationship between teacher, student, and society, and advocated for a "mutual approach" to critical pedagogy. Freire recognized "schools as a possible source/site of human emancipation and resistance" (Kahn, 2009, p. 125). The works of Paul Goodman were also popular during the 1960s and '70s and attempted to draw links between a bureaucratic and centralized society and the form of "miseducation" this resulted in, instead proposing decentralized and flexible alternatives (Goodman, 1966).

With a more explicit anarchistic political and pedagogical vision, Ivan Illich, on the other hand, argued that people have always possessed knowledge without curricula. Illich's "tools for conviviality" promoted "autonomous and creative intercourse among persons, and the intercourse of persons with their environment"—in opposition to "industrial productivity" (Illich, 1973, p. 27). Through this idea of conviviality, "Illich proposed positive norms to critique existing systems and construct sustainable options using values such as 'survival, justice, and self-defined work'" (Kahn 2009, p. 130).

The recent expression of the "free skool" is based on a community-oriented, anticapitalist, loosely structured education model. Free skools, such as the Free Skool Santa Cruz in California, often see themselves as "a direct challenge to dominant institutions and hierarchical relationships" (Free Skool Santa Cruz website, "About Free School Santa Cruz"). They consider part of their prefigurative project to be "resistance to the old [world], to the relentless commodification of everything, including learning and the way we relate to each other" (Free Skool Santa Cruz website). Free skools strive to blur the lines between teacher and student. Many of these volunteer-run and community-supported projects are decentralized, holding classes in social centers, parks, and other public or reclaimed spaces. These spaces are generally, at least attempting, to be open and inclusive, whereas university space is more often than not, increasingly corporatized, closed, and elitist.

Shantz describes a form of "constructive anarchy," or "projects that provide examples of politics grounded in everyday resistance"—which includes free skools (Shantz, 2010, p. 1). This can be viewed as the affirmative, prefigurative side of anarchist(ic) movements, which are too often described as simply reactionary or "negative" manifestations *against* the existent state of affairs. Many anarchist free skool organizers and participants consider education to be a political act—"expanding and deepening their knowledge of themselves and the world around them, sharing skills and providing an opportunity for community members at large to come together and explore alternatives" to a capitalist society (Shantz, 2010, p. 14). Free skools can act as important centers for community resources and sites for organizing struggle. In many ways, these free skools provide "infrastructures of dissent" by serving as repositories for knowledge and resources, which help to sustain mobilization and dissent (Shantz, 2010, p. 3).

However, free skools as skill-shares and resource centers for movements can be perceived as instrumentalist in terms of political action. This might explain the tendency toward sharing "

skills" rather than ideas. Perhaps in the blanket rejection of all institutions, these infrastructures of dissent hold up political action but fail to reimagine it and potentially create something new.

On the other hand, anarchist(ic) free skools as prefigurative politics have the potential to create alternative educational "institutions." Colin Ward suggests that anarchism, "far from being a speculative vision of a future society . . . is a description of a mode of human organization, rooted in the experience of everyday life, which operates side by side with, and in spite of, the dominant authoritarian trends of our society" (Ward 1973, p. 11). The Free Skool in Nottingham, UK, for example, purposefully sets itself outside of traditional education institutions, holding their classes in the local social center (see Motta, Chapter 7). However, in 2010 they decided to change the structure from a "skill-share" with a given "expert" or teacher, to a more horizontal model, focusing on general topic areas with no student-teacher dichotomy. When we spoke with some of the organizers after the Free Skool had finished, they described the difficulty of breaking out of a typical activist skill-share. People did not seem to want to come to a class to discuss "radical education" but were interested in learning specific skills, like bike maintenance. Again, there seems to be a distinction between content and form—the topics of a free skool may be radical or support a certain kind of lifestyle but the pedagogical methodology is more traditional.

### *. . . To Free Universities*

Related, but distinct from anarchist Free Skool projects are the "Free University" projects that exist across areas of Europe. These are not necessarily intended to reconstruct or replace the traditional university system but to, "establish additional means of exploring different organizational dynamics and developing new tactics, both for resistance and, more importantly, for our own creative processes by which we might constitute alternatives" (Kanngieser, 2007, p. 2). Within the current education crisis these "micro-level self-organized autonomous or free universities and classes" have been argued to help movements to, "experiment more militantly with molecular resistance activities, those that we can easily facilitate and maintain ourselves to transform the relationships between knowledge, education and capitalism" (Kanngieser, 2007, pp. 2–3).

Many experimental initiatives have been organized by student collectives—such as Meine Akademie (My Academy), the Free University of Los Angeles, the Manoa Free University in Vienna, the Copenhagen Free University, and the University of Openness in London—and have constructed "autonomous platforms dedicated to creative DIY methodologies for students and the wider public" (Kanngieser, 2007, p. 3). As Kanngieser (2007, p. 4) discusses in her paper, "Its Our Academy: Transforming Education through Self-organized Autonomous Universities," many of these initiatives are predominantly organized by current students or recent graduate activists who have an "ambivalent relationship" to the traditional university and "maintain a focus on process over terminus." For example, the University of Openness in London, is a "user led facility of learning and research with many temporary physical campuses . . . and many online presences."[8]

These free universities do not seek to be a sanctioned replacement to the normative degree-generating university, but rather an anticapitalist alternative. Instead, these projects are ways in which to neutralize the mechanisms of what some commentators see as the university-as-factory—"by denying the capitalistic endgame of the stratification of specialisation and intellectual labour" (Kanngieser, 2007, p. 5), it is suggested that the free university can create radical heterotopic spaces, "simultaneously virtual, imaginary and actual, in which to conceive, discuss and implement different modalities of knowledge" (Foucault, 1986).

However, like free skools, free universities raise the issue of voluntarism. The time and effort it takes to organize these projects limits participation for many people. The current economic and education crises exacerbates this as more students, and recent graduates, are taking on paid work to pay off their education debts. This illustrates the truism that debt is disciplinary, acting as an obstacle to participation in struggles and alternative experiments (à la "dole autonomy") (*Aufheben*, 1999). Another issue raised by these "outside" educational projects is whether they have the potential to aid the development of forms of counterpower—and whether they are fulfilling that potential—especially existing within our current capitalist society. In *After the Fall* (2010), it is suggested that, "A free university in the midst of a capitalist society is like a reading room in a prison; it serves online as a distraction from the misery of daily life."

In the next section we will turn our attention to a project we have been heavily involved with, the "Really Open University" (ROU). The ROU is, perhaps, more of an activist-orientated group than some of the Free Universities discussed above. The ROU has been agitating around a multitude of issues relating to the university, but most prominently cuts to public education and increased tuition fees. The Really Open University has also experimented with forms of Free Skools, but is not an ongoing Free Skool or Free University project like many of those mentioned above.

The ROU's most recent Free Skool project, "Reimagine the University," asks how we could transform the university, "how could students and lecturers learn differently through more creative, critical and empowering processes, is it even possible to transform the university, or do we need to create an entirely different system?"[9] As such it is attempting to experiment with a free skool transgressing the exclusionary space of the university.

## On the Periphery of the Academy

In this section we wish to look at experiments in opening radical educational spaces on the periphery of the academy. We will focus mainly on the project we helped to organize and maintain—the Really Open University (ROU)[10].

As we discussed in our introduction to this chapter, universities, as well as other educational institutions, all around the globe are facing economic instability, debt, and an uncertain future. Instead of demanding a "bailout" for education, university administrators are imposing budget cuts and austerity measures—except on capital investment projects including campus beautification and new buildings (Bousquet, 2010, p. 78). Facing an uncertain future and further alienation from educational institutions, which are increasingly "perceived to be mercenary and bureaucratic that, in the bargain, produces a commodity subject to rapid devaluation," students and education workers throughout the world are questioning and challenging the current economic model, which prioritizes profits over people, and claims that cuts in education and across the whole of society are inevitable and necessary (Caffentzis, 2010).

At the University of Leeds, the Vice Chancellor Michael Arthur announced £35 million of cuts as part of an "economies exercise" (University of Leeds, 2010). In a record ballot the university lecturers union (University College Union, UCU), voted in favor of strike action and action short of a strike (February 3, 2010). During the period in which the UCU was balloting its members, the Leeds University Student Union (LUU) started an antistrike campaign, erroneously called "Education First." This campaign urged UCU members to "vote NO to strikes" (LUU's "Education First"), and a large banner with this message was unfurled over the main entrance to the Student Union building. Furthermore, using the LUU website, students were encouraged to send generic e-mails to their lecturers, which urged them not to strike due to the alleged detrimental effects it would have on their education.

Faced with massive cuts at the University of Leeds and the antiunion response of the LUU, several students, education workers, and activists outside the university came together to discuss resistance to the cuts in education and to subsequently form the "Really Open University" (ROU) in January 2010.[11] However, in addition to rejecting the proposed cuts, the ROU also stated its opposition to the broader education crisis and emphasized the opportunity the strikes provided for students to seize control of their own education and to use the crisis as a way to open up cracks for other narratives and radical pedagogical alternatives to emerge.

The ROU linked the cuts to the general economic crisis and discussed, as both written and shouted by students in California, that it is actually *we* who are the crisis (After the Fall, 2010). The ROU's critique, therefore, was not simply one of cuts to education, but of hierarchical and exclusionary educational institutions in general, and the destructive organizing system of capitalism that accompanies them. The vice chancellor of the University of Leeds, Michael Arthur, had pronounced that he did not want Leeds to become "a battleground for the future of higher education in the UK," and the ROU responded that it is "not a battleground over education but against an economic system that puts profit before people" (Morgan, 2010).

Similar to other recent student movements, such as the "Anomalous Wave" movement in Italy, the ROU did not want to defend the university as it was, but to reform or recreate the university ("*autoriforma*," or "self-reform") (The Anomalous Wave, 2008; ROU, 2010a). In addition to forming a space for resistance, the ROU featured a call for a new model of university based on principles of "self-managed" knowledge production. The ROU adopted the refrain of "strike, occupy, transform," which it hoped to represent the transformative politics of affirmation that offers the hope of creating open and nonhierarchical institutions of research and learning, based on what has long been anarchist principle of creating and supporting prefigurative examples in the here and now. The ROU continues to seek to occupy this transformative space on the edge of the academy, which can perhaps provide a place for the merging of critical pedagogy with anarchist theory—prefigurative education (DeLeon, 2006).

We can also relate this to the idea of "mass intellectuality" developed within the post-*Operaismo* tradition (Lazzarato, 2006). Mass Intellectuality does not refer to a specific group, such as academics, nor is it spatially bound (i.e., in the academy), but is a term that describes the collective intelligence that expands across the whole of society. It recognizes that intellectuality does not develop from individuals, but from social-knowledge and cooperation. The result of this cooperation is the knowledge commons. ROU believes that we need to free the knowledge that has been enclosed within certain specialist spaces and gateways (such as the academy) and connect it with the flows of knowledge that are already, and increasingly, existent throughout post-Fordist society. As such, this is both a rejection of the traditional liberal project of the public university and the neoliberal academy—as the University of Utopia (2010) put it, "not mass education or education for the masses but mass intellectuality."

### *Strike: v. 1. To Withdraw Our Labor and Fill That Time with Other Forms of Doing*

To strike is essentially to withdraw one's labor, but it is *also* to fill one's time with other forms of "doing." Instead of the doing of labor, of capitalist exploitation, there is the doing of the picket line, or ideally of new connectivities between different parts of the worker force, other parts of the class, strike supporters, passers-by, etc. (Holloway, 2010). The *Inoperative Committee* (2009, p. 7) states that "to strike is to attack the function of a space and to suspend the rhythm of its time in a determination [*sic*] location." It is this suspension of the capitalist clock and its disciplinary regime (Thompson, 1993) that makes space for the connections and "other forms of doing," this is the self-valorizing aspect of the strike. However, it is increasingly absent.

The strike as a tactic within the UK has become very domesticated, especially since the raft of anti-trade union legislation passed under Thatcher's Conservative government. Laws about whom and how many pickets can be on a picket line and what those pickets can do, alongside the reformism of trade union bureaucracy mean that it is increasingly difficult for the strike to be anything other than a purely symbolic affair in many cases. This is especially the case with one-day strikes, where it is difficult for these connections, relationships, and other forms of doing to occur. All too often the strike and the picket line can take the form of what Foucault describes as the "sad militancy," characterized by a politics of lack, joylessness, and self-sacrifice, also criticized by Vaneigem (1983).

As discussed above, the ROU emerged in the midst of a struggle to resist cuts in education and therefore supported not only strike action by university lecturers and staff, but also workers' struggles in general.[12] The ROU planned and organized actions around the proposed strike at the University of Leeds as a way not only to support the striking lecturers, but also to critique neoliberal institutions. Importantly, the ROU attempted to come up with creative ways to transform the picket line from a few dozen pickets standing in the cold to something more vibrant. These ideas included having music and hot food present, a cheerleading troupe and games which used the campus space in reimagined ways. The ROU also published and distributed a series of newsletters called *The Sausage Factory*,[13] which sought to reveal the underlying crisis of education as well as rally support for the strikes on Leeds campus as well as throughout those taking place locally and around the world.

*Occupy: v 1. To Fill Up (time or space)*

In response to the LUU's Education First campaign and their continued attempts to undermine student resistance to the cuts, the ROU created a spoof union website[14] as well as a series of stickers encouraging support for strike action while also rearticulating the role of the student union. The ROU wanted to critique not only the LUU leadership, but also how institutions like student unions often give the impression of student participation, when they are used by university administration as a mechanism of control.

The website not only parodies the consumerism and institutionalized nature of the LUU, but also lays bare the labor practices of the university and role of the student as consumer (rather than the model of student as producer discussed earlier). In place of the apolitical volunteerism of the LUU, the ROU student union spoof site serves as a directory for other websites and information related to the struggle at the University of Leeds, as well as to the broader education and economic crises. As such it is a form of virtual occupation of the LUU aesthetic, part parody and part indicator of other possibilities.

When the strikes at the University of Leeds were called off at the last minute, the ROU continued to call for action in recognition that while strikes are important, they are normally only used as a defensive tool. The ROU highlighted that at the heart of struggle was not a return to the status quo, but a need to unravel and transform the existing university, seeing crisis as *possibility*. Part of this reclamation of the university was an opening up and redefinition of the physical space of campus. Therefore, in collaboration with *Leeds Urban Playground*—a local group that coordinated citywide games—the ROU organized a game of Capture the Flag on campus to make use of the space of the university in a reimagined way.

Participants in the ROU were—and are—interested in exploring the political importance of the idea of seizing space and using it for creative ends. The ROU organized a public discussion called the "Logic of Occupation" at the Common Place—a social center in Leeds—to discuss the recent resurgence of the use of occupation as a tool within workplace, community and university struggles—and more broadly the potential of occupations for opening up spaces for both resistive *and* affirmative politics (ROU, 2010b). This workshop was adapted and repeated in November 2010 and held in an occupied university building. This occupation was established after a several-thousand-strong march, organized as part of the escalating days of action against increased fees, culminated in around seven hundred people dancing to a bicycle-powered sound-system in what would normally have been a lecture theatre.

*Transform: "v 1. To Alter or Be Altered Radically in Form, Function, etc."*

After the strikes had been called off, the ROU held its public launch on March 2, 2010. Over fifty students, staff and members of the larger community came together to discuss, "What Is a Really Open University?" The ROU facilitated a creative, resistive space in which to have a participatory dialogue to spark a critical, reflective process about what education means and what a really open university would look like—as opposed to the neoliberal university. Through this "visioning" process, the group developed several vision statements about what an alternative to current educational system would look like. These seven statements provided a point of departure for the creation of a Really Open University. The decision was made to keep all the visioning statements that had been formulated during the meeting—rather than trying to force them into a single statement.[15]

One of the interesting things to come out of this process was that, despite the emphasis on process rather than concrete decisions or consensus, there was actually a remarkable agreement between participants and the vision statements they created. Not only did many of the statements hold themes *in common*, but the process of producing them engaged the participants in a process of "*commoning*." Commoning is the "doing" of the common(s), a verb rather than a noun, a process rather than a static resource or product (Linebaugh, 2010). The process of commoning produces new subjectivities and the generation of what Massimo De Angelis (2006) calls "other values." This emphasis on prefigurative process has been discussed as an important element of the alter globalization movement (Maeckelbergh, 2009), and we can see this influence developing within aspects of edu-struggles.

A fortnight later the ROU held another meeting, which was focused on the implementation of the alternative visions formulated in the previous meeting. This participatory process ultimately led to the creation of working groups based on the basic elements identified as necessary to make the Really Open University. The goal was to work toward manifesting a Really Open University in Leeds. Unfortunately this initially failed to get off the ground, in part because of the limitations of the student calendar, based around term time, residency in the city, etc.

However, these meetings were the groundwork for a three-day event called "Reimagine the University." This event coincided with a National Day of Action comprising of a walkout and call for direct action, which fell hot on the heels of a national anti education cuts demonstration in early November that attracted around fifty thousand people—over double what the organizers (NUS and UCU) had expected. Several thousand people broke away from the main march in London and occupied the Conservative Party headquarters at Millbank. The few police present were completely overwhelmed, and several windows were smashed, graffiti daubed, and protestors on the roof flew red and black flags.

This event effectively marked the development of a wave of student resistance that is ongoing as we write. The Reimagine the University event was timed perfectly to engage with this, as the first of the three days of activities coincided with a walkout and massive demonstration in Leeds that resulted in the occupation of one of the University of Leeds buildings. The result was a perfect mix of political antagonism, the "No!" (Holloway, 2005) to cuts and fee increases, and the affirmation and reimagination of the university in the form of workshops and discussions on topics ranging from radical pedagogies to direct action training.[16] The occupation meant that some of the events could be held in the occupied space on campus, while others were in reserve rooms across the university. Participants included students and academics from Leeds and a host of other cities, as well as a few nonstudents.

## The Risks of Living on the Edge

We have observed a number of tensions and obstacles in our experiences with the ROU. As already discussed, the ROU was initiated by a small group of students and nonstudents and the group's intention was to exist on the *edge* of the university. However, ultimately most of the nonstudents were deterred from further participation by the increasingly student-centric nature—and therefore insularity—of the group.

We think the ROU tries to occupy a precarious "cramped" space and is therefore pulled both inside/outside at times (Deleuze & Guattari, 1987). The university acts as an "apparatus of capture" (Deleuze & Guattari, 2004) that is constantly trying to reterritorialize the ROU within the realm of "student politics," or education struggles as merely the concern of a relatively privileged sector of workers. Fortunately, the explosion of anger that has recently erupted in the UK, which has included a large number of nonuniversity student, as well as university students, has to some extent helped push beyond these boundaries. Many people—inside and outside the university—seem to be taking great strength from the size and energy of the education struggles.

What makes the ROU different from other radical educational experiments is that it attempts (in theory at least) to maintain a productive tension—a dialectical relationship—between "inside" and "outside," as well as process and action. While we believe these tensions provide a unique opportunity to connect resources, struggles, and ideas, they also lead to challenges and its precarious position. There is a constant uncertainty in the periphery, which is partly due to the endemic mistrust between those inside the academy, and those outside.

In general the university does not like outsiders coming in. It either categorizes them as intellectually inferior or attempts to cite all sorts of bureaucracy (risk assessments, health and safety regulations, etc.) in order to practically maintain the campus as a territorial "bubble" or border (Counter/Mapping QMary, 2010). The insular nature of the university and student life is a barrier (or border) to many students (and faculty) thinking outside of their own university campus. Several of the Undergraduate students at the University of Leeds who are involved in the ROU, claim not to know any nonstudents.

From the perspective of those outside the university, there is a large degree of resentment and hostility toward students themselves and "student politics" in general. Many of our non-university-based friends and comrades who had been active in all manner of campaigns and anarchist-related politics for years seemed totally taken aback by the explosion of anger at the recent DEMOlition march and occupation of the Conservative Party headquarters in London.

Another tension that the ROU struggles with, is whether to defend or destroy the existing university institution—especially as these institutions are increasingly facing serious funding cuts. There was some tension within the ROU about how to confront and fight these cuts without affirming the current university system. The ROU struggled to find transformative spaces, or a creative ground between "defend" and "destroy."

This parallels debates taking place within the U.S. "occupations movement," which have become heated at times. There is a risk of self-marginalizing "ultraism" within this dialogue, which falls into a perhaps attractive (to some) militant rhetoric but fails to resonate, and, as George Caffentzis (2010) states, "what is certain is that this is a major challenge the movement must overcome in order to increase its power and its capacity to connect with other struggles." We feel that in the midst of the edu-crisis there is a possibility to develop new, open, and ephemeral forms of institution that experiment with radical forms pedagogy, based on entirely different values to those of the current educational system.

## How Do We Build the Really Open University?

So, how do we build this new kind of open and ephemeral institution? We think it is important to open up spaces in which we can both experiment with, and critically reflect upon, radical pedagogical practices. The crisis of the university is a crisis that throws up new openings and possibilities for what a university could be. These spaces can work toward pushing the boundaries of the academy by concretely asking, "what can a university do?" in praxis.

We need to engage in a discussion about how we can go forward as critical-radical researchers inside, outside and on the periphery of the academy. Is there any place for us within the institution as it is? Or as Stefano Harney and Fred Moten (2004) suggest, is the "only possible with the relationship to the university today . . . a criminal one"? This opens up the question/possibility of what Virno terms "exodus," but which might also be described as "desertion." This is not a territorial exodus, or a fleeing from, but rather a desertion of one's assigned role, in this case of the "critical" yet docile body (Foucault, 2004) of the academic. As Harney and Moten (2004) put it, "to be in but not of is the path of the subversive intellectual in the modern university."

In part, the Really Open University is an experiment in just this. The creation of spaces in which we can begin to interrogate the role of the university and of the academic, not just as theoretical exercise, but within an implicitly antagonistic, yet not wholly reactive, space of political engagement. This is a messy space that avoids any pure politics, or identitarian overcoding, neither overtly anarchist, nor Marxist, nor simply an "anticuts" group, yet neither a purely utopian reimagining.

This is necessarily a "cramped space," of (im)possibility, as Deleuze (2005) states, "creation takes place in bottlenecks." Many elements of the edu-struggle will ultimately want to close down the categories again, in order to give more weight to their ideological underpinnings, trying to make the moment fit their politics, rather than seizing the moment in all its wealth of potentiality. The ROU views 'crisis as possibility' arguing that it is "up to us to decide [the universities] future."[17]

But through what concrete actions might we actually develop a "really open university"? One way to begin may be through the occupation of the spaces where we work, play and consume, and the reappropriation of this time and space for our own (common) ends. This may help to promote new lines of questioning and open up new connectivities.

One way to discuss this occupation and reappropriation, might be the literal forced reclamation of space, though direct action. This has, of course, been a tried and tested method across history, and we have seen the tactic of occupation has begun to some extent become popular again, with the recent occupations at universities across the UK, but to a much larger extent across Europe and the United States.

We think there is an interesting dynamic, however, between *defensive* and *offensive* uses of occupation. We do not wish to set up a binary, but rather are interested in the qualitative shifts and activities that can occur within the occupied space *itself*, rather than simply the obstructive element of occupation. This problematic has been explored in the U.S. occupations movement through the often heated debate about the utility of political demands, versus occupation without demands. For example, "Occupation mandates the inversion of the standard dimensions of space. Space in an occupation is not merely the container of our bodies, it is a plane of potentiality that has been frozen by the logic of the commodity" (Inoperative Committee, 2009).

Another way to discuss the occupation and reappropriation of time and space might be through the creation of new spaces that prefigure the new forms we may wish a reimagined university to take. A concrete example of this is the model of the autonomous social center, or "infoshop," found within anarchist and autonomous activist practices (Atton, 1999).

Social centers are place-based, self-managed spaces. They can be squatted, rented or cooperatively owned (Pusey, 2010). A particularly rich history of social centers can be found in Italy, but they exist all across Europe. In the United States the closest approximation to the autonomous social centers seems to be the network of radical bookstores and "infoshops" such as Red Emma's in Baltimore and Bluestockings in New York City (Kanuga, 2010).

Some academics at the University of Lincoln are attempting to develop a cooperatively run "social science center" that utilizes a social center type autonomous space, where they can practice radical pedagogical methods (Winn, 2010). The idea is that students will be able to enroll for free and staff will still be paid. We can imagine, based on our experiences and research within social centers in the UK, that this would be controversial within anarchist circles, both for its relationship with the institution of the university, and also because of its payment of academic staff. Payment for some roles performed within some spaces has been a source of much debate and contention within social centers within the UK (Chatterton, 2008). These spaces generally rely on the good will and free time of volunteers. However, many spaces cite burnout and lack of participation as major issues within social centers (UK Social Centres Network, 2008). The "dole autonomy" (*Aufheben*, 1999), which helped facilitate earlier cycles of struggle, has been very much weakened with successive government attacks on the welfare state, and students increasingly forced to take employment while studying means that there are far fewer people around with the "free time" to help enable projects such as these.

It is, perhaps, through the establishment of self-organized alternative educational practices, and open and ephemeral institutions that we can start to value ideas for their own merit, rather than capitalist value—to create spaces and places where we can discard the price tags of commodified knowledge and instrumental learning, and instead appreciate the value of ideas and concepts themselves, while rediscovering the subversiveness of teaching.

## Conclusion: What's Next, or Where Do We Go from Here?

We started this chapter discussing initiatives inside the academy, from a course about radical social activism, to attempts to transform the position of students from one of consumer to producer. We then looked at experiments attempting to operate outside the economy, including anarchistic free skools and free university projects. These efforts attempt to translocate educational practices and skill-sharing outside of the institutions with which we traditionally associate them, into spaces such as self-managed social centers, community spaces, and other more public arenas. We have discussed our experiences engaging with the Really Open University (ROU) project at some length, including the group's attempts to navigate a precarious space on the periphery, operating both inside and outside the academy. The ROU, as a critical education activist group, continues reflectively to engage in the edu-struggles, which have been unfolding as we write this chapter, as well as to experiment in developing a praxis-based radical pedagogy.

The experiments inside university space risk cooptation and the reproduction of an elitist and exclusionary education system. The Free Skool and Free University projects can potentially run the risk of irrelevance outside of a small milieu, or disappear due to the voluntaristic nature of the endeavors. The ROU is attempting to occupy a position that is inherently precarious and could easily become drawn into being solely a university-based student group, or in its attempts to inject an irreverent creative-resistive practice, either be overcome by those who wish to continue "protest as usual" or stagnate and fail to reinvent itself, or just become an irreverent irrelevancy! But with all possibilities come risks, and this is especially the case with prospects for wide-ranging transformation.

The Really Open University byline, strike/occupy/transform, reflects a praxis of direct action—directly making the changes we would like to see. We see this as one of the most empowering and participatory ways of engaging in politics. Participants in the ROU have attempted to engage in creative-resistive tactics that reclaim space and put it to work for different ends, utilizing, for example, flashmobs, collective urban games such as "capture the flag" and participatory public assemblies. Through this process activists with the ROU hope to start an engaging, participatory process that transforms subjectivities. As the ROU states, "We wish to engage in affirmative and positive struggle, living life in different ways, even if it is only for a short time. To this end the ROU will be a series of interventions, into different ways of living."[18]

We are sure that if the current cycle of struggles around education is to continue, deepen, widen, and join up with other struggles, then the need for groups to creatively reimagine the present, so as to control the future, is essential.

## Notes

1 While we have set up an inside/outside binary for the purposes of exploring radical education experiments in this chapter, we recognize that this is a simplification, and as stated in *After the Fall (2010)*, "there is no 'outside' to the university."

2 Andre Pusey is a PhD candidate in the School of Geography (University of Leeds) and assists with some teaching on the MAASC course. Elsa Noterman studied part-time and assisted with the course for a year, before returning the United States.
3 "Home students" include students from the United Kingdom as well as those from EU countries.
4 See more about the MA at: http://www.geog.leeds.ac.uk/study/masters/courses/maasc
5 See more about TRAPESE at: http://trapese.clearerchannel.org/
6 See the following for more information: http://studentasproducer.lincoln.ac.uk
7 The word "skool" is used to distinguish these experiments in radical pedagogy from traditional learning institutions (schools).
8 University of Openness, http://uo.twenteenthcentury.com/
9 See: http://www.reimaginetheuniversity.org.uk.
10 See http://www.reallyopenuniversity.org.uk.
11 In addition to ROU, Leeds University Against Cuts (LUAC) was also formed at this time on the University of Leeds campus.
12 Specifically, at the time the ROU started, the refuse and postal workers were on strike in Leeds.
13 See: http://reallyopenuniversity.wordpress.com/sausage-factory/
14 See: http://www.reallyopenunion.org
15 To read the visioning statements, visit: http://www.reallyopenuniversity.org.
16 The full list of workshops can be found at http://www.reimaginetheuniversity.org.uk
17 http://reallyopenuniversity.wordpress.com/3-alternative-reforms/
18 From older version of "What is ROU," no longer accessible online. In authors' possession.

## References

After the fall: Communiqués from occupied California. (2010). Retrieved from http://afterthefallcommuniques.info/.

Andrew X. (1999). Give up activism. In *Do or Die,* 9, 160–66.

Anomalous Wave. (2008). *The Anomalous Wave so far: The education rebellion in Italy October–November 2008.* London: 56a Infoshop.

Atton, C. (1999). The infoshop: The alternative information centre of the 1990s. *New Library World, 100*(1).

*Aufheben*, #08 (1999). Dole autonomy versus the re-imposition of work: Analysis of the current tendency to workfare in the UK. August 1999. Retrieved from http://libcom.org/library/dole-autonomy-aufheben.

Benjamin, W. (1934). Lecture, "Author as producer" in Paris, 1934. See: The author as producer. *New Left Review* 1/62, July–August 1970.

Bookchin, M. (1998). Chapter 7: Anarchosydicalism, the new ferment. In M. Bookchin. *The Spanish anarchists: The heroic years, 1868–1936.* San Francisco: AK Press.

Bousquet, M. (2010). After cultural capitalism. *Edu-Factory, 78.*

Browne, J. (2010). Report: *Securing a sustainable future for higher education: An independent review of higher education funding and student finance in England,* October 12, 2010. Retrieved from www.independent.gov.uk/browne-report.

Caffentzis, G. (2010). University struggles at the end of the Edu-Deal. In *Mute*, 2010. Retrieved from http://www.metamute.org/en/content/university_struggles_at_the_end_of_the_edu_deal.
Castree, N. (2002). Border geography. *Area, 43*(1), 103–12.
Chatterton, P. (2002). Squatting is still legal, necessary and free. A brief intervention in the corporate city. *Antipode, 34*(1), 1–7.
Chatterton, P. (2008a). Using geography to teach freedom and defiance: Lessons in social change from "autonomous geographies." *Journal of Geography in Higher Education, 32*(3), 419–40.
Chatterton, P. (2008b). Becoming a public scholar: Academia and activism. *Antipode, 40*(3), 421–28.
Chatterton, P. (2008c). Autonomous spaces and social centres. *Shift*, 7–11.
Chatterton, P. & Featherstone, D. (2007). Editorial. Intervention: Elsevier, critical geography and the arms trade. *Political Geography, 26*, 3–7.
Chatterton, P. & Maxey, L. (2009). Introduction: Whatever happened to ethics and responsibility in geography? *ACME, 8*(2), 1–11.
Copenhagen Free University. Retrieved from http://www.copenhagenfreeuniversity.dk/.
Counter/Mapping QMary (2010). The university and border technologies. Queen Mary University. Retrieved from http://countermappingqmary.blogspot.com/2010/05/countermapping-qmary.html.
De Angelis, M. (2006). *The beginning of history: Value struggle and global capital*. London: Pluto.
DeLeon, A. (2006). The time for action is now! Anarchist theory, critical pedagogy, and radical possibilities. *The Journal for Critical Education Policy Studies, 4*(2).
Deleuze, G. (1995). *Negotiations: 1972–1990*. New York: Columbia University Press.
Deleuze, G. & Guattari, F. (1987). *Kafka toward a minor literature*. Minneapolis: University of Minnesota Press.
Deleuze, G. & Guattari, F. (2004). *A thousand plateaus*. London/New York: Continuum.
Foucault, M. (1986). Of other spaces. (J. Miskowiec, Trans.). *Diacritics, 16*(1), 22–27.
Foucault, M. (2004). Preface. In Deleuze, G. & Guattari, F. *Anti-Oedipus*. New York: Continuum.
Free School Santa Cruz. Retrieved from http://santacruztest.freeskool.org/content/about-free-skool-santa-cruz
Free University of Los Angeles. Retrieved from http://www.freeuniversityla.org/
Gilbert, D. (2009). Time to shell out? Reflections on the RGS and corporate sponsorship. *ACME, 8*(3), 521–29.
Goodman, P. (1966). *Compulsory miseducation*. New York: Random House.
Harney, S. & Moten, F. (2004). The university and the undercommons: Seven theses. *Social Text, 22*(2).
Harvie, D. (2004). Commons and community in the university: Some notes and some examples. *The Commoner, 10* (Autumn–Winter).
High Fliers Research Limited (2010). *The UK Graduate Careers Survey 2010*. Retrieved from http://www.highfliers.co.uk/
Hodkinson, S. & Chatterton, P. (2006). Autonomy in the city? Reflections on the social centres movement in the UK. *City, 10*(3), 305–15.
Hodkinson, S. (2009). Teaching what we (preach and) practice: The MA in Activism and Social Change. *ACME Journal, 8*(3), 462–73.

Hodkinson, S. (2010). Housing in common: In search of a strategy for housing alterity in England in the 21st century. In D. Fuller, A. Jonas & R. Lee (Eds.), *Interrogating alterity: Alternative economic and political spaces*. Farnham: Ashgate.

Holloway, J. (2005). *Change the world without taking power*. London: Pluto Press.

Holloway, J. (2010). *Crack capitalism*. London: Pluto Press.

hooks, b. (1994). *Teaching to transgress: Education as the practice of freedom*. London: Routledge.

Illich, I. (1973). Chapter II: Convivial reconstruction. In Illich, I. *Tools for conviviality*. New York: Perennial, Harper & Row.

Inoperative Committee (2009). *Pre-occupied: The logic of occupation*. New York: Self-Published.

Institute for College Access & Success (2010) Student debt and the class of 2009. *The project on student debt: An initiative of the Institute for College Access & Success*. Retrieved from http://projectonstudentdebt.org/files/pub/classof2009.pdf.

Kahn, R. (2009). Anarchic epimetheanism: The pedagogy of Ivan Illich. In R. Amster, A. DeLeon, L. Fernandez, A. Nocella II & D, Shannon (Eds.), *Contemporary anarchist studies: An introduction anthology of anarchy in the academy*. New York: Routledge.

Kanngieser, A. (2007). It's our academy: Transforming education through self-organized autonomous universities. Originally presented as part of the RMIT Student Union event, *Institutions, Capitalism and Dissent: A Rogue Education Conference, 2007*. Retrieved from http://academia.edu.documents.s3.amazonaws.com/1755846/Its_our_academy.pdf.

Kanuga, M. (2010). Bluestockings Bookstore and new institutions of self-organised Work. In Team Colors Collective (Eds.), *Uses of a whirlwind*, 19–36. Oakland: AK Press.

Lazzarato, M. (2006). Immaterial labour. In M. Hardt & P. Virno (Eds.), *Radical thought in Italy: A potential politics*, 133–47. Minneapolis: University of Minnesota Press.

Leeds University Union, LUU (2010). Current campaigns: Education first. Retrieved from http://www.leedsuniversityunion.org.uk/campaigning/currentcampaigns/educationfirst

Linebaugh, P. (2010). Some principles of the commons. *CounterPunch*, Weekend Edition, Jan. 8–10, 2010. http://www.counterpunch.org/linebaugh01082010.html.

Maeckelbergh, M. (2009). *Will of the many*. London: Pluto.

Manoa Free University. Retrieved from http://manoafreeuniversity.org/.

Maxey, L. (2004). Moving beyond from within: Reflexive activism and critical geographies. In D. Fuller & R. Kichen (Eds.), *Critical theory/radical praxis: Making a difference beyond the academy?*, 159–70. Vernon and Victoria, BC, Canada: Praxis (e) Press.

Morgan, J. (2010). Strike threat as job cut talks break down at Leeds. *Times Higher Education*. Retrieved from http://www.timeshighereducation.co.uk/story.asp?sectioncode=26&storycode=410292&c=2.

Neary, M. & Winn, J. (2009). Student as producer: Reinventing the undergraduate curriculum. In L. Bell, H. Stevenson & M. Neary (Eds.), *The future of higher education: Policy, pedagogy and the student experience*, (126–39). London and New York: Continuum.

Neary, M. (2010a). Student as producer: A pedagogy for the avant-garde; or how do revolutionary teachers teach? *Learning Exchange, 1*(1). Retrieved from http://learningexchange.westminster.ac.uk/index.php/lej/article/view/15.

Neary, M. (2010b). Pedagogy of excess: An alternative political economy of student life. In M. Molesworth, L. Nixon & R. Scullion (Eds.), *The marketisation of higher education and the student as consumer*, 209–24. London: Routledge.

Plows, A. (1998). Praxis and practice: The "what, how and why" of the UK environmental direct action (EDA) movement in the 1990s. Unpublished thesis. Retrieved from http://www.iol.ie/~mazzoldi/toolsforchange/papers.html.

Pusey, A. (2010). Social centres and the new cooperativism of the common. *Affinities: A Journal of Radical Theory, Culture, and Action*, 4(1), 176–98. Retrieved from journals.sfu.ca/affinities/index.php/affinities/article/view/31/124.

Really Open University (2010a). Towards a battle ground. Retrieved from http://reallyopenuniversity.wordpress.com/2010/02/07/towards-a-battle-ground/.

Really Open University (2010b). The logic of occupation: Demand nothing, occupy everything! Retrieved from http://reallyopenuniversity.wordpress.com/2010/05/12/the-logic-of-occupation-demand-nothing-occupy-everything/.

Shantz, J. (2010). *Constructive anarchy: Building infrastructures of resistance*. Farnham: Ashgate.

Shukaitis, S. (2009). Infrapolitics and the nomadic educational machine. In R. Amster, A. DeLeon, L. Fernandez, A. Nocella II & D, Shannon (Eds.), *Contemporary anarchist studies: An introduction to anarchy in the academy*. New York: Routledge.

Thompson, E.P. (1993). *Customs in common*. New York: The New Press.

Thorburn, N. (2003). Deleuze, Marx and Politics. London: Routledge.

TRAPESE, Popular Education Collective. Retrieved from http://trapese.clearerchannel.org/.

UK Social Centres Network (2008). What's this place? Retrieved from http://socialcentrestories.wordpress.com/.

University of Leeds. (2010). Economies exercise. Retrieved from http://www.leeds.ac.uk/forstaff/homepage/65/economies_exercise.

University of Leeds, School of Geography. MAASC FAQ. Retrieved from http://www.geog.leeds.ac.uk/fileadmin/downloads/school/masters/faq.pdf

University of Leeds, School of Geography. Former student testimonial: Patrick Gillett, programme participant 2008–2009. Retrieved from http://www.geog.leeds.ac.uk/study/masters/courses/maasc/student-testimonials.html.

University of Lincoln. Student as producer project proposal. Retrieved from http://studentasproducer.lincoln.ac.uk/project-proposal/.

University of Openness, online at: http://uo.twenteenthcentury.com/.

University of Utopia. (2010). Anti-curricula: A course of action. Retrieved from https://docs.google.com/View?id=df3cbtd3_0d6psn2d7.

Vaneigem, R. (1972). *"Terrorism or revolution": An introduction to Ernest Coeurderoy*. Black Rose. Retrieved from http://www.notbored.org/coeurderoy.html.

Vaneigem, R. (1983). *The revolution of everyday life*. London: Rebel Press.

Wall, D. (1999). *Earth First! and the anti-roads movement*. London: Routledge.

Ward, C. (1973). *Anarchy in action*. London: Allen and Unwin.

Winn, J. (2010). A co-operatively run "Social Science Centre." Joss Winn's blog, University of Lincoln. Retrieved from http://joss.blogs.lincoln.ac.uk/2010/09/03/a-co-operatively-run-social-science-centre/.

**CHAPTER 11**

# Anarchy in the Academy: Staying True to Anarchism as an Academic-Activist

**Caroline K. Kaltefleiter and Anthony J. Nocella II**

> Before we put so powerful a machine (education) under the direction of so ambiguous an agent (government), it behooves us to consider well what it is we do. Government will not fail to employ it, to strengthen its hands, and perpetuate its institutions. (William Godwin, 1793)

In her work *The Social Importance of the Modern School*, anarchist Emma Goldman discusses the role of schools and a state-controlled system of education and knowledge exchange. According to Goldman,

> The great harm done by our system of education is not so much that it teaches nothing worth knowing, rather that it helps to perpetuate privileged classes, that it assists them in the criminal procedure of robbing and exploiting the masses; the harm of the system lies in its boastful proclamation that it stands for true education, thereby enslaving the masses a great deal more than could an absolute ruler. (1917)

Goldman's work underscores the extent to which schools act as instruments of state power and, as such, echoes the writing of several anarchist scholars, William Godwin among them. Anarchist scholar David Gabbard (2010) notes, "William Godwin developed the first comprehensive anarchist critique of government schools in his *Enquiry Concerning Political Justice* in 1793. Godwin viewed freedom of thought as fundamental to political liberty." (p. 3). Joel Spring further contextualizes Godwin's work on anarchism and education, According to Spring (1994), Godwin believed that "since people constantly improve their reasoning power and their understanding of nature, their understanding of the best form of government is constantly changing" (p. 42). While Godwin "recognized that education was crucial toward the development of individuals' powers of rational thought that would guide them in self-government, he "considered national systems of education to be one of the foremost dangers to freedom and liberty" (Spring, 1983, p. 68).

In this essay, we examine the university not only as an instrument of state power but also as a site of cultural resistance. Our aim is to contextualize the university within an ideological framework offering both a systematic critique and alternative narratives to create new ways of looking at the university as a critical space for both theoretical discussions about anarchist studies as well as to develop locations for participatory engagement and anarchist direct action. Our work is illuminated by our respective roles in the creation of an interdisciplinary anarchist studies project/institute, the Anarchist Studies Initiative (ASI) that is housed at a state university in Upstate New York. We interrogate ongoing debates and critiques within the anarchist community as to whether an anarchist studies project housed at a state university could be successful. Finally we offer an overview of curriculum development, cocurricular programming, and community outreach taking place at the Anarchist Studies Initiative. Here, we forge a conversation that calls for an academic-activist hybrid culture; one that not only addresses the tensions that exist in the academia/activist relationship, but also advocates for creating a continuum between the academy and other sites of activist resistance.

## Universities: Ideological State Apparatuses

Critical theorist Louis Althusser (1971) argues that schools, universities first and foremost, function within a capitalist system to perpetuate its norms and values in order to smoothly reproduce itself. Althusser's work addresses a cerebral society that employs forms of physical and mental incarceration. He suggests two major mechanisms to ensure that people within a state behave according to the rules of the state, even if it may not be in their best interest (in regards to their class positions) to do so. The first is what Althusser calls the RSA or Repressive State Apparatuses that can enforce behavior directly, such as the police, criminal justice, and prison systems (Klages, 2001). Through these "apparatuses" the state has the power to force one to physically behave and restrict one's movements and actions. The second mechanism Althusser examines which is central to our discussion of anarchy in the academy is what he calls ISA or Ideological State Apparatuses. According to Althusser (1971), "Ideological practice consists of an assortment of institutions called Ideological State Apparatuses (ISAs), which include the family, the media, religious organizations, and, most importantly in capitalist societies, the education system, as well as the received ideas that they propagate. Mary Klages (2001) notes, "These are institutions that generate ideologies which we as individuals (and groups) then internalize, and in which to act in accordance. ISAs include schools, religions, the family, legal systems, politics, arts, etc. These organizations generate systems of ideas and values" (p. 239). A value system in which the notion of both economic and cultural capital is emphasized serves to reify class indoctrination.

Pierre Bourdieu (1970; 1990) notes that class domination is not only a result of economic warfare, but also a fight for cultural capital. Dominating classes use cultural capital, specifically that of knowledge, to their benefit. In the case of higher education, Bourdieu views the university system as integral to the (re)production of capitalist values, ideologies, and imperatives, such that the educational structure is designed not to cultivate knowledge and autonomy but rather to instruct students and professors how to labor in a market-dominated world. For instance, schools of journalism often focus on the mechanics of writing and producing news without asking student journalists to critically reflect on the social, cultural, political, or economic impact of stories produced and reified in various media texts. Student writers are taught to be workers (re)producing the stories of dominant elites (Kaltefleiter, 2009). In his seminal text *Pedagogy of the Oppressed*, Paulo Freire (2000) discusses what he refers to as the "banking concept of education whereby students are seen as submissive learners and merely take in information that is deposited into their brain banks by their teachers. Freire asserts that modern education is widely recognized as a chance for instructors (or "oppressors," as he calls them) to fill students with information as they submissively accept it. He explains that the ritual of schooling filters into an overall culture of manipulation whereby young minds are shaped to adhere to the agendas of the power elite. According to Freire (2000),

> Manipulation becomes a fundamental instrument for the preservation of domination. Prior to the emergence of people there is no manipulation (precisely speaking), but rather total suppression. When the oppressed are almost completely submerged in reality, it is unnecessary to manipulate them. In the antidialogical theory of action, manipulation is the response of the oppressor to the new concrete conditions of the historical process. Through manipulation, dominant elites can lead people into an unauthentic type of "organization" and can thus avoid the threatening alternative: the true organization of the emerged and emerging people. (p. 148)

He continues, "[t]he dominant elites are so well aware of [the subversive nature of free inquiry] that they instinctively use all means, including physical violence to keep the people from thinking" (p. 149). Hence, independent thought is given up in favor of obedience, with the goal of keeping people "from asking questions that matter about important issues that directly affect them and others" (Chomsky and Macedo, 2000, p. 24).

A discussion on ideology is crucial for us to better understand the systems of both repression and oppression that exist for university students and faculty today. Such an analysis extends Marxist theory which defines ideology as an instrument of social reproduction and is conceptually important to the sociology of knowledge—including the pursuit of knowledge taking place within the confines of university classrooms.

A critical investigation of ideological frameworks related to the structure of the university and avenues of intellectual inquiry opens up the possibility for (re)thinking or (re)purposing university educations, offering competing readings of how intellectual work is carried on/out of the university and allows for creative and intellectual activity taking place in the streets, union halls, and community centers. This idea is linked to the work of Stuart Hall, who discusses the notion of encoding/decoding texts. Hall (1980) emphasizes that texts through every moment in the process of communication, allow for active message composition (encoding) and message reception (decoding). The message continuum, "from the original composition of the message/code (encoding) to the point at which it is read and understood (decoding), has its own determinants and conditions of existence" (1980, p. 129). Just as the construction of the message/code is an active, interpretive, and social event, so is the moment of reception. Hall identifies three primary positions of decoding messages and signs, including the dominant position or "preferred" reading, the "negotiated" position, and the "oppositional" position/reading that can be applied to contemporary texts, institutions, and social movements. (Kaltefleiter, 1995, 2009). Therefore the space in which university learning takes place can be resisted so as to create oppositional paradigms of thought that allow for new modes of communication and direct action. Students and faculty collaborate to engage in a resistance culture: wherein individuals question the ways in which members of society come to internalize and to believe the ideologies set forth by ISAs, including universities. It is within this continuum of resistance that an anarchist studies pedagogy emerges. Students, faculty, and community members share in the development of course offerings—including readings, discussions, and evaluation, if such a system is necessary to be employed. Such actions serve to dismantle hierarchal structure of the academy and strive to create common spaces of engagement wherein one's affinity to issues of peace and social justice issues can be explored in/out of formal structures of learning.

## Labor, Anarchy, and Resistance in the Academy

> We are students of words; we are shut up in schools and colleges for ten or fifteen years and come out a bag of wind, a memory of words, and do not know a thing. —Ralph Waldo Emerson

Freire (2000) outlines the necessary steps for individuals in their everyday lives to counter deceits and regimes (im)posed by the state. To oppose such manipulation and repression, a critical thought process needs to situate its citizens in historic processes, power systems, and ideological frameworks. The academy is often touted as a space that encourages the free and unfettered pursuit of research and inquiry and yet everyday academic freedom is under fire (Kaltefleiter & Nagel, 2009). Nonetheless, this constant refusal to accept paradigms of domination is central to the development of anarchist studies dialogue within the academy. Contemporary anarchist scholar Noam Chomsky describes "the basic institutional role and function of the schools" as providing "an ideological service: there's a real selection for obedience and conformity" (Chomsky, 2003, pp. 27–28).

In order to better understand the social conditioning that exists within the academy, we draw upon the work of cultural studies scholar Paul Willis. In his ethnography, *Learning to Labour: How Working Class Kids Get Working Class Jobs*, Willis (1977) discusses ways in which youth culture prior to the Internet revolution were tracked and filtered into a menial labor market. Willis discusses a politics of resistance that was cultivated by working-class kids in the United Kingdom in their everyday life by rejecting "mental labor" and engaging in "cultural labor"—for example, hanging out in the streets, creative art/communication, and getting in and out of trouble. The dilemma of Willis's UK lads represents the catch-22 of the working and popular classes in general: "challenging power requires (credentialed) knowledge, yet the acquisition of that knowledge is organized so that it reinforces credentialed system of power" (Abercrombie and Urry, 1983, p. 17).

Willis's work has been used to ground discussions that explore schooling rituals (McLaren, 1993; Castoriadis, 1997; Aronowitz, 1998). Here the structure of learning is questioned and a politics of resistance is forged. Here we extend Willis's notion of "learning to labor" from a physical-based contest of menial work to a mental-based context of learning to do intellectual work and as such offer a rethinking of the extension of the classroom into, and onto, the streets. Everyday life experiences of colleagues engaged in anarchist and activist projects that represent interdisciplinary perspectives as well as community-based narratives serve to become a central component of a social and cultural curriculum. The sharing of information through traditional presentations as well informal publications such as zines, blogs, social media sites, and street performances allow for the creation of new forms and forums of engagement. Students, faculty, and community members study history/herstory of anarchists and contemporary events in which the lives of anarchist are examined and provide in Stuart Hall's words, an oppositional frame of analysis, disparate from a dominant pedagogical ideology, offering new ways of thinking about societal organizational structures and the ways in which fellow citizens follow directions from the State to ensure conformity and obedience that contributes to the reification of class strata. In this continuum and location of opposition, we create a dialogue and space to resist ideologies that allow for the misrepresentation of ourselves as Mary Klages (2001) puts it into "unalienated subjects in capitalism." Such dialogues lead to actions that seek to deconstruct hierarchical organizations, capitalist culture, and dominant paradigms of education, including the development of an anarchist project at a small comprehensive university in New York State.

## Anarchist Studies in the Academy

The study of anarchism in the academy is certainly not new, however, there is undoubtedly been a rise in anarchist scholarship in recent years. Significant works include: Martha Ackelsberg's (2005) rerelease on anarchist women in the Spanish Civil War; Jeff Ferrell's (2001) work on the anarchist definition of public space, anarchy, and critical animal studies (Best and Nocella, 2006) and even girls and anarchy (Kaltefleiter, 1995, 2009). Today, new forms of anarchism are being articulated and include new anarcha-feminism, environmental anarchism, and Situationist anarchism to name a few. Contemporary anarchist scholars continue to advance developments in third-wave feminism, antiracist politics, queer theories, transgender culture, disability studies, as well as environmentalism(s) and animal advocacy. Anarchist practices include actions emerging from postcolonial states and indigenous populations, giving reverence to the everyday life experiences of those involved in daily struggles of oppression. The proliferation of anarchist scholarship, coupled with historical flashpoints, aided in creating a rationale for the creation of an academic project/program that would be housed at a state university.

## Flashpoint: Battle of Seattle and the Emergence of New Anarchism

Ten years ago, anarchists and a coalition of workers' unions, feminists, antiracists, environmentalists, gay and lesbian leaders, and animal rights liberationists successfully stopped the World Trade Organization's ministerial conference. Soon after the 1999 WTO protest in Seattle there was a significant (re)emergence of scholarly and activist interest in anarchism—which opposes capitalism and envisions a society based on solidarity and mutual aid. These ideas are becoming ever more relevant as we enter a global depression that sees workers all over looking for an alternative to a corrupt and hierarchical method of distributing resources (Amster, DeLeon, et al., 2009). Since the Battle of Seattle, a number of grassroots groups and anarchist-inspired actions have gained recognition. Some of these include Food Not Bombs, Critical Mass, and Reclaim the Streets. Anarchists have a large presence in groups like Anti-Racist Action and Anti-Fascist Action. Class struggle anarchist groups can be found in various parts of the United States, Western Europe, and Latin America.

As participants of anarchist actions, including the Animal Rights movement and Riot Grrrl network, we found ourselves in the unique position being both academics and activists, in which our involvement at the WTO came through direct action and independent media projects. Our street credentials at the WTO would lead to the to the 2009 publication of essays in *Contemporary Anarchist Studies: An Introduction Anthology of Anarchy in the Academy*, coedited by Anthony Nocella. During the fall of 2009, we began to discuss the possibility of developing a center focused on anarchist studies. With the North American Anarchist Studies Network, Anarchist Academics listserv, anarchist studies lectures on a variety of college campuses, books on anarchism in every liberal arts academic discipline being published, and anarchist students from a diversity of social movements entering higher education, it seemed like an ideal and prime time to create a center on anarchist studies.

Flash forward ten years after the Battle of Seattle to Cortland, New York, where two young academic-activists decide to create an interdisciplinary institute that focuses on Anarchist theories and practices. We often get strange looks when we tell people that we are the cofounders of the Anarchist Studies Initiative at SUNY Cortland. Invariably, the first question activists and academics ask is why SUNY Cortland? A comprehensive undergraduate institution, SUNY Cortland has a longstanding tradition in social movements, direct action projects, and engaged activism that includes the work of Professor William "Bill" Griffen. He was the longest tenured faculty member in the SUNY system, serving fifty-one years until his death in 2007. Bill Griffen was a professor in the Foundations and Social Advocacy department in the School of Education, where one former student wrote upon his death, "He was kind of like Gandhi—he showed courage and bravery by being gentle and kind. He handled tough situations, never with anger, but with humor" (Geibel, 2007). Bill Griffen would become Cortland's equivalent to social historian and civil rights activist Howard Zinn. He became involved in the civil rights movement after one of his former students, Bill Moore, died while registering black voters in the South (ibid.). Griffen would go on to inspire students and faculty alike, engaging them in demonstrations against the Vietnam War, the location of a Superfund waste disposal site, and the proposed building of a Super Wal-Mart store in Cortland County.

SUNY Cortland is located in upstate in the poorest county in New York State. The ongoing need to address poverty, blight, and economic inequity of the region drove us as organizers to seek out ways to discuss and act out against the ways in which global capitalism was impacting our town—our neighbors, their kids, the unemployed, the elderly, and the dis(abled). Our university is situated between world-renowned university centers such as Syracuse, Binghamton, and Cornell universities. This action research triangle, if you will, seemed not only logical but possible to create this continuum of communication. Ongoing collaborations between area community groups such as Binghamton's Food Not Bombs collective, the Central New York Peace Consortium in Syracuse, and Ithaca Hours, an alternative currency exchange, made SUNY Cortland a logical site for an Anarchist Studies center. SUNY Cortland is also home to the Center for Gender and Intercultural Studies (CGIS) whose mission to foster and develop equity and respect for social, ethnic and cultural, economic, gender, environmental justice, and diversity. Given its mission, CGIS became an important ally in our attempt to propose what on the surface to some may have seemed like a bad idea—negative connotations associated with term "anarchist" and the ongoing images of battles in the streets of Athens, where purported anarchists were engaged in street demonstrations, some violent at times.

SUNY Cortland faculty, students, staff, and administration are open to new and cutting-edge ideas, even if they disagree with them, for instance the Ninth Annual Conference for Critical Animal Studies, which had people from around the world and more than 350 attendees mostly from colleges and universities, was embraced by SUNY Cortland. Yes, there were those that were fearful and one or two that opposed the idea of personal interest due to their research on nonhuman animals. Despite all this, our colleagues joined us in a resolution to create the Anarchist Studies Initiative. Consequently, we had an academic home that was interested and was willing to argue for our existence, which we can unequivocally attest to be the most important part of politics in and out of higher education. It should be noted while a few faculty voiced concerns about the initiative; it was not seen as a threat to status quo, but viewed as an intellectual scholarly project.

## Opposition to the Anarchist Studies Initiative in the Academy

Before the Anarchist Studies Initiative was created, we knew that we would be criticized for encouraging the institutionalization of anarchism. We had both been involved in discussions at the first North American Anarchist Studies Network (NAASN) Conference in November 2009 in Hartford, Connecticut. Discussion of the tensions in the academia/activism relationship were clear in observations made by members at the Hartford conference where academics and activists alike seem to apologize for their profession or vocation. Anarchist scholar Jesse Cohn was at the Hartford meeting and wrote on the NAASN listserv:

> I heard some moments where those who identified as "academics" seemed to feel they had to apologize for or elaborately disavow claims to expertise before nonacademics, and I heard other moments where "activists" seemed to feel almost ashamed to have no "academic" credentials, as if they had nothing to offer in the way of knowledge or insight, as if there were no other way to understand or practice scholarship. Both moments at the same conference! Because none of us is used to operating in an environment that is neither-nor and/or both-and . . . whose space is it? Wherever we locate ourselves, the answer, some of the time at least, seems to be "not yours," and that makes folks nervous. (November 23, 2010)

The strained relationship between anarchist academics and activists needs to be addressed. Academia is an institution that is at its core hierarchical—and that actively creates and maintains hierarchy—and therefore is fundamentally at odds with anarchism. Stephen Shukaitis (2007) acknowledges the awkward position of anarchist academics. He warns against the creation of a field of anarchist studies that constructs anarchism as a fixed, static object to observe from afar; the end result, he cautions, could be that the work done by anarchist academics is "turned against themselves and re-incorporated into the workings of state and capital . . . creating the image of subversion while raking in tuition fees" (p. 167). As David Graeber (2007) puts it, "to act like an anarchist would be academic suicide" (p. 107).

While we certainly understand this point of view given our own circumstances of academic repression within various institutions, our argument remains that Bakunin, Godwin, Kropotkin, and Proudhon institutionalized anarchism since day one. Moreover, we continue to interrogate the university's role as an ISA. Howard Zinn (2002) points out that educational practice is never neutral and the university is hardly benign in its spheres of influence (e.g., in the corporate, scientific, and military sectors) or its functions to perpetuate business, governmental, and social practices, however corrupt or antidemocratic. NAASN member and anarcho-blogger Kevin Carson (2010) articulates a need to move away from essentialism between academics and activists. According to Carson,

> Pushing anarchist studies into the academy is strategically smart for the movement. The University system, particularly in the United States, is a mass indoctrination factory that is essential in the functioning of

> the State and Capitalism. In the U.S. schools have a particular relationship with the population and with alternative culture/politics. The more we can [work] against authoritarian pedagogy and traditional content in the classroom the more young minds may find the path to self-empowerment. (November 23, 2010)

There were a number of exchanges on the Anarchist Academics listserv about the creation of ASI at SUNY Cortland, some of which were not so positive.

One listserv member wrote,

> I sent this to the list a while back and didn't get a response and was wondering if anyone had any answers to the questions myself and Tristan [Husby] raised below. It's about the Anarchist Studies Initiative at SUNY. I'm not against the initiative. . . . This sort of institutionalization, and the concentration of resources that comes with it, will have an effect in at least two ways (I'm sure others can point out more). First, the concentration of resources, while it will help some, will alter the balance within the movement between those who have and those who have not. The challenge for the centre will be to justify that imbalance and to equalize it again where possible. (Pritchard, 2010)

We continued to underscore our argument citing the need for anarchist studies to have a place in the academy so as to dismantle the dominant ideology or cultural reproduction apparatus. The academy is essential to state capitalism. The system relies on universities to provide trained managers and professional to perpetuate its values. Herein lies the opportunity for those in the academy to create oppositional scenarios of representation and communication and to advance narratives for direct action and social change. A number of NAASN colleagues backed up our position.

> Briefly, I'm not an organizer, but went to the unveiling and was awarded with a certificate for work I've done on anarchism and sexuality/gender (in addition to some organizing some WSAer's and I have been doing around reproductive freedom in Hartford). As far as I can tell, your guesses on their budget are way off base. Beyond that, there are ASN and NAASN folks in the associated faculty (Ruth Kinna and Jesse Cohn, for example), so they're connected to some of the other projects around anti-authoritarian education (in addition to having organizers involved in the Transformative Studies Institute and some associated popular education initiatives). (Shannon, 2010)

Criticism regarding the development of ASI at SUNY Cortland also questioned funding streams for the project as well as the "street credentials" of those involved.

> This initiative [ASI] looks pretty huge to me, with a shit load of money (please correct me if I'm wrong). I'd like to know where the money came from before I make a judgment, but it seems to me that whether the money came from trustees, benefactors, the university or elsewhere makes a huge difference. . . . The SUNY initiative seems to have oodles more and institutional support (but maybe I'm being bamboozled by fancy titles and a good website?). I think there needs to be some transparency on this if only for the sake of the integrity of the initiative and to keep the rest of the movement on side. (Pritchard, 2010)

In creating the Anarchist Studies Initiative, we knew that people would challenge our legitimacy as anarchists, academics, and as activists. In retrospect, we commend our colleagues for doing their due diligence to call for accountability and transparency of ASI's organizers. This seems even more important given the recent cases of police agents now exposed for infiltrating global activist groups, including police constable Mark Kennedy of Great Britain. Kennedy worked undercover for seven years to expose the interworkings of global climate change protesters and provided information to authorities about planned actions and demonstrations (Lewis et al., 2010).

Despite criticism and skepticism of our intentions and the mission of ASI, our defense was clear, we were activists, academics, and anarchists. Too often on the listservs and in academic anarchist groups there are those that study anarchists and proclaim to be anarchists, but have no history in social movements, activism, youth resistance, or community organizing. Anthony Nocella offered this response:

> Yep, I am on the list, a little about my self in my defense—lovable Queer and person born with severe mental disabilities, long-time animal and Earth liberationist (first activist framed in the movement), beaten severely in jail, prison abolitionist, Quaker, on the Board of American Friends Service Committee, founded more than 15 activist political organizations, working on my Ph.D., while teaching at SUNY Cortland at Le Moyne College, co-founder of one of the first youth incarcerated re-entry programs in the US, and a volunteer in NY prisons for the last 7 years. I also have published 12 books including *Igniting a Revolution* and *Academic Repression*. Both published by AK Press. (Nocella, 2010)

In addition, Nocella offered information about members of the ASI Collective to attest to the fact those involved with the project had legitimacy in the anarchist community. "Caroline Kaltefleiter, one of the leading figures back in the day of the Riot Grrrl movement and girl studies, and now the Chair of the Women's Studies Department. Colleen Kattau, a very respected peace activist and musician and major organizer against the School of the Americas and teaches Spanish at SUNY Cortland. Finally, long-time Transnational Feminist and prison abolitionist Mecke Nagel, who teaches in philosophy" (Nocella, May 17, 2010).

On the subject of institutional funding, we remained resolute in our decision to move forward with creating ASI with the understanding that there was no institutional support and had in fact always planned on adopting a DIY (do-it-yourself) strategy. As Nocella notes, "We have no money and I am very very poor, but I am a long-time organizer with many anarchist and radical organizations and can make my money stretch" (Nocella, 2010). At the same time we were launching ASI, the State University of New York, including our own faculty union, was in the midst of struggle with the governor over contractual obligations. Our efforts were being torn between advancing ASI and standing in solidarity with our union colleagues. Anarchist colleagues responded in tandem with us to this discussion. Anarchist scholar Jesse Cohn writes,

> I don't think the organizers are on this list, and even if they were, they've got other things to worry about right now (in addition to the usual end-of-semester work crunch): the governor of New York has threatened to "furlough" them for one day per week, meaning, in effect, that they have just been presented with a non-negotiable 20% pay cut. They're fighting it in the courts, but I can only imagine the kind of precarity that would introduce to my life. (Cohn, 2010)

## Unveiling ASI and Anarchist Pedagogies: Being An Academic-Activist

On April 9, 2010, in commemoration of the sentencing to death of two Italian anarchists, Nicola Sacco and Bartolomeo Vanzetti, SUNY Cortland held the unveiling and dedication the Anarchist Studies Initiative. The day included panel discussions and informal presentations from faculty, students, and community organizers, including members from the zine collective Silent Distro. Attendance for the unveiling exceeded room capacity and included members from countries around the world, including Italy.

Today, the project organizers work to create a project relates the practice of (media) theory relates to the larger field of cultural studies and anarchist studies. Work undertaken at ASI incorporates a discussion of identity politics that allows for self-reflexivity and direct action and the use of do-it-yourself media. ASI features a number of events each year—including William Godwin Spring Lecture, Emma Goldman and Lucy Parson Fellowship Programs, and Mikhail Bakunin Film Series. Analysis of contemporary anarchist studies actions and media representations of such events allows for critical analysis in the continuum of production of information about anarchists to "the reception of a given text" (Rossiter, 2003, p. 106).

Althusser's conception of ideology can therefore aid anarchist scholars in tackling a broader perspective in their work. Having established that ideology is lived relations or social practices organized by sensibilities of symbolic realms (1971, p. 131), an anarchist scholar may observe how the mass media which is both a product and a shaping force of existing institutions and social practices seeks to present a "mediated" version of anarchism. Arze-Bravo, Murray, et al. (2010) note, "Because the 'imaginary, as such, is constituted by material practices located within institutional settings' (Rossiter, 2003, p. 116), media manages to be both materialistic and imaginary. Thus not only is media a product of the social and creative imaginary, but it also reflects political and economic systems." Subsequently it is through continual interrogation and analysis of Ideological State Apparatuses (ISAs) such as schools, universities, and the media that an authentic (anarchist) activism, in and out of the academy, might emerge, or, as anarcho-blogger Kevin Carson put it, "When a student happens to perceive the internal self-contradictions of the official ideology (e.g., the contrast between 'free market' rhetoric and the actual state-subsidized and -protected nature of capitalism, the contrast between the 'peace and freedom' rhetoric of the national security state and the death squad reality, etc.). When an instructor is actively pointing out these contradictions, the effect is profoundly subversive" (November 23, 2010).

The concept of putting theory into practice has often been a desired outcome in higher learning; however, limited exposure to direct action projects by academics continues to be one of the most frustrating issues for us as activists in the academy. There are anarchists who write books, articles, and organize forums on the topic, but are not rooted in true action including, but not limited to civil disobedience ending in arrests, economic sabotage, and prisoner support. Many have only participated in activism because of their graduate work, thus justifying their political activity to academic administrators. Further, their detachment from activism like all careerists was justified because of not having a job, tenure, or still negotiating higher education. Many other academics that proclaimed their activism cannot be found within blogs, listservs, collectives, or other forms of social movement historical documentation, only to conclude that they were either against being documented or that they were "weekend warriors" up for a thrill or to tell their friends or children how they were once radicals. While wanting to remain positive about the anarchist interactions in the academy, we realize there remain a number of careerists and opportunists, who invariably steal and adopt new cutting-edge areas of interest without a true commitment or dedication to the field. They are simply moving up the ranks being collegial and collaborating with others in order to receive legitimacy within the given field of study.

Anarchism—similar to disability studies, critical animal studies, and women's studies—is rooted in struggle and liberation, and while many fear repression and are controlled by social norms, to challenge oppression and domination many are willing to write about it. A most obvious example, without saying names, is many academics who have written on the leftist revolutionary group the Zapatistas and have gotten tenure and made a career on them, with posters on their walls, but who have never been to Mexico at worst and at best never given back to them financially.

Therefore, it is not enough to organize conferences in academia or to write articles or books, or to be on Facebook shooting out comments about how the anarchist revolution is tomorrow, by their students. Moreover, how these academic-anarchists will not be involved because they have to write in an academic press or journal to gain the movement creditability and legitimacy, or that they have to be the spokesperson for the students, when the students get in trouble, which they are so proud of. We say, stop writing and stop posing and hit the streets every day, for as the quote goes, "If not you, who? If not now, when?" Social change has never been possible by people playing it safe or trying to be collegial. It was about being oneself and believing in something so much that one had to take serious extreme action to protect it such as in the case of animal liberation, the Animal Liberation Front (ALF) go underground and mask-up to liberate nonhuman animals from laboratories, fur farms, and factory farms and burn down McDonalds and research laboratories. We are not saying that academics need to take these actions, but instead if one is going to write on these actions to give back financially to political prisoners that do risk their lives for these causes. One should not use students as shields or tokens, but instead be a role model for students in engaging in democracy, such as protesting, engaging in civil disobedience, and conducting sit-ins with students, staff, and fellow faculty.

## Toward Anarchist Pedagogy: Activist Principles

Here are few principles to follow in pursuit of staying true to being an activist in and out of the academy:

1. To follow the footsteps of great role models such as Angela Davis, Howard Zinn, Bill Ayers, Bernardine Dohrn, Andrea Smith, Kathleen Cleaver, and Ward Churchill, who have challenged systems of domination prior to entering high education.
2. To be a role model for a student means to support them and take the same risks they do.
3. To actively engage in student groups not as an advisor, but as a member willing to learn as well as share.

4 To participate in community organizations and collectives regularly so as to not only have a presence on university campus or be a representative of a college.
5 To engage in antioppressive work such as volunteering at a prison or at a domestic violence prevention center.
6 To publish not in academic, corporate presses but in public activist presses such as AK Press, Arissa Media Group, PM Press, South End Press, and Lantern Books.
7 To publish in activist journals and magazines rather than in academic journals that are only read by a handful of scholars and are only useful for career advancement.
8 To publish in alternative methods such as Youtube, blogs, Twitter, film, and radio.
9 To be a public intellectual such as Michael Eric Dyson or Cornell West, who share their views, opinions, and beliefs on the radio, television, and in documentaries.
10 Finally, to be willing to be challenged and willing to accept and to work on one's dominant position as a college professor in society.

## Conclusion

Through our work at the Anarchist Studies Initiative, we continue to interrogate assumptions about various subject positions in our daily lives and our actions and interactions that that are conducted according to the cultural and ideological norms or protocols associated with them. Our work incorporates an anarchistic pedagogy of everyday life wherein whenever we read a blog, watch a movie, respond to a Facebook post, or listen to a political speech or our favorite rap artist, we become aware of how or why we resist or accept certain views.

To be above the world as a scientist examining people's behaviors, society's constructions, the natural world, and historical patterns, as if the scientist experiences did not taint the lens that the scientist examined the world through, is a detached approach that allowed for horribly oppressive and repressive actions to take place in the name of normalcy, such as eugenics, segregation, prison-industrial complex, and capitalism. Rather we embrace an evolving anarchist pedagogy, that as Graeber (2007) suggests, positions anarchism as a process, as a means, and, thus, suggests that the role of anarchism in academia (or of academia in anarchism) is to provide space and resources for "the elaboration of ideas and knowledge useful to further developing anarchist politics . . . approached from a way that is deeply connected to questions posed by social movements and struggles" (p. 169). This process of critical engagements gives us power to actively shape our lives on our own terms and creates spaces of resistance wherein learning moves beyond classroom walls, creating a two-way flow of community and ideas between the academy and the activity community.

## References

Abercrombie, N. & Urry, J. (1983). *Capital, labour and the middles classes.* London: Allen and Unwin.

Ackelsberg, M. (2005). *Free women of Spain: Anarchism and the struggle for the emancipation of women.* Oakland: AK Press.

Althusser, L. (1971). Ideology and ideological state apparatuses (notes towards an investigation). In *Lenin and philosophy and other essays.* (Ben Brewster, Trans.). New York: Monthly Review Press.

Amster, R., DeLeon, A., Fernandez, L., Nocella II, A. & Shannon, D. (2009). *Contemporary anarchist studies: An introductory anthology of anarchy in the academy.* London/New York: Routledge.

Aronowitz, S. (1998). Introduction in *Pedagogy of freedom.* Boulder, CO: Rowman and Littlefield.

Arze-Bravo, M. et al. (2010). *Athusserian ideology website.* Retrieved from *http://froberto.dnsalias.org/shared/Althusserian_Ideology/index.html* (accessed December 15, 2010).

Best, S. & Nocella A. (2006). *Igniting a revolution:* Oakland: AK Press.

Bourdieu, P. (1990). *Reproduction in society, education, and culture.* (Richard Nice, Trans.). London: Sage. (Original work published in 1970).

Carson, K. (2010, November 23). Anarchist Academics listserv (accessed December 13, 2010).

Castoriadis, C. (1997). Democracy as a procedure and democracy as a regime. *Constellations,* 4(1), 1–18.

Chomsky, N. & Macedo, D. (2000). *Chomsky on miseducation.* Lanham, MD: Rowman and Littlefield.

Chomsky, N. (2003). The function of schools: Subtler and cruder methods of control. In K.J. Saltman & D.A. Gabbard (Eds.), *Education as enforcement: The militarization and corporatization of schools.* Routledge, New York.

Cohn, J. (2010, May 16). Anarchist Academics listserv (accessed November 24, 2010).

Ferrell, J. (2001). *Tearing down the streets.* New York: Palgrave, 2001.

Forgacs, D. (1971). *An Antonio Gramsci reader.* New York: Schocken Books.

Freire, P. (2000). *Pedagogy of the oppressed.* New York: Continuum.

Gabbard, D. (2010). The outlook for social justice in our compulsory schools: An anarchist forecast. *Peace Studies Journal,* 3(1), 119–26.

Geibel, E. (2007, February 17). Making a difference. Longtime SUNY Cortland professor and activist dies. *Cortland Standard.* Retrieved from http://www.cortlandstandard.net/articles/02172007n.html.

Godwin, W. (1793). *An enquiry concerning political justice.* Charlottesville, VA: Electronic Text Center, University of Virginia Library. Retrieved from http://etext.virginia.edu/toc/modeng/public/GodJust.html (accessed December 12, 2010).

Goldman, E. (1917). The social importance of the modern school. Emma Goldman Papers, Manuscripts and Archives Division, The New York Public Library, Astor, Lenox and Tilden Foundations. Retrieved from http://dwardmac.pitzer.edu/anarchist_archives/goldman/socimportms.html (accessed December 13, 2010).

Hall, S. (1980). Encoding and decoding in the television discourse. In S. Hall (Ed.), *Culture, medial language working paper in cultural studies*. London: Hutchinson.

Kaltefleiter, C. (1995) *Revolution girl style now: Trebled reflexivity and the riot grrrl network*, unpublished manuscript.

Kaltefleiter, C. (2009). Anarchy girl style now: Riot Grrrl actions and practices. In R. Amster, A. DeLeon, L. Fernandez, A. Nocella II & D. Shannon (Eds.), *Contemporary anarchist studies: An introductory anthology of anarchy in the academy*. London/New York: Routledge.

Kaltefleiter, C. & Nagel, M. (2009). The carceral society: From the prison tower to the ivory tower. In S. Best, P. McLaren & A. Nocella (Eds.), *Academic repression: Reflections from the academic industrial complex*. Oakland: AK Press.

Klages, M. (2001). Louis Althusser's ideology and ideological state apparatuses. Course handout. Retrieved from http://www.colorado.edu/English/courses/ENGL2012Klages/1997althusser.html (accessed December 12, 2010).

Lewis, P., Evan, R. & Wainwright, M. (2010, January 10). Mark Kennedy knew of second undercover eco-activist. *Guardian*. Retrieved from http://www.guardian.co.uk/environment/2011/jan/10/mark-kennedy-second-undercover-ecoactivist.

McLaren, P. (1999). *Schooling as a ritual performance*. New York: Rowman & Littlefield.

Nocella, A. (2010, May 17). Anarchist Academics listserv (accessed November 24, 2010).

Pritchard, A. (2010, May 16). Anarchist Academics listserv (accessed November 24, 2010).

Rossiter, N. (2003). Processual media theory. *Symploke, 11*(1–2) 104–31.

Shannon, D. (2010, May 16). Anarchist Academics listserv (accessed November 24, 2010).

Sjukaitis, S. & Graeber, D. eds (2007). *Constituent imaginations: Militant investigations and collective theorization*. Oakland: AK Press.

Spring, J. (1994). *Wheels in the head: Educational philosophies of authority, freedom, and culture from Socrates to Paulo Freire*. New York: McGraw Hill

Willis, P. (1977). *Learning to labor*. Farnborough UK: Saxon House.

Zinn, H. (2002). *You can't be neutral on a moving train*. Boston: Beacon Press.

SECTION III

# Philosophical Perspectives and Theoretical Frameworks

# DIALOGUE 3

## *(On a mountaintop, between two who are in fact one)*

**Alejandro de Acosta**

**A:** See, there are movements. They issue calls, call out to each other, too.

**B:** Yes, other self, and I hear, in their distant calls, discourses, stories.

**A:** Look, somewhere someone finds or loses a self, as if one of us were to vanish to the other.

**B:** Yes, and look, somewhere, a political act, one or more, unfolds, unfold. Already here, on this mountaintop, you and I, other self…

**A:** I am not so sure. From up here all of this might come to seem strange, unlikely, incomprehensible.

**B:** Fragile, at least.

**A:** No homogenous space…

**B:** … no plinth, no socle…

**A:** … on which it is all gathered.

**B:** What negotiations were necessary to begin telling this story…

**A:** … or to jump in somewhere in the middle, saying, see, look…?

**B:** What anamnesis…

**A:** … or healthy amnesia…

**B:** … to say: this is and is not a self;

**A:** … to say: this is and is not politics.

**B:** Ah. This story folds back upon itself.

**A:** It involutes, yes.

**B:** …

**A:** One answer, for us, here on the mountaintop: ethical negotiations.

**B:** If so, their aftereffects are what we by custom call consent, consensus, assembly, consulta… do you remember how we spoke before our ascent?

**A:** Yes, those sessions in which it was in bad taste to assume ahead of time what was under discussion, its ramifications.

**B:** Another answer, kind other self: we are folding not just speech but life back on itself.

**A:** The most paradoxical lesson?

**B:** It would concern power that is not power…

**A:** … an ethics that is finally amoral. Can we even speak of this here?

**B:** Some like to ask what such-and-such would "look like"… as I wonder what you, other self, look like.

**A:** But it is not a matter of representation, is it? I can't see you at all.

**B:** The desire that the lesson could matter, that speech could come to feel concrete…

**A:** … some say "real," but here on the mountaintop…

**B:** Yes, even here, other self, direct action in discourse.

**A:** A story that, atomic, reinvents life?

**B:** I know this: it is our ever-receding goal.

**A:** It is also our ever-present discovery, if you remember the experiment that brought us here.

**B:** It is for others to take up now. For us it is a goal that is finally not a goal.

**A:** And yet we are not without the lesson that is a sign, a place-holder that is not a compromise. That is why we are two.

CHAPTER 12

# To Walk Questioning: Zapatismo, the Radical Imagination, and a Transnational Pedagogy of Liberation

**Alex Khasnabish**

> Terrible have been the struggles between those of above and those of below, between the powerful and the dispossessed. Much has been written of the reasons and causes for these clashes. The truth is, they all have the same foundation: the powerful want to bring down the world the ceiba holds up; those of below want to keep the world and memory, because that is where the dawn comes from.[1]
>
> The powerful fight against humanity.
>
> The dispossessed fight and dream for humanity.
>
> This is the true history. And if it does not appear in primary school textbooks, that is because history is still being written by those above, even though it is made by those below.
>
> But even though it's not part of the official curricula, the story of the birth of the world and the map that explains where it is, is still being held in the scars of the mother ceiba.
>
> The eldest of the elders of the communities entrusted the secret to the Zapatistas. In the mountains, they spoke with them and told them where the note was left by the first gods, those who gave birth to the world, so memory wouldn't be lost.
>
> Ever since, because they were born without faces, without names, and without individual pasts, the Zapatistas have been students of the story taught by the land. One dawn in the year 1994, the Zapatistas became teachers; consulting the old note of memory, they could teach how the world was born and show where it is to be found.
>
> That is why the Zapatistas are students and teachers.
>
> From "Democratic Teachers and the Zapatista Dream" by Subcomandante Insurgente Marcos (2001, pp. 275–76)

## Lessons in Dignity

Standing in the streets of San Cristóbal de las Casas in the first hours of the new year in 1994, Zapatista spokesperson and military strategist Subcomandante Insurgente Marcos explained the presence of the army of masked, armed indigenous insurgents occupying the central plaza, administrative offices, and streets of the old colonial capital of Chiapas, Mexico, to a group of reporters and other anxious onlookers. Rather than speaking the doctrinaire language of modernist revolution, Marcos unapologetically described the Zapatista uprising as an urgently needed "lesson in dignity" given to the rest of the Mexican nation and, as would soon become clear, the rest of the world by the insurgents and support bases of the Zapatista Army of National Liberation (Ejército Zapatista de Liberación Nacional, EZLN) in the face of the creeping oblivion materialized in the form of colonialism, imperialism, racism, genocide, and capitalism (Subcomandante Insurgente Marcos 2002, pp. 211–12). Marcos elaborated upon the significance of this lesson by extending his pedagogical analogy:

> [the uprising] should be a lesson for all. We cannot let ourselves be treated this way, and we have to try and construct a better world, a world truly for everyone, and not only a few, as the current regime does. This is what we want. We do not want to monopolize the vanguard or say that we are the light, the only alternative, or stingily claim the qualification of revolutionary for one or another current. We say, look at what happened. That is what we had to do. (ibid.)

Marcos's description of the Zapatista uprising as a "lesson in dignity" invokes the language of pedagogy not only as a morally powerful justification for the EZLN's insurgency, it would also turn out to be prophetic in terms of Zapatismo's resonance transnationally.

From a geopolitical perspective, January 1, 1994, marked the first day the North American Free Trade Agreement (NAFTA) came into force, binding Canada, the United States, and Mexico together in a continental neoliberal capitalist market. It also marked the end of the short-lived neoliberal "end of history" rhetoric that had been so enthusiastically trumpeted by capitalist elites and their intellectual defenders in the wake of the fall of the Berlin Wall and the collapse of the Soviet Union. This rhetorical invocation of "the end of history" was a phrase meant to stand for the end of the great ideological conflicts that had marked so much of modern history and the ascendance of neoliberal capitalism along with some tattered trappings of liberal democratic practice. It also signified the defeat of traditional actors of the established Left on a global scale as organized labor, communist and social democratic political parties, progressive social movements, and institutionalized social justice actors found themselves rudderless and bereft of credibility and grassroots capacity after decades of tepid and uninspired political practice aimed, at best, at ameliorating the worst consequences of capitalism and other oppressive systems such as racism and patriarchy and, at worst, angling to get a seat at the table with powerholders and thereby join their ranks. The challenge to the proclamation of history's end would not come from these disciplined, defeated, and coopted sectors—especially not from those in the global North; instead, the most profound challenge to this hegemonic claim would come from the far southeast of Mexico in the state of Chiapas where, in the early hours of the new year, thousands of armed and masked indigenous Mayan insurgents emerged from five centuries of indigenous resistance and persistence in the face of genocide, racism, and exploitation and declared "*¡Ya basta!*"—"Enough!"—to the systems of power that sought to deny them their very right to exist. Identifying NAFTA and neoliberal capitalism as only the most recent incarnation of five centuries of creeping oblivion manifested in the form of genocide, slavery, colonialism, imperialism, racism, exploitation, and brutal marginalization, the insurgents of the EZLN also positioned themselves as the legitimate heirs to the unfulfilled radical promise of the Mexican Revolution (1910–1917) and its most storied and uncompromised hero, Emiliano Zapata.[2]

Seizing several towns and hundreds of ranches throughout the state, the insurgents of the Zapatista Army of National Liberation declared war on the federal executive of the Mexican government and the Mexican Army while announcing their intention to march on Mexico City and allow the Mexican people to freely and democratically constitute a government of their own choosing. After the first day of January, the Zapatista rebellion would take a path that no one could have anticipated as armed insurgency was met by massive state repression and both, in turn, were met by the spontaneous and unexpected force of Mexican and international civil society organizing massive demonstrations in order to compel an end to the hostilities and bring the government and the Zapatistas to the negotiation table. Under the weight of massive national and international pressure, the Mexican government declared a ceasefire on January 12, 1994, and while it would hardly mark the end of violence in Chiapas, it would mark the beginning of an entirely new phase of the Zapatista struggle—one reliant much more upon the word than the gun. As Subcomandante Insurgente Marcos would remark, "We did not go to war on January 1 to kill or to have them kill us. We went to make ourselves heard" (Womack, 1999, p. 44). The Zapatistas were certainly heard—throughout Mexico and around the world and while they were clear from the outset that they were not the vanguard of some new monolithic revolutionary movement, that they were always only one pocket of rebels seeking to struggle for a new world alongside other rebellious pockets elsewhere (see Subcomandante Marcos, 2004), as a movement they would take on the roles of both student and teacher in a vital, urgent, and creative pedagogy of radical resistance and alternative-building that would engage a diversity of others in struggle far outside the borders of Zapatista territory in rebellion.

The Zapatistas' New Year's Day uprising has, in the years since, come to be widely regarded as one of the most important sparks to light the fuse of what would become the global anticapitalist/alter-globalization "movement of movements" (see Ronfeldt et al., 1998; Callahan, 2004; Cleaver, 1998; Khasnabish, 2010, 2008; Kingsnorth, 2003; Klein, 2002; Midnight Notes, 2001; Notes from Nowhere, 2003; Olesen, 2005; Solnit, 2004). Despite this recognition—in fact, at least in part because of the Zapatistas' idealization as icons of militant resistance—many observers and activists in the global North have failed to come to terms with one of the most significant lessons offered by Zapatismo: namely, that liberation is an imperfect and ongoing practice, one that necessitates not only the construction of a new world capable of holding many worlds but the nurturing of new subjectivities inspired by new imaginations who are capable of inhabiting such a world. But new imaginations and new subjectivities cannot simply be rhetorically ushered into being, they have to be socially produced and reproduced. Against this backdrop, in this chapter I take up Zapatismo—the radical imagination and political practice of the Zapatista movement—as a pedagogy of liberation directed toward the cultivation of new ways of being in the world that aim to take us beyond the failures of past revolutionary struggles. Drawing on research conducted with alter-globalization activists in Canada and the United States as well as a critical history of the Zapatista movement and insights from contemporary radical political theory, in what follows I explore the relationship between a radical imagination of sociopolitical possibility and the formation of new subjectivities in the context of the encounters and affinities provoked by Zapatismo's transnational resonance in the north of the Americas.

## Beautiful Myths and Radical Imagination

Few radical movements have had as much attention directed at them as the Zapatistas. Any number of factors could be said to account for this, including: the EZLN's seemingly anachronistic appearance as a revolutionary insurgent force at "the end of history"; the unmatched communicative skills of the Zapatistas' spokesperson Subcomandante Marcos; the Zapatistas' deft use of a variety of strategies to engage "civil society" at national and transnational levels; the romanticization and projection of revolutionary hope and desire onto the Zapatista movement by others located far beyond the living context the movement occupies. For many observers located in the global North, the resonance of Zapatismo has been described in terms of a facile and consumptive romanticism (Hellman, 2000; Oppenheimer, 2002), a product of digital communications infrastructure (Knudson, 1998), and a phenomenon driven by "globalizing" discourses such as liberal democracy and human rights (Olesen 2005; Tarrow 2005), to name only a few of the dominant iterations. This list could surely be endlessly elaborated and no doubt include various attempts to "prove" that the Zapatista movement is just another manifestation of a basic struggle for inclusion and recognition, is reducible to a narrow set of material grievances and inequalities, or is an example of the cynical and self-serving manipulation of poor, child-like indigenous peoples by self-proclaimed revolutionaries.

Equally prevalent of course is the valorization of the movement, characterizations which could be thought of as "beautiful myths" that celebrate very selective aspects of it while omitting others, particularly those that relate to the living, imperfect, and uneven experiences of struggles for radical social transformation. While "myth" is a term often deployed in a pejorative and denigrating sense, it is worth considering that myth is not merely something untrue or a constructed origin story, rather, it is perhaps best understood as a kind of interpellating mode of signification or speech, one which "calls" to subjects and in so doing simultaneously works to form them (Barthes, 1972, p. 124). Every system of meaning-making and power makes use of myth; the real question is how and to what end. For example, without using it as a basis from which to launch a delegitimization of Zapatismo or its resonance, Adrienne Russell (2005) has identified three central "myths" that have been central to the constitution of a network identity among international supporters: first, that of Subcomandante Marcos as a universal, "timeless," "uberhuman" figure; second, that of the Indigenous peoples of Chiapas as "noble warriors" paradoxically "backward" and "advanced"; and finally, the myth of the "neoliberal beast" that functions as the adversary to be confronted. The point to understanding these myths is not to affirm or debunk them, rather, it is to understand what they make possible with respect to emerging fabrics of resistance and alternative-building, as well as what their circulation and consumption might inhibit and obscure. Rebecca Solnit's (2004) inspiring characterization of the Zapatista struggle is an example of the promise and limitations of deploying such beautiful myths:

> The Zapatistas came as a surprise and as a demonstration that overnight, the most marginal, overlooked place can become the center of the world. They were not just demanding change, but embodying it; and in this, they were and are already victorious . . . They understood the interplay between physical actions, those carried out with guns, and symbolic actions, those carried out with rods, with images, with art, with communications, and they won through the latter means what they never could have won through their small capacity for violence. (pp. 34–35)

Solnit's assessment of Zapatismo is compelling and it contains many truths but it also celebrates dynamics (communicative action, moral victory, change through symbolic contestation) that have played very well among sympathetic activists and observers primarily in the global North for whom symbolic and communicative resistance to systems of power and domination have become fetishized because materializing collective resistance and alternatives to the status quo often seems so difficult in a context so thoroughly colonized by capital.

There is, of course, nothing wrong and very much right with the identification of the importance of strategies of symbolic and communicative resistance, nor is there anything misguided in celebrating the successes of struggles like the Zapatistas'. That said, when these beautiful myths become the dominant tropes that circulate about the Zapatistas, other equally or even more important lessons slide from view—and not without consequence. The assertion that "overnight" the Zapatistas managed to draw the world's attention or that they were simply "embodying" change obscures the decades-long work that went into making such things possible. Such assertions also do no justice to the fact that the attention of "the world" has been fickle and the work of sustaining it has required a great deal of time, energy, and creativity on the part of the Zapatistas. These myths also obscure the fact that the Zapatistas' struggle is a work-in-progress, one that demands constant renewal and revisioning and is also a site of contestation and conflict. Rather than locating their struggle at the apogee of a revolutionary trajectory the Zapatistas have sought from the moment of their public appearance to explicitly and self-consciously locate their struggle as one among many. Not only this, they have also repeatedly affirmed that theirs is not a revolutionary blueprint, it is a living and imperfect process that requires constant reflection, critique, and reformulation. The Zapatista narrative of radical collective social transformation being a long-term, difficult, and uncertain process that is nonetheless necessary is something that has not been picked up as enthusiastically by those who have been receptive to Zapatismo's resonance as have their rhetorically brilliant slogans. Finding fault with radical social change movements is a fashion and is often linked to generating political or academic capital, but it is also not the same thing as engaging in a process of respectful and solidaristic critical engagement with other radical social transformation processes. If we do not attend to the much more complex and nuanced lessons Zapatismo has to offer as opposed to reveling in the beautiful myths circulating about it, we miss what is most urgent and timely in the Zapatistas' pedagogy of liberation. At a moment when radicalized mass movements in the north of the Americas are conspicuous in their absence in the face of a rising protofascism aimed at engineering a new sociopolitical order predicated on permanent war, surveillance, oppression, exploitation, and misery, it is all the more urgent to attend to the "lessons in dignity" that movements like that of the Zapatistas have to teach.

So how can the reasons for and consequences of Zapatismo's resonance, particularly at the level of the transnational, be productively engaged in a way that takes us beyond the celebration of beautiful myths? How can the significance of Zapatismo be understood not only as a discrete phenomenon but in terms of what it reveals about the relationship between radical social change movements, radical social transformation, and radical knowledge production? Rather than myth, critically exploring this dynamic foregrounds the inherently political work of meaning-making and bring the production and circulation of narratives of resistance and possibility into focus. As Jeff Conant (2010) argues in his examination of the poetics—"the making of meaning through language"—of Zapatismo, "[s]tories of resistance . . . help to strengthen resistance, rooting it more deeply in belief and in practice, and thus sustain it" (11).

In the same vein, Eric Selbin (2003) contends that it is necessary to understand "the role played by stories, narratives of popular resistance, rebellion and revolution which have animated and emboldened generations of revolutionaries across time and cultures" (p. 84). This focus upon the importance of the work of meaning-making in relation to radical struggle is absolutely central in terms of understanding the lessons offered by Zapatismo as a pedagogy of liberation.

Indeed, many activists and organizers I spoke with who had experienced Zapatismo's resonance emphasized precisely this point. Describing his own experience with Zapatismo during our conversation in the fall of 2004, Rick Rowley, a radical filmmaker with Big Noise Tactical, noted that "Zapatismo's not like an ideology that's easy to lay out; it's not structured like that.[3] It's more like a structure of myth and parables but so much of it just so clearly articulated something that was in the water already just waiting to be spoken," specifically in relation to new forms of radical organizing and strategies for social transformation. Patrick Reinsborough, cofounder of the smartMeme Strategy and Training Project, used similar imagery in his own explanation of the significance of Zapatismo when we spoke in the spring of 2004: "even having had that brief stint as a military struggle [the Zapatistas] were very clear right from the beginning that their battleground was really being set on their own terms. They said it was a war of ideas, a war of words, more than a war of guns or bullets." Elaborating on this, Reinsborough pointed to the lessons taught by the Zapatistas in terms of the nature of radical struggle. Zapatismo, Reinsborough contended, illuminated the vital need for radical struggles to work to "decolonize people's imaginations" by stressing "the importance of networks, the importance of contesting idea space and that the system really is most vulnerable not where a line of riot police might be gathering or most vulnerable in a military sense, it's most vulnerable at its intellectual underpinnings." At the same time, it is worth repeating that a critical and engaged analysis of the work of meaning-making as it relates to the living experience of radical struggle is precisely the opposite of the uncritical, romanticized, and facile consumption of rhetoric and the celebration of a movement as if its primary purpose is that of icon or inspiration for others.

During our conversation in the winter of 2004, Justin Podur, a regular contributor to *ZNet*, member of the Canada Colombia Solidarity Campaign, and a self-described "camp follower" of the Ontario Coalition Against Poverty, powerfully articulated the danger of making a fashion out of a movement. Describing Zapatismo's resonance within activist circles in Canada and the United States, Podur noted that in fetishizing Zapatismo, all too often activists have drawn the wrong lessons from the Zapatistas and, in so doing, have actually undermined the struggles they saw themselves as contributing to:

> There are really cynical people who will say that [the Zapatistas are] a fashion, a fad. I think [the Zapatistas have resonated among northern activists] sometimes for the wrong reasons too. I think a lot of people who could and should continue to help a movement in a place like Venezuela [haven't] because they can't handle the idea that Chávez tried to take power in a coup in 1992 [but] they didn't have a problem with the Zapatistas doing the same in '94, that's not even on the spectrum. [These activists believe that] the Zapatistas, they don't want to take power, they're Indigenous, they want to transform the way that power's exercised, but Chávez is after power [and] we can't support something like that, that's old style Marxism. It's crazy, and it's crazy because the target of the US foreign policies, of the economic policies, of the militarism is the populations of these countries, is the population of Mexico, is the Indigenous population of Chiapas, exactly the same way as is the population in Venezuela. They're the obstacle in people's plans to exploit the resources of the region and to exploit the labor of the people and because of these fetishes I think people don't see that. In that sense the fad about Zapatismo has been really destructive because there are other groups, there are other processes, and nobody cares about them because they don't understand why the Zapatistas are important and why the Zapatistas are not important. Long before 9/11 in the anti-globalization work people were doing there were a lot of debates about violence and the debates were really superficial. The non-violence people would say, "we want to be non-violent like Gandhi" and the violence people said, "we want to be violent like the Zapatistas" and it was just the stupidest thing in the world because

> the non-violence people didn't know a damn thing about Gandhi and the violence people didn't know a thing about the Zapatistas. I really wish that people would see [the Zapatista struggle] in that context as one piece of a struggle that's going on all over the world but all over the continent especially.

The fetishization of Zapatismo as a struggle activists elsewhere can project all their desires for "authentic" and "revolutionary" struggle on to leads not only to a consumptive appropriation of other people's struggles, it also contributes to a narrative about radical social transformation where certain actors play the role of protagonist while others are accorded the status of supporting cast. This is much more than an academic distinction because the way in which we narrate genealogies of struggle frames our imagination of what possibilities exist for resistance and alternative-building. As Podur points out here, the valorization of the Zapatistas' "revolutionary model" or, even worse, a facile romanticization of their tactics and structure in fact works directly against what the Zapatistas have worked so hard to do since their public emergence on January 1, 1994: connect themselves and others to a larger fabric of struggle in which no one stands above anyone else and to explicitly reject the notion that there is only one path to revolutionary change.

The language of myth, parable, and imagination invoked by the analysts and activists above is profoundly significant. Elsewhere, I have described Zapatismo as an "insurgent" or radicalized imagination of political possibility (Khasnabish, 2010, 2008, 2007) and this dimension is core to understanding its resonance among and significance for the fabric of radical sociopolitical struggle. So what is radical imagination? Put simply, it is a process by which we collectively map "what is," narrate it as the result of "what was," and speculate on what "might be." It is both cognitive and corporeal and, rather than being necessarily spectacular or dramatic, it can be quite mundane. While the capacity to envision that which does not yet exist is obviously a human capacity, the radical imagination is also necessarily a collective process, something that arises out of dialogue and encounter rather than emerging fully formed from the mind of a gifted individual. Furthermore, while imagination is a terrain of political struggle it is not reducible to "ideology" in any simplistic sense of "false consciousness" or "fetishism." Instead of the interpellating force of myth, which calls to and creates subjects, the radical imagination embodies a more rich, complex, agent-driven and ongoing working-out of affinity (see Haiven and Khasnabish, 2010). It is in the space of radical imagination that Zapatismo's resonance, particularly transnationally, acquires its power and significance and it is within this same space that it becomes possible to refer to Zapatismo as a pedagogy of liberation in the sense that it is not a roadmap for revolution but a constant provocation to rethink radical sociopolitical struggle even as we live it. So what are some of the core tenets of the radical imagination of Zapatismo? To begin with, issues of power, autonomy, and dignity are central to it. As autonomist Marxist theorist and longtime Zapatista supporter John Holloway eloquently explains, "What is at issue is not who exercises power, but how to create a world based on the mutual recognition of human dignity, on the formation of social relations which are not power relations . . . This, then, is the revolutionary challenge at the beginning of the twenty-first century: to change the world without taking power. This is the challenge that has been formulated most clearly by the Zapatista uprising in the south-east of Mexico." (2002, 17–20). Elaborating on the Zapatista challenge Holloway identifies, in an interview in 2001 during the March of Indigenous Dignity, Subcomandante Marcos described what made the Zapatistas so different from other revolutionary movements:

> Our army is very different from others, because its proposal is to cease being an army. A soldier is an absurd person who has to resort to arms in order to convince others, and in that sense the movement has no future if its future is military. If the EZLN perpetuates itself as an armed military structure, it is headed for failure. Failure as an alternative set of ideas, an alternative attitude to the world . . . .You cannot reconstruct the world or society, or rebuild national states now in ruins, on the basis of a quarrel over who will impose their hegemony on society. (García Márquez and Pombo, 2004, pp. 4–5)

This refusal to claim a "power-over" others and the affirmation of a collective "power-to" create a world rooted in dignity, democracy, justice, and liberty is an essential element with respect to Zapatismo as a radical imagination. It also offers important lessons with respect to rethinking revolutionary action in light of the grotesque failures of past movements that sought to build ambitious transformative visions atop the persecuted, imprisoned, tortured, and murdered bodies of all those who opposed them.

Marcos has furthered this point, which challenges the familiar modernist dynamic of revolutionary movements aiming to seize the state through arms in order to actualize the revolution, noting, "The EZLN has reached a point where it has been overtaken by Zapatismo," and, in so doing, rhetorically affirmed a critical distance between Zapatismo and the EZLN (ibid., p. 5). While the EZLN is the armed wing of the insurgency and exists to defend Zapatista territory in rebellion, Zapatismo is "a political strategy, an ethos, a set of commitments claimed by those who claim a political identity" (Callahan, 2004, pp. 218–19). This "ethos" identified by Callahan hinges on an approach to politics based on the pursuit of "democracy, liberty, and justice"—

the banners of the Zapatista struggle from the moment of its public emergence—for all. While notions such as "justice," "democracy," and "freedom" are inherently plastic in that their meaning depends on the subjectivity espousing them and the context in which they are deployed, they become radical signifiers within the discourse of Zapatismo precisely because of its radical critique of power. For those activists who have been most receptive to Zapatismo as a radical imagination, concepts such as "democracy," "liberty," and "justice" are not limited to their liberal democratic interpretations, rather, they are markers for a radical political practice aimed at contesting and moving beyond both the systemic nature of marginalization, violence, and exploitation as well as revolutionary praxes that operate according to a logic of hegemony or which claim to know the "true" revolutionary path. But in order to explore Zapatismo as a pedagogy of liberation, it is necessary to examine it not only as a radical imagination of political possibility but to take it up in the context of some of the radical lessons learned by the Zapatista movement in the process of its formation, lessons that would come to deeply inform Zapatismo as radical imagination and liberatory pedagogy transnationally.

## Encounters between Worlds in *la Montaña*

The history of the Zapatista struggle can be traced back decades and even centuries to indigenous struggles against colonialism, nationalist struggles for independence, and radical struggles for revolutionary sociopolitical and economic transformation. For my purposes here, it will suffice to begin this lesson drawn from Zapatista history in the 1950s. At this time, and in a state marked by extreme inequality, enduring racism, and seemingly endless capacity for violence and brutal repression by elites in defense of their own interests, many young indigenous people sought exodus from the lack of land and opportunity in established highland communities, forming new communities in the Lacandón Jungle that would become experiments in social and political organization. Left to themselves, confronting common concerns, and bereft of their traditional leaders and ranks of honor, these migrants chose to emphasize the importance of community over hierarchy and thus turned to the community assembly where all people over the age of sixteen would meet to reach consensus over all decisions concerning the community (Womack, 1999, p. 18). The assembly materialized the principle that it was not the authorities who ruled the community but the community that ruled the authorities—a principle that the Zapatistas would make central to their movement and enshrine in the slogan *mandar obedeciendo*, "to lead by obeying" (ibid., p. 19).

While these migrant communities and their directly democratic practice would become the Zapatista base and backbone, the other vital element needed to generate this movement would arrive in the form of cadres from the urban guerrilla struggles in Mexico that took place in the late 1960s and through the '70s. Indeed, contemporary Zapatismo originated out of the encounter between indigenous communities in the Lacandón Jungle and highlands of Chiapas and the urban revolutionaries who arrived in the state in the early 1980s. The EZLN itself was born in a camp in Chiapas on November 17, 1983, with six insurgents—three *mestizos* and three indigenous—present (Muñoz Ramírez, 2008, p. 21).[4] While these urban revolutionaries—cadres from the Fuerzas de Liberación Nacional (Forces of National Liberation, FLN)—arrived in Chiapas to organize *campesinos* for a revolution, the outcome of this encounter would be significantly different than this classically modernist revolutionary objective. In fact, rather than "revolutionizing" these communities, the urban insurgents experienced profound challenges to their ideological perspectives and found them reshaped by indigenous realities, a grounded and critical pedagogical moment that actually allowed for the emergence of the Zapatista struggle itself. Amid the mists of the highlands and the heat of the jungle, indigenous communities and urban revolutionaries encountered one another and found that the defeat of revolutionary dogmatism was not enough to catalyze a new social change movement. To bring a new radical politics into being—what would ultimately become Zapatismo—required a new praxis, one born of the urban revolutionaries' critical reading of Mexican history and current economic and political context combined with the communities' own experiences of resistance and persistence in the face of genocide, racism, exploitation, and marginalization.

While Subcomandante Marcos, who would become the Zapatistas' spokesperson and one of their chief military strategists, and the other guerrillas had come to Chiapas to educate the masses about the necessity of a Marxist revolution, the indigenous communities they encountered understood their world in ways revolutionary orthodoxy could not possibly speak to fully. In the course of the difficult process of clandestine survival and organization, Marcos and the other urban revolutionaries began to realize that indigenous notions of time, history, and reality were fundamentally different from what they had been taught to believe (Harvey, 1998, p. 165). In order to be taken seriously by the communities, Marcos and the other *guerrilleros* needed to demonstrate their capacity to understand and survive in the rugged, mountainous terrain not as a physical rite of passage but because of the significance of this context for the communities as "a respected and feared place of stories, myths, and ghosts" (ibid., p. 165). While Marcos had come to teach politics and history to the communities, he quickly discovered that this revolutionary education, steeped in its own assumptions, made no sense to the communities (ibid., p, 166). In effect, the urban *guerrilleros* had to be reeducated and become new subjects capable of inhabiting the realities of the indigenous southeast if they were to be anything other than another failed group of radicals preaching incomprehensibly and ineffectually in a vain effort to recruit followers to their cause. This reeducation process included: learning indigenous languages; slowly coming to comprehend radically different ways of making sense out of the world; renouncing a politics based on Euro-Enlightenment assumptions and subordinating their own political expectations to the needs of the communities themselves; and giving up on a revolutionary politics of the vanguard and embracing a collective decision-making process grounded in the collective. The nondogmatic, radically democratic, and self-reflexive approach to radical social struggle and transformation that would come to characterize the Zapatista movement is poetically encapsulated in another Zapatista slogan, *preguntando caminamos*, "asking, we walk." Ultimately, of course, this process of radical, grounded education transformed not only the urban *guerrilleros* but the communities as well. In the canyons and Lacandón Jungle of Chiapas, the Chol, Tzeltal, Tzotzil, and Tojolabal Mayan migrants who had been practicing communal decision-making in a directly democratic way through community assemblies found their political practice further radicalized in light of the emerging politics of Zapatismo. The outcome of this radical reeducation process cannot be overstated. As Neil Harvey explains, "[i]nstead of arriving directly from the city or the university, the EZLN emerged out of *la montaña*, that magical world inhabited by the whole of Mayan history, by the spirits of ancestors, and by Zapata himself" (ibid., p. 166).

By the time members of the Zapatista base communities voted to go to war against the federal executive and Mexican Army in 1992, the EZLN had severed all ties with the Forces of National Liberation and the Clandestine Indigenous Revolutionary Committee had been created as its highest body of authority (Womack, 1999, p. 192). Tellingly, by the time the communities voted for war, geopolitical conditions seemed everywhere to point to the fallacy of such an action. With the collapse of the Soviet Union, the disarray of the traditional Left in the face of neoliberal capitalism's ascendance, and the now uncontested place of the United States as lone remaining superpower, in the eyes of the Zapatista military leadership an armed uprising in the Mexican southeast seemed strategically unwise. The Zapatista base, however, arrived at a very different conclusion, and this discrepancy says much about the way authority, knowledge, experience, and power circulate within the movement. As Mexican historian Adolfo Gilly (1998) explains:

> The channels through which communities, on one side, and the leadership of the EZLN (or for that matter any other left-wing organization), on the other, get their perceptions of the surrounding society are not

> the same; nor are the filters and the codes according to which they are interpreted. This difference, invisible to all in "normal" times when the capital decision—insurrection—is not in play, comes to light at the moment of making that decision. For that reason, while some see in the "disappearance of the Soviet Union" a negative factor, others who are distant from that interpretation of an upheaval, regarding which they are not concerned, measure by other methods—against the arc of their own lives—the maturation of conditions for rebellion. (p. 303)

In place of geopolitical analysis, theoretical sophistication, or even narrow pragmatism, the Zapatista base communities in Chiapas measured the conditions, cost, and possibility of rebellion "against the arc of their own lives," a perspective that would deeply infuse Zapatismo as political praxis in the years following the uprising and explain much about what has made the movement so compelling to others transnationally. Rather than seeking validation in abstract laws or theoretical orthodoxy, Zapatismo espouses a commitment to radical social transformation that is grounded ethically in the lives of those who constitute the movement. These same subjects are the ones who are responsible for collectively elaborating the way the movement *knows* the world, imagines possibilities beyond what exists now, and articulates paths toward liberation. As the Zapatistas have repeatedly demonstrated since their public emergence in 1994, none of these processes is static and none of the destinations are forever fixed because real revolutions are made not through blueprints or the insight of an enlightened vanguard, they are paths made by those who walk them.

## Zapatismo as Radical Pedagogy

As this fragment of Zapatista history should make clear, neither the EZLN nor Zapatismo are products of a pure revolutionary trajectory. Indeed, this is what has made both of them so significant within the Mexican context and outside of it. At the intersection of urban guerrillas seeking favorable ground for revolutionary organizing, migrant indigenous communities practicing a new kind of politics, and a sociopolitical and economic context marked by extreme violence, exploitation, and repression, Zapatismo emerged as an audacious declaration of hope and possibility. At the crossroads of this encounter it was actually the defeat of the Marxist, modernist revolutionary ideology of the FLN cadres in the face of a radically different lifeworld where the roots of Zapatismo lie. Taking the best lessons from the urban revolutionary legacy conveyed by the FLN guerrillas, and perhaps most importantly by Subcomandante Marcos, Zapatismo as radical politics and radical imagination only emerged once it was deeply grounded in the social fabric of the communities that came to constitute it.

This is not to suggest there is some essential indigenous core to the Zapatista project, that it is simply an extension of the *nature of being indigenous*. Indeed, as many of my research partners engaged in a variety of radical struggles emphasized, it is a dangerous and reductive form of romanticism that wants to see in the struggles of indigenous peoples some eternal, premodern, naturalistic identity that can show nonindigenous peoples and societies *the way* out of the overlapping crises we now confront. As indigenous media-maker and activist Rebeka Tabobondung explained to me during our conversation in the winter of 2004, "I think that people are increasingly becoming unsatisfied with Western institutions, belief systems, systems in general, and looking towards Indigenous people for hope, for fulfillment, spiritually or inspirationally." Tabobondung went on to describe the limits of this desire to find fulfillment in someone else's being, identity, or struggle when she discussed attempts made in the early 2000s to convoke an Intercontinental Encuentro for Humanity and Against Neoliberalism on indigenous territory inside the borders of the Canadian state:[5]

> [the problem of essentialism and romanticism was] something that [the organizers talked about in the process of planning] the Third Encounter. . . . To non-Native people who were part of it [we wanted to make it clear that this wasn't about coming] here to help Native people, don't come here just to help us, but when we understand what capitalism is doing to people and to the planet then, in fact, our struggles are your struggles, so people can take ownership over that and I think that the Zapatistas were trying to appeal to that as well—this has been happening forever, now it's just happening to everybody.

Stephan Dobson, member of the Canadian Union of Public Employees, academic, and a member of the planning committee for the Third Intercontinental Encuentro for Humanity and Against Neoliberalism, echoed Tabobondung's comments when he discussed the critical problem with romanticism as it relates to sociopolitical struggle during our conversation in the fall of 2003:

> I've seen [romanticization] in action and it's a problem of sustainability. People find out that it's not real or that they're dealing with the image rather than the really existing conditions [and they then feel betrayed by that]. 'Cause, from my perspective, while you're imagining a better world, how do you actualize it? My frustration with that kind of imagination way up here [is it] strikes me as dogmatic idealism. . . . It's always the revolution's elsewhere, Nicaragua was really the one when I was an undergraduate, here it is, opportunity, it's happening, you have to be a part of it, you have to mobilize because it's the leading edge, it's something new and it takes on all of the hopes and dreams

> and the aspirations and ambitions, but those struggles [are] directly here, so while you have all this wonderful solidarity going on with Zapatistas you've got a thousand Patricia Pats moving in on Oka.[6] No justice on stolen land.

This is certainly not to say that indigenous struggles do not occupy positions of primacy with respect to a wider fabric of radical social justice struggle—indeed, both Tabobondung's and Dobson's reflections above point in precisely the opposite direction. In the context of settler states like Canada and the United States, for example, coming to terms with the enduring reality of coloniality and finding ways to radically *unsettle* it in solidarity with indigenous struggles for autonomy should be a principle pillar of any radical social justice struggle and yet it is often rhetorically invoked without being manifested materially (see Alfred 2005). But what this points to, beyond the necessity of addressing coloniality as the material basis critical to the very existence of settler states, is that there is no retreat to an "other"—pure, uncontaminated, authentic, holistically grounded—that can save us from the systems of violence, domination, and exploitation that structure people's lived realities.

So what of Zapatismo as radical imagination and radical pedagogy at the level of the transnational? Throughout this piece I have brought the words of my research partners to bear on elements of Zapatismo in order to shed critical illumination on them from the perspective of those who experienced the resonance of this radical movement. These reflections are only a very small fragment of work I have done elsewhere (see Khasnabish 2010, 2008a, 2008b, 2007) that has sought to explore Zapatismo as a radical and transnationalized political imagination. These brief reflections are by no means meant to be representative of the depth of Zapatismo's resonance among radical social justice activists elsewhere but they do stand as a testament to it. In more than a year of ethnographically grounded research that engaged activists and organizers from across Canada and the United States who self-identified as having had politically significant encounters with Zapatismo. These encounters took a tremendous variety of forms as Zapatismo has circulated transnationally through diverse channels, including: the Internet; academic, activist, and journalistic writing; solidarity delegations and report-backs; Zapatista communiqués, denunciations, speeches, and the writing of Subcomandante Marcos; visual media and a host of other artifacts associated with the Zapatista movement. Many of the people with whom I worked had direct experience with the Zapatista struggle on the ground in Chiapas, although the depth of such commitments varied widely, while others had only encountered Zapatismo in mediated forms. The collectives and organizations represented by the organizers and activists with whom I spoke were similarly diverse ranging from non-governmental organizations such as Global Exchange to radical media-making collectives like Big Noise Tactical to transnational anticapitalist networks such as Peoples' Global Action to groups engaged in direct action struggles against the daily realities of capitalist violence and exploitation like the Ontario Coalition Against Poverty. Of course, one need look no further than writing that has emerged from the ranks of the alter-globalization movement itself to encounter a rhetorical confirmation of the significance of Zapatismo to this "movement of movements" (see Kingsnorth, 2003; Klein, 2002; Notes from Nowhere, 2003; Solnit, 2004).

Far from merely celebrating them as icons of militancy, the conversations I had with diverse activists and organizers in Canada and the United States as well as activist media produced about the Zapatistas and Zapatismo situate them as vital pieces of a global rebellion against neoliberal capitalism and elite domination of people and the planet. Transmitted via diverse channels, Zapatismo found resonance in the midst of a multiplicity of different struggles because it did not offer an answer to the challenge of building mass movements capable of changing the world, rather, it served as a constant source of provocation and inspiration for radical struggles seeking paths beyond the violence, oppression, and exploitation of current systems of power as well as the failures of past movements in attempting to address them. Of course, Zapatismo as a transnationalized radical pedagogy also foreground elements of the Zapatista struggle while downplaying others. Prominent in activists' writings and reflections about the significance of Zapatismo for their own understanding of struggle are notions of hope, inclusivity, imagination, dignity, communication, democracy, and a radical sense of possibility as well as an equally radical critique of power. These elements are most certainly present in Zapatismo, particularly with respect to the communiqués and communicative actions directed toward "civil society" transnationally; however, the prominence of these concepts as opposed to others relating more directly to the difficult work of building a living revolutionary struggle in the midst of formidable challenges from state repression to lack of resources also speaks to the subjectivities and contexts for which Zapatismo has proven such a potent imagination.

The emphasis upon a powerful rejection of neoliberalism, the affirmation of human dignity, peace, autonomy and interconnectedness, and the desire for dialogue, coupled with a valorization of communicative and symbolic action rather than violent insurrection cannot be divorced from the Northern context within which Zapatismo as radical pedagogy and radical imagination has resonated. This has always been a problematic dynamic as people view movements elsewhere through the lens of their own desire for change and their own understandings of struggle, and this has certainly happened with respect to the Zapatistas (see Hellman, 2000; Meyer, 2002). However, this ambiguity has also been a fundamental element of the Zapatistas' appeal. In transmitting Zapatismo and its radical lessons about revolution to people living, working, and struggling outside of the indigenous communities of Chiapas, Marcos's writing in particular has foregrounded those elements of Zapatista discourse most likely to speak compellingly across a variety of disparate contexts. In addition, activists outside of Chiapas have also actively participated in reading the Zapatista struggle from their own position, a reading necessarily colored by one's own experience. None of this makes the encounter between activists transnationally and the Zapatistas—however this encounter has been mediated—inauthentic. Rather, it suggests that the significance of the Zapatistas as rebels on a transnational political scale has to be understood less in terms of a monologue-like "inspiration" and more as a dynamic dialogue given shape by the contexts it occurs within. Once again, we return to the space of pedagogy in order to explore and explain Zapatismo's radical significance: issues of power, privilege, context, and subjectivity necessarily impact the way one learns about themselves, others, the wider world, and the possibilities therein. This is not a debunking of the transnationalized encounters between Zapatismo and those who have proven so receptive to its radical, unclosed lesson plan, rather, it is to suggest that this process of encounter and the pedagogical moments attached to it are deeply enmeshed in the living contexts in which they occur.

Indeed, what Zapatismo demonstrates so compellingly is that powerful, socially transformative movements emerge not from some singularly important revolutionary subject but through an unending process of critical encounter that reshapes all those involved. As Fiona Jeffries—an activist, writer, and academic who has done considerable solidarity work with the Zapatistas—expressed during our conversation in the winter of 2004, "that is [the Zapatistas'] strength, their historical subject is not in any singular being, their historical subject is people's desire for freedom and justice and dignity." This description applies not only to the migrant indigenous communities who would eventually constitute the Zapatista base and the urban guerrillas who would join them in the jungle and mountains, it also speaks to the experience of those who would encounter Zapatismo as a transnationalized radical imagination. In this sense, the movement itself needs to be thought of not only in organizational and political terms but also as a space for experiments in knowledge production, radical imagination, subjectification, and concrete alternative-building. Alberto Melucci (1985) once said of social movements, "The medium, the movement itself as a new medium, is the message. As prophets without enchantment, contemporary movements practice in the present the change they are struggling for: they redefine the meaning of social action for the whole society" (p. 801). In this sense, radical movements like the Zapatistas are spaces of prefiguration and possibility, living processes of resistance and alternative-building that are vital to the elaboration of ways of envisioning and enacting radical and even revolutionary social transformation.

## Notes

1 The ceiba is a silk-cotton tree and is regarded as sacred by the Maya.

2 It is significant to note that in calling themselves "Zapatista," the insurgents of the EZLN and the civilian base that comprises the bulk of the movement have adopted the name of one of the greatest Mexican revolutionary heroes, but also one who was neither active nor particularly well known in Chiapas until relatively recently (Collier and Quaratiello, 1999, p. 158). In fact, the source of the image and ideology of Zapata in Chiapas can be traced primarily to urban revolutionaries who went out into the countryside in the aftermath of 1968 to work with the rural population (Stephen, 2002, p. 150). In the statutes of the Forces of National Liberation—the guerrilla organization whose cadres would help found the EZLN—written fourteen years before the Zapatista rebellion, the choice of Emiliano Zapata as the icon for the revolution is attributed to the fact that "Emiliano Zapata is the hero who best symbolizes the traditions of revolutionary struggle of the Mexican people" (Fuerzas de Liberación Nacional, 1980, cited in Womack, 1999, p. 196). By invoking the man, his image, and his legacy, the Zapatistas are currently engaged in a process not only of reaffirming the "Mexicanness" of their movement, but also of asserting its legitimacy while laying claim to the authentic and uncompromised legacy of the Mexican Revolution.

3 Big Noise Tactical is a radical media-making collective that has produced well-known alter-globalization films such as *Zapatista*, *This Is What Democracy Looks Like*, and *The Fourth World War*.

4 "Mestizo" is a term used frequently in Latin America to refer to people of mixed European and Indigenous descent.

5 The Intercontinental Encuentros (Encounters) for Humanity and Against Neoliberalism emerged from the Zapatista movement's engagement with individuals and social movements around the world following the Zapatista uprising. More than three thousand grassroots activists from over forty countries attended the first Encuentro held from July 27 to August 3, 1996, in Zapatista territory in Chiapas, Mexico, to discuss the dynamics of and alternatives to neoliberal capitalist globalization (Kingsnorth, 2003; Neill, 2001; Notes From Nowhere, 2003). The most significant outcome of the first Encuentro, aside from bringing such a diversity of activists together, was the commitment on the part of the participants to create an intercontinental network of resistance and communication and to hold a second Encuentro a year later in Europe. One year later, the second Encuentro, organized by a variety of groups, was held in Spain. Drawing more than three thousand activists from fifty countries, the second Encuentro was directed toward building the networks of communication and resistance which emerged from the first Encuentro (Esteva, 2001; Flood, 2003). Two additional Encuentros have since been held in Zapatista territory in Chiapas, Mexico, one in December 2006–January 2007 and the other in July 2007. These Encuentros have been aimed at reinvigorating a global movement of resistance and alternative-

building to neoliberal capitalism as well as reconnecting the Zapatista struggle with other movements around the world.

6 In the summer of 1990, a conflict erupted between the Mohawks of Kanehsatake and settler Canadians from the town of Oka, Quebec. When a decision was taken by the town to expand a golf course onto contested territory—some of which contained burial land sacred to the Mohawks—members of the Mohawk Nation, including the Warrior Society, erected barricades and engaged in direct action to prevent construction from proceeding. The local, provincial, and federal governments all chose the path of escalation, first sending in police and then the army to deal with the situation. The conflict lasted seventy-eight days with the Mohawks eventually putting down their weapons and ceding the barricades to the army while the mayor of Oka cancelled the plans for the golf course expansion. The conflict became an iconic moment in the long history of Indigenous struggles for sovereignty and land reclamation against the Canadian state.

## References


Alfred, T. (2005). *Wasáse: Indigenous pathways of action and freedom*. Peterborough: Broadview Press.

Barthes, R. (1972). *Mythologies*. New York: Hill and Wang.

Callahan, M. (2004). Zapatismo and global struggle: "A revolution to make revolution possible." In E. Yuen, D. Burton-Rose & G. Katsiaficas (Eds.), *Confronting capitalism: Dispatches from a global movement*. Brooklyn: Soft Skull Press.

Cleaver, H. (1998). The Zapatista effect: The Internet and the rise of an alternative political fabric. *Journal of International Affairs* 51 (2): 621–40.

Collier, G. (1999). *Basta!: Land and the Zapatista rebellion in Chiapas*. Rev. ed. Oakland: Food First Books.

Conant, J. (2010). *A poetics of resistance: The revolutionary public relations of the Zapatista insurgency*. Oakland: AK Press.

Esteva, G. (2001). The traditions of people of reason and the reasons of people of tradition: A report on the Second Intercontinental Encuentro. In *Auroras of the Zapatistas: Local and global struggles of the fourth world war*, 55–63. Brooklyn: Autonomedia.

Flood, A. (2003). Dreaming of a reality where the past and the future meet the present. In Notes from Nowhere (Ed.), *We are everywhere: The irresistible rise of global anticapitalism*, 74–79. New York: Verso.

García Márquez, G & Pombo, R. (2004). The hourglass of the Zapatistas. In T. Mertes (Ed.), *A movement of movements: Is another world really possible?*, 3–15. New York: Verso.

Gilly, A. (1998). Chiapas and the rebellion of the enchanted world. In *In* D. Nugent (Ed.), *Rural revolt in Mexico: US intervention and the domain of subaltern politics*. Durham: Duke University Press.

Haiven, M. & Khasnabish, A. (2010). What is the radical imagination? A special issue. *Affinities: a journal of radical theory, culture, and action* 4 (2): i–xxxvii.

Harvey, N. (1998). *The Chiapas rebellion: The struggle for land and democracy*. Durham: Duke University Press.

Hellman, J. (1999). Real and virtual Chiapas: Magic realism and the left. In L. Panitch & C. Leys (Eds.), *Necessary and unnecessary utopias: socialist register 2000*, 161–86. Rendlesham Nr. Woodbridge Suffolk: Merlin Press.

Holloway, J. (2002). *Change the world without taking power: The meaning of revolution today*. London: Pluto Press.

Khasnabish, A. (2007). "Insurgent imaginations." *Ephemera: Theory and politics in organization* 7(4): 505–26.

Khasnabish, A. (2008a). *Zapatismo beyond borders: New imaginations of political possibility*. Toronto: University of Toronto Press.

Khasnabish, A. (2008b). "A tear in the fabric of the present." *Journal for the Study of Radicalism* 2: 27–52. doi:10.1353/jsr.0.0006.

Khasnabish, Alex. 2010. *Zapatistas: rebellion from the grassroots to the global*. London: Zed Press.

Kingsnorth, P. (2004). *One no, many yeses: A journey to the heart of the global resistance movement*. London: Free Press.

Klein, N. (2002). Rebellion in Chiapas. In *Fences and windows: Dispatches from the front lines of the globalization debate*, 208–23. Toronto: Vintage Canada.

Knudson, Jerry. 1998. "Rebellion in Chiapas: Insurrection by Internet and public relations." *Media, Culture & Society* 20: 507–18.

Marcos, Subcomandante Insurgente. (2001). Democratic teachers and the Zapatista dream. In J. Ponce de León (Ed.), *Our word is our weapon: Selected writings*, 274–77. Toronto: Seven Stories Press.

Marcos, Subcomandante Insurgente (2002). Testimonies of the first day. In T. Hayden (Ed.), *The Zapatista reader*, 207–17. New York: Thunder's Mouth Press.

Marcos, Subcomandante Insurgente (2004). The seven loose pieces of the global jigsaw puzzle (neoliberalism as a puzzle). In Ž. Vodovnik (Ed.), *¡Ya basta!: Ten years of the Zapatista uprising*, 257–78. Oakland: AK Press.

Melucci, A. (1985). "The symbolic challenge of contemporary movements." *Social Research* 52(4): 789–816.

Meyer, J. (2002). Once again, the noble savage. In T. Hayden (Ed.), *The Zapatista reader*. New York: Thunder's Mouth Press.

Midnight Notes (Ed.). (2001). *Auroras of the Zapatistas: Local and global struggles of the fourth world war*. Brooklyn: Autonomedia.

Muñoz Ramírez, G. (2008). *The fire & the word: A history of the Zapatista movement*. San Francisco: City Lights.

Neill, M. (2001). Encounters in Chiapas. In Midnight Notes (Ed.), *Auroras of the Zapatistas: Local and global struggles of the fourth world war*, 45–53. Brooklyn: Autonomedia.

Notes from Nowhere (Ed.). (2003). *We are everywhere: The irresistible rise of global anticapitalism*. New York: Verso.

Olesen, T. (2005). *International Zapatismo: The construction of solidarity in the age of globalization*. London: Zed Press.

Oppenheimer, A. (2002). Guerrillas in the mist. In T. Hayden (Ed.), *The Zapatista reader*, 51–54. New York: Thunder's Mouth Press.

Ronfeldt, D., Arquilla, J., Fuller, G. & Fuller, M. (1998). *The Zapatista social netwar in Mexico*. Santa Monica: RAND.

Russell, A. (2005). "Myth and the Zapatista movement: exploring a network identity." *New Media & Society* 7(4): 559–77.

Selbin, Eric. 2003. Zapata's white horse and Che's beret: Theses on the future of revolution. In J. Foran (Ed.), *The future of revolutions: Rethinking radical change in the age of globalization*. New York: Zed Books.

Solnit, R. (2004). *Hope in the dark: Untold histories, wild possibilities*. New York: Nation Books.

Stephen, L. (2002). *Zapata lives!: Histories and cultural politics in southern Mexico*. Berkeley: University of California Press.

Tarrow, S. (2005). *The new transnational activism*. Cambridge: Cambridge University Press.

Womack, J. (1999). *Rebellion in Chiapas: An historical reader*. New York: New Press.

CHAPTER 13

# Anarchism, Pedagogy, Queer Theory and Poststructuralism: Toward a Positive Ethical Theory, of Knowledge and the Self

Lucy Nicholas

Many anarchist pedagogical practices and perspectives can be understood alongside poststructuralism and queer theory because they are concerned with subjectivity, in terms of shaping individuals according to maximum possible "autonomy."[1] This is a process that both perspectives tend to consider as fundamentally situated and collective. As such,anarchist approaches to pedagogy can easily be allied with poststructuralist ideas about the subject as nonfoundational and, therefore, while not predisposed to any particular way of being, having the potential to be fostered according to a particular ethic. My concern in this chapter is to offer a formulation to anarchist approaches to pedagogy, of what, according to poststructuralist ideas of the subject, autonomy *can be*, and how it can be fostered, maximized, and maintained.

This chapter will argue that poststructuralism and queer theory share the ethical impulse of anarchism, that is, a dedication to a kind of "autonomy," but offer to anarchism a pedagogical praxis that overcomes the possible impasse of nonfoundational poststructuralist ontology, while acknowledging the complex terrains on which power operates to restrict this autonomy. Queer theory shares with the poststructuralist anarchist perspective the ethical impulse that the self (especially the sexual self) must be a willed creation, a result of some kind of agency free from coercion, alongside a more complex ontology that rejects a simplistic individualistic autonomy as the root of this.

Poststructuralism and poststructuralist-influenced queer theory widen the definition, terrain, and mechanisms of power and subjectivity in a way that has deep implications for attempts to construct transformative educative processes that are premised on an ethics of freedom or autonomy.

They widen what can be considered the terrain of power such that the way that we become subjects is implicated in power that can either be dominating and restrict our "autonomy," or more positive and enabling. This has implications for the concerns of pedagogical theory such that the terrain of learning must also be expanded so that anarchist pedagogy, I argue, should [and sometimes already does] include a concern with how we learn to be subjects, and with making this process as "autonomous" as possible. I argue that because poststructuralism gives a more central role to discourse production in this process of the formation of subjectivity and the maintenance of power (understanding discourses as Michel Foucault does as "bodies of knowledge"), poststructuralist-informed anarchist pedagogy should also be concerned with the centrality of discourses in learning how to be a self. I argue that the concept of learning should be widened to include all of the ways that subjects learn how to "be," which are often implicit and informal, and often prelimited by discursive contexts.

Poststructuralism has famously been criticized as ethically lacking (Seidman, 1995). Likewise, queer theory has also been widely understood as merely an oppositional mode of thinking. For example, Dynes surmises that "At best . . . they [queer studies] amount to a revolution of subtraction, eroding existing norms and verities, rather than a revolution of addition, creating new values. What passes for reinventing is merely disinventing" (1995). This chapter will (along with a wide body of literature) contrarily argue that this very "disinvention" and deconstruction of poststructuralism and queer theory is able to offer an ethical impulse and a pedagogical praxis that, while similar in telos to anarchism, avoids the traps of foundationalism, individualism, and closure.[2]

## Implications for Anarchism of Poststructuralism and Queer Theory

This section will consider the ways in which poststructuralism and queer theory impact on anarchism that have implications for anarchist epistemology and pedagogy. It will argue that they widen the terrains and definitions of power such that the constitution of the self and subjectivity should be a concern for an anarchist ethics of "autonomy." It will argue that the account of subjectivation offered by poststructuralism and queer theory has the implication that the notion of "autonomy" must be transformed to avoid assumptions of a reductive liberal individualism at its root and take into account the unavoidable constitutive aspects of relations with others, discourses, and social context that shape what autonomy can be. The ways that we learn to be selves (identity formation), and the extent to which they are as "autonomous" as possible should be a concern for those concerned with developing pedagogical practice that departs from anarchist ethics. This then shifts what the aim of an anarchist-informed pedagogical practice can and should be, from the assumption of the possibility of an atomized autonomous self, to a practice concerned with making the *social* constitution of selves as explicit, participatory and nonoppressive as possible. How this could be achieved will be the concern of the second and third sections.

Foucault's primary challenge to and development of conceptions of power is in the idea that power does not operate through a top-down repressive mechanism wherein the source of domination is easy to posit. Instead, ze posits a productive conception of power, in that power operates by constituting the discourses within which we are "subjected":[3]

> In a society such as ours, but basically in any society, there are manifold relations of power which permeate, characterise and constitute the social body, and these relations of power cannot themselves be established, consolidated nor implemented without the production, accumulation, circulation and functioning of a discourse. There can be no possible exercise of power without a certain economy of discourses of truth which operates through and on the basis of this association. We are subjected to the production of truth through power and we cannot exercise power except through the production of truth. (Foucault, 1980, p. 93)

The implications of this for a practice dedicated to fostering autonomous subjects, then, is that it can no longer be understood as the liberation of preexisting autonomous subjects from a repressive power. It must shift to a coexisting concern with individual subjects and the "economy of discourses of truth" within which they have the possibility of existing.

Foucault suggests that, due to this constitutive nature of power, power relations are unavoidable. This again renders definitions of anarchism that depart from a repressive notion of power and merely oppose power *over* others, and advocate the freeing of an essential cooperative and free subject, as limited in their strategies. This is not to deny that there has always been an element of a more productive understanding of the subject in anarchist theory, especially that concerned with pedagogy, which has often used metaphors of cultivation to illustrate the ways that subjects require fostering toward anarchist ideals. For example, Geoffrey Fidler (1989) charts that classical anarchist texts concerned with education made reference to "the naturalist metaphor of the educational gardener or farmer" and discussion of the "art or technique of cultivation" (p. 23). However, Fidler also identifies that this discourse of cultivation was often situated in a broader ontological discourse of subjects being cultivated or shaped toward a preexisting, natural proclivity to cooperation or autonomy.

However, the concept of productive power and of the subject as fundamentally constituted in discourse elaborates on and lends theoretical weight to these tendencies in anarchist thought, as well as limiting the conditions under which autonomy can be fostered. This ontological point of departure impacts heavily on what should, then, be understood as the terrain of the political, that is, the terrain on which domination and power can operate and on which anarchists must attempt to resist it.

Cooper and Blair (2002) argue that one of the implications of Foucault's redefinition of power is the extension of the terrain of the political to culture, such that "doing culture work—changing behaviour, attitude, norms—is just as important, if not more important, than changing laws." (p. 523). This is not to deny that there has always been an understanding within anarchism of "the internal tyrants, far more harmful to life and growth . . . [of] ethical and social conventions" (Goldman, 1969, p. 227), but poststructuralist approaches to anarchism explicate and emphasize this focus. For example, Saul Newman (2001) in the germinal poststructuralist anarchist text *From Bakunin to Lacan* summarizes this redefinition of power and domination: "I employ a deliberately broad definition of *authority*: it refers not only to institutions like the state and the prison etc.; it also refers to authoritarian discursive structures like rational truth, essence, and the subjectifying norms they produce" (pp. 12–13).

The discourses that constitute the self, and the process of this constitution, what Foucault calls "subjectivation" now become primary sites of authority and dominating relations and therefore matters of concern for those dedicated to anarchist ethics. Poststructuralism, then, offers a full account of the way that subjectivity and intersubjectivity is a site of power and dominance by narrating the way that they are produced according to dominant hierarchical ethics and assumptions, an account that can supplement the ever-present anarchist concern with what Foucault would call the "colonization of souls" (Amster, DeLeon, Fernandez, Nocella II & Shannon, 2009, p. 124). However, this necessarily impacts on the "telos" of anarchism, in that there can no longer be some ideal of a pure site of individual autonomous volition that needs to be freed from repressive power.

There is now a tension, then, which means that a focus only on how discourses limit and restrict subjects would be to negate how subjects may negotiate this contradictory position of a "subjection [that] consists precisely in this fundamental dependency on a discourse we never chose but that, paradoxically, initiates and sustains our agency." (Butler, 1997, p. 2). For my concern with learning, then, the important insight is "the way in which the discursive practices constitute the speakers and hearers in certain ways and yet at the same time is [*sic*] a resource through which speakers and hearers can negotiate new positions" (Davies & Harre, 2003). This is the "doubled vision" (de Lauretis, 1987, p. 10) of poststructuralist notions of agency that allows for a refined understanding of it from within a firmly social and intersubjective, situated ontology. This "doubled vision" suggests that discourses, in their nature as both enabling and restricting, have the possibility of being fostered as more or less enabling.

While it is clear that this poststructuralist conception of power refines the notion of autonomy, there is still a clearly "autonomous" or anti-authoritarian impulse in much poststructuralist, queer and deconstructionist thinking. Dynes (1995), for example, while critical of queer theory, rightly identifies in my view that the theory contains "a substantial heritage of nineteenth-century romantic anarchism and utopianism" and that "The hidden goal, the longing in fact, is untrammeled self-affirmation without bonds or boundaries." Indeed, Judith Butler's (1990) clearly stated aim in per germinal work *Gender Trouble* is that per vision is a politics "that will take the variable construction of identity as both a methodological and normative prerequisite, if not a political goal." (p. 5). However, Dynes finds this dedication to "self-affirmation" alongside a radical critique of the subject to be paradoxical and makes these claims of anarchist utopianism alongside charges of solipsism. I would argue the opposite, that this autonomous impulse is grounded in, and developed from, the firmly social ontology outlined above, which has implications for practices that seek to maximize this autonomy.

But how is this dedication to autonomy possible within the delimited conception of autonomy resulting from the restrictions of productive power? And how can it be ethically justified if power is *always* the source of subjectivation? I will argue that autonomy can be understood not as a natural proclivity but as a *situated capacity*. In being constituted by discursive power regimes as opposed to precultural entities (May, 1994; Newman, 2001), subjects, then, can be understood as having no proclivity toward either mutual disinterest *or* mutual aid, but rather as having capacities that are shaped by a discursive context that is constantly being (re)constituted. This is Foucault's "thin" conception of humyn nature that has often been charged with precluding agency. However, the key to "agency" in this conception, and in Butler's (1990) similar notion of "performativity," is that the discourses within which we learn how to "be" are not fixed and transcendental, but are being constantly reconstituted, and engaged with "in a living and reflective way" (Butler, 2005, p. 10). This is a process that allows reconstitution on different terms, albeit terms that always depart from the discourses they are wishing to transform. Thus, according to this ontological basis, it is possible to posit humyn nature as a situated potentiality that is not always predetermined by discourses not of its making, but has the *possibility* of being fostered according to anarchist principles. This leads Butler (1997) to conclude, "the subject is *neither* fully determined by power *nor* fully determining of power (but significantly and partially both)" (p. 17). In Paul Patton's (1994) words, Foucault can be understood as offering "an historically grounded belief in the human capacity to transcend limits to the autonomous use and development of human powers." (p. 61). This means that the ethical aim of anarchism, while ontologically possible, can no longer be justified by this ontology alone, and must be argued for on ethico-political terms, such that it may be demonstrated that a purposive "stylistics of existence" (Foucault, 1990, p. 71) would be the most ethically desirable way of being as a result of a nonfoundational ontology. In Foucault's words: "From the idea that the self is not given to us, I think that there is only one practical consequence: we have to create ourselves as a work of art." (Foucault, 1984, p. 351). The corollary of an ontology that posits an inherently nonfoundational but situated subject endowed with capacities for purposive existence, then, is that the most beneficial and effective means of achieving this type of "autonomy" would be a purposive and willed collective intervention into the discursive production of subjectivity.

To summarize, the limits to traditional notions of autonomy presented by this ontological reconceptualization do not need to present an obstacle to the principle of freedom but, rather, aid in considering the *real* conditions of agency and therefore for maximum possible autonomy. They lift the veil of misdirected hopes for a foundational autonomy that must be freed from repression or an atomised personal autonomy and lend the concept a more social premise and social goal. Contemporary approaches to anarchism that depart from a nonfoundational conception of the subject but maintain a normative stance of freedom (Bey, n.d.; CrimethInc., n.d.; Holloway, 2002; May, 1994; Newman, 2001), demonstrate how a constructivist ontology does not obviate a value-stance. The fact that there is no "I" that is not a set of relations does not preclude a "ground for moral agency and moral accountability" (Butler, 2005, p. 8).

## What Would a Poststructuralist Anarchist Pedagogy "Look Like"?

Given that power is pervasive in interaction, how, then, to distinguish which discourses, and which pedagogical practices, are positive and maximize collective autonomy, and which are exploitative and dominating? And how to ensure that discourses do not congeal into authoritarian compulsarities? A distinction between "extractive" and "developmental" power developed from Foucault (Patton, 1994) can help me to resolve this possible impasse of value distinction. And deconstruction offers strategies that are useful for considering how such positive, developmental discourses and ways of being could be maintained and prevented from sliding into dominating, "extractive" power.

### *"Developmental" Power Not "Extractive" Power:*

If, as Foucault claims, power is pervasive because of this ontological situation of subjects being constituted by their relations with others and their sociocultural discursive contexts, how can we distinguish between positive relations and contexts that are fostering "freedom" and negative ones that are fostering dominance? Despite per positing of this pervasiveness, ethical distinctions can still be made from Foucault's redefinition of power that prevent it from postmodern nihilism and make it possible to use this analysis of power as a point of departure for a poststructuralist anarchist ethics. Foucault implies that positive and negative manifestations of constitutive power relationships can be distinguished. The most explicit clue to Foucault's ethical telos is in the following statement: "I do not think that a society can exist without power relations . . . The problem, then, is . . . to acquire the . . . morality, the *ethos*, the practice of the self, that will allow us to play these games of power with as little domination as possible" (Foucault, 1997, p. 298). This demonstrates that there is the possibility of power relations that are nondominating, that Foucault's favor lies with these, and that they must be fostered through particular "practices of the self." Foucault offers examples of practices of (co-)constitution that ze considers positive, and others considered negative. For example, ze states that "the care of the self also implies a relationship with the other insofar as proper care of the self requires listening to the lessons of the master. One needs a guide, a counselor, a friend, someone who will be truthful with you." (Foucault, 1997, p. 287) Some examples are specifically pedagogical, for example Foucault has illustrated this distinction between desirable and nondesirable power relations through recourse to the example of different learning relations:

> I see nothing wrong in the practice of a person who, knowing more than others in a specific game of truth, tells those others what to do, teaches them, and transmits knowledge and techniques to them. The problem in such practices where power—which is not in itself a bad thing—must inevitably come into play is knowing how to avoid the kind of domination effects where a kid is subjected to the arbitrary and unnecessary authority of a teacher, or a student put under the thumb of a professor who abuses his authority. (Foucault, 1997, pp. 298–99)

The aspects of learning valorized here, then, are guidance and the transmission of knowledge, and the aspects opposed authoritarian. Paul Patton (1994) has developed this distinction, and similarly emphasizes how Foucault's positing of "power over" (understood as one agent affecting the action of another agent) as an inherent aspect of social relations still allows for normative distinctions between desirable and undesirable types of "power over." Patton summarizes how:

> So long as human capacities do in fact include the power of individuals to act upon their own actions, we can see that Foucault's conception

> of human being in terms of power enables us to distinguish between those modes of exercise of power which inhibit and those which allow the self-directed use and development of human capacities. (p. 68)

From C.B. Macpherson, Patton develops and applies to Foucault a distinction between "extractive" power over and "developmental" power over, a distinction which has a clear normative premise. Departing from a nonfoundational ontology, then, developmental power must maximize the *capacities* of subjects. Patton (1994) offers the following as examples of developmental power relations: "I can affect the actions of another by providing advice, moral support, or by passing on certain knowledge or skills" (p. 63). Similarly, Amy Allen (2005) has argued that, despite Butler's insistence that subjects are formed in the context of norms (akin to Foucault's discourses) that precede and shape them, these norms can be distinguished between those that are subordinating and those that are nonsubordinating. Ze states that "If we resist the idea that subjection per se is subordinating, then this opens up the possibility of conceptualizing forms of dependency, attachment and recognition that are not subordinating." (p. 210). In terms of educational alternatives, while the learning relationship necessarily entails power relations according to the Foucauldian ontology, "there are . . . structural alternatives to the carceral school, classroom, and society, because there are power relationships and technologies that are not dominating" (Wain, 1996, p. 358). The focus of transformative projects must, then, become the participatory creation of discourses within which subjects can develop and to which they can attach and identify with, that are not subordinating and extractive. The third section of this chapter will consider some examples of alternative, noncarceral discourses and relationships in specific relation to sexual subjectivity and how knowledge about how "to be" sexual is transmitted in these examples.

Gayatri Chakravorty Spivak (1994), heavily influenced by Jacques Derrida and deconstruction, has charted how, when engaging unavoidably with power relations, what can distinguish positive, nonsubordinating, and "developmental" relations from normative engagements that uncritically replicate dominating relations, is engaging in them in a "scrupulously visible political interest" (p. 153). I take this to mean that in order for such practices to not betray their own premises, it is necessary to make this developmental power "scrupulously visible," for it to be an open and consensual process and to prevent it from congealing into further tyranny. In the following section I chart how a constant deconstructivist impulse is indispensible for the continuation of "scrupulous visibility" central to the developmental power relations that I argue characterize a poststructuralist anarchist approach to pedagogical praxis.

*Deconstruction as an Ethical End:*
If individual autonomy and the over throwing of power per se can no longer be considered the end or "telos" of anarchism, what alternative end can poststructuralism offer to anarchists? Anarchist activists have long noted the potential for anarchy interpreted as "lawlessness" to reconstruct hierarchy, and the potential for the "tyranny of structurelessness" (Freeman, 1996) due to its individualistic tendencies. Likewise, critics have suggested that Judith Butler's oppositional "postidentity order" lacks a more programmatic vision of what a nonoppressive identity order *would* look like (Seidman 1995, p. 136; Stoetzler, 2005). Alongside others (Stoetzler, 2005), I argue that for many poststructuralists and theorists of deconstruction, this absence of programmatic visions is an ethical and purposive strategy in order to avoid just this closure of individualistic tyranny mentioned above. I argue that there is a clear deconstructive ethic in Butler's *Gender Trouble*, an implicit normative ethic that values critical modes of thought and nonclosure in an attempt to make the ongoing processes of subjectivation "scrupulously visible." I suggest that this minimal ethical principle as an end-point or "telos" is the strength of queer theory and something that both reflects and develops a similar impulse in anarchism, and is a strategy that should be applied to anarchist pedagogy as a means to maintain nondominating practices. Any other positive ethical principle risks closure and the replication of authority.

Anarchists are often reluctant to elaborate what anarchism would or should "look like" and what an ideal anarchist subject would or should "be like," for fear of being prescriptive and betraying anarchist principles. For example, Chomsky (2003) states, speaking specifically to the subject of education and drawing on the ideas of Bertrand Russell, that owing to "how little we really know about the aims and purposes of human life . . . the purpose of education . . . cannot be to control the child's growth to a specific, predetermined end, because any such end must be established by arbitrary authoritarian means" (Chomsky, 2003, p. 164). Likewise, Butler found that any attempt to illustrate per theory with examples that subvert the normative constitution of gender or demonstrate "performativity" resulted in the canonization of these examples as programmatic prescriptions of how to "do" queer or nonheteronormative gender correctly. In Butler's (1993) later book, *Bodies that Matter*, Butler addresses the ways that *Gender Trouble* was understood, and states that "by citing drag as an example of performativity . . . [it] was taken then, by some, to be *exemplary* of performativity." (p. 230). Likewise, Butler also addresses the way that "queer" has become an identity or a noun, so that queer is taken to be a subject position that one can *become* rather than a strategic act or something that is *done*. For Butler, then, queer, (or some other term for this same deconstructive impulse that has not yet been normalized—Butler remains open to renaming this impulse), must remain a verb, an act of de-normalizing, and never congeal into a noun. It must remain a critical perspective that can take a discourse and make it "queered from prior usage" (p. 228). This ideal of queer as a verb has led Butler to conclude that "the critique of the queer subject is crucial to the continuing *democratization* of queer politics" (Butler, 1993, p. 227). I suggest that this constant critique of discourses must be the primary function of pedagogical practices that seek to maximize the autonomy of subjectivation. This constant critique would avoid the tyranny of what Butler would call the "forcible production" of the "compulsory practice" (Butler, 1993, p. 231) of certain subjectivites, of which normatively gendered subjectivity is a paradigmatic example.

Likewise, in order to maintain this ethical principle of nonoppressive subjectivation and to evade the ever-present possibility of closure, many other poststructuralist, deconstructionist, and queer theorists have refused to posit an ethical "end-point" or "telos" any more clear than a perpetual critical relation of openness. For example, Diana Fuss's (1991) germinal concept of "'analysis interminable,' [is] a responsibility to exert sustained pressure from/on the margins to reshape and to reorient the field of sexual difference to include sexual differences" (p. 6). Indeed, this fluidity and self-criticalness, along with the reluctance to define what anarchism might "look like," preferring instead to define it around a common ethic, has been identified as an aspect of "postmodern and poststructural methodological trends of contemporary anarchism" (Armaline, 2009, p. 137). Anarchist pedagogues have summarized this line of thinking: "If ideas and accepted practices have a way of hardening, of rigidifying over time, then criticism must not be an isolated event but an ongoing practice. If thinking differently, seeking freedom by creative engagement with new possibilities, is the objective, then there is no end to ethical criticism" (Cooper & Blair, 2002, p. 529).

Butler's (1993), and other queer theorists', normative bottom line, then, a bottom-line that I argue can be usefully applied to anarchist pedagogy, can be understood as a strategy of deconstruction *as an end in itself* which would have the corollary of inexhaustibly expanding "available schemes of intelligibility" (p. 224) such that nobody's subjectivity was prerestricted by a limit to existing modes of being. And the agency to undertake this deconstructive process, this critical mode of being or "stylistics of existence" (Foucault, 1990, p. 71), is a fundamentally relational, intersubjective capacity. Due to the enabling of "agency" by our location in discourses we did not choose, the attempt to expand the "available schemes of intelligibility" (Butler, 1993, p. 224) will necessarily depart from the discourses in which we become subjects but did not choose. This leads me to argue that a poststructuralist anarchist pedagogical praxis would entail the dual strategies of inexhaustible deconstruction of prevailing discourses, and ongoing reconstruction and "reiteration" (a

Butlerian term developed from Derrida) of these discourses through various strategies such as subversion and transformative reiteration.

*Pedagogical "Strategies of Freedom"*

Theorists have emphasized the important way that the discourse of pornography serves a pedagogical function in informally and tacitly "teaching" people how to "be" a sexual subject (Hunter, 1988; Hurley, 1990). This example illustrates the very implicitness and uninterrogated nature of normalising subjectifying discourses that is at odds with the principle of autonomy as purposive and "scrupulously visible" outlined above. The taken-for-granted nature of discourses is what allows subjects to be constituted according to a dominant discourse, in which individuals are not participants, but merely subjects. Hunter (1988) describes for example "the 'moral machinery' of popular education aimed, as Foucault puts it, at the 'normalisation of the population'" (p. 75). However, I would like to consider what pedagogical practices would need to entail in order to embody the moral machinery of *autonomous* subjectivation, specifically in terms of sexual subjectivation. I argue that, due to the queer impulse of the self-willed "doing" of being sexual, anarcho-queer communities and practices offer rich strategies and examples.

According to the ontological premise that power is unavoidable, and the normative distinction I have drawn on between extractive and developmental power, developmental pedagogical practices, in order to avoid dominating relations, must be in the interests of fostering nonrestrictive "schemes of intelligibility" (Butler, 1993, p. 224) that develop the capacities of subjects toward a purposive "stylistics of existence" (Foucault, 1990, p. 71). In order for such normative practices to not betray their own premises, they would need to be explicit and transparent and open to constant critique by all participants. It is not my place here to chart the ways in which mainstream institutions and practices of education *do not* embody this process of subject formation, but anarchists have long charted how mainstream education embodies processes of subjectivation quite at odds with purposive and transparent practices. (See Gabbard, Chapter 2, and Todd, Chapter 4 in this volume)

For a poststructuralist anarchist pedagogical praxis, the transparency of processes of subjectivation needs to be fostered, as well as a means of making this process more purposive. This needs to take into account that subjects are constituted in collectively shared discourses. I argue that these two needs can be addressed through the dual processes of de-construction—a strategy discussed above that could ensure against uninterrogated implicit and normative processes of the constitution of selves—and a purposive reconstruction of discursive contexts according to the will of those constituting. I say "dual processes" as I posit that these practices must be constant, inexhaustible, and concurrent to avoid the possibility of domination by closure.

*Deconstruction/Reconstruction: "A riot for the mind":*

Kenneth Wain (1996), in considering the usefulness of Foucault for thinking about education, analogizes Foucault's strategy of genealogy to deconstruction, as a transformative process whereby understanding the historical constitution of discourses and practices and ways of being allows us to understand how it could be otherwise. Foucault implies that deconstructive thinking is a strategy of freedom: "Since these things . . . have been made, they can be unmade, as long as we know how it was they were made" (Foucault, 1988, in Cooper & Blair, 2002, p. 517). Cooper and Blair (2002) argue that Foucault's ideal of problematization as an intellectual imperative opposed to polemics holds the function of "opening possibilities for transformation" (p. 521). Thus "genealogy provides us with the tools for a project of freedom, of going beyond our 'limits'" (Wain, 1996, p. 355). The implication of Wain's, Cooper's, and Blair's arguments is that education should be reunderstood as a process of deconstructive analysis that helps us to understand why things are as they are and to make it possible to make them otherwise.

Much of anarchist practice is dedicated to this very project of deconstruction and constant critique to ensure that relations do not congeal into uninterrogated authoritarianism, as well as the creation of alternative ways of being. Below I will chart some anarcho-queer practices dedicated to the deconstruction of gender and sex norms. However, because the "critical relation depends . . . on a capacity, invariably collective, to articulate an alternative, minority version of sustaining norms or ideals that enable me to act" (Butler, 2004, p. 3), a deconstructive pedagogical strategy that is compatible with poststructuralist anarchist ethics must be supplemented with reconstructive practices that create *enabling* and *developmental* discourses. I am reluctant, given this inexhaustibly critical impulse, to offer any examples as the "summary moment" (Butler, 1993, p. 223) of these ideal discourses of poststructuralist anarchist pedagogy given the warnings above. However, there are and have been some practices that illustrate such an approach to praxis.

The "prefiguration" noted as an ever-present but growing aspect of anarchism (Franks, 2006, p. 97; Greenway in Purkis & Bowen, 1997, p. 175; Heckert 2005) can be understood in just these terms, as a *re*-constructive supplement to oppositional critique, according to the desires of the participants: "breaking rules for the sake of breaking rules is merely transgressive. Breaking rules to produce new realities is prefigurative" (Heckert, 2005, p. 42). Because poststructuralist ideas about discourse as constitutive of subjectivity extend the notion of learning, all aspects of a culture or subculture can now be understood as instrumental in the constitution of the subjectivities of the members of that culture. This has led me to argue elsewhere (Nicholas, 2007) that an example of this positively developmental and pedagogical culture is embodied in prefigurative practices and discourses in the DIY punk scene/culture. For example, the creation of zines (hand-made, often photocopied amateur publications), lyrics to songs and their dissemination in lyric sheets, spoken-word explanations of songs at shows, workshops and discussion groups, festivals, and the alteration of language.

As I have discussed elsewhere (Nicholas, 2009), the approach to sharing information in anarchist communities often represents an attempt at doing so through developmental pedagogical relations. For example, free skools, skill-shares, workshops, discussion groups, and book groups are often features of anarchist spaces such as social centers and festivals.[4] These modes of sharing knowledge are noncompulsory, explicit, and noncoercive and nonhierarchical in their form and content. They tend to encourage maximum participation from all attendants and emphasize the sharing—rather than administering—of knowledge. This embodies Bakunin's ideal of "mutual instruction, an act of intellectual fraternity" (Bakunin, 1970, pp. 41–42). It is the ideal of "work-partners" (Bhave, 2008, p. 10) instead of instructor and pupil, a relationship far more conducive to a collective and nonhierarchical reiteration and recreation of discourses or bodies of knowledge. The byline on the Toronto Anarchist Free University website is "a riot for the mind" (See Jeffery Shantz, Chapter 7 in this volume), neatly summarizing how such practices are premised on the mind as a terrain of anarchist struggle.

An interesting aspect of such knowledge sharing that further demonstrates an alliance with the notion of subjectivation as a terrain of struggle, is that there is often a central emphasis on discussing, and deconstructing, aspects of identity and selfhood. For example, Between the Lines DIY fest held at the Cowley Club Social Centre in Brighton in 2008 and 2009 held a workshop on the topic of "different kinds of relationships" that was a discussion concerned with deconstructing traditional relationship structures (including sexual relationships) and considering possible alternatives, and the possibilities of conducting relationships premised on anarchist ethics while attempting, through its title, to avoid prescription. Additionally this fest held a discussion group on deconstructing gender, a common feature of many DIY, punk, and anarchist fests, such as Belladonna DIY Fest held in Wollongong, Australia, which also held a workshop on sexuality. I have also charted elsewhere (Nicholas, 2009) how anarchist free skools and similar practices are often concerned with deconstructing gender and sexuality norms. For example, Freeschool Vancouver holds Sexuality Learning Groups that depart from collectively reading Foucault's *History of Sexuality*. Additionally, Free Skool Santa Cruz describe their workshop series "Unpacking Gender Norms" as follows: "We will examine where the gender-binary system and heterosexism come from, how they are carried out, and how we reproduce them within our own communities." (Free Skool Santa Cruz, 2008). This is paradigmatic of the concurrent deconstructive/reconstructive practice that I am referring to in that it is concerned with deconstructing the genealogy of sexuality norms, and with analyzing how these are reproduced in the interests of transformative practices of learning how not to reproduce them.

Queer anarchist communities are particularly engaged in prefigurative practices that are concerned with transforming gender and sexual identity. Many of these practices can be considered pedagogical in the sense developed here in that they offer discursive contexts in which participants reconstitute their gender and sexual identities, that is they widen the resources and bodies of knowledge within which subjects learn to "be" and learn to be sexual. The urgency of this prefigurative impulse among gender nonconformists is no surprise given the compulsory nature of binary gender identity, that one cannot "be" without "doing" gender (Butler, 2004). For example, empirical researchers have noted the discursive, as well as institutional, borders to possible ways of being gendered: "Transgendered individuals' understandings of themselves and their ability to formulate alternative identities depend[s] . . . upon existing *cultural categories* as well as institutional pressures to be one gender or the other." (Gagne & Tewkesbury, 1998, p. 95, emphasis added). This reemphasizes the necessity of "a capacity, invariably collective, to articulate an alternative, minority version of sustaining norms or ideals that enable me to act" (Butler, 2004, p. 3).

The emergence of explicitly anarchist prefigurative queer spaces that set out to do just this has grown since the 1990s. These include the annual international convergence Queeruption, local Queeruption collectives, events and convergences, and similar practices under the moniker of Queer Mutiny. It has been noted in both sociological and human geography contexts (Brown, 2007a; Brown, 2007b; Nicholas 2009, pp. 8–9) that these spaces embody the poststructuralist conception of anarchism outlined above. A primary way in which they do this is by being premised not on a positive identification with a particular gender or sex category, that is by using queer not as a noun or subject position but, rather by being premised on a shared deconstructive impulse. Brown (2007a) notes that in "these activist spaces . . . queer is still more than simply an umbrella term for all those who are 'othered' by normative sexuality. Indeed, 'queer' in these spaces is as opposed to homonormativity as it is to heteronormativity . . . [Here] Queer celebrates gender and sexual fluidity and consciously blurs binaries. It is more of a relational process than a simple identity category" (pp. 196–97).

Additionally, Brown (2007a) has noted that these spaces and practices fit with poststructuralist concepts of power as productive and ontology as situated in that "queeruptors are interested in making modest, low-key attempts to reengage their 'power to-do,' which is always part of a social process of doing with others." (p. 197).

It is interesting that, in the aspects of these queer spaces concerned with (the erotic aspects of) sexuality such as the play spaces, play parties, or sex parties at events such as Queeruption, or at events organized by various Queeruption or Queer Mutiny collectives internationally, the central concern of their behavioral policies is not with regulating practices, but with regulating the relations between people. Such events often have a "safer spaces policy" collectively created according to consensus models that outlines the desired behavior of participants that must be consented to before participation. The principle concerns of anarchist approaches to erotic desire and sexuality included in such policies are neatly summarized by a description of the "Radical Sex 4 Sexy Radicals" workshop series held by Free Skool Santa Cruz: "autonomy, consent, negotiation, respect, and pleasure." (Free Skool Santa Cruz). This demonstrates that the ethos is relational, not prescriptive, through a concern with consent and mutually positive relations between participants, but that specific sexual practices are otherwise not usually mentioned in *re*-constructions of sexuality, only in *de*-constructions.

It is obvious why such projects of deconstruction and reconstruction are so urgent for those with transgressive sex and gender identities and why anarcho-queer communities offer such rich examples of prefiguration with the intention of expanding the "fund of ideas" (Archer, 1996, p. xiii) from which we can perceive ourselves and others. However, while my examples are mostly restricted to the examples of deconstructive and reconstructive interventions into gender and sexual socialization due to space restriction, this process is allegorical to all aspects of subjectivity or "ways of being" and is just one illustration of a restrictive, congealed, uncritical, and preexisting compulsory discourse that is at odds with anarchist principles of maximizing a collective but purposive self-willed way of being.

However, it is interesting to note that, even in a community specifically dedicated to and premised on the principle of inexhaustible freedom of sexual identity and practices, there is still the risk of the congealment of dominant norms. This is one of the criticisms leveled at the Queeruption gathering in Amsterdam in 2003 by a collective from the Queeruption Berlin group. They suggest that there has been "the establishment of a queer 'convention'" (Queeruption, 2003) in terms of compulsory hypersexuality.

To reiterate, and return to Butler's concern over the congealment of "queer" into a fixed subject position, Butler (1993) argues that this reconstruction and this self-naming must not be understood as a singular act of transgression and empowerment that follows from deconstruction and overthrows previously dominating discourses and replaces them with inherently developmental ones. Rather, this reconstruction of discourses must be an ongoing process alongside the ongoing process of *deconstruction* of discourses. In Butler's terms, "As much as it is necessary to . . . lay claim to the power to name oneself and determine the conditions under which that name is used, it is also impossible to sustain that kind of mastery over the trajectory of those categories within discourse" (p. 227). Returning to Butler's concern, then, and offering a possible alternative for rethinking this deconstructive impulse, those activists who critiqued queer spaces for just this type of normalising congealment suggest as an alternative conception the German term "Freiraum," a word that they suggest needs to enter the English language. They define it as "Literally 'free-room'; more like 'freedom.' Defined as 'the opportunity to move freely and develop one's individual ideas'" (Queeruption, 2003). Perhaps this, then, is just the term that is needed when Butler (1993) suggests that queer "will doubtless have to be yielded in favor of terms that do that political work more effectively" (p. 228).

## Notes

1 I have placed the term autonomy in quotations to problematize it and to make clear that it is a contested notion in poststructuralism, the particular usage of which I follow I will elaborate on in the body of this chapter.

2 I use "telos" in the Foucauldian sense as "the kind of being to which we aspire when we behave in a moral way" (Foucault, 1984, p. 355).

3 I use gender-neutral pronouns in this chapter as an act of prefiguration. S/he will be replaced with "ze," and her/his replaced with "per." Additionally, I use "humyn" in place of "human."

4 For example, The Cowley Club social center in Brighton, UK, regularly holds skill-share days, free skool days, and book groups. See http://www.cowleyclub.org.uk/. For an example of a festival that includes many workshops and skill-shares, see Belladonna DIY Fest that was held in Australia:http://www.revleft.com/vb/belladonna-diy-festival t38804/index.html?s=6d9b80cbe974a8bca0e00603acfca79e&

## References

Amster, R., DeLeon, A., Fernandez, L., Nocella II, A. & Shannon, D. (2009). *Contemporary anarchist studies: An introductory anthology of anarchy in the academy*. London/New York: Routledge.

Anarchist Free University Toronto. (n.d.). *Anarchist Free University Toronto*. Retrieved from http://anarchistu.org/cgi-bin/twiki/view/Anarchistu (accessed November 24, 2010).

Archer, M.S. (1996). *Culture and agency: The place of culture in social theory.* Cambridge: Cambridge University Press.

Armaline, W.T. (2009). Thoughts on anarchist pedagogy and epistemology. In R. Amster, A. DeLeon, L. Fernandez, A. Nocella II & D. Shannon (Eds.), *Contemporary anarchist studies: An introductory anthology of anarchy in the academy*, 136–46. Oxon: Routledge.

Bakunin, M. (1970). *God and the state*. London: Dover Publications.

Bey, H. (n.d.). *The dinner party.* Retrieved from http://delza.alliances.org/taz/taz13.html (accessed November 19, 2009).

Bhave, V. (2008). Intimate and ultimate. In M. Hern (Ed.), *Everywhere all the time: A new deschooling reader*, 7–12. Edinburgh: AK Press.

Brown, G. (2007a). Autonomy, Affinity and Play in the Spaces of Radical Queer Activism. In K. Browne, J. Lim & G. Brown. (Eds.), *Geographies of sexualities: Theory, practices & politics*, 195–201. Hampshire: Ashgate.

Brown, G. (2007b). Mutinous eruptions: Autonomous spaces of radical queer activism. *Environment & Planning A, 39*, 2685–98.

Butler, J. (1990). *Gender trouble: Feminism and the subversion of identity*. New York: Routledge.

Butler, J. (1993). *Bodies that matter: On the discursive limits of sex*. New York: Routledge.

Butler, J. (1997). *The psychic life of power: Theories in subjection*. Stanford, CA: Stanford University Press.

Butler, J. (2004). *Undoing gender*. New York: Routledge.

Butler, J. (2005). *Giving an account of oneself*. New York: Fordham.

Chomsky, N. (2003). *Chomsky on democracy and education*. D. Macedo (Ed.). New York: Routledge.

Cooper, M. & Blair, C. (2002). Foucault's ethics. *Qualitative Inquiry, 8*, 511–31.

CrimethInc. (n.d.). *Harbinger (of a new dawn)*. Olympia: CrimethInc. Workers' Collective.

Davies, B. & Harre, R. (2003). *Positioning: The discursive production of selves*. Retrieved from http://www.massey.ac.nz/~alock/position/position.htm (accessed July 18, 2003).

de Lauretis, T. (1987). *Technologies of gender: Essays on theory, film, and fiction*, Bloomington: Indiana University Press.

Dynes, W.R. (1995). *Queer studies: In search of a discipline*. Retrieved from http://www.fc.net/~zarathus/other/queer_studies_in_search_of_a_discipline.txt (accessed July 6, 1997).

Fidler, G.C. (1989). Anarchism and education: Éducation intégrale and the imperative towards fraternité. *History of Education, 18*(1), 23–46.

Foucault, M. (1980). *Power/knowledge: Selected interviews and other writings, 1972–1977*. Brighton: Harvester Press.

Foucault, M. (1984). On the genealogy of ethics: An overview of a work in progress. In P. Rabinow (Ed.), *The Foucault reader*, 340–72. New York: Pantheon.

Foucault, M. (1990). *The care of the self: The history of sexuality: 3*. London: Penguin.

Foucault, M. (1997). *Ethics: Subjectivity and truth*. New York: New Press.

Franks, B. (2006). *Rebel alliances: The means and ends of contemporary British anarchisms*. Edinburgh: AK Press.

Free Skool Santa Cruz. (2008). About. *Free Skool Santa Kruz*. Retrieved from http://santacruz.freeskool.org/e107_plugins/content/content.php?content.1 (accessed June 4, 2008).

Freeman, J. (1996), *The tyranny of structurelessness*. Retrieved from http://flag.blackened.net/revolt/anarchism/pdf/booklets/structurelessness.html (accessed February 8, 2010).

Fuss, D. (1991). *Inside/Out: Lesbian theories, gay theories*. London: Routledge.

Gagne, P. & Tewkesbury, R. (1998). Conformity pressure and gender resistance among transgendered individuals. *Social Problems*, 45(1), 81–101.

Goldman, E. (1969). *Anarchism*. New York: Kennikat Press.

Heckert, J. (2005), *Resisting orientation: On the complexities of desire and the limits of identity politics*. Retrieved from http://sexualorientation.info/thesis/ (accessed August 9, 2005).

Holloway, J. (2002). *Change the world without taking power: The meaning of revolution today*. London: Pluto Press.

Hunter, I. (1988). *Culture and government: The emergence of literary education*. London: Macmillan.

Hurley, M. (1990). Homosexualities: Fiction, reading and moral training. In T. Threadgold & A. Cranny-Francis (Eds.), *Feminine/masculine and representation*. Sydney: Allen & Unwin.

May, T. (1994). *The political philosophy of poststructuralist anarchism*. University Park, PA: Pennsylvania State University Press.

Newman, S. (2001). *From Bakunin to Lacan: Anti-authoritarianism and the dislocation of power*. Oxford: Lexington Books.

Nicholas, L. (2009). A radical queer utopian future: A reciprocal relation beyond sexual difference. *Thirdspace: A Journal of Feminist Theory and Culture, 8*(2). Retrieved from http://www.thirdspace.ca/journal/article/viewArticle/lnicholas/248 (accessed November 25, 2010).

Nicholas, L. (2007). Approaches to gender, power and authority in contemporary anarcho-punk: Poststructuralist anarchism? *E-Sharp Journal, 2007*(9). Retrieved from http://www.gla.ac.uk/departments/esharp/issues/9/issue9abstracts/ (accessed November 25, 2010).

Patton, P. (1994). Foucault's subject of power. *Political Theory Newsletter*, 1994(6), 60–71.

Purkis, J. & Bowen, J. (1997). *Twenty-first century anarchism: Unorthodox ideas for a new millennium*. New York: Cassell.

Queeruption. (2003). *Queer is hip, queer is cool: Dogmas in the queer scene*. Retrieved from http://www.queeruption.org/ (accessed November 25, 2010).

Seidman, S. (1995). Deconstructing queer theory, or the under-theorisation of the social and the ethical. In L. Nicholson & S. Seidman (Eds.), *Social postmodernism: Beyond identity politics*, 116–41. Cambridge: Cambridge University Press.

Spivak, G.C. (1994). In a word: Interview. Gayatri Chakravorty Spivak with Ellen Rooney. In N. Schor & E. Weed (Eds.), *The essential difference*, 151–84. Bloomington: Indiana University Press.

Stoetzler, M. (2005). Subject trouble: Judith Butler and dialectics. *Philosophy & Social Criticism*, *31*(3), 343–68.

Wain, K. (1996). Foucault, education, the self and modernity. *Journal of Philosophy of Education*, *30*(3), 345–60.

CHAPTER 14

# Anarcho-Feminist Psychology: Contributing to Postformal Criticality

**Curry Stephenson Malott**

> In their search for ways to produce democratic and evocative knowledges, critical constructivists become detectives of new ways of seeing and constructing the world. (Joe L. Kincheloe, 2005, p. 4)

Considering how Kincheloe's postformal psychology as critical revolutionary practice might be extended and contributed to through the engagement with *new*, or too often ignored, *ways of seeing and constructing the world*, what I understand to be the more democratic impulses of the vast, diverse tradition known as anarchism will be explored here. I will situate this focus on anarchy within the history of the feminist movement, which played a central role in Kincheloe's (2008) critical pedagogy. For example, in Kincheloe's (2008) *Critical Pedagogy Primer*, he argues that black feminist and cultural studies scholar bell hooks is one of a handful of "important figures in the emergence of critical pedagogy" (p. 59). Hooks's (1984) contribution to critical pedagogy through feminism, according to Kincheloe (2008), was to challenge the white, middle-class point of view of the women's movement that assumed their experiences represented the experiences of all women. That is, hooks (1984) argued that Betty Friedan's *The Feminine Mystique*, which served as the basis for 1970s feminism, was based on "the plight of a select group of college-educated, middle and upper class, married white women—housewives bored with leisure, with the home, with children, with buying products, who wanted more out of life" (p. 1). That *more* that Friedan alluded to has famously become known within feminist literature as *careers*. Hooks's (1984) critical contribution here is that she extended feminist discourse to include considerations of race and class. Challenging Friedan, hooks (1984) notes that what was not being addressed was the question of who would be taking care of the kids of white, middle-class women once they began their more fulfilling careers. Summarizing this crucial point, hooks (1984) notes that white, middle-class feminism "did not speak of the needs of women without men, without children, without homes. She ignored the existence of all non-white women and poor white women" (pp. 1–2). Summarizing this contribution Kincheloe (2008) notes that "hooks and other women of color moved many feminists toward an effort to challenge an entire system of domination" (p. 83). Critical pedagogy, partly because of the feminist work of hooks, is not just focused on the notion of rights and access, but on the ability to "identify and eradicate the ideology of domination that expresses itself along the axes of race, class, sexuality, colonialism, and gender" (Kincheloe, 2008, p. 83).

This focus on ideology has allowed critical pedagogy to better understand how sexist oppression is based on the belief that women are inferior, primitive, less advanced, more emotional and less rational than men. Because oppression is based on worldviews or interpretive frameworks that are internalized and perpetuated by all members of society, even those most negatively hurt by the idea, the structure of domination is always more complex than simple dichotomies suggest. Sexism is therefore not just a struggle between men and women, but it is a social system that becomes part of the cultural, taken-for-granted, hegemony of the dominant society. Consequently, women internalize and perpetuate sexism *with* men. Kincheloe (2008) interprets this insight concluding that, "one's actions in pursuit of resistance to oppression are more important than one's race, class, or gender—one's positionality" (p. 83). Not only is ideology more important than positionality when it comes to the work of resisting the doctrinal system and oppressive structures and arrangements, but their abolition (such as patriarchy) not only benefits those who are most hurt (i.e., women) by them, but those who benefit the most (i.e., men) by them are also better off under more positive conditions. Hooks (2000) makes this point crystal-clear in *Feminism Is for Everybody: Passionate Politics*, in the following somewhat lengthy, but highly significant, passage:

> Males as a group have and do benefit the most from patriarchy, from the assumption that they are superior to females and should rule over us. But those benefits come with a price. In return for all the goodies men receive from patriarchy, they are required to dominate women, to exploit and oppress us, using violence if they must to keep patriarchy intact. Most men find it difficult to be patriarchs. Most men are disturbed by hatred and fear of women, by male violence against women, even the men who perpetuate this violence. But they fear letting go of

> the benefits. They are not certain what will happen to the world they know most intimately if patriarchy changes. So they find it easier to passively support male domination even when they know in their minds and hearts that it is wrong. (p. ix)

It is this complex context where those who benefit the most from an oppressive ideology and practice would actually, in the long run, be far better off if it ceased to exist, rendering hooks's feminism so foundational to critical pedagogy in general and Kincheloe's approach in particular. In *Teaching Native America across the Curriculum: A Critical Inquiry* (Malott, Waukau, and Waukau-Villagomez, 2009) I contribute to this line of reasoning arguing that those "goodies" referred to by hooks (2000) are not as objectively beneficial as they may seem. Consider:

> While those deemed "white," on average, receive more material privileges than non-whites, most people who fit within current definitions of whiteness would also be better off without the institutionalization of white supremacy. Simply stated, a united working class/human species would be far better equipped to create a socially just world than a divided one. In *A Call to Action* (2008) I made the point that white people, while at times made to feel special or superior because we are white, have been left to rot and die of cancer at alarming rates in de-industrialized areas such as Niagara Falls, New York. My intentions here are similar. That is, this book, in part, is designed to offer white people (and others) a worldview not based on the false supremacy of Europeans, but one that acknowledges the contributions of Africans, Native Americans, and others to modern democracy and scientific knowledge production. Solidarity, in this context, is not a polite gesture made by the assumed *superior* to the assumed *inferior*, but rather, it is an acknowledgement of the awe-inspiring achievements of the non-European world that paved the way for Europe (and those of European descent) to begin emerging from the Dark Ages—a process still underway. (p. 3)

It is within this context of universal improvement that our epistemological bazaar begins to overlap in significant ways with anarchist theory. For example, like the bourgeoisie feminist movement that ignored issues of race and class, which hooks and others confronted during the 1970s and 1980s, Emma Goldman and other female anarchists around the end of the nineteenth century confronted the sexism of foundational male anarchist scholars such as Proudhon and Kropotkin (Leeder, 1996). Making this point in "Let Our Mothers Show the Way," Elaine Leeder (1996) notes that "anarchist women added new dimensions to the tradition which could not be found in the teachings of Proudhon, Kropotkin, and Bakunin. Anarchist women believed that changes in society had to occur in the economic and political spheres but their emphasis was also on the personal and psychological dimensions of life" (p. 143).

For example, Proudhon, it is argued, believed in patriarchy and that the role of women as the domestic force in life represents the natural division of labor rendering them subordinate to men and thus unable to divorce. However, Emma Goldman still drew on Proudhon's work borrowing his conclusion that *property is theft*, and turning it on the sexist discourse and practice informing it by "arguing that woman, as private property of man, was having her freedom and independence stolen" (Leeder, 1996, p. 144). Unlike the white, *color-blind* feminists, bell hooks challenged in the United States in the 1960s and 1970s, Goldman (1969), a Jewish woman who emigrated to the United States (New York City) in 1885 at the age of sixteen, was conscious that "the true patron saints of the black men were represented" not in Lincoln, who only "followed when abolition had become a practical issue" (p. 76), but in the radical white abolitionists such as John Brown and others. Goldman, as an anarchist, recognized the importance of the abolition of all forms of coercive power from capitalism, slavery, to patriarchy. One critique of Goldman's work might be that she focused on white abolitionists without sufficiently recognizing the agency and resistance of Africans themselves in America. However, because this sophisticated focus is not universal within the feminist tradition, there are those who see no future in feminism as a theoretical framework for political praxis.

For example, some anarchists, such as Susan Brown (1996), argue that because feminism does not possess, as a central, universal commitment, the overthrow and abolition of the basic structures of power, it is not able to provide the theoretical relevance to liberate all of humanity. Consequently, Brown (1996) argues for a more general theory for "human freedom" as part of the process of moving beyond feminism. While coming to essentially the same conclusion as the like of hooks and others in the resistance to a larger system of domination and exploitation—white-supremacist, patriarchal capitalism—she chooses to abandon the language of feminism for anarchism. While this might seem like a minor issue, much can be said about the power of language and the importance of naming the world and therefore the importance of calling ourselves feminists so as to name and oppose sexist oppression, calling ourselves antiracists so as to name and oppose institutionalized white supremacy, and calling ourselves anarchists and Marxists so as to name the capitalist relations of production and oppose the process of value production. However, in the educational Left there are hard, deep lines of division drawn between Marxists (including anarchists, radical environmentalists, and others who take industrialism and a class-based approach to analysis and practice) and postmodernists (including, among others, feminists and critical race theorists).

To the new generation of critical educators and those who are curious or interested, I say *nonsense, resist choosing sides, we should embrace our critical diversity to the fullest extent possible*. This requires humility and a refusal to take oneself too seriously. *It is, in fact, all good*. We need to realize that there are legitimate critiques regarding our own practices and conclusions. For example, postmodernists tend to be correct when they charge Marxists with being transmissive/banking/traditional in terms of pedagogy. Marxists, at the same time, tend to be correct when they charge postmodernists with not challenging the basic structures of power and obsessed with identity and triviality. I do not believe the solution is to argue the Left needs to adopt a new theory. I believe the solution resides within a more conscious effort to engage in honest, critical self-reflection and not get so defensive and threatened when we are challenged. Another related component of moving forward, as suggested by the title of this chapter, is to expand and engage more critical traditions. With this spirit of solidarity in mind, let us move into a discussion of the history of anarchy and how it might contribute to our postformal, feminist approach to educational psychology.

* * *

In my study of anarchy I begin by considering the philosophical and historical roots of what we might call an *anarchist conception of human nature*. After this first section, we explore how these insights might inform a postformal, feminist psychology contributing to our move toward a new discipline. Finally, we consider barriers and challenges we will continue to face in the foreseeable future in our attempts to put into practice, as part of a larger critical education movement, postformal approaches to teaching and learning for life after capitalism and without the white supremacist, homophobic, patriarchal hierarchies of what we hope to be distant memories of a time no longer thriving. Throughout this chapter we continue to revisit central aspects of the dominant psychological paradigm as we make our postformal anarchist case against it.

## Anarchist Psychology

We begin our investigation with the scientific anarchist work of Noam Chomsky. Because there are so many talented anarchist writers, and therefore so many potential places of departure, it is worth pausing for a moment to reflect upon why Chomsky was chosen. As not only a leading scientist in linguistics since the 1950s, where he has more precisely connected the field to the essence of human nature, but also one of the world's leading public intellectuals known for his anarchist politics and ceaseless critique of U.S.

foreign policy and its ongoing *imperialist ambitions*, Chomsky's astonishing achievements and critical credentials demand we *actively* pay attention to and learn from his point of view, yet without *passively* accepting all his ideas dogmatically and mechanically. Rather, the challenge is to engage them with as much scientific objectivity as humanly possible, aware that our own subjectivities and interpretive frameworks always serve as our first lens or filter as we construct knowledge about the external world.

* * *

Of particular importance to our present investigation are the connections between Chomsky's scientific investigations regarding human nature and his anarchist politics. As we will observe in the following discussion Chomsky's choice to embrace and contribute to anarchism is based on his assessment that anarchy most closely matches the essence of human nature. In other words, Chomsky's anarchism, in many fundamental ways, is informed by the conclusions of science. The significance of Chomsky's work as a scientist cannot be overstated, especially situated in the context of the early twenty-first century, when an anti-Western science postmodernism has come to dominate critical theory. That is, while many postmodern, cultural critics, anarchist writers, and other critical activists brilliantly outline and contextualize the social context in which anarchism and other forms and modes of counterhegemony exist through struggle, Chomsky's point of view, that is, the biological context of human nature, offers a unique perspective that I believe is valuable in constructing a postformal anarcho-feminist psychology socially situated.

Chomsky (2005) situates the heart of what I will refer to as *his anarchist psychology* firmly within the revolutionary impulse of the Enlightenment and the scientific tradition of Western counterhegemony. While postmodernists tend to focus on the oppressive nature of how Western science has come to be dominated by imperialist and capitalist interests, they too often present this tradition as if domination over non-Western knowledge systems was all it was ever about. Chomsky, on the other hand, focuses his energy on contributing to the democratic nature of early Enlightenment science, more or less ignoring the indoctrinating and exclusionary tendencies. I include Chomsky's point of view because anarchist thought and practice, when not demonized by the *discourse of domination*, tends not to be traced any further back than to nineteenth-century anarchists, however important, such as Max Stirner, Pierre-Joseph Proudhon, Mikhail Bakunin, and Peter Kropotkin (see, for example, Guérin, 2005; Morland, 1997), suggesting that critical/revolutionary theory and the European Enlightenment, and the subsequent scientific revolution, are separate and unrelated developments. Locating the roots of anarchy within science and the Enlightenment, as argued by

Chomsky, reclaims *both* anarchy from demonization *and* science from the boss's reductionistic process of colonialist wealth extraction and the subjugation of non-European-ruling elite peoples and perspectives/knowledges. That is, making these connections challenges the hyperdecontextualized reductionism that falsely disconnects science and politics.

Again, the significance of Chomsky's scientific approach is highlighted by its uniqueness. For example, while many anarchist writers correctly understand that one's view of human nature is going to determine one's understanding of what kind of societies humans are capable of successfully creating thereby shaping future possibilities and interpretations of historical events, they tend to fail to transgress the idea that ones conception of human nature is purely subjective and a matter of personal preference or political commitments. Representing this point of view in *Demanding the Impossible? Human Nature and the Politics in Nineteenth-Century Social Anarchism*, David Morland (1997) notes that

> ... there is no universal agreement about the meaning of human nature. Broadly speaking, the controversy centers on whether human nature should be thought of as something innate to the entire species of Homo Sapiens or whether it ought to be viewed as a reflect of particular environmental circumstances. Human nature, it is argued, either is universal and something that is inherent in all of us, or is socially constructed within a given human and social environment ... Political ideologies, including social anarchism often rely on a conception of human nature that draws on both dimensions of this argument. (p. 3)

The debate regarding the innate qualities of human nature in this context described by Morland (1997) tend to be centered around the issue of whether it is inherently good or evil. However, while this debate and foci are important, they fail to consider the insights of science, which, I argue, is an unfortunate oversight. It is curious that the only mention of Chomsky in Morland's (1997) book is his observation that there are too many competing theories within anarchism to be able to identify a generalizable ideology. While it is true that Morland's (1997) work is specifically centered on nineteenth-century anarchists, Chomsky, a twentieth-century anarchist, as demonstrated below, provides the Western scientific/Enlightenment link between sixteenth and seventeenth-century counterhegemonic scholars, such as Galileo, Descartes, and Newton, with the likes of Proudhon and others from the nineteenth century. In other words, Chomsky's focus not only contributes to the debate regarding human nature, but his historical contextualization offers invaluable insights for understanding nineteenth-century anarchy.

* * *

One of the clearest examples of Chomsky's historical understanding of what we might call an *anarchist psychology* is outlined in his essay entitled "Language and Freedom," originally published in 1970, but recently reproduced in *Chomsky on Anarchism* (Chomsky, 2005). What follows is therefore an engagement with an anarchist psychology taking Chomsky's work as a place of departure. Arguing that Western, "libertarian . . . thought and revolutionary acts of the late eighteenth century" (p. 102) are *echoed* within the work of Schelling (1775–1854), who identifies the *essence* of the *human ego* as *freedom*, Chomsky (2005) locates the roots of anarchy within the *Romantic* branch of the Enlightenment. As we observe below, Rousseau, one of the principal architects of Romanticism, has also played a significant role in anarchist psychology.

Although deemed to be *not important* by many leading historians of philosophy, such as Bertrand Russell (1945, 1972), Schelling, who was a student with Hegel, had such an inflated sense of self, it has been reported (see Gutmann, 1936), that his friendships were almost always sacrificed, would be absolutely livid to know he has been reduced to the status of *unimportant*. Whether such conclusions are justified is a matter of debate, but outlining Chomsky's anarchist psychology leads us to his work nevertheless.

Highlighting the magnitude of his ego, Gutmann (1936), in an introduction to *Philosophical Inquires into the Nature of Human Freedom* (Schelling, 1936), argues that Schelling fashioned himself a leader of what he understood to be the *new* revolution that takes the notion of freedom to be the center of all philosophy and science (Gutmann, 1936). That is, Schelling argued that philosophy itself is an act of freedom, and thus the product of a *free human*, carried out by a species *born for action*, not just *speculation*, rendering philosophy's place of departure being the announcement of said freedom. The connection to the Romantic Movement within Schelling's focus on *freedom* here is instructive for understanding the philosophical roots of Chomsky's anarchism. It is therefore not surprising that Chomsky (2005) identifies Rousseau's insistence that the essence of human nature is *freedom* and *consciousness of that freedom*, which, he argues, is an endowment unique to the human species.

Examining the historical development of these ideas Chomsky (2005) locates Rousseau's conclusions that mechanical philosophy can explain nothing of our *freedom*, that is, *free will* or *consciousness*, therefore identifies anarchy as contributing to this tradition of opposing what has developed into a behaviorist ontology dominant in today's increasingly corporate-controlled system of mass schooling. That is, Chomsky (2005) notes that it is "striking" that "Rousseau's argument against the legitimacy of established authority, whether that of political power or that of wealth . . . follows a familiar Cartesian model" where "man is uniquely beyond the bounds of physical explanation; the beast, on the other hand, is merely an ingenious machine, commanded by natural law. Man's freedom and his consciousness of his freedom distinguishes him from the beast-machine" (p. 106). Any political or social system that assumes or treats the human species as not essentially free and independent therefore represents an attack on human nature.

While Descartes's conception of mind, that it is unique to the species and beyond mechanical explanation, remains intact, his conception of body has been abandoned by the scientific community. Further contextualizing this history, Chomsky (1988) notes:

> The Cartesian conception of body was refuted by seventeenth-century physics, particularly the work of Isaac Newton, which laid the foundations for modern science. Newton demonstrated that the motions of heavenly bodies could not be explained by the principles of Descartes' contact mechanics, so that the Cartesian concept of body must be abandoned. In the Newtonian framework there is a "force" that one body exerts on another, without contact between them, a kind of "action at a distance." Whatever this force may be, it does not fall within the Cartesian framework of contact mechanics. (p. 143)

While the notion of gravity as *action at a distance* with a physical explanation has been widely accepted in the scientific community, the implications for the mind as a sort of *action at a distance* holds the biological explanatory key for human freedom and therefore largely ignored. This negligence is astonishing given Chomsky's conclusion that the notion of *action at a distance* continues to be the best explanation science has for human intelligence or free will. The brain might be matter designed to produce thought electrically, but the source of that animation remains clouded in mystery. This mystery represents, for many scientists, such as Chomsky, the *limits* of our species' intellectual endowments. Simply put, there are some questions that are beyond the reach of human intelligence, such as, *What is the scientific explanation for the source of the* action at a distance *that gives animation to life?* For Chomsky, all species have limits. This should not be viewed as controversial. That is, most species of birds have built in genetically determined navigation systems, which humans and most other species, could never acquire.

Chomsky's rejection of the racist and sexist pseudoscience that attempted to manufacture consent for stereotypical differences, which led him to focus on similarities among the human species coincided with feminist psychologists that objected to science informed by a hegemonic and thus unconscious sexist worldview. Outlining this history, Judith Worell (2000), in "Feminism in Psychology: Revolution or Evolution," elaborates in great detail:

> They pointed out that researchers and the people they studied were predominantly male; the topics they studied, such as aggression and

> achievement, reflected male concerns; and the results of research based on male samples were assumed to apply also to women. When women were studied, they were evaluated according to a male standard, so that women's personality and behavior were seen as deviant or deficient in comparison. For example, early research that focused on sex differences claimed that in comparison to men, women were less motivated to achieve, less assertive, and less proficient in science and mathematics. These presumed deficiencies were then seen as stereotypes of all women and were used to deny women entry or advancement in male-dominated employment settings. (p. 185)

Extending this *second-wave* critique of modern, Western science's tendency to produce knowledge informed by a process whereby the world is socially constructed as a series of hierarchically constructed dualities, such as *male and female* and *white and nonwhite*, Colleen Mack-Canty (2004) argues that *third-wave* feminism deconstructs the very notion of duality itself. Mack Canty (2004) critiques second-wave feminism for working "within foundational Western political theories such as liberalism and socialism" (p. 155). Third wave feminists, according to Mack-Canty (2004), on the other hand, "works to begin from the situated and ambodied perspectives of different(ing) women" (p. 155). Mack Canty (2004) identifies three main camps of third-wave feminism in the twenty-first century—generational/youth feminism, postcolonial feminism, and ecofeminism. Similarly, in *Feminist Theories and Education Primer* Leila Villaverde (2008) highlights many feminisms—Black Feminist Thought and Womanist Feminism; Latina/Chicana Feminism; Native American/Indigenous Feminism; Asian-American Feminism; Islamic Feminism; Lesbian Feminism; and Feminist Studies of Men. Contributing to this epistemological diversity, consider:

- "Theorizing the Politics of 'Islamic Feminism'" by Shahrzad Mojab (2001)
- "Queer Black Feminism: The Pleasure Principle" by Laura Alexandra Harris (1996)
- "The Development of Chicana Feminist Discourse, 1970–1980" by Alma Garcia (1989)
- "Postcolonial Geographies of Privilege: Diaspora Space, the Politics of Personhood and the 'Sri Lankan Women's Association in the UK'" by Tariq Jazeel (2005)
- "Puerto Rico: Feminism and Feminist Studies" by Alice Colón Warren (2003)
- *Politics of Masculinities: Men in Movements* by Michael Messner (1997)
- *The Agony of Masculinity: Race, Gender, and Education in the Age of "New" Racism and Patriarchy*. By Pierre Orelus (2010)

While all of this work and all of these critiques, which barely scratch the surface of all that has been produced and is available, certainly affirm Chomsky's focus on basic human similarities (i.e., a creative, self-actualizing drive), feminism emerged as part of the postmodern resistance movement against the reductionistic tendency of modern science's exclusionary and colonizing impulse. It is therefore my intention here, as stated above, to argue that Chomsky's democratic approach to Enlightenment science (rejecting hegemonic science) combined with postmodernism's challenge to the Western scientific tendency to subjugate nonelite-Western knowledge systems and worldviews, work together to form a larger, complex whole.

For example, while there are many feminisms due to the complex nature of power and culture and therefore experience, humans, in general, seem to be genetically designed to creatively use and develop the ability to instantly understand language and be conscious of our own consciousness or freedom through self-reflection, freeing us, in part, from the impulse of reaction and internal drive, which, again, it is argued, is an endowment unique to humans. In other words, even those species such as apes, that are the most closely related to humans, do not possess the same genetically determined brains as us, rendering freedom and the consciousness of freedom outside their genetically determined endowments. Human nature is therefore, at its core, a question of defining the parameters of human cognition or intelligence. Because the notion of free will, for scientists such as Chomsky, is a little known property, human intelligence itself is not a well-defined property. While *human freedom*—a characteristic common to the species—appears to be a unique property, the independent essence of life is universal. That is, the primary quality of *life* (i.e., to be *alive*), in whatever species one refers, is that it is not driven or guided by external sources, even though intelligence can be manipulated. The limits and achievements of any given species are determined not by external factors, but by physical genetics, including brain structure and subsequent intellectual endowments. From this point of view the notion of race and gender are social constructs designed to perpetuate exploitative relationships with no real legitimate connection to objective science.

The above insight that intelligence is not a well-defined property and often manipulated to serve political interests of power is particularly important to education, which the extraenvironmentalism of behaviorism assumes, if not in theory, then in practice, the opposite. That is, behaviorism, and education in general, is based on the assumption that intelligence is well defined and therefore precisely measurable and externally controllable. However, further challenging the hyperenvironmentalism of this behaviorist pseudoscience, Newton's conclusions also strongly suggest that the source of our free will is not external, but is a fully integrated aspect of the living human. Science can therefore help intellectuals understand that the alienation observed by externally controlled and manipulated wageworkers is a direct, negative consequence of the oppression and subjugation of free will. If the essence of the human species is freedom, then those whose authority is derived from their association with science should, therefore, adopt the social arrangements that most centrally embrace this democratic value—as a conclusion of science with political implications, and in the current neoliberal context, revolutionary implications.

For Chomsky, as previously mentioned, these arrangements are called *anarchy*. An anarchist psychology—Chomsky's anarchist psychology in particular—is therefore consistent with accepted knowledge regarding the nature of human intelligence and free will within the scientific community. Chomsky (2005), always the rigorous scientist, rejects the use of detailed proposals to plan what a future society might look like because we do not know enough about the nature of human beings, institutions, society, and the implications of introducing humans to new social structures to validate such an approach. Rather, Chomsky (2005) suggests that the building of an anarchist society should be "experimental, guided by certain general ideas about liberty, equality, authority, and domination" allowing and encouraging people to "explore different ways of working through the maze and see what comes natural to them" (p. 221). It is within this practice that notions of *spontaneous learning* and *informal learning* take on new meaning.

An anarchist psychology is therefore based on the uncompromising respect for the intellectual freedom of the learner. The many subjugated knowledges represented within neocolonialist feminism, to take just one example, offers deep insight into the richness of intellectual freedom. It offers a global perspective that finds joy and solidarity in complexity and tension like when Chomksy's fifty-plus years of fearless resistance to U.S. imperialism leads postcolonial, feminist, Marxist scholar Gayatri Chakravorty Spivak to passionately exclaim in her Columbia University office suite that she is *no Chomsky* because she comes from an elite class in India that exploited a lower class for thousands of years rendering her unwilling to forfeit complexity for unification.

However, there is a contradiction here, because of our current state of indoctrination and hegemonic internalization, most of us are not conscious of the insights offered by our unique positionalities. That is, most of us have never had the opportunity to pause and take the necessary years to reflect on the ideas, values, and beliefs of the dominant, capitalist society that we have internalized throughout our lives. As a result, capitalism, behaviorism, the idea that people need leaders because human intelligence is so extremely variable that the average person is incapable of making intelligent decisions concerning important matters such as the structure and nature of the economy and foreign policy, have been so normalized and naturalized that we reproduce these structures without realizing it. The role of anarchist psychology, it seems, is to pose challenges to students that would require them to critically self-reflect on the worldviews that they have acquired over the course of their lifetimes. Again, one of the primary reasons why this self-reflective work tends not to be practiced in schools is because of the continuing dominance of behaviorism and the banking model of education.

While the scientific community has long abandoned mechanical explanations for human consciousness, behaviorists, which Chomsky names environmentalists because of their external explanations of human intelligence, have based their entire framework and conception of human nature on the assumption that human intelligence and consciousness posses no unexplainable force and are therefore merely the consequence of external conditioning (i.e., operant conditioning). That is, by reducing human intelligence and learning to the low-level conditioned responses performed by dogs and rats, behaviorism—which continues to be the dominant educational theory informing capitalist schooling (i.e., NCLB and Race to the Top)—ignores the self-reflective, complex intelligence, and free will that render humans a unique sociocognitive, intellectual species. In other words, behaviorism ignores the human endowment that leading Enlightenment thinkers such as Galileo have identified as *our most noble gift* (see Malott, Waukau, and Waukau-Villagomez, 2009). Reflecting on the insistence of certain scholars to base their behaviorist work on refuted conclusions, Chomsky (1988) provides insightful reflections: "One possible answer lies in the role that intellectuals characteristically play in contemporary—and not so contemporary—society . . . The standard image is that the intellectuals are fiercely independent, honest, defenders of the highest values, opponents of arbitrary rule and authority, and so on. The actual record reveals a different story. Quite typically, intellectuals have been ideological and social managers, serving power or seeking to assume power themselves" (p. 165).

Given this hegemonic role of science in the contemporary era, it should be expected that the universities, the official centers of knowledge production, should serve the interests of power and privilege before truth and the democratic values of the Enlightenment/science/philosophy—represented in Chomsky's anarchist psychology. Because the official channels of knowledge production that are most centrally implicated in social reproduction or engineering, that is, colleges of teacher education, science alone, as argued above, is not enough to ensure structures of power are not designed to betray what we know about human nature—that is, its propensity for freedom and the create use of labor power and language. What our anarchist approach to postformal psychology therefore needs is a political militancy in defense of science against the behaviorist tendencies of neoliberal capitalism as a current manifestation of the life and legacy of which Columbus represented. Before we move on to the next section we can summarize some of the more central ways Chomsky's anarchist psychology might inform our postformalism:

- Unlike a lot of recent anarchist literature that seems to focus on that which is out of our immediate control, such as mainstream psychology's devastating grip on not just the field of psychology but on society more generally (Fox, 2004), the driving force behind Chomsky's work, from linguistics to anarchist critiques of foreign policy, is an untiring celebration of humanity's most noble gift—our free will—expressed through our infinitely creative use of language. From this linguistic perspective the essence of humanity is therefore *freedom*—the freedom to think, engage, and create. Social arrangements that fundamentally betray this inherently human freedom, from Chomsky's scientifically informed anarchist perspective, must therefore be condemned and deposed. For Chomsky it is Newton's discovery of the previously mentioned action at a distance that contributes to the vast complexity and sophistication of human intelligence. The Cartesian insight regarding the uniqueness of human intelligence, which Newton, to his own displeasure, affirmed, led Descartes (1637, 1994) to the conclusion that "good sense is, of all things among men, the most equally distributed" (p. 3). Kincheloe's (2004) postformal cognitive theory is based on a similar conclusion, that "most students who don't suffer from brain disorders or severe emotional problems can (and do) engage in higher-order thinking" (p. 19) in their daily lives, even if not encouraged or nurtured in formalized school settings.
- Again, Chomsky's anarchist psychology challenges postformalists to be cautious when waging wholesale attacks against Descartes, Newton, and Western science in general because there are, as demonstrated above, counterhegemonic insights too important and potentially revolutionary to disregard—the notion of *action at a distance* in particular, which could be used by postformalists to rightly argue that, in many ways, their work represents the conclusions of science than do those free-will-denying behaviorists claiming to be doing scientific work.
- In other words, postformalism, unfortunately, has too often made the same mistake as behaviorism by rejecting science. The difference is that behaviorists reject science to advance an indoctrinating agenda, but call themselves scientists, whereas posformalists reject, in many ways, Western science in the name of social justice and embracing diverse epistemologies, but do not, of course, call themselves

scientists. However, I would argue that the underlying liberatory, transgressive *purpose* of postformalism and contemporary anarchist movements is essentially the same as the democratic habits of the scientific mind embodied by the likes of Galileo, and more recently, Noam Chomsky. Science, after all, did emerge in Southern Europe as a revolutionary movement against the oppressive dogma, divine-right mysticism, and utterly brutal and barbaric colonizing impulse of the Roman Catholic Church.

- Anarchist theory, from a Chomskian perspective, can legitimately invoke the authority of science and simultaneously expand the possibilities for taking postformalism to the streets, as it were. In other words, anarchists pride themselves on being *practical* or at the forefront of revolutionary movement (Graeber, 2002). Postformalism, with its emphasis on democratic knowledge production as part of the process of resisting dominant forms of oppressive and coercive power, can too easily fail to move the theory and practice or critical constructivism from the classroom to other areas of society such as places of employment and public places (i.e., parks, sidewalks, streets, etc.).

## Toward a New Field: A Constructed, Situated, and *Militantly* Enacted Discipline

Beginning with Kincheloe's ideas about a constructed and situated psychology, or the notion that the ideas people hold about the world, such as Western Europeans' construction of Orientalism during the eighteenth and nineteenth centuries (see Said, 1978), are not objectively fixed, but are rather socially constructed through historically developing relationships of power, is, no doubt, of extreme importance and thus a central component of our postformal approach to educational psychology. Similarly, dominant ideas about the nature of women are social constructions designed to manufacture consent for patriarchy from men and women. Postformalism therefore rejects the one right answer grand narrative ontology of formal science embracing, rather, a multilogicality that appreciates and learns from the knowledges and epistemologies subjugated, disrespected, and, in many instances, all but eradicated, by the enslaving and colonizing European forces that have transformed into neoliberal capitalism maintaining the same insatiable appetite for the accumulation of wealth that led Columbus and his hired hands to commit some of the most horrendous, barbaric forms of genocide never before witnessed by humanity.

For postformalists learning is consequently not just the passive transmission of facts, or the objective, decontextualized cognitive development of learners, but it is a form of development that is always socially and politically mediated in increasingly complex and contradictory ways by dominant and subordinate forms of power. Continually seeking ways of seeing and logics that are counterhegemonic is thus a drive force behind postformalism. Many of these worldviews/philosophies are the interpretive frameworks of those most oppressed and exploited women *and* men by the capitalist relations of production and the formalism of dominant society intended to normalize and naturalize the insane logics of capital.

Analysis alone, however, as our above engagement with anarchist psychology suggests, is not enough to transform the basic structures of power embedded within capitalist, industrial society. The contributions anarchist ways of seeing might inform Kincheloe and others' postformalism are particularly instructive, especially at this time of crisis when the world's people are growing ever more tired of the irresponsible practices and damages inflicted by an industrial, global capitalist ruling elite—the positivistic formalism of the boss's science for plunder.

Aware of this challenge posed by critical theory, many of us on the educational Left argue that our work in teacher education challenging future teachers to assist their future students in developing critical consciousnesses and viewing themselves as creators of history rather than mere spectators or objects of historical developments constitutes action beyond analysis. On some levels this is correct. However, at the same time, our assumption that revolutionary change will automatically happen if enough people become critically conscious because of our biologically determined intelligence as a species, is, in some respects true, but at the same time naïve and I would argue even irresponsible. That is, revolution, or the displacement of ruling class power in the form of large multi-billion- and trillion-dollar corporations and corporate/ruling elite-controlled governments, has historically proven to be a very dangerous and costly (in terms of both resources, wealth, and human life) endeavour.

If teacher educators (and others), in sharing with the students they work with the revolutionary conclusions the evidence regarding the basic structures of power suggests, encourage future teachers to teach the importance of revolutionary action, then they must themselves demonstrate through action what this might look like in practice. The challenge, from the postformal perspective outlined in this volume, is therefore to model democratic, nonviolent revolutionary agency, or a *militantly enacted* postformal anarcho-feminist psychology. Operating within the parameters of institutional learning facilities poses significant barriers to such movement because, by design, as argued above, they are constructed against the conclusions of science to serve the elite interests of reproducing capitalist society. Aware of the domesticating impulse of institutions of education, another related barrier for the critical educator is overcoming the immobilizing fear of speaking *for* rather than *with*.

That is, aware of the historical role education has played in subjugating the knowledge of Native American and African peoples, for example, by speaking for and representing the other, many academics, especially whites, in their attempts not to reproduce this paternalistic tendency, too often resort to doing nothing as a safe way to avoid the negative effects of their internalized hegemonies. However, for the critical educator, this is not an option. For change to occur, risks must be taken, but with a persistent dedication to critical self-reflection. In our efforts to become transformative agents of change we must therefore not become too dogmatically wedded to a particular analysis or conclusion. For example, we must be conscious of the significant role of positionality in informing ones analytical place of departure.

## A New Generation of Anarchists: Possibilities for an Enacted Militancy

First and foremost, we can reiterate by noting that the anarchist challenge is a challenge to more completely transgress the institutions of formalism, such as schools, colleges, and universities. While these spaces offer opportunities to produce knowledge from a diversity of epistemological frameworks, the qualitative limits to this work are defined by the institution itself. An anarchist psychology would extend Kincheloe's insistence that learning is a libidinal, full-body experience, arguing that the revolutionary development of the mind flowers into full bloom only through the collective struggle against the indoctrinating institutions themselves and the capitalist relations of production.

Offering substantial hope here in "The New Anarchists," David Graeber (2002) draws attention to the democratic organizing practices of a new generation of anarchist challengers to neoliberal domination. Often overlooked by Marxists and mainstream, academic, critical pedagogues and demonized by corporate media as violent, Graeber (2002) argues that such a mistake could not be more serious in these desperate times. Outlining who these new anarchists are and what their philosophy has looked like in practice, Graeber (2002) begins with the Indigenous, revolutionary Zapatistas of Chiapas, Mexico (see Khasnabish, chap. 12). The Zapatistas' subjugated knowledge is precisely what Kincheloe's postformalism argues is needed at this historical juncture.

Arguing that today's global action networks against neoliberalism, such as the famous protests against the World Trade Organization (WTO) in Seattle in 1999, can be traced to the Zapatistas' 1994 uprising and call for a worldwide network of opposition to neoliberalism, Graeber (2002) underscores the postformalism of today's new anarchists. Important here is the meaning of globalization, which has incorrectly been identified as a negative development. This analysis stems from the negative consequences of the liberalization of capital. However, the international movement of capital is actually antiglobalizing because it limits the free movement of people, possessions, and ideas across borders (Chomsky, 1999; Graeber, 2002). In other words, deregulating capital has strengthened the ruling class and, as a result, limited the freedom of people creating a less globalized world. The Zapatistas' call against neoliberalism is therefore a call for a more globalized world—a global movement against the abuses of ruling class power that takes the form of an international "network" rather than an "organizing structure" with a "central head or decision maker" and therefore has "no central command or hierarchies" (Graeber, 2002, p. 64).

Beginning with the Zapatistas' black ski masks, rubber boots, and white flags on their rifles symbolizing a paradox—guns that want to be silent—the new anarchists have embraced a playful engagement with outrageous symbolism matching the equally absurd era of neoliberal capitalism—an economic system that calls itself globalization while effectively limiting actual globalization (i.e., the free movement of people and information across borders) through such means as an explosion in the world's border guards and the restriction of immigration from the underdeveloped so-called third-world to first-world or industrially developed areas.

Again, responding to the absurdity of the contemporary global context Graeber (2002) points to the street pedagogy of the ridiculous where anarchists in overstuffed, padded clown costumes lob fluffy stuffed animals at riot police confusing the military-minded police of the bosses. This pedagogical approach allows even the riot police themselves an opportunity to reflect on the absurdity of a system that treats humans like chattel and denies the creative impulse of the human biological endowment. Summarizing the spirit within these new anarchists Graeber (2002) notes that, "the general anarchistic inspiration of the movement, which is less about seizing state power than about exposing, delegitimizing and dismantling mechanisms of rule while winning ever-larger spaces of autonomy from it" (p. 68) is not necessarily about rejecting all organization but is about "creating new forms of organization" (p. 70). For example, Graeber (2002) points to "spokecouncils," which are:

> Large assemblies that coordinate between smaller "affinity groups." They are most often held before, and during, large-scale direct actions like Seattle or Quebec. Each affinity group (which might have between 4 and 20 people) selects a "spoke," who is empowered to speak for them in the larger group. Only the spokes can take part in the actual process of finding consensus in the council, but before major decisions they break out into affinity groups again and each group comes to consensus on what position they want their spoke to take. (p. 71)

Such organizational structure, not unlike the ancient governing model practiced by the Mayan-based Zapatistas offers exciting prospects for what life after neoliberal capitalism could possibly look like in practice. In other words, a more horizontal and less hierarchical society is not just an impossible ideal, but is actually realistic. However, such prospects are not without real challenges.

## Barriers to an Anarchist Postformal Pedagogy

The barriers to enacting an anarchist postformal psychology are many, both interpersonal and institutional. What follows is a brief summary of these two types of barriers. However, before we proceed I should pause for a moment and acknowledge that the *interpersonal* and the *institutional* are not separate and unrelated entities, but are rather part of the same larger whole. In other words, institutions exist because groups of individuals constructed them and even larger groups of individuals either support and uncritically reproduce them or challenge and oppose them. Many scholars have identified this type of relationship as dialectical because it represents a tension of competing interests where institutions determine who individuals develop into while individuals simultaneously shape institutions through both critical and uncritical agency.

### *Institutional*

First and foremost, social structures, such as institutions of formalized education, have been constructed and developed around behaviorist models of lesson planning, curriculum development, and classroom management, and internalized by policy-makers, educational leaders, teachers, students, and caregivers to such an extent that they are viewed as *just how it is*, or a *nonperspective*. No Child Left Behind and Race to the Top, for instance, are examples of how behaviorist practices have been federally enforced through legislation. Of course nowhere within these examples of legislation does it say they are informed by behaviorist principles. Rather, they are presented as the objective results of what science tells us are the best methods of teaching literacy. The message is that they are not embedded with a political agenda, but represent an objective approach to learning.

Supporting this propaganda approach to education is the corporate media, which also has played a significant role demonizing the anarchist movement. Even many Marxists use the term *anarchy* to describe that which is assumed to be unorganized, undesirable, and unproductive, such as *the anarchy of the market*. While this tendency has historical presidents between Marx himself and prominent anarchists such as Bakunin, it is certainly not helpful to the movement for democratic globalization. However, the corporate media's attack on anarchy has undoubtedly had far greater effects than Marxists who themselves tend to be ignored or demonized by the same media outlets.

Graeber (2002), for example, points to the media's repeated insistence that the anarchists of the Seattle WTO protests were violent, despite the fact that they hurt no one. What the mainstream, corporate media seemed to be most frustrated with, argues Graeber (2002), was the fact that *the new anarchists* were decidedly not violent. That is, it is a lot more difficult to demonize and ignore a group's ideology and position when they are nonviolent. The mass media would have had a much easier time convincing people anarchists were scary monsters had they actually been physically assaulting police officers and civilian bystanders.

It is therefore the challenge of critical postformal educators to demonstrate through our teaching and scholarship the practical reasons why critical theories and practices, such as anarchy, are favorable alternatives to the neoliberal order that currently dominates. People must come to understand that the current neoliberal trajectory is not only unsustainable, but it is dangerously irresponsible. The media has conditioned millions of people to equate democracy and freedom with capitalism rendering the struggle for genuine democracy an incredibly difficult undertaking. Consequently, many critical pedagogues have given up hope believing the only way paradigmatic change will come is through the catastrophic physical and economic collapse of the current system. What these institutional barriers suggest is that part of the solution requires an individual approach.

### *Interpersonal*

While Chomsky's anarchism provides us with much insight regarding the biological context of human nature, other anarchisms and critical psychological theories are needed to better understand the social cognitive context of the mind *in* and *through* society. To begin recovering from the psychological damage done by an indoctrinating, white-supremacist, patriarchal, neoliberal society necessary to more fully embrace an anarcho-feminist, postformal psychology and critical pedagogy, we need something more. In keeping with our anarchist theme of expanding the circle of criticality, we can turn to the anarchist psychology of the late Paul Goodman (2010) who understood that conforming to this society would lead to illness, but not conforming would lead to dementia because this is the only society there is. That is, there are no other realities to escape to.

Similarly, feminist reinterpretations of Freud's work in the 1970s began to observe how women internalize sexist oppression as a result of living under patriarchy rendering the psychological life unhealthy for most women (LeLand, 1989). Others (Sa'ar, 2005) argue that the story of how women consent to patriarchy is more complex than just the result of the normalizing consequence of socialization. For example, Amalia Sa'ar (2005) notes that some women consent to the larger system of sexist oppression because they benefit materially from their racial and class associations and affiliations. The challenge for critical educators, as suggested above, is therefore to demonstrate that the result of a world without oppression and crude exploitation would be far better for everyone, even those who currently benefit the most from the negative system that exists.

## Conclusion: A Postformal, Anarchist Self-Reflection

The pressures are great living in this neoliberal, hyperconservative U.S. context where the value of ones identity is measured by their position within capitalist society. Based on the values of that *capitalist society*, at this moment in its development, most people are defined as redundant, losers, failures, and therefore not useful to the system. Consequently, from the dominant set of values most peoples' current circumstances are a mark of shame and worthlessness. However, from another marginalized and subjugated set of values it can be viewed as a badge of honor to refuse to participate in the process of value production, wealth extraction, and plunder. Most people who find themselves on the margins, however, are not there by choice and therefore do not necessarily posses a critical understanding of their circumstances. As a result, we either live with those internal tensions and try to help push ahead, or we resort to our capitalist conditioning and assume our tacit place within Jung's collective unconsciousness. Transgression of our identities in capitalist society, however, requires a collective uprising where society liberates itself from its old roles as wageworkers and subservient to elite power. An informed and empowered population understands how dominant forms of power operate and takes action to deny its existence so democracy and the power of the people can flourish. In other words, our identity cannot fully transform if the larger economic and political social structure and distribution of power remain the same.

To be successful, radicals, especially the most privileged (i.e., white) radicals, must engage in this scholarship and movement building without romanticizing oppression and suffering so many of us fail to correct within ourselves. For example, it is a romantic, privileged point of view or belief that the most oppressed citizens are critical thinkers *because* they are oppressed. This is a naïve idea informed by a simplistic and wrong understanding of the role of ideas in creating consent to the basic structures of power. Believing that all white people are rich and uncritical because of white-skin privilege is an equally inadequate and essentializing interpretive framework. Taking these precautions heightens the prospects of reaching others counter-hegemonically, which, I believe, is one of the primary responsibilities of the postformal, anarcho-feminist critical pedagogue. In other words, it is our task to oppose the power structure we benefit from, which means reaching its primary supporters—white people as a socially constructed political, economic force and ideology. Again, this is done not just because it is unfair, but because it is the necessary for all people to reach their full, supported, independent potential. Otherwise, we're missionaries, and missionary ideology is colonialist. To reiterate, we do not only pay attention to white people, hardly, we also work in solidarity with diverse communities from around the world. This is fundamental to our work and global movement against power and privilege. Again, this work is not simple or clear-cut; it is complex, too easily contradictory, and never straightforward. We nevertheless continue to negotiate these spaces of tension and contradiction as we oppose dominant forms of exploitative and oppressive power—sometimes with success, and other times suffering bitter defeats, but always knowing the struggle will continue.

## References


Brown, S. (1996). Beyond feminism: Anarchism and human freedom. In H.J. Ehrlich (Ed.), *Reinventing anarchy, again*, 149–55. San Francisco: AK Press.

Chomsky, N. (1988). *Language and problems of knowledge: The Managua lectures*. Cambridge, MA: The MIT Press.

Chomsky, N. (1999). *Profit over people: Neoliberalism and global order*. New York: Seven Stories.

Chomsky, N. (2005). *Chomsky on anarchism*. Oakland: AK Press.

Colón Warren, A. (2003). Puerto Rico: Feminism and feminist studies. *Gender and Society, 17*(5), 664–90.

Ehrlich, C. (1996). Socialism, anarchism, and feminism. In H.J. Ehrlich (Ed.), *Reinventing anarchy, again*, 169–88. San Francisco: AK Press.

Fox, D. (2004). Interview: Antiauthoritarianism, anarchism, critical psychology, law . . . Retrieved from http://www.dennisfox.net/papers/antiauthoritarian.html#3 (accessed June 2, 2010).

Garcia, A. (1989). The development of Chicana feminist discourse, 1970–1980. *Gender and Society, 3*(2), 217–38.

Goldman. E. (1969). *Anarchism and other essays*. New York: Dover.

Goodman, P. (2010). *Drawing the line once again: The anarchist writings of Paul Goodman*. Oakland: PM Press.

Graeber, D. (2002). The new anarchists. *New Left Review, 13*, January–February.

Guérin, D. (2005). *No gods, no masters: An anthology of anarchism*. San Francisco: AK Press.

Gutmann, J. (1936). Introduction. In F.W.J. Schelling, *Philosophical inquires into the nature of human freedom*. La Salle: Open Court.

Harris, L.A. (1996). Queer black feminism: The pleasure principle. *Feminist Review, 54*, Confronting Feminine Orthodoxies, 3–30.

hooks, b. (1984). *Feminist theory: From margin to center*. Cambridge, MA: South End Press.

hooks, b. (2000). *Feminism is for everybody: Passionate politics*. Cambridge, MA: South End Press.

Jazeel, T. (2006). Postcolonial geographies of privilege: Diaspora space, the politics of personhood and the "Sri Lankan Women's Association in the UK." *Transactions of the Institute of British Geographies*, 19–33.

Kincheloe, J. (2004). *Multiple intelligences reconsidered*. New York: Peter Lang.

Kincheloe, J. (2005). *Critical constructivism primer*. New York: Peter Lang.

Kincheloe, J. (2008). *Critical pedagogy primer*, 2nd ed. New York: Peter Lang.

Kornegger, P. (1996). Anarchism: The feminist connection. In H.J. Ehrlich (Ed.), *Reinventing anarchy, again*, 156–68. San Francisco: AK Press.

Leeder, E. (1996). Let our mothers show the way. In H.J. Ehrlich (Ed.), *Reinventing anarchy, again*, 142–48. San Francisco: AK Press.

LeLand, D. (1989). Lacanian psychoanalysis and French feminism: Toward an adequate political psychology. *Hypatia, 3*(3), 81–103.

Mack-Canty, C. (2004). Third-wave feminism and the need to reweave thenature/culture duality. *NWSA Journal, 16*(3), 154–79.

Malott, C., Waukau, L. & Waukau-Villagomez, L. (2009). *Teaching Native America across the curriculum: A critical inquiry*. New York: Peter Lang.

Messner, M. (1997). *Politics of masculinities: Men in movements*. Thousand Oaks, CA: Sage.

Mojab, S. (2001). Theorizing the politics of "Islamic feminism." *Feminist Review, 69*, 124–46.

Morland, D. (1997). *Demanding the impossible? Human nature and politics in nineteenth-century social anarchism*. London: Cassell.

Orelus, P. (2010). *The agony of masculinity: Race, gender, and education in the age of "new" racism and patriarchy*. New York: Peter Lang.

Russell, B. (1945). *The history of Western philosophy*. New York: Simon & Schuster.

Sa'ar, A. (2005). Postcolonial feminism, the politics of identification, and the liberal bargain. *Gender and Society, 19*(5), 680–700.

Said, E. (1978). *Orientalism*. New York: Vintage.

Schelling, F.W.J. (1936). *Philosophical inquiries into the nature of human freedom*. La Salle: Open Court.

Villaverde, L. (2008). *Feminist theories and education primer*. New York: Peter Lang.

Worell, J. (2000). Feminism in psychology: Revolution or evolution? *Annals of the American Academy of Political and Social Science, 571*, Feminist Views of the Social Sciences, 183–96.

**CHAPTER 15**

# Paideia for Praxis: Philosophy and Pedagogy as Practices of Liberation

**Nathan Jun**

## Introduction: A Pilgrimage to Forest Home

It is easy for academic workers, even those of us who consider ourselves anarchists, to become detached and disengaged from the sad realities of the world. During the two or so years I was writing my dissertation, I was often so engrossed in philosophical minutiae that I'd forget that the richest 2 percent of the world's adults control more than half of the world's wealth, while the bottom half owns barely 1 percent; that the combined wealth of the three richest individuals is greater than the combined Gross Domestic Product of the forty-eight poorest countries; that of the one hundred largest economies, more than fifty are corporations; that three billion people are living on less than one dollar a day; that twenty-five million people in Africa are dying of AIDS; that eight-hundred million people lack access to basic health care; that eight-hundred and seventy million people are illiterate; that seven-hundred million people are starving or malnourished. My reaction to these lapses of memory was always the same: I felt ashamed of myself. How could I sit in the comfort of my apartment in a clean, safe, middle-class neighborhood, an alien to the struggle, and write a dissertation about the evils of poverty and state-sponsored violence, all the while aware of my own complicity in the very system which generates these evils and unleashes them upon the world?

The role of intellectuals in general and academic workers in particular within the anarchist movement is famously ambiguous. Anarchists have long harbored skepticism toward formal academic institutions, which they tended to regard, rightly, as ancillaries of the existing social, political, and economic order. "It was not for the People," Proudhon writes, "that the

Polytechnic, the Normal School, the Military School at St Cyr, the School of Law, were founded; it was to support, strengthen, and fortify the distinction between classes, in order to complete and make irrevocable the split between the working class and the upper class" (Proudhon, 1972, p. 111). In a similar vein, Bakunin argues that "just as Catholicism once sanctioned the violence perpetrated by the nobility upon the people, so does the university, this church of bourgeois science, explain and condone the exploitation of the same people by bourgeois capital" (Bakunin, 1992, p. 124). Academics, in turn, are "by their very nature inclined to all sorts of intellectual and moral corruption," chiefly a tendency toward arrogance and pomposity (Bakunin, 1990, p. 134). (Anyone who has spent more than five minutes at an academic conference can scarcely take issue with this observation). At their worst, Bakunin says, they are "modern priests of licensed political and social quackery [who] poison the university youth so effectively that it would take a miracle to cure them" and who produce "doctrinaire[s] full of conceit and contempt for the rabble, whom [they are] ready to exploit in the name of [their] intellectual and moral superiority" (Bakunin, 1992, p. 74). Regrettably all of Bakunin's claims, though written in the 1860s and '70s, remain just as true in the present day. As Peter Gelderloos writes:

> We do not want to be like these people [bourgeois academics] . . . There is honor among thieves, and we prefer that kind to the honor of titled professionals. Imagine the hypocrisy, the blindness, of the social scientists studying "hierarchy and power" evident in one particular scene, the reception dinner at the end of the conference. A hundred ladies and gentlemen in expensive dresses and suits, gobbling up *hors d'ouevres* in a building guarded by private security in the capital of a poor country, only aesthetically aware of the dozen t-shirt-and jeans-clad anarchists among them, some packing weapons because their very real struggle against hierarchy puts them in constant risk of attack by fascists, casually stealing silverware and filling plastic bags with banquet delicacies to feed themselves for the next few days. I recall one conversation: a flirty prof mentioned the lovely seaside hotel he stayed in during a conference in Barcelona. I couldn't help but interject: "ah yes, there used to be a fishermen's village there before they demolished it and built the artificial beach. It was really nice." He didn't get the irony. Let me repeat: we do not want to be like these people. (Gelderloos, 2007)

Even honest, clear-eyed, and well-intentioned academics—the kind of academics we *want* to be—constantly run the risk of valorizing the abstract and theoretical at the expense of the concrete and the practical. This is a serious problem since, as Bakunin notes, "abstraction can easily conceive the principle of real and living individuality but it can have no dealings with real and living individuals" (Bakunin, 2004, p. 35). In other words, theoretical analysis and other forms of intellectual work do not by themselves guarantee any meaningful connection with the concrete, lived experience of human beings, which is precisely why theoretical analysis tends to invite disengagement and detachment from reality. For this reason, Rocker writes, "all higher understanding, every new phase of intellectual development, every epoch-making thought, giving men new vistas for cultural activities, has been able to prevail only through constant struggle with . . . authority" (Rocker, 1997, p. 84). This illustrates one of the major challenges which anarchist academic workers face—namely, how to marshal our intellectual work in the lived struggle against authority and the service of human liberation. Two years after completing my dissertation, an assistant professor of philosophy in a provincial North Texas military town, it is a challenge which I myself face on a daily basis.

On July 17, 2010, the seventy-fourth anniversary of the beginning of the Spanish Civil War, my wife and I visited Forest Home Cemetery outside Chicago, where some of the most famous and beloved figures of the historical anarchist movement are buried. It was in that spot, in the shadow of the Haymarket Martyrs Monument, that a dear comrade of ours had chosen to celebrate his commitment ceremony. As happy as I was for Bill and his partner, the experience of standing amid the remains of those heroes was infinitely more harrowing than it was the first time I visited the cemetery. That was in 1999 when, newly radicalized in the aftermath of Seattle and flushed with a romantic revolutionary fervor, I ventured out to lay roses at the base of the Monument and upon the graves of Emma Goldman, Lucy Parsons, and Voltairine de Cleyre.

Having been raised in a religious household, I am no stranger to the concept of pilgrimage; indeed I continue to appreciate it even though I have long since abandoned all religious creeds. To religious people, the point of pilgrimage is to draw near to holiness, to immerse themselves in the sacred. While most anarchists are not religious, we are nonetheless people of great and unwavering faith—faith in the values of liberty and equality, in the capacity of humankind to construct a world free of greed, oppression, and violence. More importantly, we belong to an old and august tradition populated by others who have shared this faith and have even laid down their lives in its name. Whenever I visit Forest Home, I feel a deep and profound connection to these heroic forebears; a profound sense of belonging to something larger and more powerful than myself; a visceral pride in the accomplishments and sacrifices of "my" movement throughout history. That was the point of past pilgrimages: to keep silent and solitary company, however brief, with giants—the giants upon whose shoulders we stand upon today. This most recent pilgrimage, however, was different. Gazing at the Haymarket

Monument, looking down at the graves of Goldman and Parsons and de Cleyre, I thought about what these people did and wondered how I could dare to count myself among them. After all, what was I doing to merit the honorable title of "anarchist"? As Beckett would say, "very little, almost nothing."

In my scholarly work I join Bakunin in condemning abstraction as politically, socially, and economically oppressive, yet isn't there something incredibly hypocritical about this? Isn't Bakunin right, after all, in intimating that scholarly work is itself a form of abstraction? More importantly, does not this abstraction entitle me to privilege—privilege which is denied to others, privilege which prejudices my work and alienates me from the class struggle, privilege which I consistently and constantly take for granted? And what, at the end of the day, does this abstraction do to promote the liberation of humankind? Does it perhaps do nothing? Worse, does it actually serve to perpetuate domination? In the face of such suspicion, it is little wonder that so many online anarchist and Left-socialist forums are constantly brimming with invective against "academics," or that I often find myself feeling ashamed and guilty in the presence of comrades. Whether such suspicion and the accompanying self-doubt are warranted remains to be seen. My point is that I find myself thinking and worrying and getting depressed about these issues all the time, and I know that I am not alone in this. Any honest anarchist who finds himself or herself toiling in the bowels of academia and kindred institutions cannot avoid these feelings. The salient question, and one which I am keen to discuss in this essay, is whether they are rational or at least understandable; whether they can be overcome with a mind to transforming us for the better; whether they can impel us to think or act differently. I think they can, but only if we think carefully about our roles as teachers and scholars.

## Anarchists as Intellectuals and Academics

Malatesta writes, "All of us, without exception, are obliged to live more or less in contradiction with our ideals" (Malatesta, 1993, p. 142). This, in my view, is the first and most important lesson of modern politics: that we are all hypocrites, that purity and authenticity are vain aspirations, that we are all accomplices with State and Capital whether we like it or not. What matters for anarchists, Malatesta continues, is that "we suffer by this contradiction and seek to make it as small as possible" (Malatesta, 1993, p. 142). We strive to be *aware* of our complicity and to do whatever we can to minimize that complicity without compromising our individuality and personal ideals. Clearly this recognition was enough to ameliorate Malatesta's shame, if indeed he had any in the first place. But then again, Malatesta was a professional revolutionary, whereas I am simply a teacher and a writer of books. If I am being truly honest with myself, I cannot help but think this makes a difference. Surely people like Malatesta—people whom I admire very much, people whom I envy because they seem so much stronger and braver than I, because they accomplished much more than I could ever see myself accomplishing—could afford to be a bit bourgeois. Yet when I try to take Malatesta's lesson to heart, it inevitably ends up seeming like a cop-out.

At the same time, are other comrades' choices really that different from mine? After all, one must earn a living whether she likes it or not, and whether she chooses to work in a factory or in a university, she necessarily remains an accomplice to the very system she seeks to abolish. So the question becomes: given one's distinctive talents, interests, and passions, how can one do the best for herself and for humanity as a whole? Clearly for some of us, the answer to this question lies in intellectual work. As Alexander Berkman writes:

> Do not make the mistake of thinking that the world has been built with hands only. It has also required brains. Similarly does the revolution need both the man of brawn and the man of brain. Many people imagine that the manual worker alone can do the entire work of society. It is a false idea, a very grave error that can bring no end of harm. In fact, this conception has worked great evil on previous occasions, and there is good reason to fear that it may defeat the best efforts of the revolution. The working class consists of the industrial wage earners and the agricultural toilers. But the workers require the services of the professional elements, of the industrial organizer, the electrical and mechanical engineer, the technical specialist, the scientist, inventor, chemist, the educator, doctor, and surgeon. In short, the proletariat absolutely needs the aid of certain professional elements without whose cooperation no productive labor is possible. (2003, p. 190)

Bakunin, too, stresses the essential role of the intellectual proletariat which, he insists, "must now be imbued with a passion founded on reason for the socialist-revolutionary cause if it does not want to succumb shamefully to total ruin; it is this class henceforth that is called to be the organizer of the popular revolution" (Bakunin, 1990, p. 212). Unlike bourgeois intellectuals, whom Bakunin resolutely condemns, the intellectual proletariat is "upright, sincere, and devoted in the extreme . . ." (p. 212). Its mission, accordingly, is to "go to the people, because today, all over the world . . . outside of the people, outside of the millions and millions of proletarians, there is neither existence, nor cause, nor future" (p. 212). And although the intellectual proletariat by itself is too small to "organize a revolutionary force apart from the people," it is sufficient to produce such a force if it works with and among the people (p. 212). The question, of course, is whether, how, and to what extent the intellectual proletariat can "go to the people" from within the universities, or whether there are other, more productive avenues for it to pursue.

In his "Prison Notebooks," Gramsci famously argues that every socioeconomic class organically generates a network of intellectuals which administer and organize that class and construct a cohesive and uniform class identity within and across the social, economic, and political fields (Gramsci, 2001, p. 1138). At the same time, every class which "emerges into history out of the preceding economic structure, and as an expression of the development of this structure" finds "categories of intellectuals already in existence," which, in contrast to "organic intellectuals," Gramsci terms "traditional intellectuals" (p. 1139). Because traditional intellectuals—such as philosophers, artists, and the clergy—have continued to exist despite "the most complicated and radical changes in political and social forms," (p. 1139) they have gradually come to believe in their own autonomy and independence from the ruling class and have erected a variety of self-serving mythologies to reinforce this belief. In reality, however, their continued existence has been permitted, not only by the ruling class, but by the "stratum of administrators, etc., scholars and scientists, theorists, non-ecclesiastical philosophers, etc." organically generated within capitalist society. Once these traditional intellectuals have been "conquered and assimilated," their function, like that of bourgeois intellectuals, is to organize, promote, and maintain "social hegemony and state domination" (p. 1143). In this capacity, they work chiefly as "creators of the various sciences, philosophy, [and] art . . ." and "'administrators' and divulgators of pre-existing, traditional, [and] accumulated intellectual wealth" (p. 1143). Their value consists precisely in their putative "independence" (or, as we say nowadays, "objectivity"), which in turns gives them the magical ability to transform contingencies into timeless, universal truths or mere propaganda into "common sense." Ultimately, Gramsci argues for the development of "organic intellectuals" within the working class coupled with the radicalization of bourgeois intellectuals (both traditional and organic).

Despite the flaws inherent in Gramsci's analysis of intellectuals, most of which are already well known to the readers of this essay, it is clear that anarchists like Bakunin and Berkman are sympathetic to several of its key components. Both recognize, for example, that intellectual work in bourgeois society has been co-opted by capitalism and that, as a result, the vast majority of intellectuals consciously or unconsciously serve the interests of the ruling class. So, too, both recognize and appreciate the importance of the intellectual proletariat and argue for the incorporation of academics and other intellectuals into the revolutionary movement regardless of class origins. But what might these thinkers have to say about anarchists working in the universities? In fairness, there are many careers, such as military service or the chairmanship of Halliburton, which would appear to be closed to anarchists on the basis of prefigurative ethics. The reason, in both cases, is that conventional armies and capitalist firms are intrinsically hierarchical, centralized, authoritarian, and exploitative institutions. Is the same true of universities? I don't think so. Although it is true that the vast majority of contemporary colleges and universities are hierarchical, bureaucratic, centrally organized, and deeply authoritarian institutions—and that's just the beginning of their problems—these aren't intrinsic features of "the university" itself. One can imagine a university (or university-like institution) that is nonhierarchical and decentralized (in fact, the original universities were marked by both features to greater or lesser degree), whereas one cannot easily imagine a capitalist firm that is nonhierarchical, decentralized, nonexploitative, and worker-owned. The fact is that universities, despite their myriad problems, serve useful and valuable functions in society. What is more, there are no viable alternatives which, at least at the present time, could even begin to accomplish the same ends.

This is all the more reason why at least some anarchists ought to work in universities: to direct the existing power and influence of universities toward anarchist goals and to work toward transforming the universities from within *with a mind to eventually making the current university model obsolete*. As Kropotkin writes:

> Repeating the formulation of Proudhon, we say: if a naval academy is not itself a ship with sailors who enjoy equal rights and receive a theoretical education, then it will produce not sailors but officers to supervise sailors; if a technical academy is not itself a factory, not itself a trade school, then it will produce foremen and managers and not workmen; and so one. We do not need these privileged establishments; we need the hospital, the factory, the chemical plant, the ship, the productive trade school for workers, which, having become available to all, will with unimaginable speed exceed the standard of present universities and academies. (1993, p. 22)

At present universities provide narrowly focused and hyperspecialized training that serves the interests of State and Capital. But what if we created universities that genuinely served the interests of humanity? Such institutions would be, to paraphrase Kropotkin, naval academies on ships, or trade schools in factories—places, in a word, where theory and practice are united and harmonized. To my mind, it makes sense to affect the transformation of existing institutions while simultaneously developing alternative institutions. To simply abandon existing institutions, especially those which contain so much transformative and revolutionary potential, strikes me as the height of folly.

## Philosophy, Paideia, and Anarchist Praxis

Now I cannot speak for all academic workers, but about 75 percent of my own intellectual work is devoted to teaching, the remaining 25 percent to research and scholarship. Whether and to what extent this work is at all useful or valuable as anarchist praxis depends crucially on (a) what, how, and why I'm teaching; and (b) what, how, and why I'm writing, and here I think my discipline could ultimately provide some saving grace. There is not now, nor has there ever been, any consensus among philosophers regarding the definition of philosophy as such. Historically this has proven both a blessing and a bane, for although philosophy's lack of any narrowly circumscribed subject matter has afforded a degree of flexibility and openness which few other disciplines can match, it has also given philosophy an unsavory reputation, memorably lampooned in Aristophanes's *The Clouds*, for hairsplitting and abstraction.

This is why Russell, Ayer, Carnap, Quine, and various other early and mid twentieth-century "analytical" philosophers are so often characterized as reformers; by rejecting metaphysical speculation, shifting attention to linguistic and conceptual analysis, and seeking to reconstruct philosophy on the model of logico-mathematical and scientific inquiry, they collectively transformed philosophy into a "modern" discipline The truth of the matter is far more complicated. The early analytical philosophers were fiercely committed to Enlightenment thought and practice, the "distinctive assumptions" of which, according to Philip Pettit, can be roughly described as follows:

1 There is a reality independent of human knowledge of which we human beings are part.
2 Reason and method, particularly as exemplified in science, offer us the proper way to explore that reality and our relationship to it.
3 In this exploration traditional preconceptions—in particular, traditional evaluative preconceptions—should be suspended and the facts allowed to speak for themselves (Pettit, 2005, p. 7).

Although there is no doubt that analytical thinkers were reacting in part against what they saw as the muddle, imprecision, and opacity of their philosophical peers, they were far more troubled by those philosophers (e.g., Hegel, Kierkegaard, Marx, Nietzsche) and movements (e.g., German Idealism, Romanticism, Marxism, Nietzschean perspectivism, phenomenology, etc.) which posed a challenge to their key assumptions. These same assumptions, after all, not only provided the foundations of modern philosophy but also made possible:

> The positive self-image modern Western culture [had] given to itself, a picture born in the eighteenth-century Enlightenment . . . of a civilization founded on scientific knowledge of the world and rational knowledge of value, which places the highest premium on individual human life and freedom, and believes that such freedom and rational-

ity will lead to social progress through self-controlled work, creating a better material, intellectual, and political life for all, (Pettit, 2005, p. 12)

As Anthony Giddens notes, this "set of attitudes towards the world, the idea of the world as an open transformation by human intervention" is the condition of possibility for all the other salient characteristics of modernity, a society "vastly more dynamic than any previous type of social order . . . a society—more technically, a complex of institutions—which unlike any preceding cultures lives in the future rather than the past" (Giddens and Pearson, 1999, p. 94). This "complex of institutions" includes "economic institutions, especially industrial production and a market economy" and "a certain range of political institutions, including the nation-state and mass democracy" (p. 94). To this list Cahoone adds "new, powerful technique[s] for the study of nature, as well as new machine technologies and modes of industrial production that have led to an unprecedented rise in material living standards . . . capitalism, a largely secular culture, liberal democracy, individualism, rationalism, humanism" (Cahoone, 1996, p. 11). If certain strands of nineteenth-century philosophy developed in reaction to the Enlightenment project, then analytical philosophy developed first and foremost in defense of its emerging status quo.

I agree with Aaron Preston that "it is a mistake to regard analytical philosophy as a philosophical school, movement, or tradition, and that, instead, it is (and always has been) a purely social entity unified by what interactional memes, maintained at high frequency by conformist transmission" (Preston, 2005, p. 292). But even as a "social entity" analytical philosophy has distinguished itself in two ways: first, by successfully achieving the total professionalization of philosophical practice—that is, by redefining philosophy as a highly specialized academic discipline that is taught, studied, and practiced exclusively by trained experts within Anglo-American universities; and second, by narrowing the focus of the discipline to minute, technical, and highly specialized problems. When analyzed from a Gramscian perspective, it is not difficult to make sense of these phenomena. By the beginning of the twentieth century, philosophers-qua-"traditional intellectuals" were in direct competition with the new "organic intellectuals" (e.g., scientists and technicians) of modern industrial society. Facing obsolescence and desperate to prove their ongoing relevance, the philosophers rebranded themselves in the image of their competitors. It is important to recognize, however, that in doing so the analytical philosophers have largely renounced their role as traditional intellectuals, retreating into the minutiae of logical and linguistic analysis instead of serving the status quo as apologists armed with "eternal verities." Unlike traditional intellectuals they do not think of themselves as serving God or mankind, let alone the ruling class, but rather the "profession." To this extent we might say they serve the status quo "by omission"—that is, in virtue of their irrelevance.

Yet the irrelevance of analytical philosophy to society at large has deep repercussions for the practice of philosophy in general. As a result of analytical hegemony, a de facto definition of philosophy has long since taken root that is considered normative for those who teach and conduct research within the Anglo-American academy, a definition which makes an engaged, socially and politically relevant philosophy virtually impossible. According to that definition, philosophy just is the set of "interactional memes"—the methodologies used, the topics studied, etc.—by those philosophy professors employed by elite philosophy departments in the United States, Canada, the United Kingdom, and Australia. Professional advancement and recognition within the discipline is determined in accordance with this definition; those who adopt alternative methodologies or study alternative topics will almost certainly be marginalized in various ways precisely because they are seen, at best, as doing "bad philosophy" and, at worst, as not doing philosophy at all. Most "elite" departments are invested with this status by tradition or, what comes to the same, because a preponderance of their faculty can trace their professional and philosophical lineages back to past analytical luminaries in a more or less unbroken succession. The underlying assumption, in all events, is that these philosophers—who ultimately share the same general concerns, discuss the same general topics, and utilize the same general methodology—should be regarded as the supreme arbiters, either implicitly or explicitly, of what counts as philosophy. They occupy the uppermost echelons of what might be called "the philosophical establishment"—the hierarchical network of professional relationships that determines topical, methodological, and disciplinary orthodoxies. What must be emphasized is that these "professional relationships" are nothing more than relations of power. The network they constitute is a purely social phenomenon that does not (and probably should not be expected to) act on the basis of "philosophical" considerations.

To this picture we must add an additional contour—namely, that philosophers employed by elite departments are generally paid obscenely high salaries compared to their lesser colleagues in the profession. The main duties they perform in order to receive such compensation are two: first, they publish research that is directed almost exclusively toward other members of the disciplinary ruling class; and second, they strive to replenish their numbers via the training and credentialing of graduate students. In order to meet the first duty, they must employ only those methods, discuss only those topics, and publish only in those journals that are met with the approval of their peers. More importantly, they must have ample time at their disposal, which means that they must avoid teaching undergraduates as much as possible. This necessitates the second duty, as the responsibility for teaching undergraduates is mainly outsourced to graduate teaching assistants. Of course, the overwhelming majority of Anglophone colleges and universities are not able to provide their faculty with these sorts of luxuries and privileges. Yet most junior faculty, having been trained in research-centered departments, are predisposed to regard publishing as their main priority even at institutions which emphasize undergraduate teaching. (It is little wonder that teaching is met with such disdain among academic philosophers, at least in my experience.)

The academic philosophical establishment regards philosophy as an essentially scientific and theoretical discipline for which rigorous argumentation and valid reasoning are the highest virtues. The goal of philosophical pedagogy, accordingly, is to instill basic familiarity with, and comprehension of, the range of theoretical problems that are regarded as distinctively "philosophical" and, more importantly, to cultivate the critical skills necessary to "philosophically" analyze these problems. It is important to recognize that this approach to philosophical practice and pedagogy differs markedly from that of our Greek and Roman predecessors, to say nothing of philosophers from ancient India, China, and other non-Western climes. Socrates famously claimed that the aim of those who practice philosophy is "to prepare for dying and death" (Plato 1950: II. 59), while Seneca upbraided teachers for reducing philosophy to argumentation, contending that their single-minded emphasis on logic demonstrated a "love of words" rather than a "love of wisdom" (Seneca 1925: epistle 108). This "love of words" has won the day, the result being that modern philosophy exists "to train [people] for careers as clerks or professors—that is to say, as specialists, theoreticians, and retainers of specific items or more or less esoteric knowledge" (Hadot, 1995, p. 38). The modern philosophy professor can ruminate for hours at a conference or in the classroom only to go home, spend an evening in front of the television, and never give his or her lecture a second thought. The same is true of any working professional whose "career" has been separated from his or her life.

There is no doubt that the study of philosophy is extremely conducive to the development of those general critical thinking and reasoning skills which are universally regarded as beneficial in every field of inquiry and endeavor. Indeed, to the increasingly limited extent that professors of philosophy are regarded as useful at all in higher education, it is mostly for our ability to help students develop these sorts of skills, not (or not mainly) to teach philosophy. Critical thinking and reasoning skills are also *sine qua non* for freethinkers and revolutionaries of all stripes, but that is obviously not why they are stressed by college and university administrators. Their goal, of course, is to produce the highly educated technical-managerial-professional class that is necessary to administer capitalist society on behalf of the ruling elite. In order to do their jobs well, members of this class not only require rote vocational training but also a moderate degree of critical intelligence (coupled, ideally, with an anemic or altogether nonexistent moral sensibility). This is by way of saying that while critical acumen may be necessary for the development of what we might call a "liberated consciousness," it is scarcely sufficient.

"All rational education," Bakunin writes, "is at bottom nothing save the progressive immolation of authority for the benefit of freedom, the final aims of education necessarily being the development of free men imbued with a feeling of respect and love for the liberty of others" (Bakunin, 2004, p. 41). Anarchists have long claimed, after all, that liberation is coextensive with education, which in turn requires a practiced ability to read, write, and think critically. The problem, which I have just illustrated, is that there is nothing inherently "radical" about teaching students "how to think." Many students simply don't *want* to engage in critical thinking even if they are able to learn how, and those that do are just as likely to marshal critical thinking in the service of self-interest or the manipulation and oppression of others. In order to make philosophical pedagogy a potentially anarchistic practice, one must pay serious attention to *what* students are thinking *about, how* they're thinking about it, and *to what end*. Again, the goal cannot merely be to teach students "how to think." If a student never learns what is worth thinking about, what questions are worth asking, what issues are worth caring about, et cetera, then her ability to think well is at best pointless (because she will never use it) and at worse dangerous (because she will apply it in harmful ways). The goal must be something altogether different.

The philosophical establishment, which is already inclined to regard teaching as a "necessary evil," does not recognize this. Its goal, as I have already stated, is to protect itself and the larger political, social, and economic system of which it is a part. To this extent, it has a vested interest in keeping its pedagogical vision as vacuous and unthreatening as possible. "Teaching students to think" sounds gutsy, but in reality it is a soft-footed and conservative approach that leaves the status quo fundamentally unchallenged. So what is the alternative? What is philosophy ("the love of wisdom") if it is not (or not *just*) a narrow, hairsplitting, logic-chopping discipline? In looking for an answer to this question, many are immediately drawn to Socrates, the spiritual godfather of Western philosophy. Socrates, after all, was not what we could call a "professional philosopher." He wasn't a specialist or a retainer of esoteric knowledge. He wasn't interested in obtaining a tenure-track position at a university or padding his CV. He wasn't offered a named chair or paid an extravagant salary to conduct research. In fact, he vehemently criticized the Sophists for teaching in exchange for money and, if we take the words of Plato at face value, insisted that these so-called "professionals," with their trumped-up claims to knowledge and wisdom, were actually charlatans.

Socrates had no ideas of his own. Instead, he traveled from place to place in search of those who *did* have ideas (or at least claimed to) and, guided by nothing but a relentless desire for truth, subjected these self-proclaimed sages to persistent and even obnoxious interrogations. The inevitable result of these interrogations, as we all know, is that the sages were shown again and again to be fools. Socrates, meanwhile, was left with even more unanswered questions, increasingly convinced that he knew nothing at all. The fact that Socrates was willing—indeed, unshakably determined—to die for the sake of philosophy strongly suggests the converse—that is, that he *lived* for his beliefs. Preparing for dying and death isn't about mastering a specialized academic discipline. On the contrary, as Plutarch noted, "at all times and in every place, in everything that happens to us, daily life gives us an opportunity to do philosophy" (Plutarch, 1936: no. 4). Philosophy is a praxis—a process by which an idea, concept, skill, or theory is realized, actualized, or implemented. Life itself is the idea or concept which philosophical praxis embodies.

It is precisely this openness to life, coupled with a desire to experience and understand it in all its richness and complexity, which underlies the ancient Greek educational philosophy of *paideia*. In the simplest and most general terms, *paideia* is analogous to Bakunin's "integral education"—it is well-rounded, broad-based and holistic training, the goal of which is the cultivation of sensibility and excellence of character rather than the accumulation of knowledge. The Greeks believed that training in a wide range of scientific, theoretical, and artistic disciplines placed students in a better position to successfully overcome the internal and external challenges posed by human life and so to achieve happiness. Philosophical acumen, historical knowledge, aesthetic sensitivity—these are all skills necessary for the pursuit of excellence (*arête*).

Philosophy is in many ways the heart and soul of *paideia*, emphasizing as it does the *process of seeking* rather than the *act of finding*. If we take seriously the sentiment which is repeated time and again throughout the works of the Stoics, the philosophical way of life is a search for knowledge about oneself and others. This search, which is something that one lives rather than lectures or writes or debates about, is coextensive with the development and practice of *arête*. Understood as a way of life, philosophy has the potential to make better people and better worlds. Understood as a scientific or theoretical discipline, as philosophy is today, it is seldom more than an accomplice of the status quo. This is best confirmed, perhaps, by asking what modern philosophers are willing to give up in defense of their doctrines and theories. If the answer is "not much"—and I suspect without cynicism that it is—we ought not to be surprised. After all, academic philosophy portrays itself as a dispassionate attempt to understand the world, a project that gets by perfectly well without martyrdom. Philosophy as a way of life is far more risky, since it calls upon the philosopher to examine and, ultimately, *change* herself.

This view of philosophy has never disappeared entirely but has continued to flare up here and there throughout history. Marx, to cite just one example, expands it by suggesting that the philosopher's goal isn't just to change herself but to change the world as well. In other words, philosophy as a way of life isn't just an introspective spiritual exercise or a voyage of self-discovery but a conscientious attempt to unite theory and practice with a mind to opening up new and heretofore unforeseen possibilities for the human race at large. It is no mistake that Marx was first and foremost a *political* philosopher, because it is within the realm of the political that the unity of theory and practice finds its most visible expression. From this perspective, the goal of a philosophical way of life isn't to offer solutions to abstract, universal problems but to immerse oneself in the dialectic of questions and answers, problems and solutions, etc. in order to discover what is possible, what might be done that hasn't be done before. In an important sense, this process of immersion precedes all inquiries about what is the case or what ought to be the case. If modernity has been guided, at least in part, by a "love of words" (or, what comes to the same, the "love of images"), if it has been directed toward solutions rather than to problems, we ought not to be surprised if alternatives to modernity have presented and continue to present very different approaches. This does not automatically imply a simple recuperation of premodern philosophical methodologies. I would suggest, however, that anything that can be genuinely regarded as "postmodern" (in the sense of "going beyond" the modern, not just coming after it) has important lessons to learn from the ancient ideal of *philos sophia*, understood, again, not as a theoretical discipline but as a lived experience.

My own philosophical pedagogy, then, may be summarized as follows. First, it situates philosophy within a broad-based, multifaceted, and holistic learning context whose goal is the cultivation of a strong, sensible, principled, adaptable, and resourceful character. (Bakunin called this "integral education, the Greeks called it *paideia*). Following Emma Goldman's advice, I draw heavily upon "the larger human expression manifest in art [and] literature . . . the strongest and most far-reaching interpreter of our deep-felt dissatisfaction," recognizing with her that "an adequate appreciation of the tremendous spread of the modern conscious social unrest" cannot be ascertained from any one kind of source (Goldman, 2004, p. 2). Second, my pedagogy treats philosophy not as a theoretical or scientific discipline, but as a way of life founded on the *praxis* of seeking, questioning, complicating, problematizing, potentiating, "possibilizing." To be sure, I am often compelled to ask students to think about traditional philosophical questions and arguments, as this is more or less unavoidable in the context of ordinary philosophy classes, but I strive as much as possible to avoid both abstraction and hairsplitting and to keep discussions grounded in the harsh and often frightening realities of the contemporary world.

Third, and most importantly, my pedagogy is an *anarchist* pedagogy because it seeks to advance, however minimally, the cause of total human liberation from oppression and inequality. To achieve this goal, it is not enough to teach students how to think; as an anarchist, I strive to help at least some of them learn to *care*, as caring is the condition of possibility for all of us to "break [our] mental fetters," to "think and judge for [ourselves]" and to escape "the dominion of darkness" (Goldman, 2008, p. 38). If I am doing my job well, at least a few students will remember and puzzle over topics we discuss in class; they will think about and be troubled by issues they read about in our books; in short, they will be *haunted*. Initially, perhaps, this haunting will take the form of nagging, intransigent thoughts; over time, it has the potential to become something else: a deeply held conviction that something is wrong with oneself and the world coupled with a desire to do something about both. It is this feeling that brings a person, eventually, to anarchism. The aim of my anarchist pedagogy is to help students discover that feeling in themselves using the tools of philosophy.

## Going to the People

How might these same ideas apply, if at all, to the issue of academic research? This is a thorny question, since research is something academic workers must do as a condition of employment and to this extent is often limited by more or less arbitrary and repressive institutional and professional standards. By and large, adhering to these standards tends to be severely at odds with the task of making one's work interesting, relevant, or useful to individuals outside one's discipline, let alone to radicals or other nonacademics. For this reason, even the most well-intentioned academic writing tends to be utterly useless as a form revolutionary praxis. That said, I take strong exception to the idea that academic writing as such is *inherently useless*, even in institutionalized forms. The foremost challenge faced by radical academic workers is overcoming the outmoded and elitist model of knowledge production that remains dominant in academic institutions. A secondary challenge is producing work within that model that actually contributes in some way to the possibility of revolutionary change.

Research, according to Gelderloos, is one "major area where the academy can be useful to anarchists." He continues:

> [Academics] have us cornered when it comes to investigation and critical debate. Anarchists are lazy researchers. Many prefer religion to research. Objective, and objectively false, statements that bear great

> importance for anarchist theory circulate freely in our circles. Some of the basic premises of primitivist, vegan, and historical materialist strains of anarchism would have been abandoned long ago if we'd had a culture of serious inquiry and debate. Instead we have name-calling on internet forums. I think we also could have made some headway on the eternal debate about the nature of formal and informal power and the extent to which each allows hierarchies to be established or challenged. But alas, in our circles it's still anybody's guess. (Gelderloos, 2007)

Certainly in the last ten years anarchist-related research has become increasingly acceptable within academia. This means it's possible to safely pursue an academic career with anarchism as a principal research focus; it does not mean that all or even most anarchism-related research is or will be relevant, interesting, or useful to the anarchist movement. For that to even become a possibility, anarchist academics must be something like Gramsci's organic intellectuals. That is, we must be a natural and integral part of the anarchist movement. Our work must emerge from within that movement and serve to reinforce and promote its interests (which are ultimately inseparable from the interests of humankind as a whole) rather than those of discipline, profession, institution,the academy, or the social and political system to which the academy belongs. This is not a matter of "activism" in some narrowly defined sense, but of passion, awareness, commitment, and historical sensibility. The last is pivotal, since anarchism, as I suggested earlier, is as much about the past as it is about the present. It is as much a lived tradition or history as it is a contemporary phenomenon. As such, a certain kind of historical consciousness would seem indispensible in making one's work relevant from the standpoint of praxis.

If I am right about all of this, then it is not difficult to understand how a certain kind of intellectual work, even of a specialized academic kind, can be valuable. First, and most obviously, it is extremely beneficial for anarchists and other revolutionaries to apply the model of *paideia* to their own lives by actively seeking out the broadest possible range of practical and theoretical knowledge. In particular, it behooves anarchists to know as much as possible about our own past, which Bakunin rightly refers to as our "mental capital, the sum of the mental labor of all previous generations" (Bakunin, 1973, p. 351). Academic workers have a crucial role to play in this respect, for, although we are not the only individuals capable of engaging in historical research and other forms of productive and valuable intellectual work, we are ideally placed to pursue it owing to our greater share of access to time, resources, and institutional support.

Anarchist academics and other intellectuals are also well disposed to engage in "theoretical work, direct communication with lots of people outside our circles . . . intervention in public discourse" (Gelderloos, 2007)—in short, what Marx called "the ruthless critique of everything existing." We are called to be, as Gramsci says, "constructers, organizers, permanent persuaders and not just . . . simple orators" (2001, p. 1143). Without theory, anarchism becomes a dogma on par with Leninism and most organized religions. Its principles become empty axioms whose truth is simply taken for granted and which have no purpose other than to mechanically justify practices. I strongly suspect there would be many more anarchists in the world if those principles were really as self-evident as we often take them to be. In fact, it is precisely our failure to better articulate and defend such principles that has fueled our ongoing historical insignificance across several key segments of Western society. No wonder Kropotkin writes, "The most important thing is to spread the truths already acquired, to practice them in daily life, to make of them a common inheritance" (Kropotkin, 2002, p. 265).

Obviously the task of "going to the people" and uniting with them in struggle involves writing to, as well as for the benefit of, nonacademic audiences. Even those non-tenured or non-tenure-track academic workers who must address a portion of our work to academic peers should strive as much as possible to make this accessible and relevant to non-academics. "With both irony and seriousness," writes Gelderloos, "I call for the excommunication of all academic anarchists who produce not for the movement but for the academy. If you study networks, find ways to explain to [the movement] how to effectively extend networks to people currently plugged into the system (or some other useful question), not how to analyze our networks so they can be understood by outsiders, as intellectually stimulating as that task may be" (2007). In offering such explanations, moreover, we ought to strive as much as possible to avoid needlessly technical language and other self-consciously "academic" conventions which serve no purpose except to alienate outsiders and ingratiate ourselves to other academics. In short, academic workers should only observe academic writing standards to the extent that doing so is practically and professionally expedient; beyond this, our foremost goals in writing should include clarity, accessibility, sincerity, relevance, and effectiveness.

To what kind of nonacademic audiences should our work be addressed? The answer, which is the same as it was more than a century ago, has already been divulged. It is "the people," which is to say, the whole mass of human persons who have been systematically oppressed, exploited, and disinherited irrespective of age, race, class, gender, sexual orientation, religion, ethnicity, or national origin. Among these, it has always been clear that our foremost attention, at least for the foreseeable future, ought to be focused on those who have suffered the most—for example, members of the poor and working classes, racial and sexual minorities, displaced indigenous populations, and so on. This does not mean, however, that the better-off, including students and bourgeois intellectuals, should be completely neglected. Kropotkin is right to point out that "propagandizing" among them "requires so much erudition . . . that it involves a terribly unproductive waste of time and distraction of energy from incomparably more urgent matters" (Kropotkin, 1993, p. 45). But we obviously need to reach young people (and, to a lesser extent, fellow intellectuals) in order to replenish and maintain the strength of our own intellectual proletariat

In all of this, we must remember that our enemies are ready and willing to use our own intellectual work against us. As Gelderloos notes:

> Simply producing information aids the system, even if that information seems to be revolutionary in its implications. This is because in democratic societies, people are pacified, and even if they are well informed they will not have gotten what they need to fight back. Information is not what's lacking. It is the institutions of power, and not the people, that are positioned to act on this information, and even critical information coming from dissident academics can help these institutions correct themselves. (2007)

To prevent this sort of thing from occurring, we need to be careful when working within the academic establishment and exercise discretion in what we choose to study, publish, and write. In the long run, we need to build up networks of reliable alternative institutions that successfully bridge the academic/anarchist divide. Publishing houses such as AK Press and PM Press and organizations such as the North American Anarchist Studies Network (NAASN), the Transformative Studies Institute, and the Institute for Anarchist Studies are slowly but surely helping anarchist academics and independent scholars to produce, disseminate, and share work that is not only "credible" to their academic peers but also useful and relevant to their comrades in the anarchist movement.

I close by enjoining academic workers to always think about what we do in terms of what came before as well as what could be. We must remember that our work is in the middle, the present, the space of "what's happening now," and to this extent we can never afford to become distanced from the realities of the world. This doesn't mean that we should all be activists *as well as* academics; it means that we should see our work itself as activism, and we should do so proudly and without shame. As Alexander Berkman writes:

> It is sad to admit that there is a tendency in certain labor circles, even among some socialists and anarchists, to antagonize the workers against the members of the intellectual proletariat. Such an attitude is stupid and criminal, because it can only harm the growth and devel-

> opment of the social revolution. It was one of the fatal mistakes of the Bolsheviks during the first phases of the Russian Revolution that they deliberately set wage-earners against the professional classes, to such an extent, indeed, that friendly cooperation became impossible . . . (2003, p. 192)
>
> In justice to the intellectuals, let us not forget that their best representatives have always sided with the oppressed. They have advocated liberty and emancipation, and often they were the first to voice the deepest aspirations of the toiling masses. (2003, p. 193)

As I made clear at the outset, I am still trying to come to terms with all of this myself. I'm nowhere near overcoming self-doubt; I have absolutely no idea how important intellectuals in general or my own intellectual work in particular are in the grand revolutionary scheme. Then again, I'm not sure that it matters. Over and above everything I've just outlined, I suspect what really matters for academics and intellectuals is just giving a real, honest-to-goodness, and passionate *damn* about what's happening outside the classroom and the conferences. Only then, it seems, can we determine whether what we do in the classrooms and at the conferences is worth giving a damn about, too. In the meantime, I hope I've offered an honest appraisal of our situation and a fair case for the potential value and usefulness of our work within the anarchist movement. For my part, I continue to wrestle with self-doubt and will probably do so for a long time. But maybe the next time I visit Forest Home I won't feel so alienated from my forebears. Maybe next time I will feel like I am part of their, *our* tradition once again.

## References


Bakunin, M. (1973). *Mikhail Bakunin: Selected writings*. A. Lehning (Ed.), (S. Cox & O. Stevens, Trans.). New York: Grove Press.

Bakunin, M. (1990). *Statism and anarchy*. (M. Shatz, Trans.). Cambridge: Cambridge University Press.

Bakunin, M. (1992). *The basic Bakunin*. R. Cutler (Ed.). Buffalo, NY: Prometheus.

Bakunin, M. (2004). *God and the state*. Whitefish, MT: Kessinger.

Berkman, A. (2003). *What is communist anarchism?* Oakland: AK Press.

Cahoone, L. (1996). *From modernism to postmodernism*. Cambridge, MA: Blackwell.

Gelderloos, P. (2007). The difference between anarchy and the academy. Retrieved from http://theanarchistlibrary.org/HTML/Peter_Gelderloos_The_Difference_between_Anarchy_and_the_Academy.html.

Giddens, A. & Pearson, C. (1999). *Conversations with Anthony Giddens: Making sense of modernity*. Stanford, CA: Stanford University Press.

Goldman, E. (2004). *The modern drama*. Whitefish, MT: Kessinger.

Goldman, E. (2008). *Anarchism and other essays*. Rockville, MD: Serenity.

Gramsci, A. (2001). The Formation of intellectuals. In V. Leitch (Ed.), *Norton anthology of theory and criticism*. New York: Norton.

Hadot, P. (1995). *Philosophy as a way of life*. Oxford: Blackwell.
Kropotkin, P. (1993). *Fugitive writings*. Montreal: Black Rose.
Kropotkin, P. (2002). *Anarchism: A collection of revolutionary writings.* Mineola, NY: Dover.
Malatesta, E. (1993). *His life and ideas*. V. Richards (Ed.). London: Freedom Press.
Pettit, P. (2005). The contribution of analytical philosophy. In R. Goodin & P. Pettit (Eds.), *A companion to contemporary political philosophy*. Oxford: Blackwell.
Plato (1950). *Phaedo*. (F.J. Church, Trans.). New York: Macmillan
Plutarch (1936). *Moralia*, Book X. (H.N. Fowler, Trans.). Cambridge, MA: Loeb Classical Library.
Preston, A. (2005). Conformism in analytical philosophy. *The Monist, 88*(2), 292–319.
Proudhon, P.-J. (1972). The general idea of revolution in the nineteenth century. In M. Shatz (Ed.), *The essential works of anarchism*. New York: Quadrangle Books, 81–123
Rocker, R. (1997). *Nationalism and culture*. Montreal: Black Rose.
Seneca (1925). *Epistles 93–124*. (R. Grummere, Trans.). Cambridge, MA: Loeb Classical Library.

CHAPTER 16

# That Teaching Is Impossible

Alejandro de Acosta

## 1

That *teaching is impossible* is not a proposition to be argued for. It would be of little interest to offer it up for debate. It would be useless to defend it against the evidence of history or common sense. To consider that teaching is impossible is to open ourselves up to an experience of the most outlandish sort. In staging this experience I wish to contemplate the happy frustration of the urge to teach, and to affirmatively invoke the limits of all pedagogies.

It is useful for anyone who thinks that they teach to explore their urge to do so. This urge is an intimate matter, the libidinal support for the innocent claim that good ideas ought to be passed on to others. I call the claim innocent in that it usually leaves the good of ideas (and the Idea of the Good) implicit and unexamined; since the good remains unexamined, people may obtusely invoke their mere participation in efficient schooling as evidence that teaching is possible. That the school, as institution, survives; that the role of teacher is understood primarily in reference to the survival of the institution: these seem to be the only evidences necessary. But one can at least begin to account for and explore the complex of desires that aim at the role of teacher. Some of them wear the mask of the ego: "I am the one who impresses the lessons."

Beyond the ego-mask, moving, that is, from what appears as inner to what appears as outer, one may observe the inevitable calcification of the urge to teach into the kinds of systems we call pedagogies. These may be described as organizations, not just of knowledge and methods of passing it on, but primarily of desire. They are institutional manifestations of the urge to teach, or rather, they are the ways in which the urge to teach, combined with other urges, invents for itself a gregarious existence, a school: "This is where the lessons are impressed." In this sense, pedagogies may also be characterized as the fantasy of the efficacy of the urge to teach.

To say or think that teaching is impossible is to let go, however temporarily, of both the urge to teach and its more or less precisely formed collusions with other urges in gregarious forms, affirming rather that study is interminable, and so learning is endlessly frustrated and frustrating. To say or think that teaching is impossible is to assert that teaching *on purpose, for a purpose*, is impossible. For the urge in its gregarious form has other purposes, which concern the person of the teacher, his role, her specialization, in the context of the school; it has nothing in particular to do with learning. I am inclined to think that neither do schools. What anyone who thinks they are a teacher *can* do purposely is mainly of two natures:

- One can transmit data, information. This is better known as *communication*. It is commonly assimilated to teaching, but, as students well know, really has nothing to do with it. This transmission is eminently possible and does not require a teacher.
- One can *model* behaviors and practices, silently offering them up for imitation. This is not only possible, but inevitable. But to whatever extent we do it for a purpose, it is for one other than to teach them In this modeling we exceed the role of the teacher.

Pedagogy, then, is precisely the in-between of the ego-mask and the school, their mutual insertion, the becoming-method or becoming-gregarious of an urge in a fantasy: "This is how the lessons are impressed." In this sense to say or think that teaching is impossible is also to invoke the countless ways that learning takes place despite and beyond pedagogy. This is the beginning of the antipedagogical lesson. Let us consider it.

## 2

Sometimes, I think that I teach. When I do so I imagine I am not alone in underlining the evident gap between discussing practices and engaging in them. Classrooms have this virtue, that in them almost anything may be said; but to the degree that the desires that allow us to survive in such spaces remain unexamined, we will tend to confuse the ability to say almost anything with the ability to do almost anything. This gap in capacity is especially manifest for me in the context of philosophy or anthropology, in courses that take up topics such as spiritual exercises, mysticism, shamanism, or the many practices that P. Hadot calls "philosophy as a way of life." I mean any topic where what is posited is not merely thinking differently in the context of a given way of life, but a thinking that (because it is not just a thinking) requires a conversion. Becoming someone or something else, living differently, in short. One can certainly talk about such matters endlessly, treating them as historical or sociological facts, without grasping what is vital in them—without, that is, being transformed in the doing.

The minimum form of the affirmation *that teaching is impossible* would then be that with regard to practices that require a conversion, at least, teaching is impossible. I found in myself, not just an urge to teach, to be the teacher, but to teach these topics, and the urge was frustrated. The role of teacher became, if not impossible, at least somewhat laughable. The reason was clear enough. No one can teach such practices in a school unless it is the school of such practices: Epicureanism needs the Garden . . . Thinking I taught, I communicated information concerning these practices, but at a great remove; I did not model them. Moreover, some of them seem separate from any known pedagogy: mystics don't seem to me to have a school, but rather to be those who are usually expelled from schools. This is not because schools are dogmatic or authoritarian (though of course most are), but because of the sort of experience that mysticism seems to entail. (Or maybe not. One might go so far as to consider the maximum form of the claim, that the problem has to do with practice as such, with any practice other than those peculiar to schools as we know them.)

So what is left in such situations? The mere intention to teach what is impossible to teach, I suppose: the urge in its raw and complicated form, not its calcification into a pedagogy. We can try to collectively give in to the will to knowledge, to more than idle curiosity. That is, to what is in fact possible given the practices and ways of life that make schools as we know them possible. (As opposed to, and without in any way devaluing, those that destroy them, or mutate them until they are unrecognizable.) But I find that this will and that curiosity are unevenly distributed. You, teacher, must seduce your students into a certain fascination. That is what I call modeling, at least when modeling has a chance of success. It is akin to what psychoanalysts call the transference, or to hypnosis when it is grasped that what is at stake in it is something other than mind control, that the one hypnotized must at some level accept the process. It must involve your body, teacher, your gestures, movements, laughter: the mask, its generation, and its corruption. Those particulars can never be bypassed in the mimesis of the model.

But even if the will to knowledge or more than idle curiosity can be modeled and imitated, (and I do think that they can, on purpose and accidentally as well!) I do not think it is wise to therefore claim that teaching has happened, and is therefore possible. Something else is at stake. In modeling, the teacher's ego-mask is revealed in its development (from the urge to the role), but also in its happy failure: the failed transition from the urge through the role to its calcification as pedagogy and its sedimentation in schooling are all provisionally laid bare. In at least one important sense, the teacher is naked. What has been modeled and perhaps imitated is still quite separate from the topics in question, from the experiences at stake in them. What has been staged is rather an antipedagogical problem.

## 3

Can one pass on anything other than the will to knowledge and more than idle curiosity? What about less exotic practices, those that seem more at home in what we know as schools? For two years I was part of a university committee concerned with feminist studies. Once, in the course of a review of our work, we tried to define what constituted, for us, a specifically feminist pedagogy. The conversation was both frustrating and (at least for me) quite amusing. ("Giving students a greater role in planning the curriculum," someone suggested. "Allowing people to speak from their experience," another said. "Encouraging connections between class readings and real-world issues," a third added. And so on.) The more concepts and examples that we collectively proposed, the clearer it became that we could produce no difference between a specifically feminist pedagogy and good pedagogy in general. It seemed as if the problem was that we had it as our goal to stay away from the humdrum of the generic, unmarked good, and to cleave rather to a more rarefied good, the sharp edge of feminist politics. But in that humdrum, generic, unmarked mainstream, there are said to be good teachers, are there not? Is their pedagogy not good? Many, arguably most, of them are in no way feminists. Our true problem was not our desire to cling to the specificity of feminism—it was that we assumed that were the ones who impressed its lesson, that our school was where the lesson was to be impressed, and that feminism, our method, our pedagogy, was to be how the lesson was to be impressed. We had supposed that teaching is possible.

Do these assumptions have anything to do with feminism as a way of life? If feminism can be learned, not as a set of theories or "studies," but as an attitude, as something that can grow into a resistant politics, it is because some of us are capable of modeling it as it exists and develops in our lives. As such it has zero informational content, or its content is incidental. That something like feminism exists at all suggests that it was, at some point, invented. At that time those who invented it were not producing new information (at least that was not what was remarkable in their invention). They were problematizing existing practices and the ways of life they flowed out of and into, proposing new ones. That something like feminism is still possible, still remarkable, suggests that someone can stage that problematization anew, in effect reinventing feminism. What does any of this, however, have to do with schooling?

The committee's troubling, unstated conclusion was that that we, presumably experts in feminism as "study," could not guarantee that, in teaching classes with feminist content, we were teaching feminism. (A student could, for example, pass a course with flying colors and in some fundamental way remain oblivious to sexism. The same went us as teachers of the course). Or, if we *were* teaching feminism, we could not define in what ways we were doing so in the context of "feminist studies."

It ought to be clear by now that this version of the antipedagogical problem does not merely concern feminism. So, where to go from here? One familiar path is that of a certain ressentiment, leveraged in this case against the good teachers who do not mark the differences that we do, leveraged against students who do not become feminists or whose feminism is alien to us, leveraged ultimately against ourselves, in our inevitable failure. This ressentiment is fed by the failure of an ideal of representation and inclusivity (its index: the presence of a certain sort of data, of information) to effect anything other than a reform in schooling—in the curriculum, I mean, in "studies," defined according to the standards, the good, of what we know as schools.

Another path, which I admit I fell into as if by instinct, would be that of bemusement. It would be to simultaneously admit that teaching is impossible and that feminism, if it is a form of resistance and not just of study, will be reinvented quite despite those of us who, well-meaning, might think we are teaching it.

## 4

Let us consider, then, the lesson of resistance, turning from reformist to revolutionary pedagogies. Another university tale: I was once asked to speak at a symposium called "Achieving Success as a Latino." I was asked by the organizers to address the difficulties Latinos and Latinas might encounter at a predominantly Anglo institution: "obstacles," more generally, that all minorities face in the educational system. I said more or less the following: I don't want to speak purely in praise of schooling, the overcoming of obstacles as progress, confusing the efficacy of schooling with the unqualified good of learning. I want to affirm learning in its entirety and as a process, with all of its conflicts and breakdowns, not to adopt a narrative of successes in the face of hardships. I regard phenomena such as Latinas dropping out of school, not going to college, feeling alienated in college, not just as problems to be solved institutionally, by schools or by groups in schools acting as their proxy. If we view all of these "problems" as negativities, deficiencies, bad attitudes, we miss their complexity, what in them is positive, is desire. I think Latinos and everybody else have countless reasons and ways to engage with schools. I also think that Latinas (and everybody else!) have good reasons to resist some or all of what is institutionalized as education. Among other things, I am referring to what we know as schools: generally, spaces where training, discipline, authoritarianism, bureaucracy, are made more or less efficacious; spaces that are often culturally hostile or indifferent, etc.

A young Latino indeed ought to ask himself, "What is school to me? Why should I risk my life for this?"—of course "life" here is not the life taken away by the gun or torture, but the life of one's barrio, community, friends, family—because many aspects of what it means to feel in one's own skin, at home, or in a community are threatened in schools. That's on the side of the construction of identity, a sense of self. On the side of the destruction of identity, the desire that so many of us have to overcome what we've been told we are—that process and its freedom are also threatened in that schooling has always had to do with acculturation to a dominant culture, language, religion, etc. And also in the sense that schools neither teach nor favor rebellion. Institutionally this is discussed in terms of curriculum and catchphrases like "campus climate," "diversity," etc., but I think the real issue is one of power and gregarious desires: the school's explicit and implicit hierarchies and their insertion into greater social arrays. Let us consider those seen as "problems" or at least having "problematic attitudes" as resisting. I think that they are right to do so, at least as right as the schools in exercising power and modeling gregariousness. Some are more at home here than others. People inhabit, move through, move in and out of a school, at different speeds, for different reasons, in different moods, using different gaits. To regard resistance as a problem to be resolved by the school, or by us as its proxy, is to fully reinforce the role of the teacher in the school: "I am the one who solves this problem"—"I transform this problem into the good of the lesson."

The critical question is: how are we using the school? What are we doing here if teaching is impossible? And this implies its converse: how is it using us? What is it doing with or to us (acknowledging that "it" is not a thing or subject, but the anonymous, gregarious actions of others)?

## 5

That talk ended with a proposal that I now recognize as well-intentioned (perhaps influenced by the good intentions of the symposium's planners) but poorly thought out. It was a gesture characteristic of a certain anarchism that claims for itself the side of the good, that proposes its revolutionary politics as the staging of the ultimate good.

I said: So much for the side of the institution! Schooling doesn't—can't—end there. Gregariousness certainly does not. It is part of being engaged with an institution, resistantly or not, that one tends to orient much of one's discourse and practices around the institution. (Supposing one wanted to define institutions, it might be worthwhile to begin by describing the various forms of this operation of capture). It takes some distance (and dropping out, along with the other forms resistance takes, is a way to attain that distance) to be able to speak of schools as I have been doing, or of pedagogy as an outgrowth of the urge to teach. But really, there are schools everywhere. If I were to discuss the other possibilities for schooling I could of course talk about activism, popular education, etc., but I would rather race to the utopian end and propose that schools should have the ultimate goal of abolishing themselves as particular, separate, specialized spaces. My political proposal is that all of society be a school: that the social field be coeval with the space of learning. This means, of course, that there would be a series of spaces, remarkable places of learning, rather than one megainstitution. It could come about through a collaboration between those happiest with schools as we know them, and those who resist or refuse schooling, relatively or absolutely.

My antipolitical criticism of that political proposal is that making a plan for all of society (especially one with a grandiose slogan such as "abolish schools as separated spaces!") without aiming at annihilating what we know as society is to give ourselves a Cause. The Cause of Making All of Society into A School. Now the mask is transformed. I am no longer in the role of teacher, but that of teacher-activist: "I am *still* the one who resolves this problem"—now putatively through revolution instead of reform. Schooling would be coeval with society in the worst sense, fostering in people not only the illusion that teaching is possible, but that freedom can be taught (anarchist pedagogy in its most nightmarish form). We would have set out with the best of intentions and ended up with the most grotesque gregariousness. It is true that study is interminable and that schools are everywhere; but schooling is not for all that omnipresent—it can and does end.

I would rather restate *that teaching is impossible* (and this time perhaps the modesty of the claim, so hard to see at first, begins to shine through). To focus our efforts, our analyses, on failure and resistance is to grasp the eccentric but vital role of modeling in the transmission of practices. It is inevitable that modeling will meet resistance. A model may be imitated, counterimitated, or met with sovereign indifference. We might cooperate, we might fight, or we might ignore each other. In that social chaos, in its interstices of order and stillness, someone might learn something. But nothing about this can be guaranteed. Why assume, why hope, even, that we will all collaborate? Why sculpt the mask in a way that arrogantly banks on success? It is the urge to teach, again reaching for the form of its survival. "I impress the lesson that schooling is interminable."

## 6

I have already said that modeling is inevitable, and implied that it may be done more or less purposefully. This is difficult because we habitually vibrate in sync with others who share our models, and in this local phenomenon the entirety of our interactions is to effect tiny variants, microimitations and counterimitations, of each other's practices. The micropolitics of power; or, a day in school. But modeling is also impersonal and indefinite. Its tautological claim: "I am the one who lives as I live" or even "I am the one who expresses the model that I am modeling."

The fullness of a self or a person is, as far as I am concerned, always and only an artifice, that of an apparently completed mask. The mask of the teacher, however, is incomplete. To think, to say, to embody "I am the one who impresses the lesson" is to simplify, to fool ourselves into identifying with our own mask, to frustrate the many other desires clamoring against the role, demanding, if you will, other masks. To seduce anyone else (to seduce oneself!) into fascination with a model is something else than to mistake oneself for the one who impresses the lessons. It is rather to display the urge, the mask, the frustrated tendencies to pedagogy and schooling, with all of their defects and failures—the failures of the simple mask of the teacher, the gregarious phenomenon of the school, and ultimately the failure of method, of all pedagogy. This impersonation shows what in the urge to teach is impersonal.

One way to conceive of this impersonality is the "silent teaching" R. Blyth reports on in his books on Zen. "We teach silently and only silently, though we may be silent or talk." Silence: the offering up of the model for imitation, with no attendant command to imitate (or maybe with the most parodic of commands). Informationless speech, laughter, sighs . . . your body, again, teacher, in its becoming-mask. Everything else is a dance of data.

Irreparably, to live is to offer one's life up for imitation. "People teach what they can. People teach what they teach. Everybody teaches everybody else." This is what I was getting at in deemphasizing the distinction between what can be passed on purposely and what is passed on inevitably. I am more interested in whether such things are done gracefully, as one may live one's life more or less gracefully. And perhaps the most graceful lesson is that teaching is impossible. But how is *that* to be passed on? "The only way to teach not teaching is really not to teach."

## 7

One final antipedagogical lesson, this one specifically for my friends, the anarchists. I hope it is clear that I have written from my own resistance. I like to think that, despite my several decades of study, I have resisted schooling. But my distance is double, since I observe that I maintain a willful incompetence when it comes to political movements that amounts to a form of resistance. There are, after all, schools everywhere! It is my style, my predilection, my *wu-wei* regarding schooling, regarding the roles of academics and activists. I believe that everything I have proposed about the urge to teach, about schools, and about pedagogy applies mutatis mutandis to activism, organizing, movements. Try the experiment yourself: go to a rally or meeting looking for teaching. You will find it. Ah, the pedagogy of rallies and meetings!

Some activists and their theorist friends are busy looking to the primitive past or the utopian future for a humanity without social institutions, as though discovering their absence someplace, somewhere, could lead to their amelioration or eradication today. Now, the absence of a given institution, especially one that I find intolerable, such as money or the police, is indeed a fascinating question for study. But study is interminable; it only leads to more study. I prefer to add to study another practice, to model a kind of disappearance, an incompetence that is a way to absent oneself from routinized activities on the side of schools as well as the side of the movements. It is possible to live this as something other than a negation. And as in all modeling, what I can do is simply to offer up the urge to teach and the urge to act as some desires among many. We can try to (and I suppose that we should) eradicate whatever social institutions we find to be intolerable; but we can also do what we can, silently, to lay bare our desires as we discover them, our social teachings as they meet resistances that, after all, have their reasons. We can be naked, with a mask on. Naturally, to call oneself an anarchist is to wear a fanciful mask: "I am the one who . . ." But if anarchism is our perhaps inevitable pedagogy, anarchy could be something else: our antipedagogy.

## References

Blyth, R. (1964). *Zen and Zen classics, Vol. 2*. Tokyo: Hokuseido Press.
Hadot, P. (1995). *Philosophy as a way of life*. Oxford: Blackwell.

CHAPTER 17

# Against the Grain of the Status Quo: Anarchism behind Enemy Lines

Abraham P. DeLeon

> Everyone is undercover. It's just a matter of degree. Look around—just about everybody you see is in disguise, terrified of being unmasked as the complex human beings they are. (CrimethInc., 2005, p. 306)

*Infiltration*: a word that may evoke a host of thoughts and fantasies from soldiers operating behind enemy lines, police informants gaining access to criminal organizations, or to scenarios of radicals inserting themselves into corporations or research labs. Whatever the scenario, infiltration can be tactic that anarchists pursue when thinking about operating within current institutional realities, especially if interested in teaching in public schools. Although this claim is entangled within complex relationships of power and privilege, struggle arises wherever domination coalesces, especially within institutional structures and settings (Sharp, Routledge, Philo & Paddison, 2000). Power conjures, "the threadings, knottings and weavings" of social relationships through a intertwining of the social, political, moral, educational, and historical realities of a given society. In this way, power is "crucially and unavoidably spun out across and through the material spaces of the world" (Sharp, et al., 2000, p. 22).

This chapter thus looks to situate itself and build radical pedagogy within the threads and knots of contemporary relationships of power; in-between what Holloway (2010) has called the "cracks" of capitalism, trying to "desperately find . . . faults beneath the surface, or to create cracks by banging the walls" (p. 8). Cracks have emerged through environmental disaster, economic collapse, psychological alienation, a crisis of identity, and decades of war and imperial aggression conducted by the West. It is under these historical conditions that resistance needs to be conceptualized. Creating, finding and exploiting "cracks" within a diffused and networked capitalism demonstrates that *dated narratives of revolutionary struggle are no longer viable* and there is "no guarantee of a happy ending" (Holloway, 2010, p. 9). Unfortunately, although these narratives may provide comfort amid an onslaught of capitalism, war, death, terror, and alienation, they do not open up, nor allow, alternative possibilities of resistance to form outside the boundaries they construct. In some ways, these may only help to reproduce the current order we find ourselves in. This does not mean that we should resign ourselves to the throngs of nihilistic defeat, as there is indeed potential for radical hope within the cracks of Empire. The multitude, with its potential for infinite possibilities, can build a complex and dispersed resistance through the breaks, tears, and folds of our social order (Deleuze, 1992), and the tactics and pedagogies that we envision as radicals can *attempt* to capture this spirit. Although the manifestations of these cracks and folds is yet to be seen, I leave the reader to their own radical imaginations in devising ways to subvert a networked and diffused machine (Shukaitis, 2009).

Evoking the metaphor of a "machine," as I describe the multifaceted nature of contemporary capitalism, harkens to Trotter's (1990) claim that colonialism operated in a very similar way, divorced from individual interactions and operating abstractly through "official" and "unofficial" discourses, forms of knowledge, ways of knowing, the morality of a given era, and the reproduction of knowledge to name a few. The analogy of a machine also challenges that human agency is solely at the center of how social system operate, because machines, "create, distribute, and organize populations and impose regimes of conduct, agency and effectivity" outside of individual actors and agency (Grossberg, 2010, p. 36). Radicals (within and outside the labor movement) had ingenious ways in which to deal with the machines of capitalism, occurring through tactics that spanned strikes, sit-ins, walking out, and subversion to even more direct forms like sabotaging machinery, bringing production to a halt. Sabotage is a tactic that anarchists need to rethink in light of how labor is now dispersed among a wide variety of institutional realities (factories, banks, corporations, and public institutions, for example), as well as the contemporary knowledge and abstract economies. The machines of capitalism that produced goods during the height of the Industrial Revolution of the nineteenth century provide us a way in which to think of societal machines and tactics that can be adapted for current conditions. How do we as anarchists, who want to teach and work with students, deal with the contradictions of being located within the same institutions that seek to discipline bodies and coerce us? How do we sabotage these machines and build a radical pedagogy from this perspective?

Sabotage provides a provocative conceptual framework in which to think about building alternative forms of resistance and aligns with ways in which anarchists have historically conceptualized direct political action. This is even more interesting when we think of how this will emerge through educational practice, as teaching allows us to directly engage ideology, challenging students' conceptions about the world around them. With this type of important, dare I say *political* work, why do some anarchists shun the world of public teaching and service? Education is at the "front lines" of the contemporary ideological war conducted by corporate media, official organs of the State, and influential economic institutions. Whether that emerges through corporate textbooks that omit subaltern experiences and worldviews, standardized testing that stress rote memorization, or a curriculum that reproduces Eurocentrism and Western ways of knowing, education is invested in reproducing dominant conceptions of the world. However, sabotage can take myriad forms, and this chapter will build on the conceptual idea of building *politics of infiltration*.

It has been well established that police and other State agents have infiltrated radical political movements, especially with the rise of anarchist praxis over the past two decades (Borrum & Tilby, 2004). Anarchists should think about assuming this same tactic, using the idea of infiltration as a guiding way to think about our praxis within institutional realities and as a way to think about diffused forms of sabotage. Although anarchism is rife with identity and lifestyle politics that detests any signs of "selling out," this has only proven to further marginalize us in the eyes of the larger society that we must work at convincing how terribly oppressive the current social arrangement is. In the end, our movement is going to have to be broad-based and span multiple identities, social locations, political affiliations, and a renewed sense of politics that seeks to look at how, "the contemporary world has been made to be what it is [and] make visible ways in which it can become something else" (Grossberg, 2010, p. 1).

Stoler (2010) discusses the idea of reading and analyzing "against the grain" of archival documents to unearth new interpretations and voices. This chapter urges radicals to think of our social actions along these same lines of thought: *against the grain* of dominant ideologies that serve to support historically oppressive realities. In this chapter, I will attempt to propose a politics of infiltration through a peculiar anarchist lens that seeks to subvert capitalism and its accompanying institutional realities through a diffused resistance stemming from bodies; bodies immersed in oppressive institutional realities. I dance through theoretical traditions to demonstrate how infiltration can be conceptualized as not only a physical practice (such as our work in classrooms), but also can be a theoretical framework in which to situate our practice, always looking for cracks, weaknesses, and opportunities to sabotage dominant conceptions of the world that demonstrates another world is possible. Although radicals may think of this action as "selling out," I want to reframe teaching and working within institutions as a potential form of infiltration, inserting other ways of knowing and being into the academy to challenge systemically oppressive realities. Shannon (2009) reminds us that cooptation lurks around every corner and Shukaitis (2009) warns us of the recuperative nature of capitalism. Both of these realities are firmly acknowledged as risks, however, it should not immobilize us into inaction. Nor should this resign us to "ghettoizing" ourselves into intellectual enclaves where conversations are more about nodding our collective heads in agreement rather than challenging our own practices with alternative voices and tactics. Indeed, tensions can be the basis for a critical reflection about what we are actually doing in our practice and engaging a wide variety of techniques and approaches to explore these, such as writing and political organization. Communities of practice, whether in activism or through qualitative research, are an essential feature of building bridges with other like-minded activists and scholars (Rossman & Rallis, 2003). Cooptation and recuperation are indeed challenges we will face but should not stop us from doing *something*, keeping in mind the question that Lorde (2003) had when she struggled with the tools of the master (p. 25). This chapter will hopefully allow the conversation to continue about the role of anarchist theory in building alternative forms of praxis, pedagogy, and direct action, especially within the context of public education and the contradictions that anarchists face within hierarchical and coercive institutions.

## Anarchism and Education

To say that anarchists have a complex relationship with education and its accompanying structures is an understatement. Anarchism seems to fall along a wide continuum of theories and ideas about the role(s) of education (Suissa, 2010). Anarchists in Spain during the revolution relied heavily on the potential of education (Gribble, 2004) while other more recent anarchists have demonstrated the necessity in sometimes dropping out (see the literature from CrimethInc. for a full context). My own work has tried to integrate anarchist critiques in how we think about education and our sense of self (DeLeon, 2008, 2009a, 2009b, 2010a, 2010b). Being located in position of privilege (as a university professor) but also being self and institutionally identified as an indigenous man (I self-identify as Mestizo, which captures my cultural experiences; see DeLeon, 2010b for a richer explanation) has also brought an interesting perspective maneuvering within institutions that do not support values or perspectives we currently hold about the world around us.

Speaking from my own positionality as a man of color, schooling has always been a personally coercive experience, particularly the highly effective ways in which the machines of schooling marginalize and erase cultural ways of knowing that are not enveloped within the dominant Eurocentric culture that exists in the United States, or what Grossberg (2010) calls "European or North Atlantic modernity" (p. 71). Because my parents never taught me to speak Spanish for the retribution they faced when they spoke it at school in the 1950s and 1960s, it never connected me to a crucial component to my own identity and sense of self that language provides (Reagan & Osborn, 2002). In other words, historically oppressed peoples (spanning ethnic, racial, class, gender, dis(ability), etc. locations) have always dealt with the contradictions faced when working within institutions of the dominant culture, especially within the context of past historical and colonial relationships (Tuhiwai Smith, 1999). Despite this, work still has to be done inside of these institutions of domination or they will reproduce unabated. Although I realize a subject is never whole but a fractured self comprised of multiple identities (Barker, 2008), the machine will continue to produce a specific type of disciplined and fractured subject unless they are subverted.

As an intellectual that produces knowledge and has classroom responsibilities and for those that have similar experiences, we are at the "frontlines" of engaging dominant ideology as our students walk into our classrooms with perspectives, identities, and subjectivities that are mired in corporate media and other dominant discourses. Knowing and understanding our mutual roles in a larger social movement is an important facet of critical work. Anarchists have critiqued education for its reproductive and coercive realities, echoing the concerns of many radical theorists in education today (Darder, Baltodano & Torres, 2009). Education domesticates desires, disciplines bodies, and tries to stifle creativity and imagination for rote standardization and high-stakes testing. The perils of education are felt along class, gendered, and racial lines, along with disability and sexuality. Anarchists have tried to think about the possibilities of education through a variety of critically engaged societal assemblages, comprised of different social movements, living arrangements, intimate encounters, artistic expressions, identity politics, discursive constructions, alternative claims of truth, and marginalized spiritualities. These assemblages give us, "a properly utopian confidence that things can change because it is . . . in continuous variation" (Buchanan, 2000, p. 119). Like the concept of the assemblage that comes from the work of Deleuze and Guattari, anarchism not only possesses a developed utopian "spirit" (Newman, 2009), but is also a body of theory that can be applied to a variety of different circumstances, further demonstrating that "no society has to be organized in the way it is, that there is always another way [that] can be activated by thinking differently" (Buchanan, 2000, p. 118). Education is at the center of this construction, as it also contains the potential to activate a different way of thinking about society and our problems.

Education has the potential to lead to self-transformation when its processes are guided by ideas such as cooperation, limiting coercive experiences, allowing for the potential(s) for growth and self-discovery, and learning to think critically about the production and reification of knowledge. Critical pedagogy has established this possibility through work that seeks a political project that questions the fundamental nature and purpose of education from a variety of different perspectives (Darder et al., 2009). Marxist dominated, radical thought in education has tended to follow the traditions from the Frankfurt School of critical theory, but has also been invigorated with voices from postmodernism, poststructuralism, feminism, eco-justice, and other critiques. Glaringly omitted has been anarchist theory, a radical and activist orientation that is rooted in protest politics, direct confrontation of the police, alternative ways of living/being, and is injected with theoretical work found at the university (Amster, DeLeon, Fernandez, Nocella II & Shannon, 2009). Although associated with representations of political terror and general mayhem, anarchism emerges from a wide variety of perspectives and is not easily definable, making it highly adaptable for different contexts. Because it has tended to be open-ended, anarchism has been adapted to a variety of settings, and education seems to be a location in which anarchists should concern themselves with (Suissa, 2010).

Anarchism is embedded in a politics that seeks to resist hierarchies, coercive experiences, and official and unofficial State politics. Although this is at the core of what many anarchists do, it has also integrated work that questions rigid boundaries of sexuality, class, racism, gendered oppression, and other political projects. Because it has been infused with a variety of different perspective and positionalities, it lends itself to being easily adaptable to a variety of situations, critiques, and approaches (Amster, et al., 2009). Anarchism appears to match the conception of Grossberg's (2010) vision of cultural studies, a "complex product of multiple lines of force, determination, and resistance, with different temporalities and spatialities" that has to be "constructed, narrated, fabricated" (p. 41). The multiple lines of force, to utilize his characterization, coalesce to produce an anarchist discourse that supports a relentless critique on coercive authority and inspires us toward praxis.

Although intellectuals are guilty of injecting our own biases and perspectives into the representations we construct, it is those that organize under anarchist theory and principles that seem to offer us a provocative approach in creating alternative resistance strategies toward a diffused and networked capitalism. It would appear that the autonomous and decentralized nature of anarchist theory and practice allows for an interesting set of tools in which to work with that appear to be equally diffused like the machines of contemporary capitalism. Capitalism exists over a global network that traverses boundaries, shaping ideologies and forms of knowledge to our most intimate knowledge of self (Rose, 1989). Anarchism has also traversed the boundaries of theory and history, a vibrant political project that has existed in various locations across the globe. Within the academy, anarchism has been networked with other radical theories, like feminism, eco-justice, and critical animal studies. This makes anarchist theory and practice stand apart from other radical traditions because of the alliances that have been formed with other disciplines, but is also the point that makes it so challenging to *do* anarchism and *produce* anarchist theory and research.

This challenge is also compounded with the nature of radical politics, as there are usually multiple and competing interests that need to be taken into consideration. For example, many conservatives can build their own strategies around common political, social, or economic interests (the Tea Party, "pro-life," a return to "traditional" ways of life, etc.) and appear to meet the needs of its broad constituency. Although many conservative policies directly counter the economic needs of its base support as it has been pointed out in the literature, their influence remains and is one of the paradoxes of contemporary politics in the United States (Gilbert, 2011). Radicals and progressive activists are so divided among issues surrounding race, gender, class, identity, disability, or sexuality that these common links are not so readily apparent. Despite this, anarchism provides a discourse that traverses a diverse range of political principles, but it is also guided by radical praxis that has been utilized by a variety of social movements that are equally as diverse. This makes anarchist theory a position full of possibility, becoming a broad umbrella in which to situate a wide variety of political concerns.

From the streets of Seattle in 1999, the DIY movement in many alternative communities, to the kitchens of activists feeding the homeless for Food Not Bombs, these actions have been influenced by anarchist politics and can be "read" and analyzed through an anarchist lens. For us in education that are struggling with the meaning of our pedagogy in light of the hierarchical and coercive nature of most educational experiences in the United States, this can allow us to explore diverse political strategies, praxis, and movements to search for synergies between them and what we do as teachers and educators in our classrooms everyday. As this particular edited collection is dedicated to anarchist forms of pedagogy, this diversity of thought and praxis in anarchist theory can help us formulate some ideas about situating ourselves as anarchists within coercive and hierarchical institutions that we eventually would like to see dismantled.

## Anarchism, Sabotage, and a Politics of Infiltration

It is widely accepted that State agents have infiltrated radical social movements historically (Fernandez, 2008). Whether through direct insertion into radical groups or sophisticated crowd surveillance, the State is invested in destroying and subverting social movements that question State authority or the institutions of capitalism. State agents appear to have a tremendous amount of authority and autonomy in these operations and are able to take direct action against any individual or group deemed a threat. The political and social backdrop in the wake of September 11 has granted State agents and authorities even more direct control (Parenti, 2007). Radical, progressive, and liberal political groups throughout the United States have endured wiretaps, police raids, and State surveillance aimed at arrest, incarceration, or serving as informants (Borum & Tilby, 2004). Through these types of operations, the State attempts to envelop, discredits, or destroy social and political movements from within (Fernandez, 2008).

If this is indeed the reality in which the State operates through the police and other agencies, radical and progressive traditions of marches, sit-ins, boycotts, and other vestiges from our protest past seem wholly inadequate. Combine this with the diffused nature of contemporary capitalist arrangements and how it spans the milieu of social experiences, it becomes an even greater challenge to resist. However, we know this. We have historical evidence in which to study how other past actions have been done. There is potential evidence that exists from participants and survivors who have witnessed or experienced these State interventions that needs qualitative work to explore these stories further. The initial seeds in which to build from already exist for us to grow.

Using an analogy from nature (specifically "growth") highlights my own commitment in imagining potentials that are organic in nature and reimagining traditional coercive relationships. Hierarchical arrangements, the ordering of life, spatial and architectural arrangements, and the privileging of positivist discourses and ways of knowing are by-products of Enlightenment philosophy and European colonial projects (Legg, 2007). Although these have shaped the West in fundamental ways, resistance has to move beyond positivist ways of knowing and thinking about current social, political, and economic realities. This also means dispersing ourselves throughout a variety of social locations through insertion and infiltration, disguising oneself for the current task at hand. As CrimethInc. (2006) provocatively asks the reader, "Do you find yourself wishing that a passerby would take advantage of his squeaky-clean look to do some dastardly revolutionary deed?" (p. 306). CrimethInc. has provided an interesting way to think about direct action, especially since they urge us to become "that squeaky-clean passerby . . . [that] . . . acts certain ways so they can move through a repressive social environment without arousing suspicion" (p. 306). Because they claim that everyone is acting and playing their social role anyways, we are all "experts on acting" (p. 306) which is a key component to infiltration: playing a part that might not necessarily be one that an activist would normally personally adopt, but helps to "gather intelligence, spread disinformation [and] create disruption" (p. 306).

The official role of "teacher" requires us to assume certain subjectivities and a willingness to play institutional roles deemed "true" and "acceptable." This is especially relevant for those of us who have radical politics and find the operations of schools at all levels in the United States to be particularly disturbing and repugnant. But being a teacher seems to encompass a performative spirit, as the classroom and the identity of teacher becomes a role in which to play out lived and embodied ideologies. Thinking of teaching as performance makes the classroom an exciting and invigorating space for learning, but, this performative reality of identity escapes school walls through our circumstances and those identities assumed by us through personal experiences, the media, and other forms of representation. Pelias (2008) discusses the performative role of identity, especially when it comes to gender or other socially sanctioned identities assumed valid and real.

> I have been called forth, called to the theatrical and cultural stage, called to move my performing body as an ideological and disciplined subject. This interpolation turns my body into a site that is worked upon and into a source for understanding. I maneuver and am maneuvered among the scripts I encounter, sometimes consenting, sometimes resisting, but never escaping the apparatus of it all. I am caught, tethered to the system of my own and others' making. I am an actor performing life. (p. 65)

The idea of performance and what this means for praxis and research is a provocative way in which to think how we assume our various identities because as Pelias aptly points out, resistance is also a vital component to the performances of everyday life.

Performance and performative methodologies, a burgeoning interest in autoethnography and critical qualitative research, demonstrates the importance of the body in interpreting and constructing what is considered "reality" (Markula, 2008; St. Pierre, 2008). Bodies lie at the heart of the experiential nature of human life and society, because we need to, "bring the body out from the shadow of the mind" (Hardt, 1993, p. 107) to better understand the role(s) of bodies in radical and revolutionary movements and insurgencies. Bodies can playfully resist or infiltrate historically oppressive institutions to sabotage from within: a fragmented and postmodern insurgency. "Insurgencies are the incubators of new ideas and knowledges; places where hopes and energies that there could exist other forms of social arrangements different from that what exists today, that there are alternatives, are cultivated" (Shukaitis, 2009, p. 63). What this entails though is an understanding of the importance that performance plays in the formation of our identities, but also in how we interact with others across a range of social spheres. Performance thus becomes a site of resistance that demonstrates how politics, culture, ideology, power, governmentality, and knowledge intersect through the bodies of historical actors (Denzin, 2003).

Anarchism addresses issues of identity and embodiment and thus is invested with the body, in terms of issues like race, class, or how sexuality has been constructed (discursively, ideologically, politically, economically, etc.) in the West (Heckert, 2005). Because anarchism has explored identity and its role in radical political struggles, anarchism provides a history of thinking about what identity means in contemporary society, stressing its socially constructed nature and the performative role it plays in building our inner self. CrimethInc. urges us to "spend time learning your character" (p. 308), but what does this mean within the context of education and specifically, becoming-teacher? Traditionally, *teacher* is associated with a specific way of being. Educational theories abound that tell us that behavior (usually collected under "behaviorism") of students should be the locus of educational practice and a majority of educational thought has been traditionally grouped under this mantra: punishment for rules infraction, assigning grades for work that meets specific criteria, strict demarcation of time and space, and the closed system of knowledge that "official" school curricula reproduce (Apple, 2000).

Being "in charge" and the sole authoritarian voice that delivers curriculum divorced of historical context and other ways of knowing are ways in which teachers are constructed today. With the rise of standardized testing over the past several decades, this has also intensified. Art, social studies, physical education and other disciplines that are not tied to state tests are rapidly disappearing; the logic of schooling and education now being more directly tied to systems of accountability, coercion, and control (Hursh, 2008). Higher education has also not escaped this type of thinking about practice and the role(s) and interests schooling should serve. The recent rise in a standardized approach to education is at the forefront of educational thought, as debates are constructed within tight discursive parameters. Although these are the ways in which teachers have been constructed, we can resist these ways of being and begin to spread disinformation and establish ideological critique as a basis for an invigorated critical pedagogy.

Infiltration could also possibly occur through a variety of positions in educational settings. Substitute to part-time teaching, filling adjunct positions to even pursuing full-time work are all ways in which the anarchist can insert her/himself into the machines of contemporary schooling. Integrating critical discourses, forgotten histories, new forms of media that offer critiques of contemporary arrangements, exercises that allow students to deconstruct ideology, or providing evidence that helps students question the notion of reality itself are ways in which teachers can subvert the status quo. Through reflective and critical writing assignments, students can also explore their own forms of subjectivity. In the midst of an educational climate steeped in standardized measurement, these types of actions will provide a stark contrast to the experiences that most students become accustomed to while sitting in desks and doing what they are told, devoid of historical context and purpose.

Even leadership positions can be assumed for short amount of times to assure that the logics of the institution itself does not begin to infect the infiltrator, always with an eye on the dangerous possibilities of coercion and cooptation. But within these positions for short period of times, decisions can be made that greatly influence the lives of students and these should not be underestimated. Whatever action the infiltrator decides upon is irrelevant. The more important issue is recognizing the necessity in not shunning teaching or other ways in which to enter institutions as a political misstep, defeat, or secular sin, but instead a way to engage with others and to convince a broader public that other ways of knowing and organizing society indeed can and *should* exist.

## Toward Exits: Infiltration and Lines of Escape

In this chapter I have tried to establish what anarchism can offer those who wish to teach in coercive and hierarchical educational institutions. Akin to "selling-out" in some radical circles, the desire to work with children and make direct impacts through ideological or curricular sabotage, organized under a loose network of resistance, is a strategy that seems to match the diffused nature of contemporary capitalism. Anarchism, especially when infused with other radical sensibilities, gives us an interesting set of tools and a language of the ever-present *potential* for resistance. Although anarchists have always stood in opposition to coercive institutions, anarchism can offer us ways to think about navigating the "reality" of institutional life through direct infiltration and subversion. However, I would argue, that anarchism is also about escape, or better yet, what Papadopoulos, Stephenson & Tsianos (2008) call "lines of escape" that "enables us to examine the often neglected engine of transformation which occurs without a master plan and without guarantees . . . a means, not an end" (p. 61). The work of an anarchist saboteur is not only in pointing out the inherent contradictions of contemporary capitalist arrangements, it is also in providing space for the imagination to flourish that seeks new possibilities for social organization, "transform[ing] the present as part of an organic process in which already existing tendencies are built on, nurtured, and actively engaged with" (Suissa, 2009, p. 244).

I have also highlighted the concerns anarchists face, as the recuperative and coercive nature of education, and Euro-modernity more broadly, cannot be underestimated. This means that anarchism has to be continuously aware of its own internal contradictions and its own sense of privilege, while also recognizing its marginalized space even within radical thought, fighting the dominant representations of anarchism as lawless, selfish, and individualistic, divorced of community responsibility. Even with this understanding, these words arise from an intellectual that is in the middleground of social experiences, between those of the dominant (my institutional role and its accompanying cultural capital) and the indigenous roots that I self-identify with and embody. The contradictions of contemporary capitalism are especially present in the bodies of those that exist in the margins or find their own construction of self that is torn between worlds of privilege, ambivalence, alienation, and oppression.

Despite this being a reality for some of us privileged enough to think and theorize about these issues, this does not resign us to defeat but can instead be a place to build political strategies that are adaptable to a wide variety of situations and contexts. This is also important for radicals, especially anarchists torn between wanting to perform public service but fear the coercive and institutional reality that spaces of education today now assume. Hardt and Negri (2004) argue that the multitude (comprised of you, me and everyone else) is a series of vast potentialities, from new ways to organize labor, exploring the imagination and its role in radical politics, to different ways of living together socially. "The multitude . . . might thus be conceived as a network: an open and expansive network in which all differences can be expressed freely and equally, a network that provides the means of encounter so that we can work and live in common" (Hardt & Negri, 2004, p. xiv). This is the strength and the challenge of our current historical moment. However, anarchist theory provides a way in which to think about the linking of these multiplicities and their anchor being in the notion of imaginative and radical practice: from infiltration to direct confrontation. And for teachers who also assume an anarchist stance toward social problems, this becomes even more important as we try to understand the contradictions of working in hierarchical institutions while maintaining a commitment toward a politics rooted in radical difference and reimagining coercive and hierarchical State institutions.

## References


Amster, R., DeLeon, A., Fernandez, L., Nocella II, A. & Shannon, D. (Eds.). (2009). *Contemporary anarchist studies: An introductory anthology of anarchy in the academy*. New York: Routledge.

Apple, M. (2000). *Official knowledge: Democratic education in a conservative age*, 2nd ed. New York, NY: Routledge.

Barker, C. (2008). *Cultural studies: Theory and practice*, 3rd ed. Thousand Oaks, CA: Sage Publications.

Borum, R. & Tilby, C. (2004). Anarchist direct actions: A challenge for law enforcement. *Studies in Conflict and Terrorism, 28*, 201–23.

Buchanan, I. (2000). *Deleuzism: A metacommentary*. Durham, NC: Duke University Press.

CrimethInc.. (2005). *Recipes for disaster: An anarchist cookbook; a moveable feast*. Olympia, WA: CrimethInc. Workers' Collective.

Darder, A., Baltodano, M. & Torres, R. (2009). Critical pedagogy: An introduction. In A. Darder, M. Baltodano & R. Torres (Eds.), *The critical pedagogy reader*, 2nd ed., 1–20. New York: Routledge.

DeLeon, A. (2008). Oh no, not the "a" word! Proposing an "anarchism" for education. *Educational Studies, 44*(2), 122–41.

DeLeon, A. (2009a). Sabotaging the system! Bringing anarchist theory into social studies education. In N. Jun. (Ed.), *New perspectives on anarchism*, 241–54. Lanham, MD: Lexington Books.

DeLeon, A. (2010a). Anarchism, sabotage and the spirit of revolt: Injecting the social studies with anarchist potentialities. In A. DeLeon & E. Wayne Ross (Eds.), *Critical theories, radical pedagogies and social education: New perspectives for social studies education*, 1–12. Rotterdam: Sense Publishers.

DeLeon, A (2010b) How do I begin to tell a story that has not been told? Anarchism, autoethnography, and the middle ground. *Equity & Excellence in Education* 43(4), 398–413.

DeLeon, A. & Love, K. (2009b). Anarchist theory as radical critique: Challenging hierarchies and domination in the social and "hard" sciences. In R. Amster, A. DeLeon, L. Fernandez, A. Nocella II & D. Shannon (Eds.), *Contemporary anarchist studies: An introductory anthology of anarchy in the academy*, 159–65. New York: Routledge.

Deleuze, G. (1992). *The fold: Leibniz and the Baroque*. Minneapolis: University of Minnesota Press.

Denzin, N. (2003). *Performance ethnography: Critical pedagogy and the politics of culture*. Thousand Oaks, CA: Sage.

Fernandez, L. (2008). *Policing dissent: Social control and the anti-globalization movement*. Piscataway, NJ: Rutgers University Press.

Gilbert, D. (2011). *The American class structure in an age of growing inequality*, 8th ed. Thousand Oaks, CA: Sage.

Gribble, D. (2004). Good news for Francisco Ferrer—how anarchist ideals in education have survived around the world. In J. Purkis & J. Bowen (Eds.), *Changing anarchism: Anarchist theory and practice in a global age*, 181–98. Manchester: Manchester University Press.

Grossberg, L. (2010). *Cultural studies in the future tense*. Durham, NC: Duke University Press.

Hardt, M. (1993). *Gilles Deleuze: An apprenticeship in philosophy*. Minneapolis: The University of Minnesota Press.

Hardt, M. & Negri, A. (2004). *Multitude: War and democracy in the age of empire*. New York: Penguin.

Heckert, J. (2005). *Resisting orientation: On the complexities of desire and the limits of identity politics*. Unpublished dissertation, The University of Edinburgh. Retrieved from http://sexualorientation.info/thesis/resisting%20orientation.pdf (accessed May 7, 2010).

Holloway, J. (2010). *Crack capitalism*. New York: Pluto Press.

Hursh, D. (2008). *High-stakes testing and the decline of teaching and learning: The real crisis in education*. Lanham, MD: Rowman & Littlefield.

Legg, S. (2007). Beyond the European province: Foucault and postcolonialism. In J. Crampton & S. Elden (Eds.), *Space, knowledge and power: Foucault and geography*, 265–90. Hampshire, England: Ashgate.

Lorde, A. (2003). The master's tools will never dismantle the master's house. In R. Lewis & S. Mills (Eds.), *Feminist postcolonial theory: A reader*, 25–28. New York: Routledge.

Markula, P. (2008). Affect[ing] bodies: Performative pedagogy of pilates. *International Review of Qualitative Research* 1(3), 381–408.

Newman, S. (2009). Anarchism, utopianism and the politics of emancipation. In L. Davis & R. Kinna (Eds.), *Anarchism and utopianism* (207–20). Manchester: Manchester University Press.

Papadopoulos, D., Stephenson, N. & Vassilis, T. (2008). *Escape routes: Control and subversion in the 21st century*. London: Pluto Press.

Parenti, M. (2007). *Democracy for the few*, 8th ed. Belmont, CA: Wadsworth Publishing.

Pelias, R. (2008). Making my masculine body behave. *International Review of Qualitative Research*, 1(1), 65–74.

Reagan, T. & Osborn, T. (2002). *The foreign language educator in society: Toward a critical pedagogy*. Mahwah, NJ: Lawrence Erlbaum Associates.

Rose, N. (1989). *Governing the soul: The shaping of the private self*, 2nd ed. London, England: Free Association Books.

Rossman, G. & Rallis, S. (2003). *Learning in the field: An introduction to Qualitative research*, 2nd ed. Thousand Oaks, CA: Sage.

Sharp, J., Routledge, P., Philo, C. & Paddison, R. (2000). Entanglements of power: Geographies of domination/resistance. In J. Sharp, P. Routledge, C. Philo & R. Paddison (Eds.), *Entanglements of power: Geographies of domination/resistance*, 1–42. New York: Routledge.

Shukaitis, S. (2009). *Imaginal machines: Autonomy & self-organization in the revolutions of everyday life*. Brooklyn: Autonomedia.

Stoler, A. (2010). *Along the archival grain: Epistemic anxieties and colonial common sense*. Princeton, NJ: Princeton University Press.

St. Pierre, E. (2008). Decentering voice in qualitative inquiry. *International Review of Qualitative Research* 1(3), 319–36.

Suissa, J. (2009). "The space now possible": Anarchist education as utopian hope. In L. Davis & R. Kinna (Eds.), *Anarchism and utopianism*, 241–59. Manchester, England: Manchester University Press.

Suissa, J. (2010). *Anarchism and education: A philosophical perspective*. Oakland: PM Press.

Trotter, D. (1990). Colonial subjects. *Critical Quarterly*, 32(3), 3–20.

Tuhiwai Smith, L. (1999). *Decolonizing methodologies: Research and indigenous peoples*. London, England: Zed Books.

**AFTERWORD**

# Let the Riots Begin

**Allan Antliff**

Rooted in antiauthoritarian values often at odds with the "mainstream," anarchists conceive of education as a site of critical reflection and creative license, where life and learning comingle, giving rise to ways of being that prefigure and realize our ideals on a practical level, as a lived reality. And on that score, as I read this book, I was struck again by the diversity of approaches and perspectives within anarchist pedagogy, as well as the many avenues awaiting further development. Saku Pinta's study of the Industrial Workers of the World's Finnish-American Work People's College, for example, cites a college attendee reminiscing about the school's curriculum, which included "Bogdanoff and 'Kalle' Marx." The reference is to the Russian Marxist Alexandr Bogdanov, whose theories concerning the need for workers to organize autonomous educational institutions inspired a short-lived mass "proletarian culture" educational movement (the "Prolet'kult") in the Soviet Union before Lenin intervened. Lenin, who opposed Bogdanov's theory of Marxism as a "proletarian science" (which he had critiqued in his 1909 philosophical tome, *Materialism and Empirio-Criticism*), demanded the Prolet'kult be brought under State and Communist Party control. And so the organization was subsumed into the Soviet Ministry of Education where it continued propagating Bogdanov's ideas on a much-diminished scale until it was shut down for good in the early 1930s. In its heyday, the Prolet'kult idea spread to the English-speaking world, contributing to a substantial workers' education movement in the United Kingdom during the 1920s and '30s. Some of Bogdanov's writings were translated into English and they circulated in other languages as well. Discovering his work figured in the curriculum of the Work People's College is intriguing, given Bogdanov's hostility toward anarchism, which he dismissed as "unscientific," as opposed to Marxism, which was promoted as the class-based "scientific" knowledge system of the coming "proletarian" era. How IWW activists at the WPC reconciled the tenets of proletarian culture with the educational ideas of Kropotkin and other anarchists, then, remains an open question. Perhaps Pinta will take up this issue in a future study.

Then there are the innovations realized at the Toronto Anarchist Free Space and Anarchist Free School, which I helped found (in Fall 1998) and where I cofacilitated a number of courses before Jeff Shantz, who writes on these projects, joined (in July 1999 I left Toronto for a teaching position at the University of Alberta). During the time of my involvement I was completing my first book, *Anarchist Modernism: Art, Politics, and the First American Avant-Garde* (2001), whose focal point is an anarchist educational institution and art school (a Francisco Ferrer-inspired Modern School) in World War I–era New York City. This history helped shape my contributions to the mission statement, art-related course offerings, and organizational logistics of the Toronto Anarchist Free School; and the Free School/Free Space experience, in turn, impacted on the art history I was writing. Other contributors to anarchist learning through the arts included Adrian Blackwell, who constructed an architectonic sculpture configuring the Anarchist Free School's antihierarchical principles (*Model for a Public Space*, 1999) and Luis Jacob, who created an art installation utilizing records from our founding meetings (*Anarchist Free School Minutes*, 1999) to promote anarchist education in art gallery settings. It is fair to say, then, that in addition to Shantz's focus on class-specific activism, the Toronto Anarchist Free School and Anarchist Free Space brought new ideas to the longstanding tradition of anarchist pedagogy in the arts.

But I digress. Shantz focuses on the ways in which our activities challenged the capitalist status quo for good reason. Anarchist educational projects routinely generate contestation, internally by virtue of the diversity of opinions and debates they encourage and externally by virtue of what they are: sites of learning at odds with the capitalist State-adjudicated socioeconomic system pervading today's societies. Coming to grips with contestation is important, because we need to build our projects in full knowledge of what we are up against. One of the most exciting aspects of this book is its critical engagement with this issue in chapters such as David Gabbard's analysis of the U.S. public school system or Joseph Todd's discussion of contested terrain beyond State-based compulsory education where, as the home schooling movement reveals, absence of government authority is no guarantee that anarchic values are being realized. These studies are complimented by some very rigorous examinations of anarchic educational practices which foreground the gaps between aspiration and realization. I am thinking, in particular, of Isabelle Fremeaux and John Jordan's discussion of Paideia, a long-running school in the city of Mérida, Spain, where students and instructors alike are constantly negotiating how best to realize anarchist educational values in conditions fraught with potential or real conflict. Matthew Weinstein's analysis of the spaces of learning created by street medics at protests captures a different kind of tension. Here, under conditions of stress and emergency, we have an anarchist politics of "crisis pedagogy" in which street medics, "even when denying explicit connections to anarchism, adopt much of its ethos" out of necessity, proving once again that anarchism is nothing if not practical!

What is to be gained from pursuing educational projects under anarchism's auspices?

Justin Mueller, Sarah Motta, and other contributors bring fresh perspectives to this issue in relation to many canonized theorists of antiauthoritarian pedagogy—A.S. Neill, Paulo Freire, and Ivan Illich, for example—revealing that anarchism can serve as a powerful evaluative tool for revisiting their ideas. Similarly, it is important to address relationships between anarchism, academic systems of learning, and the kind of "high" theory so valued in some quarters of the academy. Projecting anarchic values into university curriculums or creating anarchic academic spaces autonomous from such institutions is tricky terrain, as Elsa Noterman and Andre Pusey argue in their study of experimental educational projects in Leeds. Despite the problems, neither they nor Caroline K. Kaltefleiter and Anthony J. Nocella II are ready to give up on the idea that universities can serve as generative sites for anarchist politics. That said, how one goes about sustaining these politics is an important issue, particularly as more and more anarchists create spaces for themselves within the academy. Kaltefleiter and Nocella's hands-on advice to anarchist academics for sustaining their militancy in a university setting is, arguably, an integral part of the process. Equally important is a willingness to theorize from a stance of engagement, Alex Khasnabish's study of the Zapatista movement being a case in point. Now, I am not suggesting that ideas founded in academic theory have no place in anarchist pedagogy. Lucy Nicholas and Abraham DeLeon offer compelling arguments to the contrary, demonstrating "riots for the mind," to paraphrase my favorite Toronto Anarchist U slogan, can also be weapons. My point is that anarchist pedagogy is not about critiquing the present state of affairs; it's about subverting and transcending oppressive social formations so as to realize our freedom to creatively shape our lives in the fullest sense. Changing society anarchically through learning, therefore, is a process of "becoming anarchist" that necessarily eludes any final resolution.

**Allan Antliff**
**Canada Research Chair**
**University of Victoria, Canada**

# CONTRIBUTORS

**Alejandro de Acosta** writes on anarchist philosophy and aesthetics. He is currently composing amoral essays inspired by Gracián and Hume. Since moving to Austin, Texas, seven years ago, he has launched the micropress mufa::poema, publishing and freely distributing eight booklets of poetry and philosophy. He taught philosophy in the university setting for ten years.

**Allan Antliff** is Canada Research Chair, University of Victoria, and is the author of *Anarchist Modernism: Art, Politics, and the First American Avant-Garde* (University of Chicago Press, 2001), *Anarchy and Art: From the Paris Commune to the Fall of the Berlin Wall* (Arsenal Pulp Press, 2007) and editor of *Only a Beginning* (Arsenal Pulp Press, 2004), a documentary anthology of anarchist writings and activism in Canada.

**Abraham P. DeLeon** is an assistant professor of Foundations of Education at the University of Texas at San Antonio in the Department of Educational Leadership & Policy Studies. His research interests are interdisciplinary, spanning cultural studies, critical pedagogy, anarchist theory, critical animal studies, space and place, postcolonial theory, and autoethnography. Some of his writing has appeared in journals such as *Educational Studies, Equity & Excellence in Education, Critical Education*, and *Theory in Action* and in a wide variety of edited book collections. He was also a member of the editorial collective that published *Contemporary Anarchist Studies: An Introductory Anthology of Anarchy in the Academy* (Routledge, 2009) and has coedited *Critical Theories, Radical Pedagogies: Towards New Perspectives for the Social Studies* with E. Wayne Ross (Sense Publishers: 2010). He lives in San Antonio, Texas, with his partner and feline companion.

**Isabelle Fremeaux** was, until December 2011, senior lecturer in media and cultural studies at Birkbeck College, University of London. She has left academia in order to start a Utopian experiment in radical education. **John Jordan** is an art activist.

He cofounded the direct action groups Reclaim the Streets and the Clown Army, worked as a cinematographer for Naomi Klein's *The Take*, coedited the book *We Are Everywhere: The Irresistible Rise of Global Anti-capitalism* (Verso, 2004). Together they founded the Laboratory of Insurrectionary Imagination, a collective of artists and activists who develop action research projects focusing on creative forms of resistance and popular education. They cowrote *Les Sentiers de l'Utopie*, a book-film project about Utopian communities in Europe (La Découverte, 2011), which contains an initial version of the chapter published in this volume.

**David Gabbard** is a professor of educational foundations in the College of Education at East Carolina University. He has edited or coedited several important books dealing with contemporary educational policy issues, including *Knowledge and Power in the Global Economy: The Effects of School Reform in a Neoliberal/Neoconservative Age* (Lawrence Erlbaum Associates, 2008) and *Education Under the Security State* (Teachers College Press, 2008).

**Robert H. Haworth** is an assistant professor in the Department of Professional and Secondary Education at West Chester University. He teaches courses focusing on the social foundations of education, anarchism and critical pedagogies. He has published and presented internationally on anarchism, youth culture, informal learning spaces, and critical social studies education. He cofounded worker-owned and -operated Regeneration TV as well as other academic research collectives. Currently he is working on a coedited book on Critical Perspectives and Informal Learning, as well as writing a single-authored book entitled: *Horizontal Imaginaries: Education, Spontaneity, and Desire*.

**Nathan Jun** is assistant professor of philosophy and coordinator of the philosophy program at Midwestern State University in Wichita Falls, Texas. He is coeditor (with Shane Wahl) of *New Perspectives on Anarchism* (Lexington Books, 2009) and (with Dan Smith) of *Deleuze and Ethics* (Edinburgh University Press, 2010) and the author of *Anarchism and Political Modernity* (Continuum, 2011).

**Caroline K. Kaltefleiter** is coordinator of women's studies and associate professor of communication studies at the State University of New York College at Cortland and recent director of the Sacco and Vanzetti Foundation. She has over twenty years of broadcast activism experience as a news anchor and producer for public and community radio stations in Texas, Georgia, Ohio, and New York. She served as producer and director of the documentary *Burn Out in the Heartland*, which investigates the crystal methamphetamine culture among teens in Iowa and Nebraska. She continues to work on radio documentaries for National Public Radio and anchors a radio program titled *The Digital Divide* on public radio station WSUC-FM. She received her PhD from Ohio University in communication and women's studies.

She holds an MA from Miami University and participated in the Center for Cultural Studies, where she began her research on youth subcultures and activism including work on youth culture, capitalism, postfeminism, and popular culture. Her current research project articulates cyberfeminism within a discourse of new media studies. The project examines the construction, manipulation, and redefinition of women's lives within contemporary technoscientific cultures.

**Alex Khasnabish** is an assistant professor in the Department of Sociology and Anthropology at Mount Saint Vincent University in Halifax, Nova Scotia, Canada. He is the author of two books, *Zapatismo Beyond Borders: New Imaginations of Political Possibility* (University of Toronto Press, 2008) and *Zapatistas: Rebellion from the Grassroots to the Global* (Zed Press, 2010). He has also written several journal articles and book chapters about contemporary radical politics, globalization, and social movements. Khasnabish's current research focuses upon the relationship between radical social change struggles and the radical imagination. He sees his academic work as an extension of his political commitments to an anarchist-inspired anticapitalist, antioppressive, and anticolonial practice.

**Curry Stephenson Malott** is an assistant professor in the Department of Professional and Secondary Education at West Chester University of Pennsylvania. His research interests are wide-raging, focusing most recently on the history of education from a Marxist perspective. He has published and presented in many areas of critical pedagogy from countercultures, cognition, neoliberalism, and leadership, to neocolonialism and Native North America. All of his work is connected by the common goal of contributing to the emergence of a postcapitalist global society.

**Sara C. Motta** focuses her research on the politics of subaltern resistance, with particular reference to Latin America. She has written about the Latin American Third Way Governments of the Concertación in Chile and the Workers' Party in Brazil in relation to their role in stabilizing and normalizing neoliberal hegemony. A second strand of her research is focused on new forms of subaltern politics in the region, with particular reference to social movements in Argentina (unemployed movements), Venezuela (urban land movement) and Brazil (Landless Workers Movement and Solidarity Economy Movement). This research has led her to explore the politics of knowledge and the linkages between knowledge, power, and exclusion, as well as the ways in which new social movements are reinventing democratic and participatory forms of knowledge-creation that challenge the academic privilege of the academy. Methodologically, she is therefore interested in developing movement-relevant research and participatory research methods. As part of this she is also interested in the pedagogy of dissent and the use of popular education and critical education in and outside the university in the forging of struggles and practices of social justice.

**Justin Mueller** is a graduate student in political science, with a focus on political theory at Purdue University. His primary research interests include: anarchism as a movement, a political/social theory, and an analytical framework; democratic theory; politics and education; power and authority; political economy; political ideology; and U.S. foreign policy.

**Lucy Nicholas** is currently completing per PhD in Sociology at the University of Edinburgh considering the possibility of understanding the self and others without or beyond the lenses of sexual difference. Per research has focused on poststructuralist anarchism, queer theory, existentialist ethics, pedagogy, and broader gender and sexuality theory. Ze has published journal articles about poststructuralist anarchism, riot grrrl, DIY punk, sexuality and gender and presented internationally on the same topics. Ze is also a zine maker and an active member of anarchist, queer, and feminist communities.

**Anthony J. Nocella II** completed his PhD in social science at Syracuse University and has taught at SUNY Cortland and Hamline University. As an interdisciplinary scholar, Nocella has an interest in security, conflict and peace studies, cultural foundations of education, criminology, disability studies, critical media studies, critical animal studies, and environmental studies. He has taught workshops in mediation and tactical analysis, and assisted in a number of legal committees in the Americas, including working with the Mennonite Central Committee, American Friends Service Committee, and Christian Peacemaker Teams. Nocella has published more than twenty-five scholarly articles, cofounded more than twenty-five political organizations including the Sacco and Vanzetti Foundation, and serves on five boards including the American Friends Service Committee. He has cofounded four journals: *Green Theory and Praxis*, *Peace Studies Journal*, *Journal on Critical Animal Studies*, and *Journal on Terrorism and Security*, is on the editorial board of four other journals, and has published more than ten books including coediting *Contemporary Anarchist Studies: An Introductory Anthology of Anarchy in the Academy* (Routledge, 2009) and *An Economy of Sustainability: Anarchist Economics* (AK Press, 2010). Feel free to contact him at: www.anthonynocella.org

**Elsa Noterman** is Program Associate at the Community Strategies Group of the Aspen Institute in Washington, D.C., where she has worked since 2008. Her work includes research on community foundations and community groups working in rural areas of the United States. At CSG she also provides support for peer-learning sessions and publications for local groups working on social justice issues in these areas. While on a sabbatical year in the UK she helped to establish the Really Open University and coorganized several participatory workshops to collaboratively envision what an alternative university might look like and discuss the possible creation of a knowledge commons. She has a long-term commitment to working for social justice in a wide range of areas including in antiwar and anticapitalist movements, green affordable housing projects, and alternative education initiatives.

**Saku Pinta** has a PhD from the Politics, History, and International Relations Department at Loughborough University. His research examines moments of theoretical and practical convergence between class struggle and antiparliamentarian anarchisms and marxisms. He has been active in the labor movement, as a member of the Industrial Workers of the World, as well as other independent media and anticapitalist projects. His recent creative projects include work in the capacity of researcher, writer, and coproducer on the documentary film *To My Son in Spain: Finnish-Canadians in the Spanish Civil War* and as a researcher, writer, and actor in the feature-length docudrama *Under the Red Star* (2011).

**Andre Pusey** is a PhD candidate in the School of Geography at the University of Leeds, UK. His research is looking at ways in which social movements engage in "value struggles" which both defend and (re)produce the common(s). He has been active in movements, such as Earth First! and the Camp for Climate Action, as well as autonomous social centers and an assortment of anticapitalist initiatives for a number of years. Recently he has helped to establish a group called the Really Open University, which aims to both resist savage spending cuts across higher education and open a up a space for critical dialogue and debate about the both the role and methods of education and knowledge production.

**Jeff Shantz** has been a community organizer, rank-and-file union activist and anarchist for decades. He has been active in a range of groups and projects (IWW, Ontario Coalition Against Poverty, Who's Emma? Infoshop, Anarchist Free Skool, and *Kick It Over* magazine among others). His publications include numerous articles in movement publications including *Anarchy*, *Social Anarchism*, *Green Anarchy*, *Earth First! Journal*, *Northeastern Anarchist*, *Industrial Worker*, *Anarcho-Syndicalist Review*, *Onward*, *Arsenal*, and *Processed World*. His writings have also appeared in academic journals including *Critical Sociology*, *Critique of Anthropology*, *Feminist Review*, and *New Politics* as well as numerous anthologies. His book *Constructive Anarchy: Building Infrastructure of Resistance* (Ashgate, 2010) is a groundbreaking discussion of contemporary anarchist projects. Currently he teaches at Kwantlen Polytechnic University in Vancouver.

**Joseph D. Todd** is a doctoral student as Montclair State University (MSU) in the pedagogy and philosophy program and an adjunct instructor at MSU and Bergen Community College teaching both philosophy and education courses. His areas of interest involve reimagining student-teacher relationships, authority and discipline, learning and play, imagination and creativity, and learning technologies. He and his wife also homeschool/deschool/unschool their two children, who have never experienced the traditional educational paradigm.

**Matthew Weinstein** is a professor of science education at the University of Washington–Tacoma. He is the author of *Bodies out of Control: Rethinking Science Texts* (Peter Lang, 2010) and *Robot World: Education, Popular Culture, and Science* (Peter Lang, 1998), as well as many articles and chapters on the politics of human subjects and the project of critical science literacy more broadly.

# ACKNOWLEDGMENTS

I first and foremost want to thank PM Press for their support of this project. I can't say enough great things about the folks who have helped to make this collaboration happen. I also want to thank all the authors who contributed to this volume. The work you are doing is inspiring, and I appreciate that you trusted me to publish your thoughts. Additionally, I want to acknowledge my lifelong partner Holly and my kids Rachel and Dylan. Your patience and critical feedback through this process have been invaluable. Having your ten-year-old child ask, "Why do we have to go to school?" works as a great springboard for reflection, discussion, and action. I also want to thank my mom and dad for being supportive over the years. Additionally I want to thank my brother for turning me on to punk rock at an early age.

I definitely want to thank many of my friends who have always been supportive and have pushed me in far-off directions I never thought possible. To name a few, Bryan Chu, Stacey Duncan, Chris Adams, Curry Malott, Eric Alvarez, Gregory Wegner, Joseph Caroll-Miranda, Mostafa Mouheeddine, Manal Hamzeh, Marc Pruyn, Peg Finders, Will Watts, Zack de la Rocha, and many more.

I think it is also appropriate to say "thank you" to the anarchists who are no longer with us. They have been integral in reenergizing some of our current movements to contest global capitalism and reimagining how we might organize ourselves differently. I keep learning so much from their raw honesty and critical work.

Finally, I would like to dedicate this book to Don LaCoss, one of the most thoughtful and dedicated people I have met. His insights and conversations meant so much to me during a rough spot in my life and through the process of getting this book together. He is definitely missed!

# INDEX


academic-activist 178, 200–216
affinity group medics 97
Althusser, Louis
  Ideological State Apparatuses (ISA) 201, 212, 215, 216
  Repressive State Apparatuses (RSA) 201
anarchism 2–10, 69, 95, 97, 119, 120–121, 143, 176, 177, 205, 213, 214, 244–245, 250–251, 253, 255, 260, 265–267, 279, 298–299, 308, 314, 315–316, 317–318, 321, 322–323
  defined 15, 184
  equality and 14, 17–18, 22, 25, 74, 108, 114, 137, 182, 271
  liberty 17, 18, 19, 35, 73, 127, 137, 200–201, 271, 294
  praxis 3, 30, 145–160, 195, 242–243, 249, 251, 252, 253, 283–301, 314–315, 317–318
  principles 14–21, 107, 128, 140, 176, 182, 187, 246, 256, 299, 317
  solidarity 16, 18–20, 21, 22, 25, 108, 114, 138, 183, 205
  values 16–20, 22, 27, 107, 108, 109, 114, 116, 118
Anarchist Free Space and Free Skool (AFS) 124–143
Anarchist Studies Initiative (ASI) 201–214
  emergence 211–213
  opposition 207–211
  relationships SUNY Cortland 206–207
anarcho-feminism 205, 260–281
  intersections 263–264
  psychology 264–265, 267, 268–269, 271–276, 278, 279
asambleas 112–119
Athens Manifesto 93, 104
Avrich, Paul 2, 25, 112

Bakunin, Mikhail 17, 21, 111, 143, 208, 211, 254, 263, 265, 278, 284–285, 286, 287, 288, 294, 295, 296, 298
behaviorism 267, 270–273, 278, 321
Berkman, Alexander 18, 287, 288, 300–301
Bey, Hakim 124–125, 141, 247
bin Laden, Osama 33
Black Cross Health Collective 94–95
Bush, George W. 32–33
Butler, Judith 245–247, 249, 250–251, 252, 253, 255, 256–257

Canadian Auto Workers (CAW) 168, 171
capitalism 1, 2, 3, 4, 6, 8, 15–16, 18, 20, 59, 64, 82, 102, 111, 121, 145, 160, 168, 173–174, 178, 180, 185, 187, 205, 209, 212, 214, 222, 234, 263, 271, 279, 288, 291, 312–313, 314–315, 319, 322–323
  global 4–5, 207, 317
  neoliberal 4, 165–166, 181, 221, 222, 232, 236, 239, 272, 274, 277–278
Catholic 25, 274
children's rights 71, 75, 108

Chomsky, Noam 27, 35–36, 64, 203, 204, 250, 264–268, 270–274, 277, 279
*ciencia popular* 91, 94, 103–104
class 39–40, 78, 103, 111, 132–140, 178, 201–202, 204–205, 260–261, 271, 277, 284, 286, 288–289. *See also* working class
collective medics 90–91, 93–94, 96–102
commoning, defined 190
compulsory schooling 5, 6, 35, 36–39, 43–44, 69, 72, 75, 81
consensus decision-making 5, 90, 132, 140–141, 145, 149, 230, 232, 277
Copenhagen Free University 185
counterpublics 73, 76–77, 83
  feminist 77
creative economy 4
criminal justice 44, 201. *See also* prisons
critical pedagogy 2, 23, 126, 176, 183, 187, 260–262, 279, 317, 321

Day, Richard 4
debt 175, 176, 180, 185, 186
de Cleyre, Voltairine 15, 27–28, 285–286
Deleuze, Gilles 5, 8, 191, 193, 313, 316
deschooling 69–84, 159
developmental power 249, 252
Dewey, John 2, 23
do-it-yourself (DIY) 82, 125, 136, 142–143, 185, 211, 254, 257, 318
Dolgoff, Sam 163

edu-crisis 176, 192
Ejército Zapatista de Liberación Nacional (EZLN) 220–239
  history 223, 230–233
  myths 223–230
  romanticism 223, 234–235
  Subcomandante Insurgente
    Marcos 220, 221, 222, 223–224, 229, 231, 233, 235, 237
Enlightenment, the 232, 265–267, 270, 272, 290–291, 319
Escuela Moderna (Modern School) 24–26, 112, 127, 132, 183, 200
extractive power 247, 249, 252

Ferrer, Francisco 2, 7, 22, 24–26, 111–112, 127, 130, 183
Food Not Bombs 130, 206, 207, 318
Foucault, Michel 8, 36, 124, 185, 188, 193, 243–249, 251–253, 254, 257
free skools 6, 7, 182–185, 186, 195, 254. *See also* Anarchist Free Space and Free Skool (AFS)
Free Skool Santa Cruz 183, 254–255, 256
Free University 176, 182, 184–186, 195, 254
Freire, Paulo 2, 7–8, 20, 23–24, 145, 147–148, 152, 183, 202, 204

Gabbard, David 200, 252, 327
gender 8, 47, 56, 77, 122, 152–153, 177, 207, 209, 250, 253–257, 261, 270, 299, 316, 318, 320
Giroux, Henry 2, 4, 111, 112
Godwin, William 35, 37, 73, 75, 111, 200–201, 208, 211
Goldman, Emma 2–3, 15, 17, 19, 25, 26, 36, 38, 130, 143, 200, 211, 245, 262–263, 285–286, 296–297
Goodman, Paul 26, 27, 127–128, 130, 183, 279
Graeber, David 3, 5, 7, 208, 214, 274, 276–277, 279
Gramsci, Antonio 215, 288, 298, 299

heterotopia 124–126, 143
hidden curriculum 70, 74, 79–80, 81–83, 111, 115
higher education 44, 175, 177, 187, 202, 206, 207, 212, 293
  academy 30, 175–180, 186–188, 192–195, 201, 203–205, 208–209, 212–213, 297–299, 315, 318

anarchist studies 201, 203, 204, 206, 208–209, 211–213
liberalization 177
site of cultural resistance 201
state power 201
Holloway, John 6, 176, 178, 180, 188, 191, 229, 247, 312–313
Holt, John 72, 75, 78, 80
homeschooling 70–83
autonomy 73, 75, 76, 77, 79, 80, 82–84
networks 76, 78–82
politics of 70–73
hooks, bell 177, 260–263
human nature 16, 17, 20–21, 22, 29, 264–266, 267–268, 272, 279

identity 73, 76–77, 82, 83, 147, 229, 234, 243, 246, 254, 255–256, 264, 280, 288, 308, 314, 316, 318, 320–321
Illich, Ivan iii, 24, 26, 69–70, 73–84, 136, 145, 147–148, 156, 159, 183
Industrial Workers of the World (IWW) 47–54, 56–58, 59–64, 65–66
Junior Wobblies 58–59
infiltration 312, 314–315, 319, 322–323
infrastructures of resistance 125, 138, 162–165, 167–169, 171, 174

Kamiya, Gary 32–33, 35, 38
Kincheloe, Joe 260–262, 273, 274–276
Kropotkin, Peter 16, 18–19, 21, 53, 124, 143, 208, 262–263, 265, 289, 299–300

La Mascara feminist theatre 155
Leeds University Student Union (LUU) 186–187, 189
libertarian 14, 16, 20, 21, 29, 48, 50, 53, 59, 61, 65, 108, 121, 138, 183, 267

Malatesta, Errico 17, 286–287
Mann, Horace
common schools 39–40
Manoa Free University, Vienna 185
Marxism 3, 15, 49, 52, 54, 203, 290, 317
Marx, Karl 278, 296, 299
mass intellectuality 187–188
Mayer, Deborah 34–36
May, Todd 8, 20, 56, 81, 246, 247
McLaren, Peter 23, 133, 134, 138, 204
Meine Akademie (My Academy) 185
Modern School. *See* Escuela Moderna
Morland, David 265–266
mutual aid 18–19, 75, 82, 124, 137, 138, 145, 163, 168, 171, 172, 205, 246

*Nation At Risk, A* 43
Neill, A.S. 20, 21–22, 24, 25, 108, 238
neoliberalism. *See* capitalism
neutrality 22, 23, 25, 90
No Child Left Behind 28, 278
nongovernmental organization (NGO) 179–180, 236
North American Anarchist Studies Network (NAASN) 206, 207–209, 300
Nottingham Free School 145–161
Open Spaces of Dialogue and Enquiry (OSDE) 145, 146, 149–150, 152, 155, 160
Radical Education workshop 147–152
Sumac skill-shares 156–160
Trauma and Privilege workshop 152–155

Obama, Barack 33, 41–42
objectivity. *See* neutrality
occupy 189
defensive 189, 193
defined 189, 193–194
Logic of Occupation 189
offensive 189, 191, 192, 193, 221
Occupy movement 3, 192, 193–194

paideia 28–29, 289–297, 298
democratic 33
Paideia school 107–122

nonviolent conflict resolution 114–115
pedagogical framework 111–112
self-management 109–110, 112–114, 118, 121
*Pedagogy of the Oppressed* 23, 145, 161, 183, 202
peer-matching 70, 77, 79–80
Peters, Michael 4
postformal 260, 264–265, 272–275, 278–281
Postman, Neil 111, 161
poststructuralism 8, 242–257, 317
prisons 21, 36, 43–44, 139, 185, 201, 214. *See also* criminal justice
privilege 18, 21, 115, 148, 152–155, 180, 237, 262, 272, 280–281, 286, 312, 315, 323
Proudhon, Pierre-Joseph 35, 111, 208, 262–263, 265, 266, 283–284, 289
public schools 1–3, 6, 26–27, 39–40, 41, 44, 71–72, 75–76, 78, 81, 132, 312

queer anarchist communities 255–256
queer theory 8, 242–243, 246, 250

Really Open University (ROU) 159, 176, 186–196
Reimagine the University 186, 190–191
resistance culture 203
Rocker, Rudolf 7, 285

sabotage 74–75, 165, 212, 313–315, 318, 320, 322
scholar-activism 178
schooling, compulsory. *See* compulsory schooling
Seaview Street Medic Collective (SSMC) 93, 96–101
September 11 33, 34, 319
skill exchange 70, 77, 79
skills 28, 49, 53, 57, 79–80, 82, 94–95, 101, 107, 111, 115, 117, 119, 125, 128, 132, 143, 156–157, 170, 173, 177, 180, 182, 184, 293–295
social centers 163, 166–167, 176, 178, 183–184, 189, 194–195, 254, 257
spontaneous learning 271
Spring, Joel 35, 111, 126–128, 130, 132–138, 200–201
standardized testing 28, 43, 314, 316, 321
Stirner, Max 16, 23, 126–127, 135, 137, 265
street medics 90–104
education 99–104
history 91–94
practices 95–99
protest 98–99
structure 95–97
strike, defined 188
student-centered learning 112, 182
Suissa, Judith 5–6, 19, 22, 74–75, 111, 315, 317, 322
Summerhill School 21–23, 108

teachers' rights 108
freedom of expression 34
teaching 2–3, 7–8
communication 101, 203, 298–299, 304
impossibility of 303–311
modeling 156, 304, 305–306, 308, 309–310
philosophy 304–306
temporary autonomous zones (TAZ) 124–125, 141–143

unions 47–49, 51–52, 55–59, 62–63, 64, 72–73, 162–166, 167–168, 170, 171, 186, 211
universities. *See* higher education
University of Leeds, UK 186–189, 191, 196
MA in Activism and Social Change (MAASC) 175, 176–181, 196
University of Lincoln, UK 194
Student as Producer 175, 181–182

University of Openness, London 185, 196
unschooling 69–84

Ward, Colin 20, 29, 69, 75, 78, 83, 138, 173, 184
West, Cornel 33–34, 35, 214
Windsor Workers' Action Centre (WWAC) 168–172
Wobblies. *See* Industrial Workers of the World (IWW)
working class 47–51, 56, 58–59, 61, 63–64, 111, 125, 142, 146, 162–173, 204, 262, 284, 287–288. *See also* class
Work People's College (WPC) 47–66
  background 50–53
  curriculum 53–55
  *Education as Struggle* 50
  faculty 59–61
  gender equality 56
  impact 61–64
  students 49–50, 52, 55–59
  tactical sessions 55

Zapatismo 220–239
Zapatistas. *See* Ejercito Zapatista de Liberatcion Nacional (EZLN)

# ABOUT PM PRESS

PM Press was founded at the end of 2007 by a small collection of folks with decades of publishing, media, and organizing experience. PM Press co-conspirators have published and distributed hundreds of books, pamphlets, CDs, and DVDs. Members of PM have founded enduring book fairs, spearheaded victorious tenant organizing campaigns, and worked closely with bookstores, academic conferences, and even rock bands to deliver political and challenging ideas to all walks of life. We're old enough to know what we're doing and young enough to know what's at stake.

We seek to create radical and stimulating fiction and non-fiction books, pamphlets, T-shirts, visual and audio materials to entertain, educate and inspire you. We aim to distribute these through every available channel with every available technology — whether that means you are seeing anarchist classics at our bookfair stalls; reading our latest vegan cookbook at the café; downloading geeky fiction e-books; or digging new music and timely videos from our website.

PM Press is always on the lookout for talented and skilled volunteers, artists, activists and writers to work with. If you have a great idea for a project or can contribute in some way, please get in touch.

**PM Press**
**PO Box 23912**
**Oakland, CA 94623**
**www.pmpress.org**

# FRIENDS OF PM PRESS

These are indisputably momentous times—the financial system is melting down globally and the Empire is stumbling. Now more than ever there is a vital need for radical ideas.

In the four years since its founding—and on a mere shoestring—PM Press has risen to the formidable challenge of publishing and distributing knowledge and entertainment for the struggles ahead. With over 175 releases to date, we have published an impressive and stimulating array of literature, art, music, politics, and culture. Using every available medium, we've succeeded in connecting those hungry for ideas and information to those putting them into practice.

*Friends of PM* allows you to directly help impact, amplify, and revitalize the discourse and actions of radical writers, filmmakers, and artists. It provides us with a stable foundation from which we can build upon our early successes and provides a much-needed subsidy for the materials that can't necessarily pay their own way. You can help make that happen—and receive every new title automatically delivered to your door once a month—by joining as a Friend of PM Press. And, we'll throw in a free T-shirt when you sign up.

Here are your options:

- **$25 a month** Get all books and pamphlets plus 50% discount on all webstore purchases

- **$40 a month** Get all PM Press releases (including CDs and DVDs) plus 50% discount on all webstore purchases

- **$100 a month** Superstar—Everything plus PM merchandise, free downloads, and 50% discount on all webstore purchases

For those who can't afford $25 or more a month, we're introducing **Sustainer Rates** at $15, $10 and $5. Sustainers get a free PM Press T-shirt and a 50% discount on all purchases from our website.

Your Visa or Mastercard will be billed once a month, until you tell us to stop. Or until our efforts succeed in bringing the revolution around. Or the financial meltdown of Capital makes plastic redundant. Whichever comes first.

## *Anarchism and Education: A Philosophical Perspective*

Judith Suissa

**ISBN: 978-1-60486-114-3**
**$19.95 184 pages**

While there have been historical accounts of the anarchist school movement, there has been no systematic work on the philosophical underpinnings of anarchist educational ideas—until now.

*Anarchism and Education* offers a philosophical account of the neglected tradition of anarchist thought on education. Although few anarchist thinkers wrote systematically on education, this analysis is based largely on a reconstruction of the educational thought of anarchist thinkers gleaned from their various ethical, philosophical, and popular writings. Primarily drawing on the work of the nineteenth-century anarchist theorists such as Bakunin, Kropotkin, and Proudhon, the book also covers twentieth-century anarchist thinkers such as Noam Chomsky, Paul Goodman, Daniel Guerin, and Colin Ward.

This original work will interest philosophers of education and educationalist thinkers as well as those with a general interest in anarchism.

*"This is an excellent book that deals with important issues through the lens of anarchist theories and practices of education... The book tackles a number of issues that are relevant to anybody who is trying to come to terms with the philosophy of education."*
*— Higher Education Review*

## *The Paul Goodman Reader*

Edited by Taylor Stoehr

**ISBN: 978-1-60486-058-0**
**$28.95 500 pages**

A one-man think-tank for the New Left, Paul Goodman wrote over thirty books, most of them before his decade of fame as a social critic in the Sixties. A Paul Goodman Reader that does him justice must be a compendious volume, with excerpts not only from best-sellers like *Growing Up Absurd*, but also from his landmark books on education, community planning, anarchism, psychotherapy, language theory, and poetics. Samples as well from *The Empire City*, a comic novel reviewers compared to *Don Quixote*, prize-winning short stories, and scores of poems that led America's most respected poetry reviewer, Hayden Carruth, to exclaim, "Not one dull page. It's almost unbelievable."

Goodman called himself as an old-fashioned man of letters, which meant that all these various disciplines and occasions added up to a single abiding concern for the human plight in perilous times, and for human promise and achieved grandeur, love and hope.

*"It was that voice of his that seduced me—that direct, cranky, egotistical, generous American voice… Paul Goodman's voice touched everything he wrote about with intensity, interest, and his own terribly appealing sureness and awkwardness… It was his voice, that is to say, his intelligence and the poetry of his intelligence incarnated, which kept me a loyal and passionate fan."*
— Susan Sontag, novelist and public intellectual

*"Goodman, like all real novelists, is, at bottom, a moralist. What really interests him are the various ways in which human beings living in a modern metropolis gain, keep or lose their integrity and sense of selfhood."*
— W. H. Auden, poet

*"Any page by Paul Goodman will give you not only originality and brilliance but wisdom, that is, something to think about. He is our peculiar, urban, twentieth-century Thoreau, the quintessential American mind of our time."*
— Hayden Carruth, poet and essayist

*"No one writing now in America makes better sense of literary subjects. His ability to combine linguistic criticism, politics, a version of the nature of man, anthropology, the history of philosophy, and autobiographical testament with literary analysis, and to make a closely woven fabric of argument, seems magical."*
— Robert Meredith, *The Nation*

## *Teaching Rebellion: Stories from the Grassroots Mobilization in Oaxaca*

Edited by Diana Denham
and the C.A.S.A. Collective

**ISBN: 978-1-60486-032-0**
**$21.99 384 pages**

In 2006, Oaxaca, Mexico came alive with a broad and diverse movement that captivated the nation and earned the admiration of communities organizing for social justice around the world. What began as a teachers' strike demanding more resources for education quickly turned into a massive movement that demanded direct, participatory democracy. Hundreds of thousands of Oaxacans raised their voices against the abuses of the state government. They participated in marches of up to 800,000 people, occupied government buildings, took over radio stations, called for statewide labor and hunger strikes, held sit-ins, reclaimed spaces for public art and created altars for assassinated activists in public spaces. Despite the fierce repression that the movement faced—with hundreds arbitrarily detained, tortured, forced into hiding, or murdered by the state and federal forces and paramilitary death squads—people were determined to make their voices heard. Accompanied by photography and political art, *Teaching Rebellion* is a compilation of testimonies from longtime organizers, teachers, students, housewives, religious leaders, union members, schoolchildren, indigenous community activists, artists, journalists, and many others who participated in what became the Popular Assembly of the People's of Oaxaca. This is a chance to listen directly to those invested in and affected by what quickly became one of the most important social uprisings of the 21st century.

"Teaching Rebellion *presents an inspiring tapestry of voices from the recent popular uprisings in Oaxaca. The reader is embraced with the cries of anguish and triumph, indignation and overwhelming joy, from the heart of this living rebellion.*"
—Peter Gelderloos, author of *How Nonviolence Protects the State*

"*These remarkable people tell us of the historic teachers' struggle for justice in Oaxaca, Mexico, and of the larger, hemispheric battle of all Indigenous people to end five hundred years of racism and repression.*"
—Jennifer Harbury, author of *Truth, Torture and the American Way*

"*During their marches and protests, whenever the Oaxaca rebels sighted a reporter, they would chant: 'Press, if you have any dignity, the people of Oaxaca demand that you tell the truth.'* Teaching Rebellion *answers that demand, with ample dignity, providing excellent context to understand the 2006 uprising and extensive and eloquent interviews with the participants themselves; an amazing read and an important contribution to the literature of contemporary rebellion.*"
—John Gibler, author of *Mexico Unconquered: Chronicles of Power and Revolt*

Also from SPECTRE from PM Press

## *Capital and Its Discontents: Conversations with Radical Thinkers in a Time of Tumult*

Sasha Lilley

**ISBN: 978-1-60486-334-5**
**$20.00   320 pages**

Capitalism is stumbling, empire is faltering, and the planet is thawing. Yet many people are still grasping to understand these multiple crises and to find a way forward to a just future. Into the breach come the essential insights of *Capital and Its Discontents*, which cut through the gristle to get to the heart of the matter about the nature of capitalism and imperialism, capitalism's vulnerabilities at this conjuncture—and what can we do to hasten its demise. Through a series of incisive conversations with some of the most eminent thinkers and political economists on the Left—including David Harvey, Ellen Meiksins Wood, Mike Davis, Leo Panitch, Tariq Ali, and Noam Chomsky—*Capital and Its Discontents* illuminates the dynamic contradictions undergirding capitalism and the potential for its dethroning. At a moment when capitalism as a system is more reviled than ever, here is an indispensable toolbox of ideas for action by some of the most brilliant thinkers of our times.

*"These conversations illuminate the current world situation in ways that are very useful for those hoping to orient themselves and find a way forward to effective individual and collective action. Highly recommended."*
— Kim Stanley Robinson, *New York Times* bestselling author of the *Mars Trilogy* and *The Years of Rice and Salt*

*"In this fine set of interviews, an A-list of radical political economists demonstrate why their skills are indispensable to understanding today's multiple economic and ecological crises."*
— Raj Patel, author of *Stuffed and Starved* and *The Value of Nothing*

*"This is an extremely important book. It is the most detailed, comprehensive, and best study yet published on the most recent capitalist crisis and its discontents. Sasha Lilley sets each interview in its context, writing with style, scholarship, and wit about ideas and philosophies."*
— Andrej Grubačić, radical sociologist and social critic, co-author of *Wobblies and Zapatistas*

## *My Baby Rides the Short Bus: The Unabashedly Human Experience of Raising Kids with Disabilities*

Edited by Yantra Bertelli, Jennifer Silverman, and Sarah Talbot

**ISBN: 978-1-60486-109-9**
**$20.00 336 pages**

In lives where there is a new diagnosis or drama every day, the stories in this collection provide parents of "special needs" kids with a welcome chuckle, a rock to stand on, and a moment of reality held far enough from the heart to see clearly. Featuring works by "alternative" parents who have attempted to move away from mainstream thought—or remove its influence altogether—this anthology, taken as a whole, carefully considers the implications of parenting while raising children with disabilities.

From professional writers to novice storytellers including Robert Rummel-Hudson, Ayun Halliday, and Kerry Cohen, this assortment of authentic, shared experiences from parents at the fringe of the fringes is a partial antidote to the stories that misrepresent, ridicule, and objectify disabled kids and their parents.

*"This is a collection of beautifully written stories, incredibly open and well articulated, complicated and diverse: about human rights and human emotions. About love, and difficulties; informative and supportive. Wise, non-conformist, and absolutely punk rock!"*
— China Martens, author of *The Future Generation: The Zine-Book for Subculture Parents, Kids, Friends and Others*

*"If only that lady in the grocery store and all of those other so-called parenting experts would read this book! These true-life tales by mothers and fathers raising kids with 'special needs' on the outer fringes of mainstream America are by turns empowering, heartbreaking, inspiring, maddening, and even humorous. Readers will be moved by the bold honesty of these voices, and by the fierce love and determination that rings throughout. This book is a vital addition to the public discourse on disability."*
— Suzanne Kamata, editor of *Love You to Pieces: Creative Writers on Raising a Child with Special Needs*

*"This is the most important book I've read in years. Whether you are subject or ally,* My Baby Rides the Short Bus *will open you—with its truth, humanity, and poetry. Lucky you to have found it. Now stick it in your heart."*
— Ariel Gore, founding editor of *Hip Mama*

## *Rad Dad: Dispatches from the Frontiers of Fatherhood*

Edited by Jeremy Adam Smith and Tomas Moniz

**ISBN: 978-1-60486-481-6**
**$15.00 200 pages**

*Rad Dad: Dispatches from the Frontiers of Fatherhood* combines the best pieces from the award-winning zine *Rad Dad* and from the blog Daddy Dialectic, two kindred publications that have tried to explore parenting as political territory. Both of these projects have pushed the conversation around fathering beyond the safe, apolitical focus most books and websites stick to; they have not been complacent but have worked hard to create a diverse, multi-faceted space in which to grapple with the complexity of fathering. Today more than ever, fatherhood demands constant improvisation, risk, and struggle. With grace and honesty and strength, *Rad Dad*'s writers tackle all the issues that other parenting guides are afraid to touch: the brutalities, beauties, and politics of the birth experience, the challenges of parenting on an equal basis with mothers, the tests faced by transgendered and gay fathers, the emotions of sperm donation, and parental confrontations with war, violence, racism, and incarceration. *Rad Dad* is for every father out in the real world trying to parent in ways that are loving, meaningful, authentic, and ultimately revolutionary.

Contributors include: Steve Almond, Jack Amoureux, Mike Araujo, Mark Andersen, Jeff Chang, Ta-Nehisi Coates, Jeff Conant, Sky Cosby, Jason Denzin, Cory Doctorow, Craig Elliott, Chip Gagnon, Keith Hennessy, David L. Hoyt, Simon Knapus, Ian MacKaye, Tomas Moniz, Zappa Montag, Raj Patel, Jeremy Adam Smith, Jason Sperber, Burke Stansbury, Shawn Taylor, Tata, Jeff West, and Mark Whiteley.

"Rad Dad *gives voice to egalitarian parenting and caregiving by men in a truly radical fashion, with its contributors challenging traditional norms of what it means to be a father and subverting paradigms, while making you laugh in the process. With its thoughtful and engaging stories on topics like birth, stepfathering, gender, politics, pop culture, and the challenges of kids growing older, this collection of essays and interviews is a compelling addition to books on fatherhood."*
—Jennifer Silverman, co-editor, *My Baby Rides the Short Bus: The Unabashedly Human Experience of Raising Kids with Disabilities*

*"With a diverse, smart, and political collection of contributors,* Rad Dad *will be an instant classic among the new generation of parents whose parenting intersects with their politics. There's no way you can put this book down without feeling both inspired and entertained by the bold honesty and fierce love heard in these voices."*
—Jessica Mills, author of *My Mother Wears Combat Boots: A Parenting Guide for the Rest of Us*